ENGLISH PLACE-NAME SOCIETY

The English Place-Name Society was founded in 1924 to carry out the survey of English place-names. The Society has issued the following volumes:

The volumes for the following counties are in an advanced state of preparation: *Berkshire, Cheshire, Westmorland.*

All communications with regard to the Society should be addressed to:

THE HON. SECRETARY, English Place-Name Society, University College, Gower Street, London, W.C. 1.

ENGLISH PLACE-NAME SOCIETY.   VOLUME XXXVIII
FOR 1960–1

GENERAL EDITOR
A. H. SMITH

THE PLACE-NAMES OF
GLOUCESTERSHIRE

PART I

ENGLISH PLACE-NAME SOCIETY.   VOLUME XXXVIII

THE PLACE-NAMES OF GLOUCESTERSHIRE

By
A. H. SMITH

PART I
THE RIVER- AND ROAD-NAMES
THE EAST COTSWOLDS

CAMBRIDGE
AT THE UNIVERSITY PRESS
1964

PUBLISHED BY
THE SYNDICS OF THE CAMBRIDGE UNIVERSITY PRESS

Bentley House, 200 Euston Road, London, N.W.1
American Branch: 32 East 57th Street, New York 22, N.Y.
West African Office: P.O. Box 33, Ibadan, Nigeria

CAMBRIDGE UNIVERSITY PRESS

1964

Printed in Great Britain at the University Printing House, Cambridge
(Brooke Crutchley, University Printer)

PREFACE

THE survey of Gloucestershire place-names will be issued by the Society in four parts, of which this is the first. The present volume deals with the river- and road-names of the county and with the place-names of the south-eastern and eastern parts of the Cotswolds; it includes the upper Thames valley, and the valleys of the Evenlode, the Windrush, the Leach, the Coln and the Churn, which run into it; to the west it includes the Golden valley and the upper valley of the Frome; and to the north the valley of the Stour which runs into the Avon a mile short of Stratford upon Avon in Warwickshire. The principal towns and villages are Bibury, Cirencester, Tetbury, Nailsworth, Minchinhampton, Stroud, Cowley, Chedworth, Northleach, Bourton on the Water and the Slaughters, Stow on the Wold, Moreton in Marsh, Chipping Campden, Preston on Stour, and Weston on Avon.

The second part deals with the Cotswold escarpment and the Avon and Severn valleys from Winchcomb, Tewkesbury, and Cheltenham to Gloucester, Berkeley, and Dursley, whilst the third part covers the lower Severn valley to Bristol and the area beyond the Severn, including the Forest of Dean.

A list of abbreviations and sources, the historical introduction, the phonology of the place-names, the analyses of elements and personal names, the index, and parish and distribution maps, as well as my acknowledgements to the many scholars who have given help in the preparation of these volumes, will comprise the fourth part.

A. H. SMITH

UNIVERSITY COLLEGE, LONDON
1 April 1962

*The collection of material for this volume
from unpublished documents has been greatly
assisted by a grant from the British Academy*

CONTENTS

ADDENDA AND CORRIGENDA

i, 12. SWILGATE. The Swilgate, as Dr Finberg notes, seems to have been called *on tyrl* 11 (14) Finb 187; this name is of the same origin as Tirle Brook (i, 13), which joins the Swilgate in Tewkesbury. Hyde Brook (i, 111) in its Southam section (an affluent of the Swilgate) was also called *on tyrl* 769–85 BCS 246 (*on Suth Tyrl* 11 Heming); cf. Grundy 72, 78.

i, 20. WELSH WAY. This may have been a route to London used by Welsh cattle-drovers to avoid Cirencester. A similar name occurs in Witney (O).

i, 29. COLN ST ALDWYN. The form *Cungle*, as Dr Finberg points out, actually refers to land at Ablington (i, 26), which is on the R. Coln to the west of Coln St Aldwin (cf. Finb p. 55).

i, 32. FYFIELD. On the five-hide unit cf. also M. Hollings, 'The survival of the five hide unit in the West Midlands' in EHR lxiii, 453 ff.

i, 40. Joistment. Professor Dickins notes that this is probably an aphetised form of e.ModE *agistement* 'right of herbage, a rate or charge for pasture land' (cf. NED s.v.).

i, 53. *Opmanehevede*. Professor Löfvenberg compares the lost *Upmantone* (K 306), 'farmstead of the men of the upper part of the village'.

i, 60. CIRENCESTER. *The map of Roman Britain* (O.S. 1956), 21, 26 (to which Professor Jackson calls attention) identifies *Durocornovio* of the Antonine Itinerary with the Roman station at Wanborough (W 284). Mr Margery (Mg ii, 255), however, regards the identification with Cirencester as right. There is clearly a missing stage between Gloucester (*Clevo*) and Speen (*Spinis*); in view of the distance of 14 miles allowed from Gloucester to *Durocornovio* (which is substantially correct if *Durocornovio* is Cirencester), the 15 miles allowed from *Durocornovio* to Speen (which is the distance from Wanborough to Speen) is some 18 miles short, and that is the distance from Cirencester to Wanborough. Wanborough would appear to be a missing unnamed station.

i, 63. *Law-ditch-lane*. Cf. BaddeleyC 150 for a note on this; it was a moat of the former castle.

i, 64. INCHTHROP. ME *enche*, as Dr Finberg points out, was used in the 13th century of 'a manorial servant or workman' on the estates of the Bishops of Worcester (*RBB* 367). The etymology of the term is uncertain, but we may note the 15th-century gloss Lat *enencus*:*gotherd* 'goatherd' in *Dict. Grammatica* (Trinity College Cambridge MS O.5.4, fol. 152); it may be connected with the obsolete dial. *inch* 'youth, boy' as in *goad-inch* 'plough boy' (EDD s.v.).

i, 66. ALFRED'S HALL, POPE'S SEAT. On these pseudo-antiquities cf. BaddeleyC 267–271. The poet Alexander Pope, from whom Pope's seat is named, spent time at Cirencester House as friend and landscape adviser of Lord Bathurst.

i, 76. PEASTON LANE. Another possible interpretation, according to Professor Löfvenberg, is 'look-out stone' from a word connected with ModE *peer* 'to peer'.

i, 83. SOMERFORD KEYNES. Dr Finberg thinks that the BCS 671 form possibly refers to Little Somerford (W 73); cf. VCH(W) ii, 88.

i, 91. *Merchionis horne*. Professor Dickins suggests the Welsh pers.n. *Merchiawn*.

i, 93. Coombes. The first el., as Professor Dickins notes, is the surn. *Lockyer*.

i, 105. CULKERTON. Professor Löfvenberg provides the interesting suggestion that the first el. is an OE *culcor 'water-hole', which would be related to OE ōden-colc 'hollow used as a threshing-floor', OFris kolk 'hollow', MDu colc, culc 'pool, hollow filled with water', etc. On topographical grounds, however, there would be some difficulty.

i, 107. Hasyldyn. This is doubtless a variant form of Hazleton Fm (i, 106).

i, 108. le Wawes. This could be OE *wagu 'quaking bog' (cf. wagen 'quagmire' in EPN ii, 239), which, as Professor Löfvenberg notes, would formally suit better than wāg 'wall' (as also in Twenewawe i, 206), but topographically 'quaking bog, marsh' is improbable. The spelling wawes is doubtless a WMidl inverted spelling of ME wōwes (the normal development of wāg).

i, 113. Arundells. Add 'pasture called Arundell' 1460 Cl; it is from the surn. Arundel (cf. Reaney s.n.).

i, 118. BATTLESCOMBE. The pers.n. could be a nickname from OE bǣddel 'effeminate person', as Professor Dickins suggests.

i, 132. Smabryche. Add Smelrugg 1287 Ipm. This name means 'narrow ridge', but has obviously been confused in 1627 with the other name Smabryche.

i, 137. SAPPERTON. OE sāpere is used as a byname in the name of Adam le Sapere 1248 Ass 13 d (Gl).

i, 152. Scummington hill. This, according to Professor Dickins, may contain e.ModE skimmington used of 'a ludicrous rural procession intended to bring ridicule on a married man or woman who has been unfaithful to or ill-used by the other' (cf. NED s.v.); it was a Gloucestershire custom.

i, 169. LINEOVER WOOD. Dr Finberg thinks that this name and the OE name do not refer to the same feature, as the latter came between Merecombe (188) and Neatley (153), both further south of Lineover on the Withington boundary. Etymologically the names are identical and it is possible that the wood now called Lineover Wood once extended much further south, and as the woodland was cleared the name itself became restricted to the remaining part of the woodland bank. The grid reference of the OE boundary point is therefore incorrect.

i, 169. PEGGLESWORTH. The OE form might indicate an OE Pæcgel or Pecgel, a derivative of the Pæcga in Pagenhill (i, 139), but it leaves the ME -k- spellings unexplained.

i, 183. TURKDEAN. Dr Finberg points out that the OE forms do not all refer to the present day parish of Turkdean. That in BCS 356 is to be located at grid 144–063207 near the Hawling–Salperton boundary (Finb p. 189); Dr Finberg has noted two fields nearby called Turk's Dean Hill on an 1821 map (GRO); this is one of the heads of the main Turkdean valley; the stream which runs down it through Salperton disappears underground but it is not the stream which disappears near Turkdean village.

i, 187. HALES WOOD. Possibly named from Hailes Abbey (ii, 15), which Dr Finberg suggests owned the place.

i, 189. Green Stye. Dr Finberg (FinbergW 20) notes a William Grenesty, whose name is of local origin ('green path', v. grēne[1], stīg).

i, 189. Walwell. This was the spring which supplied the Roman villa at Withington; cf. also Walton (i, 185) in the adjoining parish of Whittington.

i, 189. Blokoldende. This is an erratic form, as the name also appears as Brooke-hole End 1600, Brokehall Ende (ex inf. Dr Finberg), possibly 'badger sett' (v. brocc-hol).

i, 192. SALMONSBURY HUNDRED. Mr C. R. Elrington points out that the frank-pledge court always met at Salmonsbury and the halimote court of the hundred at Lower Slaughter.

i, 201. *Mallbarnys hey.* Probably named from a woman called *Mall Barnes,* as suggested by Professor Dickins.

i, 209. *Fayrewellhull.* Mr Elrington thinks that this was in Little Rissington.

i, 213. THE BANKS. The spelling may belong to Banks Fee (i, 247).

i, 215. Quinmoor Lane. Mr Elrington states that the lane leads to a place locally known as Quimber.

i, 218. Ganborough. Probably of similar origin to Ganborough (247) in the adjoining parish of Longborough; the spelling *Grand-* for the latter shows that it is from OE *grēnan-beorge* 'green barrows' (cf. Phonol. § 13 for the development), and this Ganborough may therefore be a development of the OE *grenebeorhas* mentioned s.n. Little Barrows (218).

i, 220. *hwettan stanes wylle.* Professor Löfvenberg compares the OE pers.n. *Hwetta* with OHG *Hwezzi* and relates it to OE *hwæt* 'sharp'.

i, 223. Fulbrook. The site of *fulan ford,* Mr Elrington points out, was actually at Stow Bridge.

i, 225-6. *Duck Bath Street.* This survives as Digbeth St. Raggs Row also survives.

i, 231. LARK STOKE. Mr Elrington notes that Lark Stoke, though in Gloucester-shire, was a chapelry of Ilmington (Wa), and presumably regarded as an outlier of the latter place.

i, 244. PUDLICOTT MILL. This may in fact contain a surn. from Pudlicote (O 378).

i, 246. LONGBOROUGH. In DB the hundred of Kiftsgate merely contained the manor of *Langeberge* with Meon (254). *Langeberge* has usually been identified with Longborough, but Dr Finberg (Finberg 49) prefers to identify the manor with the Cotswold escarpment above Mickleton (where there is a Long Hills Fm); the gap between the main scarp and the outlier Meon Hill (near Kiftsgate Court) is probably the *geat* or gap of the name Kiftsgate (230), more precisely Kiftsgate Court (250). There is also a Long Hill on the ancient track leading south-west from the top of the scarp near Kiftsgate in Weston Subedge (261). How far to the south-west *Langeberge* Manor extended is not known, but the manors below this part of the scarp (Mickleton, Aston, Weston, Saintbury, etc.) were not in Kiftsgate Hundred in DB. Dr Finberg's suggestion has, therefore, much in its favour.

i, 247. GANBOROUGH. Cf. Ganborough (i, 218 and Addendum *supra*).

i, 251. *twicelan.* On the meaning of OE *twicele* cf. M. T. Löfvenberg in *Studier i modern språkvetenskap* xix (1956), 125-8.

i, 257. SEZINCOTE. Professor Löfvenberg calls attention to the difficulty of the persistent -e- forms, which are not readily explicable from *cisen.* But they may be due to analogical influence of the noun *ceosol* 'gravel' or the adj. *ceoslen* 'gravelly'.

i, 263. WILLERSEY. There is also a recorded OE pers.n. *Wilhere,* which should also be taken into account.

i, 264. Chamber de Key. This is doubtless the same as *Keys house* (i, 265), from ME *chambre* 'chamber' used of 'a dwelling' (cf. Higgin Chamber YW iii, 147-8); *Key* is the surname.

GLOUCESTERSHIRE

(to, on) Gleawe ceastre scire 11 ASC (E, F s.a. 1016), 1062 ASWrit 115, *-cestre-* 12 ASC (E s.a. 1122), *(to, on) Gleawcestrescire* 11 ASC (D s.a. 1016, E s.a. 1038, D s.a. 1052), 1042–66 ASWrit 101, *into Glæaweceastre scire* 1033–8 ASChart lxxxvii

Glowercestre scire 1042–66, 1062–6 ASWrit 100, 102

Gloucestrescire, -scira, -syra, -sira, -schire 1042–66 ASWrit 99, Wm 1 Monast, 1100–12 Glouc *et passim* to 1412 GloucHist, *comitatu(s) Gloucestrie* 1211–13 Fees, 1220 WinchLB *et freq* to 1331 RBBr, *(le) Counte(e) de Gloucestr(e)'* 1398 ib, 1426 BrCh, *the County of Gloucester* 1543 Berk, *Comitatu Gloucestrensi* 1337 WinchLB

Glouuecestre, Glowec'scire 1086 DB, *on Glowe ceastre scire* 12 ASC (E s.a. 1119), *comitatu de Glouecestra* 1358 Ch, *Þe shire of Glowcetur* 1304 Godstow.

Glucestre scyra 1119 Glouc

Gloecestre scir(a), -scyra, -scr', -sire 1130 *et freq* P, 1312 Ch, 1424 Pat

Comitatum Glovernie 1274 RH

On the name *v.* Gloucester (ii, 123 *infra*), scīr[1] 'shire, county'. Winchcomb (ii, 29 *infra*) was in OE times a separate shire, but became part of Gloucestershire in the reign of Cnut (Introd.). There have been many other adjustments of the county in relation to Wiltshire, Oxfordshire, Warwickshire, Worcestershire, and Herefordshire, and these are mentioned in the notes to the various hundreds (cf. GlAtlas 24, and for W *v.* 47, 85, iii, 22, for O *v.* 192, 229, for Wa *v.* 211, 229, ii, 75, for Wo *v.* 211, 229, ii, 41, 52, iii, 166, and for He *v.* iii, 209 *infra*). The greater part of the county was in the medieval diocese of Worcester and formed the archdeaconry of Gloucester, but Gloucester was founded as a separate bishopric in 1541; Bristol in the south was created a separate diocese in the following year (VCH ii, 48–9); much of the land between the Severn and the Wye was in the diocese and archdeaconry of Hereford (cf. *op. cit.*, Tax 161 and Introd.).

DISTRICT-NAMES

THE COTSWOLDS

montana de Codesuualt 12 Gir, *Coddeswold* 1269 Pat, 1294 Cl
Coteswaud 1250 Pat, *-wold* 1305 Cl, *-wowlde* 1577 M, *-would* 1646
 M, *Cotiswold* 1440 Pat, *Cotswold* 1592 Shakespeare (Ric 2)
Cottyswolde 1440, 1480 Cely, *Cottiswoldes* 1543 *MinAcct*, *Cottes-*
 wold, *-wald* 1577 Harrison, 1590 Camd
Cotssold 1541 Roister Doister iv, 6, *Cotsall* 1602 Merry Wives i, i, 92

'Cōd's high open land', *v.* **wald** The pers.n. is an OE *Cōd* which
appears in certain other names in this area, Cutsdean, *Codswell*
(ii, 7, 8 *infra*) and *Codesbyrig* (i, 227 *infra*); these places are in the
hills between the head-waters of the Windrush and the Dikler, and
it is possible that the same man gave his name to all four sites. The
name may originally have referred to the stretch of hill-country
between the Cotswold escarpment east of Winchcomb and the Fosse
Way in the neighbourhood of Blockley, Stow on the Wold, and
Naunton; Giraldus Cambrensis passed through the Cotswolds
between Blockley and Evesham, and in 1269 (Pat) Cotswold was
described as 'towards Clapley' (258 *infra*). The name Cotswold also
occurs as an affix in the spellings of Naunton (199 *infra*), a little to
the east, but the term *wold* itself has a somewhat wider provenance
in the earlier affixes of Withington (186), Stow on the Wold (225)
and Westington (239). In recent times the name denotes the whole
of this great upland region of Gloucestershire as far south as Northleach, Bibury, Cirencester, and Wotton under Edge.

THE VALE OF GLOUCESTER

vallis Gloecestræ c. 1125 WMP, *valle de Gloccestria* 1316 Ch,
describing the Severn valley in the neighbourhood of Gloucester.

RIVER-NAMES AND STREAM-NAMES

The names included here are those of the principal rivers and streams and
the material generally is that found in Gl sources. Stream-names which are
derived from place-names or other topographical features are dealt with in
the appropriate parishes, as are stream-names which have become the names
of settlements (like Bournstream or Lydbrook ii, 241, iii, 218 *infra*) or are in-
corporated in the names of such settlements (as in Lemington 246).

AVON (1) (affluent of the Severn at Tewkesbury)

Afen 704–9 (12th) BCS 123, (*in, onlong*) *Afene* 922 (1643) ASChart xxi, *éá Afene* c. 1025 Saints (v.l. *éa Auene, amnem Afena*), *Auena, -e, Avena, -e* 1100–35 *Tewk* 71b, 1207 ib. 87a, 1248, 1287 *Ass*, 1300 Ch *et freq* to 1496 Pat, *Avon(e)* 1535 VE, 1540 *AOMB*. A common British r.n., *v.* abonā 'river', cf. RN 21. This river in the north of the county joins the Severn at Tewkesbury, where its course was changed to provide water for the mill; the old course is called the Old Avon (*infra*). The name forms the first el. of Avon Ham and *Auenford* (ii, 64, 68 *infra*), and an affix in Welford and Weston on Avon (259, 260 *infra*).

Avon (2) (affluent of the Severn near Bristol)

Abone 4 AntIt, *Aben* 793–6 (11th) BCS 274, *in Afene stream* 883 (11th) BCS 551, *be Áfne* 9 ASC (A s.a. 652), *Au-, Avene, -a* 1236 *FF et freq* to 1434 Pat, *Abone, -a* 1240, 1350 RBBr, 1373 BrCh, *Havon'* 1540 *MinAcct*, *Avon* 1634 *FF*, *the Bristol Avon* 1779 Rudder, *v.* prec. This is the Avon which forms the southern boundary of the county and runs through Bristol, where the Floating Harbour marks the old course of the river and what is now the Avon in the city was a cut finished in 1809 (cf. BrKal 28 note). This r.n. is found also as an el. in *The Back*, Marsh Bridge (iii, 86, 96 *infra*), and Avonmouth (iii, 130).

Little Avon River (affluent of the Severn near Berkeley)

on afene 972 BCS 1282, *Avon* c. 1540 Leland, *le Haven* 1575 *TRMB*, *Auen fluuiolus* 1590 Camd, *the Berkeley Avon* 1779 Rudder, *the Little Avon River* 1830 M, *v.* Avon (*supra*). This r.n. is found as an el. in Avening, Avonscot and *Avon Mouth* (iii, 41, ii, 210, 224 *infra*).

Bladen (now the Evenlode, an affluent of the Thames)

flumen Bladon 675 (12th) BCS 37
fluvium…Bladaen, on bleadene 718 (11th) BCS 139
fluvii…Bladen 772 (11th) BCS 210, (*innon, of, andlang*) *Bladene* 777 (14th) ib 222, 779 (12th) ib 229, 969 (11th) ib 1238 *et freq* to c. 1050 (12th) KCD 963, *Bibladene* 862 (l. 13) BCS 535
on, of blædene 949 BCS 882
Bladon' 12 Oseney
Bladen' Hy 2 Eynsham, 1238 Cl, 1279 RH, 1363 Eynsham

Further material is given in RN 36 and O 7, and for the village of Bladon in O 252; Bledington (213 *infra*) is also on this river. The origin of the name is obscure. As a river-name it had fallen into disuse by the fifteenth century and was then replaced by Evenlode (7 *infra*).

BOYD (affluent of the Bristol Avon)

andland byd, on tha ealdan byd, on Bydincel, of Bydincele 950 (copy) BCS 887, *on byd, on bydyncel* 972 (10th) ib 1282, *aq' de Byde* 1287 *Ass*, *Boyd* 1712 Atkyns, 1779 Rudder. This r.n. occurs also as the first el. of Bitton (iii, 75 *infra*) and the f.ns. Boyd mead and Boyd field (iii, 50, 76). The form *ealdan byd* refers to an older course of the river (*v.* ald 'old'), and *Bydincel*, which means 'little Boyd' (*v.* -incel, a diminutive suffix) referred in BCS 887 to a small eastern affluent of Feltham Brook (itself an affluent of the Boyd) and in BCS 1282 to a part of Feltham Brook on the west boundary of Dyrham. Ekwall (RN 47) takes the name to be from an OE *Bȳd* which is possibly of Celtic origin and connected with Welsh *budr* 'dirty', *baw* 'dirt' or Welsh *budd* 'profit, benefit'. The later form Boyd is dialectal (cf. Phonol. § 30).

CAM (affluent of the Severn in Slimbridge)

'water of *Cambrigga*' 1200–10 Berk, *Cammes Brooke* 1566 BG vii, 285, *Cam amniculum* 1590 Camd, *Cambs water als. Framptons Pill* 1609 *Comm*. The r.n. is also that of the village of Cam (ii, 215) and is the first el. of Cambridge and the f.n. *Camsfeld* (ii, 248, 250); Camwell (ii, 198 *infra*, at grid point 156–768035) is the source of a small affluent which first runs into Wickers Brook and then into the Cam and may once have been regarded as its source. As Ekwall notes (RN 65), this is probably a Celtic r.n. from cambo- 'crooked'; Rudder 317 comments that 'the course of it is crooked like an arch or bow, wherefore it was called the *Cam*'.

CARRANT BROOK (affluent of the Avon (1) in Tewkesbury)

rivuli...Carent 779 BCS 232, *C-*, *Karent(e)*, *-am* 12 *Tewk* 85b, 1274 RH, 1318 *Talbot*, 1327 *SR* (p), 1365 WinchLB (p), 1376 Ipm

rivulum Cærent 780 (11th) BCS 236, *of kærent* 875 ib 541, *in, of kærente* (ðære ea) 969, 977 (11th) KCD 552, 617

Caraunt 1482 *Talbot*

Carrauntes Broke 1540 *AOMB*, *Carrants Brooke* 1626 FF

Caran 1577 M, *Carren Brook* 1777 M

The name is an affix in Aston on Carrant (ii, 52 *infra*), and the first el. of Carrant meadow and Northway mill (ii, 55, 54 *infra*) and *Carenforlong, Carentesmede* 1375 Ipm near Mitton in Bredon (Wo) on the north side of the stream. As noted in Wo 10 and RN 70, Carrant has a parallel in Charente (France), *Karantona* (Holder). Ekwall derives it from a Celtic root *carant-* related to Welsh *car* 'friend' and interprets it as 'the friendly, pleasant stream'. Another example of this r.n. occurs in Caerwents (iii, 178 *infra*).

CHELT (affluent of the Severn near Deerhurst)

Chelt c. 1540 Leland, 1830 M, (*-or Chilt*) 1760 M
Chiltenham water, Chilus 1577, 1586 M
Chilt 1712 Atkins, 1779 Rudder

The name is the first el. of Cheltenham (ii, 101 *infra*) and is regarded by Ekwall (RN 75) as a back-formation from the p.n.; at one time the river appears to have been called *Alr* (from Arle ii, 104 *infra*), and later *aqua de Incham* 1620 *FF*, 1627 InqM from Incham (a f.n. in Prestbury ii, 111 *infra*) of uncertain origin, which might, however, be compared with the modern Inchbrook (116 *infra*); cf. also Inchmore (ii, 151 *infra*). It is possible on topographical grounds, however, that Chelt is in fact an old r.n. from which Cheltenham is derived, but its origin is obscure.

CHURN (affluent of the Thames in South Cerney)

innon Cyrnéa c. 800 (11th) BCS 299 (v.l. *Cirnea*), *Cirnea, on Cyrnea*
    852 (13th) ib 466, *innan, on, andlang Cyrne* 999 (13th) KCD 703
Cheern 15 WmWo
Churn(e) c. 1540 Leland, 1577, 1610, 1695 M
Corinius fl. nunc Churne 1590 Camd

South Cerney and North Cerney (58, 148 *infra*) are variants of this name, which is also the first el. of Cirencester (60 *infra* where its origin is discussed).

COLN (affluent of the Thames near Bibury)

fluvium...Cunuglae, of Cunuglan sulhforda 721–43 (11th) BCS 166
bi Cunelgan 855 (11th) BCS 487
juxta Cunelgnan 899 (11th) BCS 580
be Culne n.d. (11th) BCS 1320, *Culna* 1257 Ipm
Colne 1248 *Ass*, 1577, 1610, 1646 M, *le Colne Streme* 1487 *MinAcct*
Coulne Broke 1574 *MBks*, *the olde Cowlne, Cowlne brookes* 1627 Inq
Cowne 1590, 1637 FF, *Coune* 1637 ib
the Cole 1631 Inq

The name also became at a very early date that of the settlements at Coln St Aldwyn, Coln Rogers, and Coln St Denis (29, 165, 166 *infra*); its origin is obscure. In its upper course it was called *Tilnoth* (13 *infra*). The r.n. is the first el. of Cawcombe (178 *infra*).

CONE BROOK (affluent of the Severn in Aylburton)

Cone c. 1270 *For*, 1276 RH, *passag' de Cone, -Kone* 1280, 1289 *MinAcct, ductus de Cone* 1355 Heref, *Cone Brook* 1830 M
C-, Kunesbrok 1282 *For*   *Corne* (sic) c. 1340 *For*

This name also occurs in Cone Pill (iii, 256 *infra*). Its origin is uncertain; apart from the *C-, Kunes-* spellings, ME *Cone* and the modern form could be from OE *cān* which occurs once in the Paris Psalter 79[10] where from the context it is thought to mean 'germ, sprout'. It is, however, a normal grade of the OE verb *cīnan* 'to gape, crack', and a possible topographical sense is suggested by e.ModE *coane, cone*, 'gap, fissure, cleft' (from 1584 NED s.v.); this might have been an appropriate description of Cone Pill, a large tidal creek on the Severn bank (156–6099). But the *Kunes-* spelling could not be accounted for by OE *cān* except as an inverted spelling of a shortened form *Cŏn-* in the compound and a WMidl over-rounding of this (cf. Phonol. § 5).

DIKLER (affluent of the Windrush in Bourton on the Water), *Thickeleure* 1241–64 Eynsham, *the Dickler* 1779 Rudder. 'Thick dense reed-bed', *v.* þicce[2], læfer, cf. Thickleather (258 *infra*), and Phonol. § 41 (*a*).

DOVERLE BROOK (affluent of the Little Avon in North Nibley)

to dofer lan, andlang dofærlan 940 (12th) BCS 764. Modern maps consistently print this name as Doverte Brook, but according to E. S. Lindley (BG lxxvii, 43 ff) it is still locally called Doverle, and Grundy 289 note cites a passage from John Smyth's *Lives of the Berkeleys* (1883–5) i, 141, where the author refers to 'a smalle river called *Doverle*' and *Doverley* (ib iii, 85); these are correctly derived from the OE form. The name is possibly referred to also in *Dovarde hurns* in Alkington (ii, 211 *infra*). Ekwall (RN 137) interprets the name as 'the pure water', from Brit **dubro-** and **glano-* 'pure' (or possibly from the root of Welsh *glan* 'bank, shore').

DRY BROOK (affluent of Cinderford Brook in East Dean), *Druybrok* 1282 *For*. The name also remains in Drybrook (iii, 217 *infra*).

ELL BROOK (affluent of the Leadon by Upleadon), *Ellbrook, a brook called the Ell* 1779 Rudder 561, 589. 'Elm stream', *v.* elm, brōc; it is crossed by Ell Bridge (iii, 175 *infra*), from which it may be a backformation.

EVENLODE (affluent of the Thames), *Euenlod(e)* 1577, 1607 M, *En-, Yenload* 1612 Drayton, *Evenload River* 1770 *EnclA*. Named from Evenlode (219 *infra*); its former name was *Bladen* (3 *supra*).

EWELME (affluent of the Cam in Uley), *æwylme* 940 (12th) BCS 764, (*the*) *Ewelme* 1453 *MinAcct*, 1487 *GR* 1349, 16, 1585 ib 1193, 8, *aquam de Elme* 1605 *AOMB* 394. *v.* ǣ-welm 'spring, source of a river'.

FROME (1) (affluent of the Severn near Fretherne)

aqua de Frome 1248 *Ass*, *From*, *Fraw* als. *Frome* c. 1540 Leland, *Froome or Stroudwater* 1779 Rudder. This r.n. forms the first el. of Francombe (73, 131), Frampton Mansell (137), Framilode (ii, 179), Frampton on Severn (ii, 196), Fromebridge (ii, 196, 205), *Fromelee* (ii, 197) and Frocester (ii, 197 *infra*). Like Frome (2) *infra* it is from PrWelsh **frōm* (Brit **frām-*), the root of Welsh *ffraw* 'fair, brisk' (cf. Ekwall, RN 167–8). In the one spelling *Fraw* and in the form of the r.n. in Frocester the nasalised *v* resulting from lenition of Brit *m* is lost (cf. Jackson 416, 488, etc.).

FROME (2) (affluent of the Avon (2) in Bristol)

andlang Frome(s) 950 (copy) BCS 887
(*aquam de*) *Frome* 12 Glouc, 1221, 1248, 1287 *Ass*, 1251 Pat *et freq* to 1695 M, *Froma* 1248 *Ass*
Frama 1221 Eyre
Froome 1610, 1646, 1648 M, 1712 Atkyns

The r.n. is the first el. in Frome Bridge & Gate (iii, 54, 88), Frampton Cotterell (iii, 116) and Frenchay (iii, 123 *infra*). For the name cf. Frome (1) *supra*. In Bristol its old course was filled up and the water diverted to the Avon near the bridge in Princes Street (cf. BrKal 28 note).

GLYNCH BROOK (affluent of the Leadon in Staunton)

ondlong Glences, on, of, ondlong Glencing 963 (11th) BCS 1109, *in, andlang glencincg* 972 (10th) ib 1282, *on glenccinc* 11 (14th) Finb 187

aquam...Clenche 12 Glouc
Glench' Hy 3 Misc, 1276 RH, 1357 *Talbot*
'water called *Glengh'* 1383 *GR* 1448
the *Glinch* 1779 Rudder

Ekwall (RN 181) derived this from a Brit **glanīc-* from the root of Welsh *glan* 'pure' (cf. Doverle 6 *supra*), with OE *i-* mutation and syncope of *glanic* to *glenc-*. In the OE form *glencing*, *-ing* is the river-name forming suffix *-ing²* as in Guiting (ii, 12 *infra*).

GORE BROOK (affluent of Dry Brook in east Dean), *Gor Brook* 1770 Comm. Probably 'dirty stream', *v.* gor 'filth, dirt', brōc, but gāra 'gore of land' is also possible.

GRAN BROOK (affluent of the Avon (1) in Weston on Avon), *on grenan broc* 1005 (12th) KCD 714, *Grandbrook* 1698 *M.* 'The green brook', *v.* grēne¹, brōc, cf. Phonol. § 13.

HAM BROOK (1) (affluent of the Chelt in Charlton Kings), *Hambroc* 1221 *Ass* (p). Named from Ham (ii, 97 *infra*).

HAM BROOK (2) (affluent of Horsbere Brook in Badgeworth), *Homme-broke* c. 1400 GlR, *Ham brook* 1839 *TA* 171. *v.* hamm 'water-meadow', brōc.

HOLY BROOK (affluent of the Frome (1) in Bisley), *Hollowwell* 1609 *AOMB* 394, *Holywell* 1658 *GR* 270. Probably 'holy stream or spring', *v.* hālig, wella.

HORSBERE BROOK (affluent of the Severn in Longford), (*aquam...*) *Horsbere* 1243–63 Glouc, a. 1263 BG vii, 148, 1263–84 Glouc, *-beor* c. 1260 GlR, *Horsberebrok* 1313 *GlCh* x, 22, cf. also *Horsbeyrebrigg'* 1363 Works, *Horspery Lodge* 1700 PR 7. 'Horse grove', *v.* hors, bearu, brōc. The second el. could formally be OE bǣr 'woodland pasture' as in Horsebear (Sx 116), but that el. is otherwise unknown in Gl. Cf. Horsbere Bridge (ii, 116 *infra*).

GREAT & LITTLE HOUGH BROOK (affluents of Lydbrook in East and West Dean), *Holebrok* 1282 *For*, *Hoebrooke* 1612 *Comm*, *Hou-*, *How-brooke* 1632 *For*, 1669 *Comm*. 'Stream in the hollow', *v.* hol², brōc. The two streams are on opposite sides of the main valley, the former in East Dean, the latter in West Dean.

HUMBER BROOK (an affluent of the Stour in Preston on Stour), *Humber Brooke* 1642 Inq, cf. also *Humber ffilde* 1575 *TRMB* (in

Admington). This is an example of the well-attested r.n. Humber of which Ekwall (RN 201–3) gives 11 examples, including a lost Gl instance *Humbyr'* (1263 AD iii) which would be an affluent in Hawkesbury of the Bristol Avon near its source. Ekwall has suggested that the name is from a Celtic root **sumbr-* meaning something like 'the good one'.

ISBOURNE (affluent of the Avon (1) near Hinton on the Green)

> *in Esenburnen* 709 (12th) BCS 125, *Biesingburnan* 862 (l. 13th) ib 535
> *Esegburna* 777 (16th) BCS 223, *on Esigburnan* n.d. (12th) KCD 1368
> *Biesingburnan, on is esingeburna, of, in esingburnan* 930 (13th) BCS
> 667, *Esingburnan, of, on, in Esingburnan* 1002 (13th) KCD 1295
> *Eseburn(e)* 13 WinchLB, 1221 Eyre, 1248 *Ass, -bourne* 16 *Hls* 12,
> *E(a)seburn(e)* c. 1540 Leland
> *Esseburn'* 1287 *Ass*   *Essborne* 1586 *Comm*
> *Esbourne* 1309 WinchLB, *-borne* 1588 *Comm*
> *Isbourne* 1779 Rudder

'Ēsa's stream', from the OE pers.n. *Ēsa* and **burna**. The OE spellings represent a variation between *Ēsan-burna* (with wk.gen.sg. *-an*) and *Esing-burna* (with *-ing*[4] denoting some kind of association of the stream with *Ēsa*); the spelling with *Esig-*, etc., is a scribal variant of *Esing-* (cf. Karlström 9–10). The river was also called *aqua de Tutington* 1248 *Ass* from Toddington (ii, 28 *infra*).

KNEE BROOK (affluent of the Stour in Todenham), *Knee Brook* 1830 M, *v.* cnēow 'knee' in the sense 'bend in a river', brōc. The stream has many sharp bends, esp. in the vicinity of Knee Bridge (236 *infra*) where it is crossed by the Fosse Way. It was formerly called *Doferburna* 977 KCD 614, which contains the Brit r.n. **dubro-** (Welsh *dwfr*) 'water', and OE **burna** 'stream'.

LADDEN BROOK (affluent of the Frome (2) in Iron Acton), '*Loden, but communely Laden*' c. 1540 Leland, *Laddon, West Laddon* 1592 *Eg* 60d, 64, *Laden* 1712 Atkyns, (*-Brook*) 1777 M, cf. also *Laddon mede* c. 1560 *Surv, Laddan meade* c. 1603 *TRMB* 39, *Laddonbrigge* 1592 *Eg* 61d. This name is discussed with Latteridge (iii, 2); cf. also *Ledden Bridge* (ii, 244 *infra*).

LEACH (affluent of the Thames in Lechlade), *æt Lec* 721–43 (11th) BCS 166, *Lachebrok* 12 Glouc, *Leche flu* 1570, 1690 M, *Lechbrooke*

1621 Inq. This has given its name to the villages of Eastleach (31, 33), Northleach (175) and Lechlade (40 *infra*). *v.* læcc, lec(e) 'stream flowing through boggy land'.

LEADON ['ledn] (affluent of the Severn in Maisemore)

in, andlang, of ledene 972 (10th) BCS 1282, 978 (11th) KCD 619, *Ledene* 12, 13 Glouc, 1221 Ass, 1263–84 Glouc, 1287 *Ass, Leden* c. 1235 GlR, 1248 *Ass, veteri Ledena* 1243 Glouc, *Ledon* 1542 *MinAcct, Leddon* 1565 GlR, *Leadon* 1619 BG xl, 130, 1627 *FF*, 1830 M, *Ledden* 1754 *EnclA*. The name occurs also in Leadington, High-leadon and Upleadon (iii, 169, 158, 189 *infra*), *Ledenebrugge* 1300 *For, Ledon' Brigge* 1542 *MinAcct*, and Ledbury (He 112). Ekwall (RN 242) suggests a Brit **litano-* (cf. Welsh *llydan*) 'broad' for this name.

LYDD (affluent of the Severn in Lydney). This name, not recorded, is an alternative name of Cannop Brook (iii, 227 *infra*) and is clearly a back-formation from Lydney (iii, 257 *infra*).

MARCHFONT BROOK (affluent of the Avon in Clifford Chambers).

NOLEHAM BROOK (affluent of the Avon (1) near Welford on Avon), *riuulum de Nolland* 1540 *MinAcct, (Brooke) Nollande, Nyllandes* 1575 *TRMB* 39, *brook...Noleham* 1779 Rudder. The first theme is an old p.n. or f.n., possibly OE *hnoll* 'top of the head', applied to a hill, *v.* land, hamm.

OLD AVON RIVER (affluent of the Severn in Tewkesbury), *Old(e) Aven* 1539, 1540 AOMB, 1542 *MinAcct, le Olde Avon* 1545 LP. This is the old course of the Avon (1) before it joins the Severn to the west of Tewkesbury at Upper Lode; the alternative course of the river runs along the edge of the town as the Avon and the Mill Avon, and joins the Severn at Lower Lode to the south-west of Tewkesbury.

PLUMMER'S BROOK (affluent of the Severn in Lydney), *Plumbers Brook* 1830 M, from the surname *Plummer* (ME *Plummer, Plumber*), *v.* brōc.

SEVERN

Sabrina(m), -e 2 Tacitus (*Annals* xii), 6 (11th) Gildas, c. 730 (8th) Bede, c. 700 (14th) BCS 121, 814 (11th) ib 350, 12–13 Glouc (*freq*), 1100–35 *Tewk* 71d, c. 1150 Land, c. 1205 *GlCh* v, 8, 1221 *Ass*, 1228 Cl *et freq* to 1584 *Comm, Sabryne* 1539 *FF Saberna, on Sæfyrne* 706 (12th) BCS 116, *Sæbrino* 816 ib 357

(in, æt, be, on, innan) Sæfern(e) 757–75 (11th) BCS 219, 9–10 ASC (A s.a. 894, 896, 910), 929 (11th) BCS 665, 956 (12th) ib 927, 10 Saints, 11 (14) Finb 187, *innan, on, to Sæfern muðon, -an* 10 ASC (A s.a. 918), 11 ib (D s.a. 915, E s.a. 997, C, D s.a. 1052)
be Sefærn 11 ASC (E s.a. 910), *of Seferne* 11 (14) Finb 187
on Sæuerne 10 (12th) ASChart cix
Sau-, Saverna, -e 1086 DB, 12 Glouc (*freq*), Ric 1 Cur, 13 Flax, 1221 *Ass et freq* to 1312 Ch, 1653 *ParlSurv*
Seu-, Severne, -a 1248 *Ass*, 1287 Glouc, 1291 Tax, 1292 Ch *et passim* to 1648 *FF*
Sevarne 1378 Works, 1401, 1461 Pat
Seaverne 1609 *Comm*, 1635 *For*, 1670 Berk

The name appears in various minor p.ns. in Gl such as *Seuernesyde* (ii, 59), Severn Ham (ii, 66), Severn Road (ii, 132), Severn Hill (ii, 189), *Severnelees* (ii, 197), Severn field (ii, 227, 234), and *Seavernes bank* (ii, 228) and as an affix in Frampton (ii, 196), Oldbury (iii, 8), Littleton (iii, 118) and Westbury on Severn (iii, 201 *infra*). Ekwall (RN 358 ff) cites a large selection of forms including many from Celtic sources (early Welsh *Havren*, etc.), and derives this r.n. from Brit *Sabrinā* from a root **sab-, *sabar-* of doubtful meaning. The change of *s-* to *h-* in Welsh and that of *-b-* to *-v-* by lenition are regular; the normal OE form is *Sæfern*, and ME *Savern* is a development of this; ME *Severn* may well be from a Merc variant *Sefern* (cf. Phonol. § 1) and the later spellings *Seaverne* would represent a ME lengthening of *Sev-* to *Sēv-* in an open syllable.

STOUR (affluent of the Avon (1) in Clifford Chambers) [stauə]

Sture 704–9 (12th) BCS 123, *Stuur, of Sture, Stures stream* c. 757 (11th) ib 183, *on Sture* 922 (17th) ASChart xxi, *Stura* 1247 *Ass*, *þe Stowre* c. 1270 Oseney, *Stoure* 1577 M, *Stower* 1638 FF. The name occurs as an affix in Clifford Chambers and Preston on Stour (239, 253 *infra*). Ekwall (RN 380) gives further forms. There is some doubt about the origin of this r.n. which occurs elsewhere; it is possibly from a Germanic root **stūr* 'fierce, gloomy, etc.' but since this is not otherwise found in English Ekwall would prefer a Celtic source, but such is not to be found either (Ekwall, RN 381–2, Jackson 195 note 1). Atkyns 105 stated that there was a stream called *Stower* which joined Ladden Brook in Iron Acton, but this is probably a confusion with Stover in Yate (iii, 44 *infra*) which has a different origin. Sturden Court (iii, 124 *infra*) may, however, provide a further instance of the r.n.

STROUD WATER (affluent of the Frome (1) near Stroud)

Strod(e)water 1475 Pat, 1477 Cl, 1484 ECP, *Strowdwater* 1547 *AOMB* 411, *Stroude fl* 1577, 1610, 1690 M, *Stroudwater* 1644 PR 15, 106, *Stroodwater* 1701 ib 5, 116. This river is named from Stroud (139 *infra*), *v.* wæter. It is an affluent of the Frome; the name is an alternative one for the Frome or for one of the channels made by it, such as that near Eastington, where it was called *Stroud old River* c. 1800 *GR* (P. 127a). The name only survives as that of the Stroudwater Canal between Stroud and the Severn at Frampton on Severn. *Burnewater* (Bourne 140 *infra*) seems to have been an earlier name for the river.

SUD BROOK (affluent of the Severn in Gloucester), *Sudbrok* c. 1250 *GlCh* ii, 3, *-brooke* 1589 *Dep*, *Suthbrok(e)*, *-broc* 1261 GlR, 1263–84 Glouc, c. 1270 *GlCh* iii, 1, *Sodbrucke* 1598 *Dep*. 'South stream', *v.* sūð, brōc, so called because it is on the south side of Gloucester.

SWILGATE (affluent of the Severn in Tewkesbury)

aqua de Swil(l)gat(e) 1540 *AOMB*, 1540, 1542 *MinAcct*, *river Swilgate* 1784 *GR* 892, *Suliet* c. 1540 Leland, *Swilgate* 1577 M, *Sw-*, *Suilliat* 1610 M, 1612 Drayton. The name enters into Swilgate Bridge (ii, 67 *infra*). *v.* swille 'sloppy mess', from OE *swillan* 'to wash, rinse', e.ModE *swill* 'to wash down, to pour liquid down', etc., with geat 'gate', which possibly had here the sense of a flood-gate or trap. Ekwall explains Swill Brook (La 139) as 'a stream where clothes were washed'; cf. also dial. *swilly* 'eddy, whirlpool', 'a gutter washed out of the soil' (cf. NED s.v.), as in Swilley Grove (123 *infra*); the name may possibly have referred to a flood-gate across the ditch or water-course near Tewkesbury Abbey.

SWILL BROOK (affluent of the Thames in Ashton Keynes), *Swillbrook* 1779 Rudder, 1830 M, *Swellbrooke* 1807 *EnclA*. *v.* swille, brōc and Swilgate (prec.), cf. Swill Brook (78, iii, 21 *infra*).

THAMES

Tamesis 51 B.C. Cæsar, 6 (11th) Gildas, c. 800 (11th) HistBr
'Ιαμῆσα c. 150 Ptol, *Tamesa* 681 (13th) BCS 56, *Tamisa* 1172 P
Temis 688 (14th) BCS 70, (*innan, andlang*) *Temese* 999 (c. 1225)
KCD 703, c. 1300 RGl

Tamyse, -ise 931 (14th) BCS 673, c. 1140 Gaim, 1247, 1287 *Ass*, *Tamese* c. 1300 RGl *Thamis'* 1220 *Ass, Thamyse* 1244, c. 1300 Godstow

Ekwall (RN 402) and Förster (*Themse* 461 ff) cite an extensive selection of forms, and also discuss its origin. Ekwall agrees with Holder's suggestion that it is from a root **teme-* 'dark' with an *-ns* or *-st* suffix, 'the dark one'. The river rises near Thames Head Bridge (76 *infra*).

TILNOTH (lost) (affluent of the Coln in Withington)

fluvium...Tillath 736–7 (11th) BCS 156, *Tillnoð* 774 (11th) ib 217, *innan tilnoð, andlang tilnoðes* c. 800 (11th) ib 299. This was the OE name of the upper part of the Coln in Withington. It is a figurative name based on an OE pers.n. type, *Tilnōð* 'the useful one' (cf. RN 408).

TIRLE BROOK (affluent of the Swilgate in Tewkesbury)

rivuli...Tyrl 769–85 (11th) BCS 246, 780 (11th) ib 236, *on North Tyrl, on Suth Tyrl* 11 Heming, *on tyrl* 11 (14) Finb 187 *le Trulle* 1487 *MinAcct, Trulle broke* 1575 *TRMB* 39 *(le) Turlebroke* 1490 *TewkCt,* 1575 *TRMB, Turl Brook* 1777 M *Thurlebroke* 1540 *AOMB* *Tyrle* c. 1560 *Surv, Tirle* 1779 Rudder, *-brooke* 1830 M

This r.n. is the first el. of *æt Tyreltune, Tireltune* 781–98 (11th) BCS 283 (in the neighbourhood of Whittington or Dowdeswell), Tyre field and Turl Meadow (ii, 56, 74 *infra*). *Tyrl* BCS 246 is the Swilgate (12) and *Suth Tyrl* Hyde Brook (ii, 111 *infra*). *v.* tyrl probably in the sense 'that which turns or rolls along, a stream' (cf. RN 409).

TRYM (affluent of the Avon (2) in Henbury), *Trin* 1712 Atkyns, *Trim* 1714, 1779 Rudder, occurring in the affix of Westbury on Trym (iii, 141 *infra*) as *Trim, Trym(m)e* 1472 Pat, 1534 LP, 1547 Pat. Possibly, as Ekwall suggests (RN 419), an OE *Trymme*, a derivative of OE *trum* 'firm, strong'.

TWYVER (affluent of the Severn in Gloucester)

Weu-, Wever(e) 1351 *GlCh* iii, 17, (*cursum aquae...*) 1455 Cole 102, 145–772 *GlCh* v, 17, 1504 ib ii, 19, (*riuoli*) 1542 *MinAcct* (*riuulum de*) *Wyver* 1537 *MinAcct,* 1779 Rudder *Twyver River* 1821 *Guise* (M. 21), *River Twiver* 1830 M *v.* wēfer 'winding stream'. Initial *T-* in the modern form is probably due to a wrong analysis of the expression 'at Wyver' as 'a(t) Twyver' (cf. Phonol. § 45).

WHETSTONES BROOK (affluent of the Severn in Newnham), *Whetstonysbroke* 1492 GlR, *Wetstones Brook* 1830 M, *Weston brook* 1839 *TA* 141. 'Brook where whetstones were found', *v.* hwet-stān, brōc.

WINDRUSH (affluent of the Thames)

> *fluvii*...*Uuenrisc, uuænrisc* 779 BCS 230, *on Wenrisc* 969 (12th) ib 1230, *éá Wenrisc* 11 Saints (v.l. *Wenrise, Wearisc, Wearise, Yearnisc*)
> *on Wenris* 949 BCS 882
> *on Wænric* 949 BCS 882, *Wenricces* 969 (12th) ib 1230, *on, of, innon Wenric* 1016 (14th) KCD 723, 1044 (12th) ib 775, (12th) ib 1360, c. 1055 Finb 171
> *Wen(e)rich(e), -rych'* 1247 Ass, 1279 RH, l. 13 Eynsham
> *Wynrysshe* 1500–15 ECP, *Winruche, Wynderusch* c. 1540 Leland, *Windrush* 1577 M

The village of Windrush (209 *infra*) is named from it. Ekwall (RN 462) has taken the name to be a compound of the older form of Welsh *gwyn* 'white' as in Welsh *Gwendraeth* 'white strand', with a Celtic root **reisko-* which survived in Irish and Gaelic *riasg* 'moor, fen' and the early Welsh stream-name *nant ruisc*. The upper part of the river was called *Gytingbroc* 780 (11th) BCS 236 (*v.* Guiting ii, 12 *infra*) and *Theodningc* 779 ib 230 (*v.* þēoden 'prince' and -ing[2], a river-name suffix); in the latter charter *uuænrisc* seems to refer to the Dikler (cf. Grundy 53).

WYE (affluent of the Severn)

> *on Wæge* 956 (12th) ASChart cix, *éá Wæge* 11 Saints (v.l. *Wege*)
> *Waia, Waya(m)* 1086 DB, 1150–60 BM, 1190 P, 1228 Cl *et freq* to 1626 *For* 28
> *Waie, Waye* 1086 DB, 1086–7 Glouc, 1227 Ch, 1282 *For et freq* to 1367 Inq
> *Wye* c. 1340 For, 1396 Works *et freq* to 1677 BG vii, 252

The name occurs as the first el. of *wægemuþan* 956 (12th) BCS 927 'the mouth of the Wye' (*v.* mūða) and Wyeseal (iii, 244 *infra*). Ekwall (RN 451–2) cites many more forms, including variants of the Welsh name of the river (*Gwy*), and explains it as a PrWelsh **weg* from the root *u̯egh- (as in Lat *veho* 'carry', etc.) denoting 'running water' or the like, but the origin is uncertain. Professor Jackson suggests that the PrWelsh form of Welsh *Gwy* would be *wē.

WYND BROOK (affluent of Glynch Brook in Redmarley D'Abitot), *Penbroc, ondlang Penbroces* (sic for *Wen-*) 875 (11th) BCS 542, *Wenbroc(es)* 963 (11th) ib 1109, 967 (11th) ib 1208, *Wendebrok* 1496 Hopt 48. The first el. is probably a Celtic stream-name from Welsh *gwyn* (fem. *gwen*) 'white'.

ROAD-NAMES

Cirencester (*Corinium*) was at the centre of a series of Roman and other roads which from Romano-British times offered communication with important places in all directions. The great Roman road going in a north-westerly direction from Silchester to Gloucester and beyond the Severn was intersected here by the Fosse Way which ran from Bath in the south-west to the central midlands. Between the arms of these roads there was on the north the ancient track called Whiteway, and on the east were Akeman Street and Welsh Way. Roman roads also ran from Avonmouth to Gloucester and Worcester up the Severn valley (Hare Lane, Portway), from Avonmouth to Bath, from the Fosse Way near Bourton on the Water north to Alcester (Buckle Street), and from Gloucester to Caerwent on the west side of the Severn; others formed a network in the Roman mining area of the Forest of Dean. Ancient tracks also include Green Street and the various Portways, Ridgeways, and Saltways. Not all these roads are named, but their existence is recognised in certain later minor p.ns. Various matters concerning these roads have been fully discussed in Bd 1–7 and Wo 2–9, the latter being particularly important in connexion with the Gl system. Cf. esp. BG xlvii, 65–80 on minor ancient roads to and from *Corinium*, ib lii, 151–86 on the later Roman road system, ib liii, 113–44 on road-planning in the Cotswolds, and I. D. Margery, *Roman Roads in Britain* (London, 1955), i, 119–47, ii, 13–22, 55–64.

AKEMAN STREET (Mg 16b), the Roman road from Cirencester east to Eastleach Turville; possibly, in view of an old name of Bath (*Acemannes ceastre* ASC(A) s.a. 973), this name also applied to the Fosse Way between Cirencester and Bath (cf. Bd 1–2), but the name is not so far found in sources for the Gl section. It is probably *Ruggeweye* 13 Glouc, *alta strata* 1306 *Ass* 6. According to Rudder 348, 'Acman Street was sometimes called *the Icknild-way*', but the latter is probably an antiquarian transference of the name of the famous Icknield Way in Wiltshire and Berks (cf. Bd 4).

BUCKLE STREET, the section of the Roman road from Bidford on Avon (Wa) to Weston Subedge (Mg 18a), marked on 1″ O.S. 144 as then going through the parishes of Snowshill, Temple Guiting and the Slaughters (where it was called *Eveshams Wayes* 209 *infra*) to the Fosse Way at Bourton on the Water. *Buggilde stret* 709 (c. 1200) BCS 125 (Wo), *bi Buggild strete* 11 KCD 1368 (Honeybourne), *in to buggilde stræt* c. 1055 Finb 171 (Upper Swell), *Bugkildweie* 1248 *FF* (Swell), *Bugkeildeweye* 1255 ib, *Buggildweye* 1258 Maddox, *Buckle-streete* 1689 Harrowby. The first el. is the OE fem. pers.n. *Burghild*, cf. Wo 2. It is sometimes called *Ikenild-*, *Rikenildstret* (Wo 2).

CONDICOTE LANE (Mg 18a), the Roman road which leaves Buckle Street in Saintbury and goes in a straight line through Condicote to the Fosse Way at Bourton on the Water. It is doubtless referred to in *to stret beorge* and *Stratburgdich* in Upper Swell (228 *infra*) and *onlong stræt* 854 (c. 1200) BCS 482 in Willersey.

THE COTSWOLD RIDGEWAY (Road A. 436 Adlestrop–Stow–Birdlip, then Sapperton–Avening–Weston Birt, A. 46 to Sodbury–Cold Ashton–Bath), following the line of a prehistoric track from the Humber to the Bristol Channel, is rarely mentioned by name, but is referred to in Banbury Lane (i, 212 *infra*), *hric weges* (Naunton 201), Rudgeway (Avening 89), *Rugwei* (ii, 240), *rycg weg* (iii, 35), and *Rugeweye* (Old Sodbury) (*v.* Ridgeway 19 *infra*), Portway (Upper Slaughter 209), *Portstræte* (Dowdeswell 171) and *Porteweye* (Hawkesbury) (*v.* Portway 18 *infra*), *Wildeneweye* (Sapperton 139) (*v. Fielden Way infra*), and *Saltherpoðe* (Cold Ashton) (*v.* Saltway 20 *infra*).

ERMIN STREET, now used of the Roman road from Silchester (Ha) to Cirencester and Gloucester (Mg 41 b, c) to be identified with *Ermingestrete* 13 Higden, and called *the Irminstreet* 1779 Rudder; this is in fact a transferred name from the great Ermin Street, which is named from an Anglo-Saxon folk, the *Earningas*, whose name appears in Armingford and Arrington (C 50, 69), cf. Bd 2–3. The Gl road is known as *hean streat* (i, 60), *Streta* 13 BG vii, 143 (p), *Dagelingstrete* (69), and *Fosse* (142), and gave its name to Stratton and *Stretfeld* (65, 70 *infra*), and *Foss ground* (70) and Foss Field (72), due to confusion with Fosse Way (17).

FIELDEN WAY (lost), occurring once as *Fildeneweye* in North Cerney (149 *infra*), where it is probably the Fosse Way or White Way; also as the name of another road, *Fildeneway*, in Upper Swell and Condicote (217, 228 *infra*); and possibly as the name of a third road, *Wildeneweye* in Sapperton (139). The name is one used for ancient roads and denotes 'road of those dwelling in the open country', *v.* filde[2], weg.

FOSSE WAY, the Roman road from Bath (So), through Shipton Moyne to Cirencester, Northleach, Bourton on the Water, Stow, and Moreton in Marsh (Mg 5c, d), (*in, æfter, andlang, etc.*) *Foss* 779 (c. 1200) BCS 229 (Donnington), 949 ib 882 (Bourton on the Water), 11 (c. 1200) KCD 1365, 1016 (14th) ib 723 (Maugersbury), c. 1055 Finb 171 (Upper Swell), (12th) KCD 1359 (Broadwell), *on fos* 852 (13th) BCS 466 (North Cerney), *stratum que vocatur fos* 931 (14th) ib 673 (Kemble), *ad metas Fose* 13 WinchLB (Aston Blank), *Foss(e)* 1221 ib (Chedworth), 1319 BG lxxiii, 169 (Rodmarton), 1374 *Rent* 248 (Maugersbury, Upper Swell), 1460 *CirenD* 18 (Cirencester) *et freq* to 1779 Rudder, (*the*) *Foss(e)way* 1457 WinchLB (Yanworth), 1621 *GR* 158 (Bourton on the Water), 1675 ib 1448 (South Cerney); the name *Fosse* appears in various minor names and f.ns. on its course, such as Foss leaze (59), Foss field and Foss Hill (66, 69), Foss Cross & Bridge (165, 166), *Fosse end* (172), *Fossebridge* (Bourton Bridge 196), *Fosse peace* (208), Foss Lane (222), etc. *v.* foss[1] 'ditch', weg, so called from its having a prominent ditch on either side (cf. Wo 3). The road was also known as *braðan stræte* in Maugersbury (223), 'the broad road', and *innan hæn streat, of ðam streate* 779 (c. 1200) BCS 229 (Donnington), that is, 'the high or chief road' (*v.* hēah, strǣt), and this use of *strǣt* for the Fosse Way recurs in the lost *Dunnestreattúnne* (*v.* Donnington 217 *infra*), Stratford Bridge in Longborough (247), which was on a field track to Fosse Way, f.ns. like Streetfold and Street Acre in Yanworth (191), and the surname *Bythestrete* 1327 *SR* in Clapton near Slaughter. Other terms referring to this road include dīc 'ditch' (in Ditchford 235 *infra*), Fielden Way (*supra*), (*le*) *Rugweie, -wey* 13 WinchLB, AD v, *Ridgeway* 1621 Inq (in Yanworth, North Cerney and Farmington respectively), *v.* Ridgeway (18 *infra*).

GREEN STREET occurs several times, esp. in late forms; the one named in Boddington (*Grenestrete* 1491 *TewkCt*), Churchdown (*Green street ground* 1840 *TA* 47) and Brockworth (Green Street ii, 118 *infra*) might refer to one road (cf. BG vii, 132), but it is not possible to trace a connexion from this to Green Street in Haresfield (ii, 183), in Stonehouse (ii, 204), in Coaley (ii, 220), where there is also a *Stretley* (ii, 221), and in Uley (ii, 255), or Green Lane in Iron Acton (iii, 2 *infra*). *v.* grēne[1], strǣt. On Green Way in Shurdington (ii, 157) *v.* Introd.

HARE LANE, formerly HARE STREET, was used of the road from Worcester to Gloucester and the south (A. 38) in Hare Lane in

Gloucester (ii, 129) and *Hereweye* in Cam (ii, 218); *herepað, -poð* was
the name of highways in Clifford Chambers (240), Olveston (iii, 123)
and Cold Ashton (iii, 64). *v.* here-pæð, here-weg 'military highway'.

PORTWAY, usually denoting 'a road leading to some important town'
(*v.* port², **weg**), occurs several times in Gl, including Portway in
Upper Slaughter (209) and *port stræte* (171 *infra*), a name for the
Cotswold Ridgeway (16) in Dowdeswell; *le, la Porteweye* 1293,
1383 AD iii (possibly a stretch in Hawkesbury of the Nailsworth–
Bath road A. 46, which is also called Portway Lane in Old Sodbury
iii, 54 *infra*). Other examples include *Porteway* 1498 AD i (the road
from Tewkesbury to Gloucester), *Portweye* in Down Hatherley
(ii, 146), *Portstret* in Hardwicke (ii, 182) and *Portway* in Haresfield
(ii, 185 *infra*), which refer to the Roman road from Worcester to
Gloucester and Bristol; Portway in Chedworth (152), possibly a
northern extension of White Way (*infra*); Port Way in Coates (69)
and *Portweye* in Bisley (126), which may refer to the Cirencester–
Stroud road (A. 419); Portway piece in Barnsley (26) and Partway
Ash in Bibury (28), denoting Akeman Street (A. 433); Port Way
(ii. 143), the old Gloucester–Painswick road; Portway furlong in
Ebrington (244); *Oldeporteweie* (ii, 28) in Sudeley and *norðmæstan
port weig'* in Roel (ii, 21), which is probably the road from Guiting
Power to Winchcomb; *portstræt* (ii, 46) in Teddington and Portway
in Ashchurch (ii, 56), which seem to be the Tewkesbury–Stow road
(A. 438), also called *Teuxbury way* in Alstone (ii, 42); *Portewey* in
Forthampton (ii, 59), the Upton on Severn–Gloucester road (B. 4211);
Portway Length in Gotherington (ii, 89); Portway in Newland (iii,
240); Portway (iii, 193) in Longhope, the road to Ross; Portoway
Top (iii, 170) in Dymock, which is near the Roman road from
Gloucester to Leominster.

RIDGEWAY, RUDGEWAY, used of several roads in various parts of Gl
(*v.* hrycg, weg): (1) as an alternative name for the Fosse Way (17
supra); (2) as an alternative name for Akeman Street at Rudgeway
piece in Eastleach Martin (32); (3) as an alternative name of Ermin
Street at *Reggeweyfurlond* in Brimpsfield (147), *Ruggewey* in Badgeworth (ii, 117) and *Rugweye* in Brockworth (ii, 119); (4) possibly of
Buckle Street or the Saltway at *Rigge Waye* in Cow Honeybourne
(245); (5) possibly as a name of the northern continuation of White
Way in *Rugwey* in Rendcomb (162) and Ridgeway in Compton Abdale
(167), and as the name of the same road in Baunton (57); (6) Ridge-

way in Alveston (iii, 112 *infra*), which refers to a section of the Roman road from Gloucester to Avonmouth; (7) Ridgeway in Stapleton (iii, 102), Rodway in Mangotsfield (iii, 99), *hric weg* in Pucklechurch (iii, 67) and Ridgeway in Marshfield (iii, 61 *infra*), which no doubt represent a road from Bristol to Marshfield to the north of the present main road (A. 420), and called *that strǣt* in Doynton (iii, 78 *infra*); (8) *Ricchwaye* in Awre (iii, 255), the Roman road from Gloucester to South Wales; and various minor or unidentified roads such as Ridgeway ground in Bibury (28); Rudgeway in Avening (89); *hric weges* in Naunton (201), which is probably the Cotswold Ridgeway (A. 436); *Ruggeweie* in Sherborne (206); Ridgeway in Ashchurch (ii, 56), which may be the Stow–Tewkesbury road (A. 438); Rudgeway in Tewkesbury (ii, 68) and in Elmstone Hardwicke (ii, 82); *Rugeweye* in Old Sodbury (iii, 56), also called *le Strete* (iii, 56), which is probably the Stroud–Bath road (A. 46), etc.

SALTWAY, SALTERSWAY, etc. The saltways in Gl are an extension of the Worcestershire system which is centred on Droitwich (Wo 285): (1) a saltway running south-east from Buckle Street in Weston Subedge is suggested by *Salteresweie* 1225 *FF* in Chipping Campden and *andlang Sealt strǣte* 969 BCS 1238 near Four Shire Stone at the north end of Evenlode (cf. also Stratford in Evenlode 220); it ran thence along the Chipping Norton road skirting Rollright (which had salt rights in Droitwich) and through Salford (O 373–4), this being Road I in Wo 7. (2) A saltway (Road H in Wo 7) from Buckle Street (15 *supra*), which was also known as *þa sealt strǣt* (972 (10th) BCS 1282), may have followed the Broadway–Stow road (A. 424) or left the Saltway (1) in Chipping Campden and passed through Blockley over Saltmore in Longborough (248), through Donnington parish, where it was called *innon, of ðere saltstret(e)* 779 (c. 1200) BCS 229, to *sæltstræt* in Broadwell (216), by *Saltuuelle* in Icomb (222) and *Saltforde* in Wyck Rissington (203), probably by Saltway Plant. in Windrush (210) and Salt hill in Southrop (46). (3) The chief saltway (Road A in Wo 5) through Hinton on the Green (*ða ealdan strǣt* near *Saltwyllan* 1042 KCD 764), perhaps by Stanway (ii, 24), along Salter's Lane in Hailes (*Salters Lane* 1586 *Comm*, cf. also Hailes ii, 15 *infra*) and Salt Way in Pinnock (ii, 20) and Winchcomb, over Salter's Hill, along Saltway in Sudeley (*Saltweye* 1256 WinchLB, *Salters Lane* 1777 M), between Sevenhampton (cf. *Hayles Way* 180 *infra*) and Hawling, where it is called *ofer þa s(e)alt stræt(e)* 816 (11th) BCS 356 and *Saltersway* 1777 M, possibly through the parish of Salperton, whose name may refer to this saltway (176), along *Saltway* (1811 Auct 5) and through Eastington (Saltway 172), then to *Saltway Hill* 1798 *EnclA* and Saltway Fm (166 *infra*), both in Coln St Denis, to *Saltway* 1768 *EnclA* and *Saltway Road* 1830 M in Bibury, with a branch from Coln St Denis through *le Saltstret* 1301 AD iii in Winson to *Saulthill* (53 *infra*) in Ampney St Mary; this is 4 miles from Cirencester where there was a *Saltewhich* (67), which was probably a centre for trading in salt. (4) A saltway (Road B in Wo 6) through Tewkesbury, which had salt-rights in Droitwich in DB, Ashchurch (Saltmore ii, 56) and Gotherington (*Salterway* ii, 89), presumably Cheltenham and Salterley in Coberley (153), perhaps by Whiteway in Miserden (131), by either Salter's Hill in Winstone (142) or Cranham (Saltridge Wood 158) to *Saltharperweie* in Rodmarton (107) and the south. (5) A saltway (Road B¹ in Wo 6) by Tewkesbury (*Salters lane* ii, 63), to Deerhurst (Salter's Hill ii, 80), Gloucester (the monks of St Peter's had salt-rights) and the south; the connexion of Salters hill in Horton (iii, 37), Saltmoors (iii, 33) in Hawkesbury, Saltterswell in Tormarton (iii, 57), *sealtherpoðe* in Cold Ashton (iii, 64, the ridgeway to Bath), and *Sealterforda* (iii, 186) with the saltway system cannot be exactly determined. Cf. also Salter St. in Berkeley (ii, 212).

WELSH WAY, now used of a lane from Fairford, formerly called *Street way* (36), to Sunhill in Meysey Hampton, where it may be referred to in Street Way (75), crossing Akeman Street at Ready Token, through Barnsley and Ampney Crucis, where it may have been called *le Waweweye* 1300–25 *CirenP*, through Barnsley, Bagendon (*Welch Road* 1792 *EnclA*) and Duntisbourne Rouse (*Welchway* 1837 ib). It is not known if *Walhweg* (116 *infra*) in Woodchester refers to an extension of this road through the Golden Valley, nor is it known where it crossed the Severn towards Wales; cf. J. H. Cooke, 'The Roman road from Corinium to Lydney' in BG iv, 156–8. The name is from OE Walh 'Welshman' or Welisc 'Welsh' and weg.

WHITE WAY (Mg 55), the name of a ridgeway from Cirencester towards Compton Abdale, where it would appear to join the Saltway which goes north towards Winchcomb and Stanway; it is possibly referred to in *ongean stretun* 852 (13th) BCS 466. If it is a branch of the main saltway the name might well refer to its use for the carrying of salt (v. hwĭt, weg). There was also a *Whiteway* in Farmington (173) and this may be another name for the Saltway. Whatever its meaning, the road clearly linked Cirencester with the Roman villas at Chedworth, Withington, etc. Cf. also H. P. R. Finberg, *Gloucestershire* 57 and Stratton (Bd 102).

Other Roman roads have no current names. (1) Sections of the Worcester–Tewkesbury–Gloucester–Sea Mills road (Mg 180, 541) were known as a Saltway (Saltway (B) Wo 6) and by various names, including 'street' as in Stratford Bridge in Twyning (ii, 72), *Strete* in Norton (ii, 151), and possibly Street croft in Ham and Street field *& ley* in Hamfallow (ii, 227, 232), Hare Lane (i, 17), Portway, Ridgeway (i, 18), and possibly Rykenild Street, cf. *Rikenel Stile* in Gloucester (ii, 141 *infra*). (2) The Roman road Cirencester–Rodmarton–Bath (Mg 542, 544) may be referred to in *le Streat heyes* in Cherington (91), Street Fm in Tetbury Upton (112); from Lasborough it followed the Cotswold Ridgeway south with a branch from Lasborough to Nympsfield, Frocester, and Arlingham (Mg 543). (3) The Roman road from Gloucester to Ross on Wye (He) (Mg 61, 611) is referred to in Oakle Street in Churcham (iii, 197); a branch to Dymock (Mg 610) is called *magnam stratam usque Newent* 1228 Cl. (4) The Roman road from Gloucester to Caerwent (Monm) (Mg 60a) is referred to in Stantway and *Stratfield* in Westbury on Severn (iii, 20, 208), Stretfield Hill, *Morefeldstrete* in Awre and *Overstreet* (iii, 254, 253, 251) and Stroat in Tidenham (iii, 265). Various other allusions to 'streets' occur in Banbury Lane and *Lodreswei* in Adlestrop (212, 213), *le Strete* in Bisley (126), Stratford Park in Stroud (140), and *Streetefurlonge* in King's Stanley (ii, 201); *strǣt* or Stanborough Lane in Notgrove (176), *strǣt* in Mickleton (251); *strǣte* and *Streteley* in Wotton under Edge (ii, 261); *Stretecrofte* in Yate (iii, 46); *strǣt* in Pucklechurch (iii, 67), *ealdan strǣt* in Elberton (iii, 115); *Mayysmorstret* (iii, 162), the road from Gloucester to Worcester on the west of the Severn, cf. also Oridge Street (iii, 147) and Wickridge Street (iii, 153), the names of two lanes that join this road (B. 4211) but which may simply denote 'village street, built-up road'. A road from Lydney through Mitcheldean to *Ariconium* (Mg 614) was called *Merring Street* in Mitcheldean (iii, 235), etc. The Sea Mills–Bitton–Bath road (Mg 54) is not named or referred to in place-names.

I. BRIGHTWELLS BARROW HUNDRED

This hundred is in the south-east of the county, bounded on the south by the R. Thames and Berkshire and Wiltshire, and on the east by the R. Leach and Oxfordshire; it occupies the lower part of the Coln valley. At the time of DB the manors of Aldsworth, Barnsley, and Bibury were in a separate hundred of Bibury (26 *infra*) but they had been transferred to Brightwells Barrow before 1221 (*Ass*). It was one of the hundreds of Cirencester (1221 *Ass* 10d, cf. 47 *infra*).

BIBURY HUNDRED (lost)

Begeberie, -briges h'd, Becheberie hond' 1086 DB, named from Bibury 26 *infra*.

BRIGHTWELLS BARROW HUNDRED

Brictv(v)oldes-, -woldesberg h'd, Bricstvoldes h'd 1086 DB, *Bricthwolde bergh* 1221 *Ass, Bricgtwoldesberwe* 1316 FA

Bristoldesberg h'd 1086 DB, *Bristewaldeberewe* 1276 RH

Brichwaldesberge 1169 P, *Brichtwoldeberga* 1176 P, *-woldes-* 1177 P, *-waldes-* 1193 P, *Brichgtwaldbergh'* 1221 *Ass*

Brithwaldesbergahundredo 1195 P, *Brethwaldesbergh* 1220 Fees, *Brithwoldesberwe* 1327 *SR*

Brikeswaldeberga 1195 P, *Brykwellbarowe* 1286 Inq

Brittewaldesbyr', -woldesbergh 1248 *Ass, Britwoldeslewe* (sic) 1276 RH, *Britwoldesburwe* 1285 FA, *Brytwell hundred* 1286 Ipm, *Brytwodesberwe* 1303 FA

Brightwaldesbergh 1248 *Ass, -bar(r)owe* 1540 *MinAcct*, 1559 *FF*, *-borowe* 1587 ib, *Brightwoldesbergh(e)* 1287 *Ass*, QW, 1346 FA, *-beriwe* 1316 FA, *Brightwaldisbarough* 1540 *AOMB* 242

Bryztwoldesberewe 1378 *Ass*

Britles Barrow 1610 M

'Beorhtwald's mound' from the OE pers.n. *Beorht-, Brihtwald* and *beorg*. The meeting-place of the hundred has been identified with Barrow Elm Fm in Hatherop (37 *infra*) where the hundred court met in 1400 (BG ix, 333) and which is in the centre of the hundred. There is a *Brighthallesbarowe felde* in 1540 *AOMB* 444, 30, 1540 *MinAcct*, but its location is not certain (40 *infra*).

Aldsworth

ALDSWORTH (144–1510)

Ealdeswy[rðe] 1002–4 ASWills, 1004 KCD 710, *-worthe* 1008
Finb 149
Aldesorde 1086 DB
Aldeswrd(e) 1086 DB, 1221 *Ass*, *-wurde* 1184–1205 Oseney
Aldesworþe 12, 1200, 1263–84 Glouc, *-w(u)rþe* 12, 13 WinchLB,
-worth(e) 1148–1271 Glouc (*freq*), c. 1184, 1271 Oseney, 1282,
1290 Episc, 1327 *SR et passim* to c. 1560 *Surv* (*-als.
Alsworthe*)
1578 *FF*, *-wrth* 1291 Tax, *-wurth'* 1248 *Ass*
Aldew(u)rth(e) 1221 *Ass*, Plea, *-worthe* 1276 Oseney
Altesworth 1287 *Ass*   *Allesworth* 1540 *MinAcct*
Aul(e)sworth 1577, 1610 M, 1675 Ogilby   *Audlesworth* 1587 *FF*
'Ald's enclosure', *v.* worð. An OE pers.n. *Ald, Eald* is not
recorded except in this and other p.ns. like Awsworth (Nt 137) and
Owdeswell (188 *infra*). It would be a shortened form of such OE
pers.ns. as *Aldfrið, Aldhelm*, etc. On the form *Aules-* cf. Phonol. § 5.

WALL FM, *Walle* 1184–1205, c. 1230 Oseney, 1221 *Ass* (p), 1287
QW, 1299 *RBB*, 1354 *FF et passim* to 1542 *AOMB* 447, *atte Walle*
1327 *SR* (p), *Wall* 1561 *GR* 540, 1639 Inq. *v.* wall 'wall', used in
p.ns. of a defensive wall, especially of Roman works, but no such
remains have been reported here; it probably denoted some defensive
or boundary bank to the north of Aldsworth.

BLACKPITS BARN, *-Downs* 1793 *EnclA*, *the Blackpitts* 18 Sherb, *v.*
blæc, pytt.   COCKLEBARROW, *-Banks* 1793 *EnclA*, *v.* beorg 'hill,
mound'; the first el. is uncertain, but is possibly OE coccel 'tares',
cf. Cockleberry (W 105).   CONYGREE FM, *the Conygrees* 1793
EnclA, *v.* coninger 'rabbit-warren'.   LAD BARROW, 1793 *EnclA*, the
name of a tumulus, possibly 'the youth's mound', *v.* ladda, beorg.
LARKETHILL WOOD, *Larcothill* 1793 *EnclA*.   SHABBINGTON PLANT.,
Shabington furlong 1793 *EnclA*, *Shabindean* 1862 *GR* 540.

FIELD-NAMES

The principal forms in (*a*) are 1793 *EnclA*. Spellings dated 1271 are Oseney
v, 30–1, 1542 *MinAcct*, 18 Sherb, 1799 *EnclA* (map) in *GR* (D 1388).

(*a*) Abbots Penn (*v.* penn² 'enclosure'); Aldsworth Downs 18 (*terr' voc'
Downes* 1542, *v.* dūn); Allens Downs (*v.* dūn 'hill'); Ashway furlong;
Berryhill (*v.* beorg 'hill'); Blackenhill furlong (*v.* blæc 'black' or the OE

pers.n. *Blaca*, hyll); the Brach (*v.* brēc 'land broken up for cultivation'); Broadbarrow Hill (*Brad-* 1799, *v.* brād, beorg 'hill'); the Butts (*v.* butte 'abutting strip'); Cathill furlong (*c.* catt, hyll); Clinkstone furlong (perhaps identical with *Cohoenston* 1355 Orig); The Deadmore Hill; Dewbrink furlong; Dialhill (*v.* dial 'sun-dial carved in the turf', hyll); Droveway-, Dunstone furlong; Ewe Yean Ground 1799 (*v.* eowu, ēan 'lamb'); the Garston ground (*Gerstuna* 1184–1205 Oseney, *v.* gærs-tūn 'paddock'); Giants Cross 1799; Gooseacres; Green Cleeves Hill & Penn; Hidespit furlong; Hitching Lane (*v.* heccing 'the part of a field sown'); Hogrick furlong; Hundred's Hill ground; Lampool acre, Lambpool 1799; the Leazow 1799 (*v.* lǣs); Leekbeds furlong; the Leys; Lousey piece 1799; Maul Croft; New Tineing (*v.* tȳning 'enclosure, fencing'); Nomans Land (usually denoting land on an undefined boundary); Oathill furlong; Oldland Penn; Palmers Bush; Picked Close; Pludds furlong (*v.* pludde 'pool, puddle'); Potshole 1799; Slat Quar ('slate quarry', *v.* slate, quarriere); Swire Hill; Wedingbush furlong; Westchestle furlong (*v.* ceastel 'heap (of stones)'); Whit furlong; Wontslades furlong; Wry furlong (*v.* wrēo 'twisting').

(b) *grangia de Aldeswrthe* 1271 (a grange of Oseney Abbey, *v.* grange); (*pastura voc'*) *Hayl(l)inge* 13 Glouc, 1271.

Barnsley

BARNSLEY (157–0705)

> *æt Bearmodes lea* c. 802 (11th) BCS 304
> *æt Beorondes lea* 855 (11th) BCS 487, *æt Bærendes lea* n.d. ib 1320
> *Bernesleis* 1086 DB, *-leia* 1154–89 *Lanth²* 32d
> *Berdesley(a)*, *-leia* 1195–6 P, 1494 *MinAcct*
> *Bardesley(e)*, *-leg(h)*, *-l'*, *-le* 12 Glouc. 1186–91, 1200–20 Oseney, 1209 Fees, 1221 Eyre (p), 1274 RH, 1276 Oseney, 1285 FA, 1291 Tax, 14 AD i *et freq* to 1553 Pat, (*-juxta Bebur'*) 1290 Episc, *Bardisleigh(e)*, *-ys-* 1544 LP, (*-als. Barnsley*) 1623 *Rec*
> *Berdel'* 1201 Cur
> *Barndesley(e)*, *-le(e)*, *-legh(e)* 1221 *Ass*, Plea, 1276 RH, 1286 Ipm, 1291 Tax, 1327 *MinAcct*, 1327 *SR et freq* to 1494 *Rogers 2*, *Berndesley* 1330 Ipm
> *Berandesleg'* 1221 *Ass*   *Barnedesley* 1353 Ipm
> *Bardeleg'*, *-leye* 1248 *Ass*, 1301 Ipm
> *Bramdesleye* 1276 RH, *Brandsley* 1316 FA, *Bradesley als. Barnesley* 1576 *MonLand*
> *Barn(e)sley* 1326, 1347 Ch, 1400 Ipm *et freq* to 1623 *FF*
> *Barmesley* 1488 Pat

'Beornmōd's glade or clearing' from the OE pers.n. *Beornmōd* and lēah; the contracted forms are interesting in the fluctuation between

Bernes- (the *-m-* in the contracted *Bermdes-* having become *-n-* before the dental *-d-* which was then lost) and *Berdes-*, etc. (with loss of the nasal); cf. Barnsleyhall (Wo 338) for a similar name.

DITTENHAM (lost), *Di-, Dyttenham* 1330, 1366 Ipm, 1494 *MinAcct, Duttenham* 1448 ib, *Ditenham* 1459 ib. Probably 'Dytta's meadow', *v.* hamm. An OE pers.n. *Dytta* is nowhere recorded, but it would be a mutated form of the OE *Dutta* which seems to occur in *duttan hamm* BCS 757, now Dutmans (W 231). The origin of the pers.n. is obscure; it might be connected with OE *dott* 'head of a boil' and *dyttan* 'to shut'. But it is possible that *Dittenham* contains the OE *Dydda* which occurs in several p.ns. (cf. Didmarton iii, 28 *infra*); the strong form *Dyddi* already appears as *Dit-* in the 14th century in Dittisham (D 322).

POULTMOOR, *Pountmor(e)* 1330, 1366 Ipm, 1380, 1414, 1459 *MinAcct, Poundemore* 1494 ib, *Poultmoor* 1830 M. This could formally be a compound of OFr *pount* 'bridge' (*v.* pont) and mōr, but although there are a few ditches about it is unlikely on topographical and other grounds. It is possibly of similar origin to Poltimore (D 444), which Ekwall (DEPN) derives from an OE pers.n. *Pulta* of obscure origin. The modern spelling suggests this; the *Pount-* forms, which are due to French influence, occur sporadically also in Poltimore and Poultney (Lei); cf. Zachrisson, ANInfl 127 ff. An obscure OE pers.n. *Punt(a)* is also possible (cf. *Puntes pirian* ii, 78 *infra*).

BARNSLEY PARK (1830 M) & WOLD (1841 *TA*, *super Waldam* 1459 *MinAcct, -Weldam* 1468 ib), *v.* park, wald (WSax *weald*). FIELD BARN, 1830 M. FURZEY FURLONG BARN. THE GROVE. HILL COPSE, 1830 M. MIDDLETON COPSE, 1830 M, *Middletons* (*Coppice*) 1841 *TA*. QUEENS WELL WOOD. THE WARREN, 1830 M. WINTERWELL, a stream, cf. Winterwell (45, 50 *infra*).

FIELD-NAMES

The principal forms in (*a*) are 1841 *TA* 17.

(*a*) Allington; Birstwells; Broadmoor; Cadmore pool; Cats sprain (the common f.n. Catsbrain, used of mottled soil consisting of rough clay mixed with stones, clay overlaid with marl, *v.* cattes-braȝen and cf. Arkell and Tomkeieff, *English Rock Terms* 19); Clay hill; Clayton green; Coney gore (*Conynger* 1366 Ipm, *v.* coninger 'rabbit-warren'); Downs ground (cf. Ampney Downs 49); Eight acres; Forehead (*Forherdesmede, -yardes-* 1488, 1494 *MinAcct* 'the front yard or enclosure', *v.* fore, geard, mǣd 'meadow');

Fount Moors; Gallows ground; Gossmoor ground; Great slade (*v.* slæd 'valley'); Halfpenny hill ('hill paying a halfpenny rent'); Hollington; Horse hays (*v.* hors, (ge)hæg 'enclosure'); Hull bush; Knowl ground (*v.* cnoll 'hillock'); the Lawn (*v.* launde 'glade, woodland pasture'); Leverbed (probably 'reed bed', *v.* læfer, bedd, cf. *le leuer bedde* KCD 632 (W), R. Dikler 6 *supra*); Nomans land; Penny lands ('strips of the common field paying a penny rent'); Portway piece (possibly a reference to Akeman Street 15 *supra*); Pourn hill; Redlands; Riding grove; Rookmoor; Shoulder of Mutton (so called from its shape); Smiths mead; Stone quarry; Tabres slud; Three acres; Waterwell hill; Wayhall hill; Webbs hays (*v.* (ge)hæg).

(*b*) *Bryggefeldes* 1494 *Rogers* 2 (*v.* brycg, feld); *le Ley(e)s* 1448, 1459 *MinAcct* (*v.* lēah 'clearing').

Bibury

BIBURY (157–1106)

Beagan byrig 721–43 (11th) BCS 166, n.d. ib 1320, *Began byrg* 899 ib 580

Begeberie, -ia 1086 DB, 1186–9 Oseney, *Begaberia* 1151, 1173 ib, 1320 Ch *Becheberie* 1086 DB, *Behebiria* 1221 Plea (p)

Bi-, Bybur' 1154–89 *Tewk* 73b, 1274 RH, 1291 Tax, 1303 FA, *-byr, -bir* 1271 Episc, 1287 *Ass*, *-bery* 1287 ib, 1349 Ipm, 1535 VE, *-buri, -bury* 1291 Tax, 1316 FA, 1319 *FF et passim* to 1610 M, (*-Northumberland, -Osney*) 1600 *FF*

Bei-, Beybir', -bur(y), -buria 1163, 1173 Oseney, 1209 Fees, 1254 Pat, 1255 Ch, 1269 Episc *et freq* to 1303 FA, *Beyeburi* 1285 FA *Biebir'* 1221 *Ass*, *Byebury* 1349 Aid

Bebiry, -bur(y) 1248 *FF*, 1275 Episc, 1281 *Heref* (p), 1284 Episc

'Bēage's fortified place', *v.* burh. The place was doubtless named from *Bēage*, the daughter of Earl Leppa, to whom the land was granted by the Bishop of Worcester in the 8th century (BCS 166). Her name may also be preserved in the local f.n. *Bywell* (*infra*). The affix *Northumberland* refers to a grant of land here to the Duke of Northumberland in 1550 and *Osney* to the land of Osney Abbey (Oseney v, 1–21).

ABLINGTON

(*æt*) *Eadbaldingtun(e)* 855, 899 (11th) BCS 487, 580

Abelinton, -yn(g)- 1207 FF, 1208 Abbr, 1248, 1287 *Ass*, 1349 Ipm *Ablinton(a), -yn-* 13 Oseney, 1209 Fees, 1210 FF, 1215 ClR, 1221 Eyre, 1263–84 Glouc *et passim* to 1501 FF, *Ablyngton, -ing-* 1286 FA, 1322 Pat *et freq* to 1601 *Comm*

'Farmstead associated with Ēadbald', *v.* ing⁴, tūn. The pers.n. is the common OE *Ēadbald*.

ARLINGTON

Ælfredin(c)gtune 1002–4 ASWills, 1004 KCD 710, *-intun* 1008
Finb 149, *Alvredintone* 1086 DB
Alurinton(a), *-yn-* Hy 2 Monast, 1221 *Ass*, 1225–50 *CirenP* i, 44,
1285 FA *et freq* to 1363 *FF*, (*-iuxta Bibury*) 1332 FF, *Alurington*,
-yng- 1233 Cl, 1337 Ch, 1359 Orig, *Alvrynton(e)* 1314, 1349 Ipm
Alfrinton 13 Oseney, 1296 Ipm, 1327 *SR*   *Alvertone* 1287 QW
Auerinton' 1221 Eyre, *Auuerington'* 1248 *Ass*
Alwrintone 1253 Oseney, *Ailwrenton'* 1287 *Ass*
Alrin(g)ton, *-yn(g)-* 13 Oseney, 1306 *Ass*, 1349, 1375 Ipm, 1550
Pat, *Elryngton* 1541 Monast
Herlingthon 1303 Ipm, *Erlyngton* 1439 IpmR
Arlington 1584 Comm, 1713 PR 17, (*-als. Alrington*) 1598 *FF*

'Farmstead associated with Alfred', *v.* *-ing⁴*, tūn. The pers.n. is OE *Ælfrēd*. On the late form *Arl-* metathesised from *Alr-* cf. Phonol. § 46.

DEANHILL, *ofer ða dene* 721–43 (11th) BCS 166, *Deane heye* 1575 *TRMB*, *Deanhill* 1840 *TA*. *v.* denu 'valley'. The identity is not certain.

ABLINGTON DOWNS, *the Downs* 1840 *TA*, *v.* dūn 'hill'.   ARLINGTON PIKE, *Pike ground* 1840 *TA*, *v.* pīc 'pointed hill or pointed piece of ground'; it is the junction of six lanes.   ASH PIECE, *the Ashes* 1840 *TA*.   BIBURY ELMS (1777 M, *the Elms* 1768 *EnclA*) & FIRS (1830 M).   BROOKLANDS, 1840 *TA*.   THE CLUMP, *Clump patch* 1840 *TA*, a long barrow; the name is from e.ModE *clump* 'a cluster of trees' (1586 NED s.v.).   DEAD MAN'S ACRE COPSE, 1830 *TA*.   DOWNS BARN, *la Dunne, la Northdoune* 1384 Inq, *Downs Lane* 1768 *EnclA*, *v.* dūn 'hill'.   FURZEY FURLONG WOOD, *Furzey furlong* 1840 *TA*, *v.* fyrs 'furze'.   GAMBRA HILL, a tumulus, *Kanbarrow* 1840 *TA*, *v.* beorg 'hill, barrow'.   THE GROVE, *Grove Barn* 1830 *TA*, *v.* grāf.   HALE BARN, *Hale* 13 Oseney, cf. *Hail withy bed* 1840 *TA*, *v.* halh 'nook of land'.   HAY BARN, 1830 M, *Arlington hay* 1768 *EnclA*, *Hay pool* 1840 *TA*, *v.* (ge)hæg 'enclosure'.   HILL BARN, 1830 M, *la Hulle* 13 Oseney (p), *v.* hyll.   HOLLOW PEN.   KILKENNY, 1830 M, formerly *New Farm* 1777 M; like Kilkenny (189 *infra*), named from Kilkenny (Ireland), which was captured by Cromwell in 1650.   KING'S HILL BARN, 1830 M.   LADYHILL COVERT, *Lady hill* 1840

TA. LAMBROUGH BANKS, a long barrow, *Longburiestle, Longe-burwesweye* 13 Oseney, *Langeberg* 1285 FA, *Longborough banks* 1840 *TA*, 'long barrow', *v.* lang, beorg (confused in the earliest forms with burh 'fort'), stigel 'stile'. LEACHBROOK COVERT, *Leach brook* 1768 *EnclA, v.* R. Leach (9 *supra*). MILL STREAM, cf. *Myll heye* 1575 *TRMB, the Mill(hill)way* 1768 *EnclA, Millbank, -pound* 1840 *TA*; there was a water-mill here in 1565 *Rogers* T. 8.   NEW BARN, 1830 M.   OLD WALLS SHEDS, *Oldwalls* 1840 *TA*.   OXHILL BARN. PITCHERWELL COPSE, (*-coppice*) 1768 *EnclA*, 1840 *TA*, 'well with a pitcher or from which pitchers were filled'.   QUARRY HILL, 1830 M, *Quarry* 1840 *TA*, formerly *Tite Quarr* 1777 M, *v.* quarriere 'quarry'. SALT WAY, *v.* Salt Way (19 *supra*).   SHAGBOROUGH BARN, 1830 M, *Shag barrow bottom* 1840 *TA, v.* beorg 'barrow'.   SHEWCROFT BARN 1830 M.

FIELD-NAMES

The principal forms in (*a*) are 1840 *TA* 2, 8. Spellings dated 721 are 721–43 BCS 166, 1151, 13 Oseney v, 17–21, 1384 Inq 145, 1575 *TRMB* 39 and 1768 *EnclA*.

(*a*) the Acre; Barrow Hill(s) (ib 1768, *v.* beorg 'barrow'); the Berry closes 1768; Beulands; Broad hill; Bury close (*claus' voc' Burie Curte* 1575, *Bury fields* 1768, *v.* burh 'fort', Burleigh Court 98 *infra*); Bywell 1760 M (ib 1690, 1695 M, the first el. is probably as in Bibury *supra, v.* wella); Cadmore; Calcott Peak Gate; Candle ground; Castle ditch; the Clover; Coln Stile; Cunninger (*Conyngar* 1575, *the Conegree* 1713 Sherb, 1768, *v.* coninger 'rabbit-warren'); Cow Down; Craslands meadow; Day bank (*v.* dey 'dairy-house'); Deadlands Copse; Deeplands; Fish pond; the Flat; Fold Cross; Fold Yard 1768; the Folly 1768 (*v.* folie); Forty acres; French mead; Gastons ground (cf. *Garsintone* 1327 *SR* (p), *v.* gærs-tūn 'paddock'); Gill-wares; Gore hill 1768 (*v.* gāra, hyll); Gosham; Gow hill; Great hold; Green hollow; Green heads; Greenway bottom; Hams (*the Hams* 1768, *v.* hamm 'water-meadow'); Hampstead yards; Hand post ground (*guide post called the Hand and Post* 1768); Hare barrow; Hasenbury; Hell fire piece; Hisbourn hill; Hodbush; Hollowell ground (*Holywell* 1768, *v.* hālig, wella); Hule ground; Hull Road 1768; Island; Kingsley hill; Kings orchard; Knowl hill (*La Knolle* 1384, *v.* cnoll 'hill'); Lagger hill (Gl dial. *lagger* 'a narrow strip of land or copse, esp. one uniting two parts of a farm'); the Lains (*v.* leyne 'tract of arable land'); Lark Slad (*v.* lāwerce, slæd); the Lext; Linnoth; Long bottom; Long hold (ME *hold* 'tenure'); Long lands; Lynefull ground; Mackley; Middle Hay (*v.* (ge)hæg); Millisetts; the Nine acres; Oat leaze; Old Kitchen; Ouzwell Hill 1768; Ox down(s) (ib 1768, *v.* oxa, dūn); the Park; Parsons folly; Partway ash; Picked closes 1768; Pudding hill; Rambury hill (*on rawan berh* 721, *v.* beorg 'hill, barrow', the first el. is uncertain but could be hræfn 'raven'); Redstone; Ridgway ground; Sands; Severals (*the little Several* 1768, e.ModE *severell* 'plot of privately owned land', cf. The

Severals YW i, 10); Swamp; Ten acres; Tithe lands; Trownshill bottom;
Water lands (*Waterlonde* 13, *v.* wæter, land); Water slad (*v.* slæd 'valley');
White hill; Whitelands; Withy bed; Woodway.

(*b*) *on ða aldan dic* 721 (*v.* ald, dīc); *Braynesdene* 1384 (denu); *Browninges
close* 1575; *Chenvichelle* 1086 DB; *Cleyputte* 13 (*v.* clǣg, pytt); *Cowe penne*
1575 (*v.* cū, penn²); *drihtnes dene* 721 ('the lord's valley', *v.* drihten, denu);
on east hleowan 721 (*v.* hlēo 'shelter'); *Echelinchbenland* 13 ('Ezelin's bean-
land' from the OG pers.n. *Az-*, *Ezelin* (Forssner 38), *v.* bēan, land); *Estfilde*
1575 (*Campo orientali* 13, *v.* ēast, feld); *Estweye* 13 (*v.* weg 'road'); *Hauekes-
bergh* 1384 ('hawk's hill', *v.* hafoc, beorg); *Hetherlessuihul* 13; *Home heye*
1575; *Huttelongeforlonge* 13; *Inhowe* 1384; *Leklond* 13 (*v.* lēac 'leek,
vegetable', land); *on leppan crundlas* 721 (named from Earl *Leppa* (cf. Bibury
supra), *v.* crundel); *Meidecliuum* 13 (probably 'maidens' cliff', *v.* mægð¹,
clif); *Middilhul* 13; *Renysham* 1299 *RBB*; *Roggerescroftes* 1384 (the OG pers.n.
Rotger, ME *Rog(g)er*, croft); *Staperslede* 13 (*v.* slæd 'valley'); *Stwywardesham*
1384 ('the steward's water-meadow', *v.* stīg-weard, hamm); *Þormoruslet* 13
(*v.* slæget 'sheep-pasture', cf. Sleight Barn 45 *infra*, the first el. is possibly
the AScand pers.n. *Thurmer* from ODan *Þormar*, cf. Feilitzen 395); *le Westfilde* 1575 (*campo occidentali* 13, *v.* west, feld); *Whitmede* 1303 FA (*v.* hwīt,
mǣd); *Wych* 1151 (*v.* wīc 'dependent farmstead', cf. *The Wick* 51 *infra*);
Wyssewellegate 1384 (*v.* wisse 'marsh', wella, geat).

Coln St Aldwyn

COLN ST ALDWYN (157–1405)

æt Enneglan (sic) 862 (late 13th) BCS 535
(*loco...nuncupatur*) *Cungle* 962 (11th) BCS 1091 (*v.* Addenda)
Colne 1086 DB   *Chulna* c. 1127 *GlCh* vii, 2
Culna, Culn(e) Sancti Ail-, Aylwyn(i), -win(i) 1154–1217 Glouc
(*freq*), c. 1243 *GlCh* i, 31, 1287 *Ass*, 1290 Episc, 1291 Tax, 1327
SR *et passim* to 1542 *MinAcct*, *-S. Alwyny* 1342 Heref, *-Ailwyns*
1535 VE, *-Sancti Alwini* 1559 *FF*
Coln(e) Sancti Aylwyn(i), -y- 1276 Heref, 1284 Episc, 1287 *Ass*,
-Sancti Alwini 1316 FA, *-aylewyns* 1544 *FF*, *-alyns* 1577, 1610
M, *-Allwyns* 1587 *FF*, *-alins* 1675 Ogilby
Cowne Allens 1620 *Rec*, *Cowlne Sainte Alewynes* 1628 *FF*

Coln St Aldwyn, Coln Rogers, and Coln St Denis (165, 166 *infra*)
all stand on the R. Coln (6 *supra*); it is not clear which of the three
places the OE spellings refer to, nor is it certain which saint's name
has provided the affix. The church was known as *ecclesia Sancti
Aylwini* (12, 1191 Glouc i, 257, iii, 11) before the 13th century when
it was dedicated to St John the Baptist (Glouc iii, 196). Baddeley and
Ekwall suggest the saint was Ealdwine the hermit, but the regular

spelling *Ail-*, *Ayl-* (which Feilitzen 104 has shown to be a normal development of *Æþel-*) makes it likely to be St Athelwine, the bishop of Lindsey from 679 (Bede iii, 27, iv, 12).

COCKRUP FM, *Cocthorpe* 1266 Glouc, *Co(c)kthrop(p)* 1542 *MinAcct*, c. 1560 *Surv*, -*thrope* c. 1603 *TRMB*, *Cockrup* 1830 M, *v.* þrop 'an outlying secondary farmstead'. The first el. is uncertain but could be OE cocc 'cock' ('farm where cocks were bred') or an OE pers.n. *Cocca*, which is evidenced only in p.ns. like Cockbury (ii, 90 *infra*), Cocking (Sx 16), or Cockenach (Hrt 172); Cokethorpe (O 324) is similarly ambiguous. The el. þrop is fairly common in Gl, cf. Introd. and Hatherop (36 *infra*).

WILLIAMSTRIP PARK
>*Hetrop* 1086 DB
>*Williamsthorp(e)* 1287 *Ass*, 1303 FA, 1498 *FF*, -*throp* 1287 *Ass*, 1327 *SR*, -*tropp* als. -*dropp* 1620 *FF*, -*troupe* 1567 *Rec*, -*trip* 1779 Rudder
>*Wyllamesthrop'* 1287 *Ass*, *Willamesthorpe* 1349 Aid, *Willamstropp* 1587 FF
>*Wallemesthorp* 1316 Ipm, *Walmesthorpe* 1335 ib

v. þrop 'outlying farmstead'. *Hetrop*, a manor separate from but adjoining Hatherop (36 *infra*), probably contains OE hēah 'high'. The later name no doubt embodies that of *Willelm*, who in 1086 held the manor of Roger de Laci.

BRATCH COPSE, *the Breatch* 1770 *EnclA*, *v.* brēc 'land broken up for cultivation'. BROADMEADOW COVERT. CUPID'S PARLOUR, 1830 M. HILL BARN, 1830 M. JOHNMAN'S FM. KEBLE BARN, cf. *Kibbles field* 1840 *TA* 8. KNOLL BARN, *Knowl-* 1830 M, *v.* cnoll 'hillock'. MILL HO, cf. *Mill lane* 1770 *EnclA*. MOOR'S FM. SWYRE FM, *Coln Swire* 1830 M, *v.* swēora 'neck of land'. TYNING WOOD, *Tineings Wood* 1830 M, *v.* tȳning 'enclosure', cf. Tyning 138 *infra*.

FIELD-NAMES

The principal forms in (*a*) are 1770 *EnclA*, 1862 *GR* 540.

(*a*) Bibury Gate; Burford Lane; Catland-house 1779 Rudder; Cibb's Sham; the Cow Downs; Dick Slade 1862; Downhalt 1723 *GR* 540; Grass Downs; Green Way; Haswells close; the Mill Mead; Net Garson (*v.* gærstūn 'paddock'); Rack close; Great and Little Several (cf. Severals 28 *supra*); Swan close; Tomb's Sitch (*v.* sīc, dial. *siche* 'brook, ditch'); Westbury's.

(*b*) *Westfelde* c. 1243 *GlCh* i, 31.

Eastleach Martin

EASTLEACH MARTIN (157–2005)

> *Lece* 1086 DB, *Lechia* 1127 AC, *Lech(e)* 1205 WinchLB, 1221 Eyre, 1227 *FF*, (*-Sci' Martini*) 1291 Tax
>
> *Estleche* 1138, 1148–79 Glouc, 1199 *FF*, 1205 WinchLB, 1215 Glouc, 1221 *Ass*, 1236 Fees, (*-Sancti Martini*) 1291 Tax, *Hestleche* 1232 *FF*, *Estletche* 1535 VE, (*-Martyn*) 1542 *MinAcct*
>
> *Estlecche* 1139–1275 Glouc (*freq*), (*-Sancti Martini*) 1302 Pat
>
> *Astlech(e)* 12 Glouc, 1221 Eyre, *Aslech* 1303 FA, *Astlegh* 1221 *Ass*, *-lugge* 1306 ib
>
> *Estlek'* 1248 *Ass*   *Estlucche* 1306 *Ass*
>
> *Estlac(c)he* 1476 Pat, 1485 Ipm, 1500 *FF*, *-latche als. Burethroppe* 1541 LP
>
> *Eastleach Marten* 1587 *FF*, *-Martin or Botherop* 1822 M

This name and Eastleach Turville (33 *infra*) are called 'east' as they lie in the east of the hundred and south-east of Northleach (175 *infra*). All three are named from the R. Leach (10 *supra*) on which they stand. The church was dedicated to St Martin (Rudder 432) and now to St Martin and St Michael. The place was alternately called *Boutherop* (*infra*).

BOUTHEROP (lost)

> *Burithrop* 1310 *GlCh* vi, 11, *Burethroppe* 1541 LP
>
> *Burthrop(pe)* 1354 Ch, 1535 VE, 1549 Pat, 1587, 1635 *FF*
>
> *Byrdthroppe* 1542 *MinAcct*
>
> *Bowthorp* 1577–1648 M, *Bouthrop* 1738 PR 13
>
> *Bootheroppe* 1718 Will, *Both(e)rop* 1749 GR 540, 1777 PR 17

'Outlying farmstead of the peasants', *v.* bū̆r², þrop; cf. Burdrop (O 405) and Hatherop (36 *infra*). It was an alternative name for the parish (1541 LP).

COATE FM, *Chotes* 12 Glouc, *la Cote* 13, p. 1412 ib, *Cotes* 1283–4 ib, 1561 GR 540, *atte Cote* 1327 SR (p), *Cootes* 1542 *MinAcct*, *Pryors Cotes* 1561 GR 540, *Coat* 1779 Rudder. *v.* cot 'cottage'. *Pryor* is doubtless the surname of some owner.

FYFIELD

> *Fishide, -hyde* (sic for *Fif-*) 12, 13, 1216–43 Glouc
>
> *Fif(h)ida, -(h)ide* Hy 1 (1313) Monast, Ric 1 (1372) ib, 1207 Cur, 1221 *Ass*, c. 1230 *GlCh* vi, 12, 1248, 1287 *Ass*, 1327 SR

Vifhida c. 1140 BM
Fyfeld 1566, 1587 *FF*, *Fifield* 1777 PR 13

'(An estate of) five hides', *v.* fīf, hīd. A hide was originally the land needed for the support of a single family, and in p.ns. it is usually found in single units or multiples of five, cf. Fi-, Fyfield (O 351, W 328, etc., EPN i, 246). On the unit of five hides as the basis of the Old English obligation to provide one soldier for the *fyrd*, cf. C. Warren Hollister in *Speculum* xxxvi, 61–74.

STAFFORD'S BRIDGE, *Stovenebrugge* 13 Glouc i, 271–2, *Stanforde* 1327 *SR* (p), *Staffords Bridge* 1830 M. 'The stone ford or bridge', *v.* stān, ford, brycg. *Stovene-* is probably for *Stonene-* (a ME variant of stǣnen 'stony'). On the loss of *-n-* before labials cf. Phonol. § 37 (*c*) and Stafford Mills (141 *infra*).

GREENHILL BARN. LOCOMBE HILL, *Lowcomb Hill* 1753 *EnclA*. RAVENSHILL HO. SHEEPHOUSE FM, *-furlong* 1753 *EnclA*, *Sepeshuswalle* 1263–84 Glouc. SMERIL PLANT., *Smerehulle* c. 1243 *GlCh* i, 31, 'hill with rich butter-producing pasture', *v.* smeoru, hyll, cf. Smerrill Fm 76 *infra*. TOM JOLLYS, formerly *Warren Ho.* 1777 M.

FIELD-NAMES

The principal forms in (*a*) are 1753 *EnclA*, and in (*b*) 13 Glouc i, 271–2. Spellings dated 12 are Glouc ii, 225, 1263 ib i, 274–5, 1349 *GlCh* ix, 18, 1561–1669 *GR* (D. 540), 1639 Inq.

(*a*) Black Bushes; Blackland; Blackmore Lands; Botherup sheep slaight (*v.* slæget 'sheep-pasture', cf. Sleight Barn 45 *infra*); Bowling Alley; Broadleaze (ib 1639, *v.* brād, lǣs 'pasture'); Broad-Mear; the Bushes; the Butts; Crowslade (*v.* crāwe, slæd); Eel-slade; Eye Mead (*v.* ēg 'island', mǣd); Fyfield Forty (*v.* forð-ēg 'island in marshland'); the Garston (*v.* gærstūn 'paddock'); Hay-neights (*v.* hēg 'hay', ēgeð 'island'); Hill furlong (*Hulle* 13, *v.* hyll); Hind Town ('land behind the village'); Hollwell Wall; Kingway close (*Kyngeswey* 1263 *v.* cyning, weg); Langford furlong; the Lockhams; Long Slades (*v.* slæd); Millham (*Mulhom* 1349 'mill meadow', *v.* myln, hamm); Oar-ditch; Old Hitching (*v.* heccing 'part of a field sown'); Oxall, Oxleighs (*v.* oxa, halh, lēah); Pig-neights (*v.* pigga, ēgeð 'island'); Plank Stones; the Quarrs (*v.* quarriere 'quarry'); Rudgeway piece (*Rugweyesende* 13, 'ridge road', *v.* hrycg, weg); Sloe-Bush (*v.* slāh 'sloe-tree'); Slow or Slough (*v.* slōh 'slough, mire'); Short Lands (*Sortelonde* 1263, *v.* sceort, land); Three lands; Two ditches; Turdy-corner; Westall Downs; the Wherns (Slow) (*v.* cweorn 'mill-stone', slōh 'mire').

(*b*) *Biesteþegore* ('by the east of the gore', *v.* gāra); *Biþerevelonde* ('by the reeve's land', *v.* (ge)rēfa); *Busshelesmulle* 1349 (the ME surname *Buss(h)el* 'one who measures out corn in bushels' (Reaney 55), myln); *Dunebrugge* ('lower bridge', *v.* dūne, brycg); *East meade* 1639; *Ferniforlong* 1263 (*v.* fearnig, furlang); *Gore* (*v.* gāra 'gore'); *Goreshoneþedepefurw* 1263 ('gores on the deep furrow'); *Hackers Mill* 1561; *Hangindelonde* 1263 ('steep land', *v.* hangende, land); *Heyruggedelonde* ('high-ridged land'); *Hemhamme* (*v.* hamm 'water-meadow'); *Humelesburiam* (possibly humol 'rounded hillock' and burh 'fort'); *Hundacre* 1263 ('hundred acres', from OE *hund*, æcer); *Illeburweslade* 13, 1263 (possibly the OE fem. pers.n. *Hildeburh*, *v.* slæd 'valley'); *Kyneborwelonde* (the OE fem. pers.n. *Cyneburh*); *Leyeplek* (*v.* lǣge 'fallow', plek 'a small plot'); *le Longeforendole* (*v.* lang, fēorða, dāl); *Longemonnesfurlong* 1263 (the ME by-name *Longman*); *Lot Medowe* 1535 VE (*v.* hlot 'lot, allotment', mǣd); *Mare*; *Newebreche* (*v.* brēc 'land broken up for cultivation'); *Northfelde* 1263; *Northgrote* (probably an example of ME *grut*, dial. *groot* 'mud, soil', cf. NED s.v.); *Oldebreche* (*v.* brēc); *Otforlonge* (*v.* āte 'oats'); *Overþeslade* ('across the valley', *v.* slæd); *Peckshay* 1669, *Perryhay* 1668, *Playhay* 1668 (*v.* (ge)hæg 'enclosure', the other els. being the surname *Peck*, pirige 'pear', plega 'sport'); *Quicheforslade* 1263; *Radeforlonge*; *Smalvern*; *le Sorthbac* (*v.* sceort, bæc); *Stapelforlang* (*v.* stapol 'post'); *Stradele*; *Suthfelde* 1263; *Tappenacre*; *Teþemede*; *Vivedinghemede* 12 ('meadow belonging to the men of Fyfield (*supra*)', *v.* -ingas (EPN i, 302), mǣd); *Voxmereforlongo* (*v.* fox, mere); *Weydene* 1263 ('road valley', *v.* weg, denu); *Wenserde*; *Wodeweye* (*v.* wudu, weg); *Wowelonde* ('crooked land', *v.* wōh, land); *Yebbelake* (*v.* lacu 'stream').

Eastleach Turville

EASTLEACH TURVILLE (157–1905)

> *in Lecche* 862 (late 13th) BCS 535   *Lecce* 1086 DB
> *Estlech(e)* 1220 Cur, 1221 *Ass*, 1285 FA *et freq* to 1372 Ch, (*-Rob' de Tureuill'*) 1221 *Ass*
> *Lecche Cecilie* 1220 Fees
> *Lech(e) Sci' Andree* 1291 Tax, 1535 VE
> *Est Lecch(e)* 1302 Pat, 1310 Ipm, 1500 Pat, (*-Turvill, -vile*) 1445, 1499 FF, *Ouer Esleche* 1554 FF
> *Lec(c)h(e)turvill, -toruill(e)* 1316 FA, 1319 FF, 1320 *Ass*, 1327 *SR et freq* to 1355 Ipm
> *Astleach* 1349 Heref, *-lech* 1366 Ch
> *Lacheturuyle* 1428 FF
> *Estlayche Turvyle* 1552 FF, *Estlatche Turveilde* 1574 *MBks*
> *Eastleach Turvile* 1587 FF

Like Eastleach Martin (31 *supra*), this is named from the R. Leach. The feudal affix is that of the family of *Turville* which held land here (*Robert de Turevill* 1200 Cur, 1221 *Ass* i, 15, Eyre 89, *Galiana de Turville* 1242 Fees), as it did in Acton Turville (iii, 47 *infra*). The affix

Sci' Andree refers to the church dedication to St Andrew (*S. Andree de Astleach* 1349 Heref, *St Andrew, Estlecche* 1500 Pat). *Lecche Cecilie* is named from *Cecilia de Evereux* (1242 Fees).

BEER FURLONG. EASTLEACH DOWNS FM, 1830 M, *the Downs* 1773 *GR* 540, *v.* dūn. EDGE PITS. THE FOLLY, 1862 *GR* 540 (a copse, *v.* folie). GREENBERRY HO, *Greenbury* 1723 *GR* 540, *Grimbury* 1773 *EnclA*, 'green fortification', *v.* grēne[1] (becoming *Grim*- by assimilation), burh; no trace of any fortification remains. GREEN LANE, 1862 *GR* 540. MACARONI FM, 1830 M. ORLINGE PLANT., *Orlinge* 1862 *GR* 540. THE SCRUBBS. SHEEP BRIDGE, 1773 *GR* 540, *v.* scēap, brycg; it is possible that in this and similar names brycg has replaced ford, and that the name was originally 'ford which could be crossed by sheep'; cf. also Mill Bridge, Horse Bridge, Durbridge (35, iii, 39, 183 *infra*) for a similar change.

FIELD-NAMES

The principal forms in (*a*) are 1773 *EnclA* and in (*b*) 1574 *TRMB* 39. Spellings dated 1711–1862 are *GR* (D. 540).

(*a*) Adams Garth; Bedwells Home close (*v.* byden 'vessel', wella); Blunts Hay (the surname *Blount*, *v.* (ge)hæg 'enclosure'); Botherway; Boults Hay (*Boles- als. Bolts Hay* 1726, the surname *Boult*, *v.* (ge)hæg); Chappell hill 1725; Chopping hill 1788; Church lane 1767; Clatley Hull 1777 M (*v.* clāte 'burdock', lēah, hulu 'shed'); yᵉ Conigree (*v.* coninger 'rabbit-warren'); Crowhay (*v.* crāwe, (ge)hæg); the Fold Yard; Frogs Corner 1773; the Grove (*Grove Corner* 1773); Hales Ditch 1862; Menham Hay ('common watermeadow', *v.* (ge)mǣne, hamm, (ge)hæg); the Michaelmas Downs 1773; Moseditch 1862; Parsons Bridge (*Parsonage-* 1711); Pudding lane 1783; the Ranging Plott 1723 ('a pasture for 600 sheep to range over'); Rubbing wall 1777 M; Sundayes·hill 1711 (cf. Sundayshill iii, 108 *infra*); Tyning ground 1773 (*v.* tȳning 'enclosure'); the West field pound; Wood Field 1773.

(*b*) *terr' voc' Rurkes*; *Styles haye* (the surname *Stiles*, (ge)hæg); *Trynnes lane*.

Fairford

FAIRFORD (157–1500)

æt Fagranforda 862 (late 13th) BCS 535 (Finb p. 154)
Fareford(e) 1086 DB, 1190 P, 1498 FF
Feir-, Feyrford 1100, 1106 *Tewk* 71, 72d, 1221 *Ass*, 13, 1231 Theok, 1276 RH, 1303 FA, *Feire-, Feyreford(e)* 1100–35 *Tewk* 71d, 1231 Theok, 1234 Cl, 1275 Episc *et freq* to 1349 Ipm, *-fort* 12 (1496) Pat, *-vord* 1290 Episc

Faire-, Fayreford(e) 12 Glouc, 1100–25 (1496) Pat, Hy 1 (1300) Ch,
  1220 Fees, 1261 Ipm, Ed 1 *Rent* 236 *et passim* to 1587 *FF*
Fair-, Fayrford 1221 *Ass* 10d, 1248 ib 2, 1261 Ipm *et freq* to 1709
  PR 17
Faierford 1204 P, 1577 M

'The fair, clear ford', *v.* fæger, ford, in contrast to Blackford
(*infra*); Camd (1590) renders it *vadum pulchrum*. The ford carried the
road from Lechlade to Cirencester across the R. Coln.

CORNFORD (lost), *Cuerneford* Hy 3, Eliz Monast, *Corn(e)ford* 1314,
1349 Ipm. 'Ford near the mill', *v.* cweorn, ford, and for the form
corn-, which is a not unusual substitution, as in Cornford (Do 35),
cf. The Querns (65 *infra*) and Corndean (ii, 32 *infra*), Phonol.
§§ 20, 42.

MILTON END & FM

  Middelton(e) 12 Glouc, 1307 Ipm
  Mid(d)leton(e) Hy 3 Monast, 1232 Ch, Eliz Monast
  Mil-, Mylton 1398 *FF*, 1487 *MinAcct*, 1527 *Rent*, 1548 Pat, (*-End*)
    1638 InqM, 1747 Will

'Middle farmstead', *v.* middel, tūn, and for the reduction cf.
Milton End (ii, 175 *infra*). Milton End is the west end of the town
across the R. Coln (*v.* ende).

BEAUMOOR FM. BLACKFORD BARN, 1830 M, *Blakeford* 1241 *FF*,
'the black ford', *v.* blæc, ford (in contrast to Fairford *supra*). BUR-
DOCKS, *Burdock ground* 1840 TA. THE CROFTS. EAST END, 1777
M, *Estende* 1398 *FF*, 1527 *Rent*, *v.* ēast, ende. FAIRFORD PARK,
1830 M. FARHILL FM, *Far Hill* 1830 M. THE GROVE, 1830 M,
cf. *Grovemed* 1314 Ipm, *v.* grāf 'copse', mǣd. HIDE COURT (lost),
Hid(e)court(e) 1540 *AOMB*, *MinAcct*, 1548 Pat, *v.* hīd 'a hide of
land' (about 120 acres), court. LADY LAMB'S COPSE, 1830 M.
LEAFIELD FM, LEA WOOD, 1830 M, *le Lee* 1314, 1349 Ipm, *Lye* 1487
MinAcct (p), *Fairfield Lays, Lay Wood* 1777 M, *v.* lēah 'clearing'.
LONG DOLES FM, *Longedole* 1314, 1349 Ipm, *v.* lang, dāl 'share of
land'. MILL BRIDGE, *Mulforde* 1327 SR (p), cf. *Mill ham* 1840 *TA*,
originally 'ford by the mill', *v.* myln, ford, cf. Sheep Bridge (34
supra). PEN BARN. WAITEN HILLS, 1830 M, *Waiting hill* 1840 *TA*.

FIELD-NAMES

The principal forms in (a) are 1840 *TA* 84. Spellings dated 1314, 1349 are Ipm, 1327 *SR*, 1487 *MinAcct*, 1527 *Rent* 8, 4, 1596 *GR* 185.

(a) Barrow ground & leys (v. beorg 'hill'); the Bassetts; Bog moor; Brake leaze; Broad ham (v. brād, hamm); the Chalace; Church acre; Clay pitt leaze; Cleve meadow (*Clyvemede* 1314, 1349, v. clif, mǣd); Crow slade (v. crāwe, slæd); Eastcotts; the Fawlake; the Garbage; Garsons (v. gærs-tūn 'paddock'); Hay green; Hemp lands; Hill coppice (*la Hulle* 1314, 1349, v. hyll); Hornham; Langet (v. langet 'long strip'); Long castle; Lot meadow (v. hlot 'allotment'); the Moors; Pack yatt; Penny field; Plies; Pressham, -hurst; Quarry ground (*Quer(e)* 1314, 1349, *Quere Wormestall* 1314, v. quarriere and *Wormestall infra*); Rack hill; Starveall barn; Street way; Sushwell ground; Thornhill barn; Vat hill; the Vineyard; Waybury bush; Washpool ground; Water slag; White lands; Wood brake & leys; Woe furlong (v. wōh 'crooked').

(b) *Cockemeade hay* 1638 (v. cocc[1], mǣd, (ge)hæg); *atte Fortheye* 1327 ('an island of dry land in marshland', v. forð, ēg, cf. O 445, EPN i, 185); *Frogmarch Barn* 1596 ('marsh infested with frogs', v. frogga, mersc); *Mercoumbe* 1314, 1349 ('boundary valley', v. (ge)mǣre, cumb); *S(c)harp(e)nesse* 1314, 1349 ('pointed headland', v. scearp, næss); *Seales croft* 1487, *Salez Crofte* 1527 (probably the ME surname *Sele* (cf. Reaney 287), v. croft); *Sheephowse close* 1639; *Sothe-, Suthward* 1314, 1349; *atte Trouwe* 1327 (v. trēow 'tree'); *Wekeslade* Hy 3 Monast (v. slæd 'valley'); *Well close* 1639; *Wormestall* 1314 *Wyrnestall* 1349 (dial. *wormstall* 'shelter for cattle', v. wyrm, stall, cf. *Wormestalles* YW ii, 136 and R. Forsberg in NoB xlviii, 137).

Hatherop

HATHEROP (157–1505) ['heiðrəp]

Etherop(e) 1086 DB, 1284 Ipm, *Ethrop* 1138 Glouc, 1232 Ch
Hadrop 1086 Glouc
Haethrop 1139–48 Glouc
Hetrop 1154–89 Glouc, 1285 FA, *Hethrop* 1154–89 Glouc, 1221 Eyre, 1281 Episc, 1291 Tax
Heythrop 1164–79 Glouc, 1211–13 Fees, p. 1421 GloucHist, -*trop* 1220 Fees, 1249 FF, *Haytrop* 1248 Ass, -*throp* 1291 Tax
Eythrop 1191, 1200 Glouc, -*trop* 1221 Ass
Hatherop(e) 13 Glouc, 1221 Eyre, 1236, 1251 Ch, 1303 FA *et freq* to 1783 PR 4, -*opp(e)* 1316 FA, 1544 FF *et freq* to 1722 PR 16, -*uppe* 1574 MBks, 1584 Comm
Het(h)erope Hy 3 Monast, *Etherop* Ed 1 ib, *Hethrep* 1287 QW

Hatrop(e) 1275 Ipm, 1291 Episc, *Hathrop(p)e)* 1287 *Ass*, 1331 *FF et freq* to 1592 FF, *-thorp* 1675 Ogilby

Since the village stands on the top of a hill overlooking the R. Coln, the name may mean 'lofty dependent farmstead' or 'farmstead on the height', *v.* hēah, þrop; the spelling *Hatherop* at least suggests the possibility of OE hǣð 'heathland'. There is a certain ambiguity in the spellings, and forms like *Etherope, Hatherop(e), Het(h)erope* with a medial *-e-* would also favour a compound of *hǣð* in which the medial *-th-* was regarded as belonging to the first el. and not to the second el. þrop, after the juncture of ð-ð was simplified to -ð-; Southrop (45 *infra*) has a few later spellings *Sowtherop* showing a similar treatment of ð-ð. It may be noted here that six of the examples of *þrop* in Gl are in this hundred between the lower reaches of the Coln and the Leach, Cockrup (30), Williamstrip (30), *Boutherop* (31), Netherton and *Overthrop* (*infra*), Southrop (45), and Pindrup (165), and that the word *þrop* in these p.ns. is of English origin and not Scandinavian; it denoted a secondary outlying farmstead or colony from a larger and older settlement.

BARROW ELM, 1766 *EnclA*, 1777 M, *la Berge* 1400 BG ix, 333, may be identified with *Brighthallesbarrowe Feld* 1540 *MinAcct, AOMB* (though that is possibly in Kempsford (40 *infra*)); it would be the name of the hundred meeting-place (cf. 22 *supra*). The name refers to a tumulus in the centre of the hundred at the crossing of the Fairford–Hatherop road and the Lechlade–Barnsley road (grid 157-161043). The modern name referred to a large elm growing on the low flat-topped barrow; *v.* beorg 'tumulus', elm.

NETHERTON (partly in Fairford parish), 1746 *GR* 540, *Nether Towne* 1574 *MBks*, probably identical with *Netheruppe* 1574 *TRMB*. 'Lower farm', *v.* neoðera, tūn, þrop (cf. Hatherop *supra*); it is on the lower part of Hatherop Hill.

OVERTHROP (lost), *Overthurppe* 1574 *MBks*, so-called to distinguish it from prec. *v.* uferra, þrop.

BROADMOOR GATE. CHURCHMEAD. DEAN CAMP & FM, *the Deane farm* 1723 *GR* 540, cf. *Weast deane* 1574 *TRMB*, *v.* denu 'valley'; the camp is an old earthwork. HATHEROP CASTLE, *le Castell* 1574

TRMB, *v.* castel; the present house is probably the site of an old earthwork. HATHEROP DOWNS & PARK. SWANHILL COVERT. SOUTH FM, 1830 M.

FIELD-NAMES

The forms in (*a*) are 1723, 1728, 1767, 1778, 1862 *GR* (D. 540) and the principal forms in (*b*) are 1574 *TRMB* 39. Spellings dated 1554, 1561, 1675 are *GR* (D. 540), 1766 *EnclA* (PRO).

(*a*) Barrow ground (*v.* beorg); Mess' called the Bell (a tavern-name); Bennetts Grave; Broadham Spring 1766; Croft Pingle (*v.* croft, pingel 'small enclosure'); the Downs (*v.* dūn); Ewepenground; Great Severall (*Severell* 1574, *Severhill* 1766, cf. Severals 28 *supra*); Green Islands; the Ham (*v.* hamm); the Heath; Isles close; Langett (*v.* langet); the Leys; Millers Close; Ragg Hill; Row hill; Bushy Stafford 1766; Stoneyhurst (*v.* stānig, hyrst); Swan's Hill; Westcroft; Withy Bed.

(*b*) *Ashe Close* (*v.* æsc); *Calf haye* (*v.* calf, (ge)hæg 'enclosure'); *Culvermead* (*v.* culfre 'dove', mǣd); *Grene haye* (*v.* grēne[1], (ge)hæg); *Grenhills close* 1554; *Hadès* (*v.* hēafod 'headland in the common field'); *terr' voc' Hamletes* (the ME pers.n. *Hamelet*, *-lot*, cf. Bardsley s.n.); *Hankeshaye* (probably the ME pers.n. *Hauk*, *v.* (ge)hæg); *Hobbshey* (the ME pers.n. *Hobbe*, (ge)hæg); *H(o)ulmore* ('marsh in the hollow', *v.* hol[1], mōr); *Mylkyn Haye* ('enclosure where milking was done'); *le Northfeld*; *le Northe Side*; *Northe thornes* (*v.* þorn); *Oxeleaze* 1639 Inq (*v.* oxa, lǣs); *St Marye Land*; *le Southfeld*; *West Crofte*.

Kempsford

KEMPSFORD (157–1696)

æt Cynemæres forda 9 ASC (A s.a. 800)

Chenemeresforde 1086 DB

Ki-, Kynemereford(e) 1086–1218 Glouc (*freq*), 1221 *Ass*, 1283 Ipm, *-meres-* 12 Glouc, 1220 Fees, 1221 *Ass*, 1236 Ch, 1303 FA, *-mares-* 1191 Glouc, 1291 Tax, *-mer-* 1221 *Ass*, 1258 Ipm, 1268 Ch, *-mers-* 1284 Episc, 1285 FA *et freq* to 1354 Ipm, *-mars-* 1303 FA, *Kynmaresford* 1327 SR, *-mers-* 1356 Ch

Kenemer(e)ford(e) 1100–22 Glouc, 1267 Ch, 1287 *Ass*, *-mers-* 1293 Episc, 1316 FA, *Kenmeresforde* 1378 *Ass*

Kymmysford 1455 Pat

Kemysford(e) 1535 VE, 1542 *MinAcct*, *Kemmysford* 1549 Pat

Kemsford 1577 M, 1587 FF, 1690 M, *Kempsford* 1610, 1696 M

'Cynemǣr's ford', from the OE pers.n. *Cynemǣr* and ford, here probably referring to the crossing of a small stream which is now a canal feeder but which doubtless formerly ran into the Thames south of the village.

HORCOTT, *Horcote* 12, 1225, p. 1412 Glouc, 1225, 1312, 1512 *FF*, *-cott* 1638 InqM, Will, *Harcutt* 1749 ib. 'Cottage in a dirty or muddy spot', *v.* horu, cot.

WHELFORD

Welford(e) 12 Glouc, 1287 *Ass*, 1387 Ipm *et freq* to 1779 Rudder 511
Weleforde 1262 Ipm
Whelford(e) 1535 VE, 1541 LP, 1542 *MinAcct*, 1822 M
Welneford 1540 *AOMB, MinAcct*

'Ford at the deep river-pool', *v.* wēl², ford; the ford crossed the R. Coln. The spellings *Whel-* (which might suggest OE hwēol 'mill-wheel') and *Welne-* are too late to be significant.

BLACKLANDS WOOD. BOWMOOR COTTAGE, 1801 *EnclA*, *Bulmer* 1542 *MinAcct*, *Bomer* 1627 Inq, 'bull pond', *v.* bula, mere. BRASEN CHURCH HILL, *Brazen-* 1830 M. COLLEGE FM, 1830 M. DOWN END BARN, 1830 M, *v.* dūn. DUDGROVE FM, 1777 M, probably 'Dudda's wood', *v.* grāf; the pers.n. is from OE *Dudda* (which also occurs in the f.n. *Dudworth* across the R. Coln in Lechlade (44 *infra*). DUNFIELD, *Downe medowe* 1540 *AOMB*, *Dunfield al. Dunvill* 1777 M, *Dunville field* 1801 *EnclA*, *v.* dūn 'hill'. FURZY HILL FM, *Furzey Hill* 1801 *EnclA*, *v.* fyrs 'furze'. HAM BARN, 1830 M, *v.* hamm 'water-meadow'. JENNER'S FM, 1830 M. MOOR GROUND BARN, 1830 M. OAK COPSE, 1830 M. OATLANDS BRIDGE, 1801 *EnclA*, *atte Oclonde* 1327 *SR* (p), possibly 'oat land', *v.* āte, land. POPE'S COURT. RAMTHORN WOOD, *Ram Thorne* 1801 *EnclA*, *v.* ramm, þorn, cf. *Rommesthurne* (ii, 145 *infra*). REEVEY FM, *Reevey* 1830 M. RHYMES BARN, *Rimes-* 1830 M, *the Rhymes* 1801 *EnclA*. STUBB BARN, *the Stubb* 1801 *EnclA*, *v.* stubb 'stump'. TOTTERDOWN LANE, 1870 Auct 43. WASHPOOL.

FIELD-NAMES

The principal forms in (*a*) are 1870 Auct 43, and those in (*b*) 1540 *AOMB* 444, 30. Spellings dated 1626 are Inq, 1801 *EnclA* (PRO).

(*a*) Ague Ham (*v.* hamm); Beanlands 1801; Break (*v.* bræc); the Brook Swarth 1801; Chelworth 1870 (*Cow Chilworth* 1801); Cleeve hill 1801; Cow Leaze (*v.* cū, lǣs 'pasture'); Ditch End; Dowles Lane; Dymer 1801; the Fishery Eyott 1801 (*v.* ēgeð 'island'); Gastonfurlong 1801 (*v.* gærs-tūn); Gossey mead 1801 (*v.* gorstig, mǣd); Green Moor; Hanplands 1801 (*v.* hænep 'hemp'); Hartmoor 1801 (*v.* heorot, mōr); the Hayes (*v.* (ge)hæg); Heron Hill; Horcutt field 1801; Hooram hill (*Horum Sty* 1801); the Hurst

1801 (v. hyrst); Joistment (*Joicements meadow* 1801); Green Langdon (*Langdon* 1801, v. lang, dūn); Langett (v. langet); the Layering 1801; Long-doles 1801 (v. dāl); Maiden Croft (ib 1801); Marra Lease (*the Mare leys lots* 1801, v. mere² 'mare', lǣs); the Mill knapp 1801 (v. cnæpp 'hillock'); Much-earing lands 1801; Ney-, Nylake (*Nilakes* 1801); Nutt Croft; Oakey; Ownham; Ox Lease (*Oxcelase* 1258 Inq, 'ox pasture', v. oxa, lǣs); Petty Toes Meadow (e.ModE *petitoe* 'pig's trotter'); Picked Lease (e.ModE *piked* 'cleared, pointed, etc.', lǣs); Red Pool Mead; Rumsey Meadow 1801; Shirt's Stirts; the Short haydes 1801 (v. hēafod 'headland'); Side Hale 1801 (v. sid 'broad', halh); Sin- or Ten Furzen piece (first el. probably a shortened form of *seven*, v. fyrs); Smithfield (ib 1801); Starve All; Streats moor 1801; Tainter Wich; Thursditch (ib 1801, v. þyrs 'giant, demon', dīc); Town ash mead 1801; Vesome Mead; Vines; Wallborough furlong 1801; Water Ham (v. hamm); Westbrooks 1801; the Whore pitts 1801; Wymore ditch 1801.

(b) *nigrum fossatum* 12 Glouc (probably a translation of blæc, dīc); *Bright-hallesbarowe Felde* (possibly in Kempsford, cf. Brightwells Barrow 22 *supra*); *Bystow medowe*; *Grafton medowe*; *Hilborough medowe*; *Middlebarowe Feld* (v. beorg 'barrow', feld); *Shulbrede Felde* ('narrow strip', v. scofl, brǣdu); *Stalbrokesfeld* (possibly stall in the sense 'stall' or 'fishery', brōc); *Stonehouse* 1542 *MinAcct*; *Westmedowe*; *le Yare ende* (v. gear 'fishery', ende).

Lechlade

LECHLADE (157–2199) [ˈletʃleid]

> *Lecelade* 1086 DB
>
> *Lec(c)helad(e)* 12 Glouc, 1111 *Tewk* 81d, 1204 P, 1205 ClR, 1211–13 Fees, 1246 Ch, 1248 *Ass*, 1252, 1255 Ch, 1255 Cl *et passim* to 1508 Pat
>
> *Li-, Lyc(c)helad(e)* 1211 ClR, 1221 *Ass*, 1234 Cl, 1238 *FF*, 1270 Ch, 1294 Episc, 1320 *Ass et freq* to 1494 *MinAcct*
>
> *Lechlad(e)* 1213 Abbr (p), 1220 Fees, 1268 Episc, 1275 Ipm, 1314 Pat *et freq* to 1822 M
>
> *Lachelad(e)* 1259 Abbr, 1549 Pat, 1576 *FF*
>
> *Leggelade* 1274 RH   *Legchelode* 1296 Episc (p)
>
> *Letch(e)lade* 1405, 1461 Pat, 1535 VE, c. 1560 *Surv*, 1721 PR 16
>
> *Leychelade* 1429 Pat   *Leachlade* 1564 *FF*

The name has been equated with OE *Hlincgelade* 966 BCS 1189 (*Licchelade* in the heading), but that is Linslade (Bk 79). Lech-lade is usually interpreted as 'passage across the Thames near its confluence with the R. Leach', v. Leach (10 *supra*), (ge)lād; the crossing would possibly be one at St John's Bridge (*infra*), which is adjacent to the outflow of the Leach but nearly a mile to the east of the present village, and which carried the old road to Faringdon. It seems more likely, however, to mean 'a water-course of the R. Leach'; if that is so it would presumably refer to some alternative water-channel of the Leach like a mill-stream; there was in fact a mill here called *Lademull* (possibly Lechlade Mill) and 'a pightle of ground called *Lade*' at the bridge-head at Lechlade in 1246 Ch. The present course of the R. Leach from north of Lechlade Mill to St John's Bridge may be the channel in question, for a second and now minor water-course runs from the former point to join the Thames 1½ miles further east of St John's Bridge and is in fact the county boundary. On these variant meanings of OE (*ge*)*lād* and on the current p.n. form *-lade* for the more usual *-lode* (as in Framilode ii, 179 *infra*) *v*. EPN ii, 8–9.

STREET-NAMES: BURFORD ST. (leading to Burford O 310). HIGH ST., 1770 *GR* 81, 'the chief street', *v*. hēah, strǣt. MARKET PLACE. ST JOHN'S ST. (cf. St John's Bridge *infra*). THAMES ST.

BRYWORTH FM, *Brywortheshamme* 1448 *MinAcct*, *-ham* 1459, 1494 ib, *Brewortheshamme* 1468 ib. *v*. worð 'enclosure', hamm 'meadow'. The first el. is not certain but an OE pers.n. *Brēga*, which is not recorded, is possible; it would be a mutated form of the OE pers.n. *Brōga*.

DOWNINGTON, 1606 *FF*, *Downend Towne* 1637 Inq, *Downinton* 1746 *GR* 540, *Downing Town* 1822 M. Probably a late name meaning 'the part of the village at the lower end of Lechlade Down', *v*. dūn, ende, tūn (*toun*); ME *ende* often becomes *-ing* in Gl as in the spellings of such names as Barton End (91), Priding (ii, 176), Oldend (ii, 203), Downend (iii, 99), Grovesend (iii, 15, 112), Walning (iii, 122), Pilning (iii, 139), Hallen (iii, 133), Rednend (iii, 139), Woodend (iii, 171), etc. Lechlade Down falls to river-level at the west end of Lechlade town.

ST JOHN'S BRIDGE, *pont' Sancti Johannis de Lichelade* 1459 *MinAcct*, *Saynt Joones bridge* 1591 FF, cf. also 'priori et fratribus de *ponte de Lichelad*' 1234 Cl, *ponte Sancti Mich' de Lychelade* 1494 *MinAcct* (possibly an error for *St John*). The bridge, which carries the Cirencester–Faringdon road over the Thames at the presumed site of an older passage (cf. Lechlade *supra*), was named from the local priory of St John; the priory was founded c. 1220 and dedicated to St John Baptist, and the bridge built a few years later (cf. BG xxii, 44, xli, 223–6).

THORNHILL FM, *Thornehill* 1448 *MinAcct*, *Thornhill* 1459 ib, 1764 Will, *Thorneshill* 1494 *MinAcct*, *Thirnehill* 1627 Inq. 'Hill with a thorn-tree or thorns', *v.* þorn, hyll.

BRIDGE WALK, 1838 *TA*, cf. St John's Bridge (*supra*). BUTLER'S COURT, (*ten' voc'*) *Botulers, -illers* 1449–1494 *MinAcct* (*freq*), *Butlers Hall* 1830 M, the ME surname or byname *Boteler* (Butler). CLAYDON FM, CLAY HILL, 1727 Will, *Cleyhill* 1627 Inq, *v.* clǣg, dūn, hyll. FOX FIELD. GREEN FM, cf. *atte Grene* 1320 *Ass*, *Collesgrene* 1626 Inq, *the Green* 1838 *TA*, *v.* grēne²; *Colles-* is doubtless the R. Coln. LEAZE FM, *Est(e)lese* (*pastur'*) 1448, 1494 *MinAcct*, *Newleaze* 1627 Inq, *Lechlade Leaze* 1839 M, *v.* lǣs 'pasture'. LECHLADE BRIDGE ('bridge of *Lechlade*' 1246 Ch), DOWNS (1830 M, *atte Doune* 1327 *SR* (p), *the Downes* 1627 Inq), & MILL (1830 M, cf. also *Millehous*, *Westmylle* 1494 ib, and Mill meadow *infra*), *v.* brycg, dūn 'hill', myln. GREAT & LITTLE LEMHILL, 1830 M, transferred from Oxfordshire in 1844. PEST HO., 1838 *TA*, from e.ModE *pest-house* 'a hospital for infectious diseases' (from 1611 NED s.v.). PRIORY MILL, named from St John's Priory. ROUGH GROUND FM, identical with *Rough Barn* 1830 M. ROUND HO., 1830 M. ST JOHN'S PRIORY, *the Priory* 1779 Rudder, cf. St John's Bridge (*supra*). SHEEP LEAZE, 1830 M, *v.* scēap, lǣs 'pasture'. STARVEALL BARN, 1838 *TA*, a common nickname for poor land. TROUTHOUSE FM, 1830 M, *Trout Inn* 1838 *TA*, a former inn 'the Trout'. VENEYMORE LANE, *Fern(e)-*, *Vernehammore* 1448, 1469, 1461 *MinAcct*, *Fearney-*, *Fernymore* 1626, 1627 Inq, *Venny Moors* 1838 *TA*, 'marsh near the ferny water-meadow', *v.* fearn, hamm, mōr; on initial *V-* cf. Phonol. § 34 (*a*). WARREN'S CROSS, (*prat' in*) *Wareng(e)*, *-ynge* 1448, 1459, 1494 *MinAcct*, *Warren Cross* 1830 M, *v.* wareine 'rabbit-warren'. WILLOWS, 1830 M.

FIELD-NAMES

The principal forms in (*a*) are 1838 *TA* 122. Spellings dated c. 1270 are Oseney v, 41, 1414–1494 *MinAcct*, 1626–1639 Inq.

(*a*) the Asses (*the Hasses* 1627, *St John's Ashes* 1779 Rudder 333, *v.* æsc, here denoting ash-trees on the site of St John's Priory); Beanlands (*Beane-landes* 1626, *v.* bēan, land); Black Barn; Blackmoors; Bladdermoor; Brake (*v.* bræc¹ 'thicket'); Branny moor (*Bronmore* 1459); the Brickbats (*Brickle-bates* 1627, probably a compound of e.ModE *brickle* 'brittle, broken' and *bat* 'lump, bit, piece of brick', used in much the same way as e.ModE *brickbat* 'fragment of brick', cf. NED s.v. *brickle*, *bat* sb.²); Bridles; Broad leaze; Browns ground (cf. *Brownesham* 1448, 1494, the ME surname *Brown*, *v.* hamm 'water-meadow'); Butter Horns; the Butts (*leȝ Buttes* 1448, *v.*

butte 'abutting strip in the common field'); Carters cross 1770 GR 81 (cf. *Cartersham* 1639, the ME occupational name *Cartere* (Thuresson), v. hamm); Cold pound; Colne meadow (cf. *Colneham* 1448, *Cowenham* 1449, *Cullenham* 1494, named from the R. Colne, v. hamm); Colstones ground; Cuckoo Pen (a jocular f.n. alluding to the folk-tale (told of the men of Gotham) of 'penning the cuckoo' to prevent the passing of summer, common in O 438, Gl, etc., cf. J. E. Field, *The Myth of the Pent Cuckoo*, London 1913); Ditch ground (cf. *Di-, Dychefurlong(e)* 1448, 1494, v. dīc); Double Moors; Dung croft (*Duncroft* 1627, 'Dunna's croft', from the OE pers.n. *Dunna*); Faringdon; Frenchey ground; Furze bank; the Grasswells (v. gærs, wella); Hambridge ground; the Hams (v. hamm 'water-meadow'); Hatchett; Hinton Moors; Horsemoor; Hounds pool (cf. *H(o)undeshale* 1448, 1459, 1494, *Hunsell* 1627, 1639, 'the hound's nook of land', v. hund (perhaps used as a byname as in ME, cf. Reaney 170), halh); Inglesham meadow (*Inglesham* c. 1270, named from Inglesham W); Knapps furlong (*Knaps* 1770 GR 81, v. cnæpp 'hillock'); Lakes meadow; Langet (*the Langett* 1627, v. langet 'long strip of land'); the Lawn (v. launde 'glade'); Lechlade Marshes; Letherham (ib 1448, 1627, *Lither(h)am* 1459, 1494, v. hamm, the first el. being possibly OE *lȳðre, lēðre* 'bad, worthless'); Marum (*Mereham* 1331 Ipm, *Merham* 1414, *Marreham* 1448, 1494, 'pool meadow', v. mere, hamm); Mill Meadow, -pond, -stream (cf. *Milham, Milleholme, -whele* 1448, *-place* 1449, *-ham* 1494, v. myln, hamm, hwēol, cf. Lechlade Mill *supra*); the Moors; Mortar Pitts (*le Morter-pittes* 1626, ME *morter* 'mortar', pytt); Pingle (v. pingel 'small enclosure'); Pollock; Quack hill (*Quatchill als. Cotchill* 1627, perhaps from OE *cwacian* 'to quake, tremble' and hyll); Rats Castle (probably a jocular name of a derelict building); (Thames) Reddies (*Redhey, -hay* 1448, 1494, 1627, *Redehey* 1459, 'reed enclosure', v. hrēod, (ge)hæg, it was near the R. Thames); Reeds; Rod-, Rudmore (*Rudmores* 1627, 'reed marsh', v. hrēod, mōr); Rumsey (*Rameshey, -hay* 1448, 1459, 1494, *Ram-, Romsey* 1626, 1627, 'ram's enclosure', v. ramm, (ge)hæg); the Sheephams (*Shepham* 1448, *hamme voc' Shepenhamme* 1494, *Sheepham* 1627, 'sheep meadow', v. scēap, hamm); Shoulder of Mutton ground (so called from its shape); Smyrrell meadow (*Smere-, Smorehilham* 1448, 1459, 1494, v. smeoru 'butter, fat' (used of rich land), hyll, hamm); Summer land; Thames furlong (near the R. Thames); Warners Moors (*Warnammore* 1494, v. warener 'warren-keeper', mōr); West Mills (*Westmylle* 1448); Westwick (*le Westewyke* 1494, *Westwicke* 1627, v. west, wīc 'dairy-farm'); Wey acre; Widney mead (*Wydney* 1448, *Wideney* 1494, *the Widney* 1627, 'wide water-meadow or island', v. wīd, ēg); Wigmore mead (*Wid(e)more* 1448, 1494, v. wīd, mōr); Withy bed; the Worn.

(b) *Akkemylle* 1448, *Atmylle* 1494, *Acte Mill* 1627 (v. myln, the first el. possibly from OE *Acca*); *Balham* 1448, *hammes prat' voc' Belham* 1494 (possibly of the same origin as Balham (Sr 33), v. balg 'rounded', hamm); *Bircheham* 1448 (v. birce 'birch-tree', hamm); *the Blackbrookes* 1627; *Blaxhamme* 1448, 1459, *-ham* 1494 (possibly the OE pers.n. *Blæc* (cf. Feilitzen 203), hamm); *Calcroft* 1459, *Calvescroft, -hous* 1494 (v. calf, croft, hūs); *Casteldyke* 1414, *-diche* 1459, 1494 (v. castel 'fortification', dīc); *Colmanstile*

1494 (the ME pers.n. *Colman*, stigel); *Devel(l)eserce, -herse* 1448, 1449, *Diwelleshers* 1494 ('the devil's arse', *v.* deofol, ears, cf. Peak Cavern Db 56, Trollers Gill YW vi, 80); *Dolemeade* 1639 (*v.* dāl 'share', mǣd); *Dudworth field* 1626 (cf. Dudgrove 39 *supra*); *le East meade* 1626; *Eldermanstile* 1494 (the surname *Alderman* (WSax *ealdormann* 'alderman'), stigel); *Emede* 1494 ('river meadow', *v.* ēa, mǣd); *Fenslade* 1448 (*v.* fenn, slæd 'valley'); *the Gaston* 1627 (*v.* gærs-tūn 'pasture'); *Grandesham* 1448, 1494 (the surname *Grand* (OFr *grand* 'great, tall'), hamm); *homme voc'* (*H*)*aselyngham* 1448, 1461, 1494 (*v.* hæsling 'hazel copse', hamm); *Hurstfurlonge* 1448 (*v.* hyrst 'wood'); *the Inlandes* 1627 (*v.* in-land 'land near the house'); 'a pightle of ground called *Lade'* 1246 Ch (*v.* (ge)lād 'water-course', cf. Lechlade *supra*); *les Latteʒ* 1494 (possibly OE lætt 'beam'); *the Leynes* 1627 (*v.* leyne 'tract of arable land'); *Lostes- Lusteshull(e)* c. 1270; *hamme voc'* *Perse* 1448, *-Pe(o)rce* 1449, 1459 (the ME pers.n. *Pers* (OFr *Piers*), *v.* hamm); *Petty dolles* 1626 (the surname *Petty, v.* dāl); *Pinborowe Laynes* 1627 (*v.* leyne); *Pipmorestrete* 1494 (*v.* pīpe 'conduit', mōr, strǣt); *Priorye Orchard* 1627 (named from St John's Priory *supra*); *Queen(e)sham* 1627, 1639 (*v.* cwēn 'queen', hamm); *Southfeilde* 1627; *Ste(e)pleacre* 1627, 1639; *Stichill Firres* 1627; *Stoneham buttes* 1494, *Stonyham* 1627 (*v.* stān(ig), hamm, butte); (*hamme, prat' voc'*) *Lytul-, Mekyl-, Mikulsturmyn'* 1448, 1494 (the ME pers.n. *Sturmyn* (Reaney 311), *v.* hamm); *Toppe* c. 1560 *Surv* (*v.* topp 'hill-top'); *Trencheham* 1494 (*v.* trenche 'ditch', hamm); *Trindersham* 1627 (the ME surname *Trinder* (Reaney 327), *v.* hamm); *Vas(e)gore* 1448, 1459, 1494 (*v.* gāra 'gore of land', the first el. possibly fæs 'edge'); *Wythekam* 1414, *Wythikham* 1448, *Whithynkeham* 1494 (*v.* wīðig(n) 'willow, willow-copse', hamm); *Whithi-, Wythyweyham(me)* 1448, 1459, 1494 (*v.* prec., weg 'way', hamm); *Wydeʒatesham* 1448 ('meadow near the wide gate', *v.* wīd, geat, hamm); *Wyndesworth* 1448, 1494 (*v.* worð 'enclosure', the first el. possibly the ME byname *Winde*, cf. Reaney 356).

Quenington

QUENINGTON (157–1404) [ˈkwenintən]

> *Qv-, Queninton(e), -tona, -yn-* DB, 1115–1261 Glouc (*freq*), 1199 ChR, 1261 FF, 1274 Episc, 1278 Cl *et passim* to 1434 Monast, *-ing-, -yng-* 1282 Cl, 1290 Ch, 1439 Pat *et freq* to 1587 FF
> *Quenton', Queniton'* 1221 Ass, *Quenton als. Queinton* 1276 Cl
> *Cunintone* 1221 Plea (p)   *Queenington* 1553 Pat
> *Quennington* 1676 PR 16, 1766 ib 4

'The women's or Cwēn's farmstead', *v.* cwene, tūn. The medial *-in(g)-* may represent, as Ekwall suggests, the OE gen.pl. *cwenena*, but the connective *-ing*[4] which denotes an association of the person with the place is also possible and we may therefore have the OE fem. pers.n. *Cwēn* or an OE *Cwēna* (a hypocoristic form of names like *Cwēnburh, Cwēngȳð*, etc.) or possibly an appellative (in this case

OE *cwene*), as we also appear to have in Arlington (Sx 408, cf. EPN i, 294). The spellings of this name and Quinton (254 *infra*), which in some respects agree, cannot easily be separated, but the later pronunciations of the two names show that they are of different origin.

SLEIGHT BARN, 1830 M, *Slaytlane* 1754 *EnclA*. The term *sleight*, Gl dial. *slait, sleight* 'a pasture, a sheep-walk' (EDD s.v.), occurs several times in the sheep-rearing parts of the Cotswolds; it is from an OE slæget 'sheep-pasture' (which is fully discussed by M. T. Löfvenberg, *Studier i mod. språkvetenskap* xvii, 87–94); it occurs as a local appellative for cattle-walk in *pecudum cursum anglice a sleyte* (1401 *Tetb* T 1, 6).

CHERRY COPSE, 1830 M.   CONEYGAR WOOD, -*Copse* 1830 M, *the Conygree* 1754 *EnclA*, v. coninger 'rabbit-warren'.   COURT FM, 1754 *EnclA*.   ELM COPSE, 1830 M.   HONEYCOMBE LEAZE FM, *Honeycomb(e) Lays* 1754 *EnclA*, -*Leaze* 1830 M, 1836 Auct 48. PITHAM COPSE, 1754 *EnclA*, v. pytt, hamm.   SIDELANDS, *Sideland* 1830 M, 'broad strip of land', v. sīd, land.   WINTERWELL COPSE, 1830 M, 'spring flowing chiefly in winter', v. winter, wella.

FIELD-NAMES

The principal forms in (*a*) are 1862 *GR* 540 (E. 10), and in (*b*) 1507 *Rent* 831. Spellings dated 1539 are *AOMB* 238, 1557 *FF*, 1754 *EnclA*, 1836 Auct 48, 1847 *GR* 540 (P. 3).

(*a*) Barnstable; Clay Pitts; Cloud Hills (v. clūd 'rocky outcrop'); Coln Bridge 1754, Coln Hill (v. R. Coln); The Downs 1847 (*le Downes* 1507, *Quenyngton Downe* 1539, v. dūn 'hill'); the Droveway 1754 (dial. *drove* 'unenclosed road, esp. one for driving cattle or one leading to the fields'); The Grandage, Grandage Hill (*Grandidge Mead* 1754); Hannington Hill 1847; the Hollow way 1754; Langet 1836 (v. langet); The Leys; Limekiln Slait 1847 (cf. Sleight Barn *supra*); Long Sands; Mill Ham 1836 (v. myln, hamm); Northffield 1754; Picked acre 1754 (cf. Picked Lease 40 *supra*); Ready Token 1754; Slovens Hill 1836; the Southffield 1754; the Townsend Green 1754.

(*b*) toft' voc' Barbers; le Eastcroft; *Iland Grove* 1545 LP; *Lanes* 1557 (v. leyne 'arable tract'); terr' voc' *Lightfotes* (the surname *Lightfoot*); *the greate- the litell parke* 1539 (v. park); terr' voc' *Simmons*; *Walkemyln*.

Southrop

SOUTHROP (157–2003) ['sɑuþrəp]
  Suthþrop 12 Glouc, *Suththrop* 1286 *FF*, 1321 Ipm
  Sudthropa c. 1140 BM

Suthrop(e) 1211–13, 1220 Fees, 1221 *Ass*, 1227, 1232 *FF*, 1236
Fees, 1263–84 Glouc *et freq* to 1327 *SR*, *Sutrop* 1248 *Ass*
Suthorp(e) c. 1215 Glouc, 1317 Ch   *Sutheorp* 1285 FA
Southrop(e) 1290 Episc, 1314 Ipm *et freq* to 1822 M
Southorp(e) 1297 Ipm, 1303 FA *et freq* to 1675 Ogilby
Sowthethrop 1552 FF   *Sowtherop(þ)e* 1584 *Comm*, 1592 *FF*

'The southern dependent farmstead', *v.* sūð, þrop. It is the most
southerly of the *þrops* in the district. Cf. Southrop (O 354) and
Hatherop (36 *supra*).

STANFORD HALL, *Stanford* 1296 Ipm, 1830 M, *Staunford* 1448
MinAcct, *Stammford* 1494 ib. 'Stone ford', *v.* stān, ford, here a ford
across a small stream.

TILTUP, *Tiltups Inn* 1830 M. This p.n. occurs several times in Gl
(93, ii, 202, iii, 164 *infra*), but not with early spellings. It could
represent a dial. pronunciation of 'the hill top' (cf. Phonol. § 45), but
is more probably the obsolete Gl dial. *tiltup* 'covered wagon' (EDD).

BEE FURLONG BRAKE, 1840 *TA*. BILLY PARK, 1830 M. HAMMER-
SMITH BOTTOM, *Hammersmith* 1840 *TA*. HOMELEAZE FM, *Momes
Leaze* (sic) 1830 M, *Home mead* 1840 *TA*. HOOK'S FM, 1840 *TA*.
MOOR LA., *-mead* 1840 *TA*. ROTTENBOROUGH COPSE, *-Barn* 1830
M, *-coppice* 1840 *TA*. SPARROW COPSE, named from the family of
Edward *Sparrow* (1771 PR 13, 142).

FIELD-NAMES

The principal forms in (*a*) are 1840 *TA* 181.

(*a*) Beastbrook (possibly 'by the east of the brook', cf. *Biesteþegore*
32 *supra*); Bradborough; Brooks downs & moor; Cooks hill; Cottenborough;
Ellenbrook furlong; Fullbrook 1764 PR 13 ('dirty stream', *v.* fūl, brōc);
Gore, Gore hill (*v.* gāra); Green heath; Kibbles field; the Langett (*v.* langet);
Mill field & mead; the Moors; Moreditch (*v.* mōr, dīc); Parish pound; the
Pen (*v.* penn); the Pits; Salt hill; Shabbing down; Standing cross; Stock
leaze; Stouts hill; Summer leaze ('summer pasture', *v.* sumor, lǣs);
Vousland; Water mead.

(*b*) *Filibertis Court* 1406 Pat (named from the family of *Philibert*, cf.
Rudder 680); *Greyes Court* 1406 Pat (named from the local family of *de Grey*,
1315 Ipm); *atte Lanende* 1327 *SR* (p) (*v.* lane, ende); *the parsonage barne*
1584 *Comm*; *atte Plodde* 1327 *SR* (p) (*v.* pludde 'pool, puddle').

II. CROWTHORNE AND MINETY HUNDRED

This hundred is in the south of the county and centred on Cirencester and the lower Churn valley. Wiltshire lies to the south. There have been various adjustments of the boundaries from time to time; Kemble, Poole Keynes and Somerford Keynes were formerly in Wiltshire and Poulton was a detached parish of Wiltshire (cf. 1822 M); Poulton was transferred to Gloucestershire in 1844 and the other three parishes in 1897; the latter are dealt with in the Wiltshire volume of EPNS (W 60, 64, 46) as well as here. Minety, transferred to Wiltshire in 1844 (W 61), was formerly a detached parish of Gloucestershire. At the time of the DB survey the hundred of Crowthorne and Minety comprised the hundreds of Cirencester and *Gersdon* which were soon merged as the hundred of Cirencester; *Gersdon* included the parishes of Ampney Crucis, Down Ampney, Ampney St Mary, Ampney St Peter, South Cerney, Driffield, Meysey Hampton, and Harnhill, and Cirencester those of Bagendon, Baunton, Cirencester, Coates, Daglingworth, Duntisbourne Abbots and Rous, Minety, Preston, and Siddington, as well as Rodmarton (which was later in Longtree Hundred). Various hundreds made up the 'seven hundreds of Cirencester' by the late 12th century (Ric 1 (1423) Pat, 1319 Cl, etc.), including Bisley, Bradley, Brightwell's Barrow, Cirencester, Crowthorne, Longtree, and Rapsgate (cf. 1587 *FF*); a hundred of *Dunhameneye* (Down Ampney) is mentioned in 1256 Ipm; this late medieval organisation is fully discussed by H. M. Cam in *Historical Essays in honour of James Tait* 17, Finberg 45–7, 59.

CIRENCESTER HUNDRED

Cirecestre hd' 1086 DB, 1169, 1177 P, 1221 *Ass, hund' de Ci-, Cyrencestr(e), -ria* 1175 P, 1220 Fees, 1221 *Ass,* 1274 RH *et freq* to 1587 FF, *Hund' de Cirincestr'* 1221 *Ass, -Cyrnescestr'* 1248 *Ass, Circestre* 1330 Ipm. *v.* Cirencester (60 *infra*).

GERSDON HUNDRED (lost)

Gersdon(es) hd', Gersdvnes hd' 1086 DB. The name means 'grass hill', *v.* gærs, dūn. The place has not been found; there is an unidentified *Gerston(a)* in Ampney (13 AD ii, vi), but this may be the common f.n. OE gærs-tūn 'pasture' and unconnected; a reference to 'the king's hundred of *Dunhameneye*' in 1256 Ipm suggests that *Gersdon* might be found in Down Ampney.

CROWTHORNE & MINETY HUNDRED

hundredo de Minti 1204 P, *Crouthorne hund'* 1327 *SR,* 1381 Cl, 1535 VE, *Hund' de Crothorne* 1540 *AOMB* 242, 1559, 1587 *FF, hundred of Myntye* 1552 Pat, *Crowthorne and Minety Hundred* 1822 M. A reference to 'land in the fields of *Strattone* on the green lane between *Crawthorne* and *Bauditon* (Baunton)' in 14 *CirenD* 12 suggests that Crowthorne was on the northern edge of Cirencester parish (grid 157-016044); there was also a Crowthorne grounds in Kemble (76 *infra*). The name denotes 'a thorn-tree haunted by a crow', *v.* crāwe, þorn, cf. *Crauthorn* (K 481), *crawan þorn* (BCS 216); but Wallenberg (KPN 481) and Anderson 26 suggest that the compound might have denoted a particular species of thorn and instance the parallel Swed *kråktorn* which is the vernacular name of *Rhamnus catharticus*. The hundred of Minety appears to have been originally a separate hundred (cf. Minety 77 *infra*).

Ampney Crucis

AMPNEY CRUCIS (157–0602)

> *Omenie* 1086 DB, *Omenai*, *-ay* 1086–1148 Glouc (*freq*)
> *Amenel(l)* 1100–35 (1496) Pat, 1100–1284 Glouc (*freq*), Hy 1 (1300) Ch, 1204 ClR, 1211–13 Fees, 1300 Ch, (*Up-*) 1221 FF, (*-Abbatis*) 1221 *Ass*, Uphamenhell, *-el* 1221 *Ass*, (*-Abbatis*) 1221 ib
> *Ameney(e)* 1215, 1263–84, 1267 Glouc, (*Up-*) 1261 *FF*, 1279 Glouc, 1303 *et freq* to 1347 Glouc, (*-Sancte Crucis*) 1287 *Ass*, 1291 Episc, Tax, 1325 *FF*, (*-Crucis*) 1328 Banco, *Hameneye* 1285 FA
> *Auenel Abbatis* 1221 *Ass*, Uphauene 1287 ib
> *Aumeneya*, *-(e)ye* 1255 Cl, 1354 Ch, (*-Sce' Crucis*) 1291 Tax
> *Hameneye* 1285 FA, *Up-Amyne* 1287 *Ass*, Up Amoney 1316 FA
> *Holyrod(e)hampney* 1509 *MinAcct*, *-amney* 1529 FF, *-ampney* 1542 *MinAcct*, Holyrood(e) Hamney 1545 LP, *-Ampney* 1549 Pat, 1725 PR 16, *-Amney* 1610 M
> *Ampney Crucis* 1535 VE, 1600 *FF*, 1713 PR 16

This place, along with Down Ampney, Ampney St Mary, and Ampney St Peter, is named from the stream called Ampney Brook or from an affluent. 'Amma's stream', *v.* ēa, ēg. An OE pers.n. *Amma* is not recorded but occurs in such p.ns. as OE *Amman broc* BCS 1110, etc. (*v.* Ekwall, RN 13); it would be cognate with OHG *Amo*. The spellings with *Aum-* are French; the form *Amenel* has the OFr diminutive suffix *-el* (cf. Vincent 101) 'the little *Ameney*', such a use being paralleled by Hampnett (173 *infra*); the sporadic form *Auenel* may be due to a scribal error in a long sequence of minims, or the substitution of -*u*- for -*m*- could be due to the influence of Fr p.ns. like *Avenelles* (Vincent 564). The affix in this name, *Abbatis* 'abbot's' (*v.* abbat), alludes to the Abbots of Tewkesbury who owned one hide in the manor t. Hy 1, but later a much larger amount (cf. VE); St Peter's, Gloucester, and Cirencester also had land here; *Up-* (*v.* upp 'higher') refers to the fact that this Ampney occupies the highest position up Ampney Brook (which rises in the parish), esp. in contrast to Down Ampney (51 *infra*); *Sancte Crucis, Crucis* and *Holyrode* 'holy cross' (*v.* hālig, rōd) are from the dedication of the church, Holy Rood Church; a fine cross is to be found in the churchyard (cf. BG xv, 297–303).

AMPNEY DOWNS, 1777 M, *le Doune* 1275 *CirenP*, *le Downe* 1540 *AOMB*, *v.* dūn 'expanse of open hill country', in the south-east of Gl usually referring to the outlying higher grounds of the Cotswold parishes which provided considerable amounts of sheep-pasturage. Ampney Downs was in the north-west of the parish adjoining Baunton.

WIGGOLD

> *Wigge-*, *Wyggewald* 1109 Monast, -*waud* 13 *CirenD* 3, -*wold*(*e*)
> 1287 *Ass*, 1327 *SR*, 1343 Orig (p) *et passim* to 1549 *FF*
> *Wige-*, *Wygewald*' 1220 Fees, -*wad* 1236 *FF*, -*waud* 1248 *Ass*,
> -*wold*(*e*) 1285 FA, 1337 Ch, 1374 Ipm
> *Wykewald* 1231 *FF*, *Wykefrod* (sic) 1291 Tax
> *Wigolde* 1587, 1609 *FF*, *Wygall* 1669 *Talbot*, *Wighill* 1777 M

'Wicga's piece of high open land', from the OE pers.n. *Wicga* (which is found also in Witpit in Preston 81 *infra*) and OE wald 'lofty woodland', but probably, as seems often the case in the Cotswolds, in the somewhat later sense of 'lofty open country' (cf. EPN ii, 240). Wiggold was formerly a detached part of Cirencester.

LITTLE ACKLEY, *Oakley close* 1770 *EnclA*, 'oak clearing', *v.* āc, lēah. AMPNEY BROOK (1770 *EnclA*), FIELD (*Westfeld* 1540 *AOMB*, *Ampney West Field, the East Field* 1770 *EnclA*, -*Fields* 1777 M), KNOWLE (*the Knowl Farm* 1770 *EnclA*), PARK (1770 ib) & RIDING (1830 M, *the Riding grounds* 1770 *EnclA*), *v.* brōc, feld, cnoll 'hill', park and rydding 'clearing'. BEGGAR HILL, *Beggar's Hill* 1770 *EnclA*, 'hill frequented by beggars'. BOWN'S FM, named from the local family of Edward and Thomas *Bown* (1756, 1759 PR 15, 109–110). DARK QUAR, 1770 *EnclA*, *v.* quarriere 'quarry'. DUDLEY FM, 1830 M.

HILLCOT END, formerly *Tiltups End* 1830 M, cf. Tiltup (46 *supra*). HUNT'S HILL, 1830 M, named from the family of Samuell *Hunt* (1696 PR 15, 107). LONG FURLONG, 1830 M. SHEEPHOUSE FM, *Shephouse* 1540 *AOMB*, v. scēap, hūs. WATERTON FM. WINTER-WELL, 1770 *EnclA*, -*Spring* 1777 M, 'spring flowing chiefly in winter', v. winter, wella.

FIELD-NAMES

The principal forms in (a) are 1700 *EnclA* (which also includes some for Ampney St Mary 52 *infra*). Spellings dated 1275–1388 are *CirenP* i, 18–23, 1540 *AOMB* 70, 1542 *MinAcct* 1248, 1575 *TRMB*.

(a) Astable hill; Bendons (*Myddulbenyndone* 1388, from OE bēanen 'bean-growing', dūn); Brandons (*Barndheme-mere* 1275, v. hǣme 'dwellers', (ge)mǣre 'boundary', *Bernedheme-* being doubtless a folk-name from some older p.n. such as Barnsley (24 *supra*), cf. *Polhemstret* 53 *infra*); the Breach Way; the Butts (v. butte); Catstone road (-*Lane* 1777 M); Cheslett's lane; Cobgo; Coneygarthstones (*Conygarshton lane* 1777 M, v. coning-erth 'rabbit-warren'); the Crow's nest; the Cuckow Pen (v. Cuckoo Pen 43 *supra*); Cynderlands (*le Sonderlond* 1275, v. sundor-land); Deadman, Dead-man's Lane (*le Dedemanne* 1275, doubtless denoting the place where a dead man was found); Easington Green; Felder Hills; the Folly (v. folie); Forty Bridge & Lane (*atte Fortheie* 1327 SR, *le Fortheys* 1388, v. forð, ēg, cf. *Fortheye* 36 *supra*); Foxhills Fern (*le Foxhole* 1275, v. fox-hol); Gallows Corner; Goding Ham (*Godwynesham* 1354, the OE pers.n. *Godwine*, v. hamm 'water-meadow'); Gorse-moor; Green Acre; Hare Hill (*Harnell filde* 1575); Haslets; Hill Oak; (Chapel) Hollington; The King's Quar; Lockway; Marland Hill; Nearstall (*Meurstals* 1779 Rudder); the Newtakein; Outlands (*le Outlonge* 1275, v. ūt, lang 'long piece of ground'); Picked Lands (cf. Picked Lease 40 *supra*); Pinchey (*Pinchinges haie* 1575, the ME surname *Pinc(h)un*, v. (ge)hæg); Ponsway ((*Bysouthe*) *Ponsesweye* 1320, *Punseweye* 1388, the ME, OFr surname *Ponce*, v. weg); Pool Ditch; Radway furlong (*Rudweis* 1575, v. weg); Reddington (*Radin(ge)den'* 1275, 1320, 'valley of Rēada's folk', from the OE pers.n. *Rēada*, v. -ingas, denu); Sands; Settle Sedge; Shipman's hay (v. (ge)hæg 'enclosure'); Shoe Croft (*Sewcrofte* 1575, perhaps to be connected with OE scēawian 'to look out, examine', v. croft); Silver Pitts; Stallings; the Stepstones; Street Wall; Totlands (*Totelinge* 1275); Venslow Gap; Westmead 1799 *CirenP* 3; White Quar (v. quarriere 'quarry').

(b) *Aishton'* 1540 (v. æsc, tūn); *Brodemede* 1470 Cl, 1542; *atte Churchheye* 1327 SR (v. cirice, (ge)hæg); *Cloysterbroke* 1470 Cl; *Frydaysham* 1540 (the ME byname *Fridai*, v. hamm 'water-meadow'); *Georges place* 1593 FF, the *Georges* 1626 Inq (the surname *George*); *Hale furrs* 1637 FF (v. halh 'nook', furh 'furrow'); *Hundhipull* 1540; *Lyuersuchelondes* 1542 (perhaps to be compared with Liversedge YW iii, 27, v. lǣfer 'reed', secg); *Morton' landes* c. 1603 *TRMB*; *Pluckenett* 1535 VE; *Pulmede* 1542 (v. pull 'pool', mǣd);

Shrouingdoles 1275, *leʒ Shrevendoles* 1540 (*v.* dāl 'share of land', the first el. being connected with OE *scrīfan* 'to shrive' and e.ModE *shroving* 'merry-making', but the context is not clear).

Down Ampney

DOWN AMPNEY (157–1097)

Omenel 1086 DB, *Amenel*(*l*) 12 (1496) Pat, 1227–1233 Ch (*freq*), (*Dun-*) 1154–89 RBE, 1211–13, 1220 Fees, 1221 *Ass*, 1236 Fees *et freq* to 1361 FF

Hamenel(*l*) 1221 *Ass*, (*Dun-*) 1221 ib, 1236 Fees

Dunhamle, -el 1221, 1248 *Ass*   *Dunhauenel* 1226–8 Fees

Dunameie 1221 *Ass*   *Dunhaumen* 1275 Episc

Dunaumeneye 1271 Ch, *Dounaumeney* 1429 Pat

Donamen(*e*)*ye* 1275 Episc, 1287 *Ass*, 1293 Cl, 1385 Ch, *Dun-* 1276 RH, 13 *CirenD* 2, 1287 *Ass*, *Doun-* 1300 FF, 1327 *SR et freq* to 1426 Pat, *Down-* 1361 FF

Dounamney 1424 Pat, 1434 Monast, *Downe-* 1445 FF, 1577 M

Down(*e*) *Ampney* 1535 VE, 1587 FF, 1725 PR 16

v. Ampney Crucis (48 *supra*). This place is the most southerly of the Ampneys at the lower end of Ampney Brook, *v.* dūne 'lower'.

THE OAK, 1830 M. It has been suggested that this place rather than Aust (iii, 127 *infra*) was the site of Bede's *Augustinaes Ác* (ii, 2) 'on the borders of the Hwicce and the West Saxons', the oak where St Augustine first met the leaders of the British church (cf. Plummer, *Bede*, II, 74). But there is nothing to establish the identity except that possibly this region generally would be on the southern border of the territory of the Hwicce.

THE WICK (lost), *Wyk' iuxta Dounameneye* 1330 FF, *Wyke* 1331 FF, 1346, 1358 Ipm, 1484 IpmR, (*-Valers*) 1332 Pat, (*-iuxta Hampton Meysy*) 1394 FF, *Dounameneyeswyk* 1345 Ipm, *-omeneyes-* 1349 Aid. *v.* wīc 'dairy-farm', sometimes used to denote a secondary settlement from an older place as here, Cerney Wick (58), or Northwick (235 *infra*). Nicholas *de Valers* was granted the estate in 1270.

BEAN HAY COPSE, 1830 M, 'bean enclosure', *v.* bēan, (ge)hæg. CASTLE HILL FM, 1830 M. THE FENS, *Fenns Farm* 1830 M, *further, hither Fenn* 1843 *TA*, *v.* fenn 'marshland'. GALLY LEAZE COPSE, *Gallows leaze* 1843 *TA*, 'gallows meadow', *v.* galga, lǣs. THE GROVE, 1830 M. HORSEGROUND COVERT, *House ground* 1843 *TA*.

4-2

LITTLE HOOK, *middle, further Hook* 1843 *TA*, *v.* hōc 'bend'.   MUD-
DOCK COVERT, *Muddock* 1843 *TA*.   PEASBURGE BARN, *Pease bridge*
1843 *TA*, *v.* pise 'pease', brycg.   WETSTONE BRIDGE, *Whetstones*
1843 *TA*, *v.* hwet-stān 'whet-stone'.

FIELD-NAMES

The principal forms in (*a*) are 1843 *TA* 70 (which may also include some
for Ampney St Peter (55 *infra*)).

(*a*) Bakenhursts; Bickney; Black knoll (*v.* blæc, cnoll 'hillock'); the
Breach (*v.* brēc 'land broken up'); Bullhams (*v.* bula, hamm); Bull Vane;
Chaincot field; Coneygree (*Coninggores* 1275 *CirenP*, *v.* coninger 'rabbit-
warren'); Drowned hazard; Dunsworth; Farndells field ('quarter', *v.* fēorða,
dǣl); Gogmire; Gooselake; (long) Laines (*v.* leyne 'arable strip'); the Langat
(*v.* langet 'long strip'); Larborough mead; Lertle (Wilts Archæol. Soc.
1900–1, 275–9, a well associated with St Augustine, *Letherwelle* 12 BaddeleyC
167, OE *hlēoðor* 'noise, song'); Lime pitts; Long hades (*v.* hēafod 'headland'); Mere lands; Millham (*Millhamme* 1575 *TRMB*, *v.* myln, hamm);
Ox leaze; the Patch; the Picks; Putt hazard; Rushey hazard; Slade field;
Swan neck field; Swinham (*v.* swīn, hamm); Syndrams; Thorn bush; Water
beds; White lands; Withy bed.

(*b*) *le Hamme* 1535 VE (*v.* hamm).

Ampney St Mary

AMPNEY ST MARY (157–0802)

Omenie 1086 DB, *Amenel(l)* 1100–1220 *Tewk* (*freq*), 1220 Fees,
1221 Eyre, 1251 Theok, *Auenel* 1220 Fees, *Ameneye* 1269 Episc, 1287
Ass, *Ammeneye* B. *Marie* 1291 Tax, *Ampney Bte' Marie* 1535 VE,
-Sce' Marie 1600 *FF*, *Ampney Marie* 1587 ib, *Seynt Mary Ampney*
1570 ib, *St Mary Ampney als. Ashbrooke* 1626 Inq, *Amney-Mary*
1700 PR 3. *v.* Ampney Crucis (48 *supra*). The small church here
was dedicated to the Virgin Mary (Rudder).

ASHBROOK

Estbroc(e) 1086 DB, 1221 Eyre, 1225–50, c. 1300 *CirenP*, *-brok(e)* 12,
1279 Glouc, *FF*, 1287 *Ass*, 1354 *CirenP*
Esbroc 1086 DB
Astebrok 1303 FA, 1374 Ipm, *Eastbrooke als. Astbrooke* 1600 *FF*
Asebrok(e) 1300–25, 1388 *CirenP*, 1535 VE, (*le*) *Asse-, Asbroke* 1540
MinAcct, 1542 *AOMB*, 1575 *TRMB*
As(s)hebroke 1509, 1533 *MinAcct*, 1592 *FF*, *Ashbrooke* 1621 *Rec*

'(Land) east of the brook', *v.* ēast, brōc. The later form *Ash-* is due to folk-etymology. The small stream, from which the place is named and which is in the west of the parish, is an affluent of Ampney Brook.

ASHBROOK FIELD, 1770 *EnclA*, *v.* feld. CAN COURT, *Cancourt(e) farm* 1633 *Rogers* 7, 1639 Inq, possibly from the ME surname *Canne* (Reaney 59), *v.* court; cf. also Canford (iii, 142 *infra*). QUARRY FM, formerly *Talland Quarry* 1830 M.

FIELD-NAMES

Some modern f.ns. may be included in those of Ampney Crucis (50 *supra*). The principal forms in (*b*) are 1275 *CirenP*; spellings dated 1225–1425 are *CirenP*, 1540 *MinAcct* 1240, 1575 *TRMB* 39.

(*b*) *Byllesbrock* 1320 (the OE pers.n. *Bil*, *v.* brōc); *Brownesham* 1575 (the ME surname *Broun*, *v.* hamm 'water-meadow'); *Caples-*, *Capulles hey(e)* 1540, 1575 (the ME surname *Capel* (Reaney 60), *v.* (ge)hæg 'enclosure'); *Cleydych* 1300–25 (*v.* clǣg, dīc); *Fayrfordesweye* (*v.* Fairford (34 *supra*), weg); *Folewelle* 1320; *Fouracres*; *Galecrofte* 1374 (held by William and Richard *le Gale* (*CirenP* i, 24), *v.* croft); *Ganne-*, *Jannegor(e)* 1300–25, 1320 (*v.* gara 'gore of land'); *le Gores* (*v.* prec.); *Gosemersshe* ('goose marsh', *v.* gōs, mersc); *le Inlonde* (*v.* in-land); *Lilles-*, *Lyllusbrok* 1275, 1388 (the OE pers.n. *Lil*, *v.* brōc); *le Lithlemor* 1300–25 (*v.* lȳtel, mōr); *le Merechastles* (*v.* mere 'pool' or (ge)mǣre 'boundary', ceastel 'heap of stones'); *le Newebrugg*, *le Nyweburgg'* (*v.* nīwe, brycg, cf. Phonol. § 46); *Opmannehevede* (cf. also *Upmanfeld* 1425, possibly an otherwise unrecorded ME byname *Up-man* 'upper man', *v.* hēafod 'headland'); *Osmondes heye* 1575 (the OE pers.n. *Ōsmund*, *v.* (ge)hæg); *Polhemstret* ('road of the dwellers at Poulton (79 *infra*)', *v.* hǣme, strǣt, and for the elliptical form *Polhem-* cf. Weston Subedge (261 *infra*), Poulton is an adjacent parish); *Saulthill* 1575 (*v.* salt, hyll, probably on the Salt Way 20 *supra*); *Sevenacres* 1320; *le Shortebreche* (*v.* sceort, brēc 'land broken up'); *Therling(h)* 1275, 1320, *-lygth* 1388; *Þikkeforlond* (*v.* picce[1] 'thicket', fore, land); *Toppedebu* 1225–50; *Woldgroue* 1575 (*v.* wald, grāf).

Ampney St Peter

AMPNEY ST PETER (157–0801)

  Omenie 1086 DB, *Omenai* 1138 Glouc
  Omenel 12 Glouc   *Amenel(l)* 1122 Glouc, 1220 Fees
  Hameneye 1285 FA, *Ameneye Petri* 1290 Episc
  Aumeneye St. Peter 1425 CirenP
  Ampney Petri 1535 VE, *-Sci' Petri* 1542 MinAcct, *-Peter* 1587 FF,
    -St. Peter 1638 InqM

Peter amney 1577, 1610, 1646 M, *Peter Amni als. Eastington* 1626 InqM

v. Ampney Crucis (48 *supra*). The church is dedicated to St Peter, but the affix refers to the Abbey of St Peter, Gloucester, which held lands here; in DB the land was held of St Peter's.

CHARLHAM HO, *Cherlham* 1275, 1354 *CirenP*, 1381 *MinAcct*, *Charleham* 1540, 1542 *AOMB*, 1600 *FF*, 1626 Inq. 'The churls' meadow', *v.* ceorl, hamm, cf. Charlton (111 *infra*). It is of course difficult here and in other Gl p.ns. to distinguish hamm 'meadow, water-meadow' from hām 'homestead', but hamm is common in local ME f.ns., and topographically and chronologically it is more appropriate.

EASTINGTON, *Estinton'* 1250–75 *CirenP*, *Esterston'* (sic) 1320 *Ass* 2, *Estyngton* 1535 VE, *Estenton* 1609 *FF*, *Eastington* 1626 Inq. This type of p.n., which is repeated in Siddington (81 *infra*) and Westington (239 *infra*) as well as in another example of Eastington (171 *infra*), is discussed in Wo 60 (s.n. Sodington) and Bd 109 (s.n. Seddington), where the latter names are interpreted as 'farmstead of those dwelling south of the village' from an OE *sūðinga-tūn*. There can be no doubt about the general sense on topographical grounds and from the fact that some of these p.ns. have alternative forms, like *Sudtone* 1086 DB for Sodington (Wo 60), *Suþtun* 825 BCS 386 for Sinton (Wo 128), both from sūð 'south', and *Sudurton* c. 1200 for Suddington (Wo 271) from sūðerra 'southern'. But no spellings in OE -*inga*- or ME -*inge*- have been found for any of these names which would point to a folk-name in -ingas (gen.pl. -*inga*); the OE form of Sodington (Wo) *Suþintuna gemæru* c. 957 (11th) BCS 1007 and most ME spellings have medial -*in*- (and not -*inge*- which we should expect from *Sūðinga-tūn*). Ekwall's suggestion (DEPN xviii) that these are in fact elliptical names and denote '(land) east, south, etc. in the village' has much to commend it (cf. also EPN i, 281, and *v.* sūð, ēast, etc., in, tūn). Normally we should expect such names to denote part of the main village settlement, and certain names like Eastington itself (which lies immediately east of Ampney St Peter village) or Westington (which is the south-western part of Chipping Campden) in fact satisfy this condition. But there are others like Siddington and Eastington (81, 171 *infra*) or Sodington (Wo) where the places are not a contiguous part of the parent settlement and the meaning '(land) south in the village' is not strictly accurate unless tūn is used in some such sense as 'township, district'; this seems to be the most acceptable explanation, esp. in cases like Downton (ii, 198 *infra*), or Sinton (Wo 128) which is not south of the village of Grimley but is in the southern part of the parish. In some of these names we may also have the OE adverbial form (be) sūðan, (be) ēastan, etc. again used in elliptical formations to denote '(land) south, east, etc. of the village'.

THE MOOR, *Mora* 12 Glouc, *v.* mōr.   RANBURY FM & RING, -*farm* 1779 Rudder, -*Camp* 1830 M, an old encampment.

FIELD-NAMES

The principal forms in (*a*) are 1843 *TA* 7; some modern f.ns. may be included in those of Down Ampney (52 *supra*). Spellings dated 1250–75, 1414 are *CirenP* i, 26–7, 1543 *MinAcct*, c. 1603 *TRMB* 39, 1626–1639 Inq.

(*a*) Cow leaze (*Trinders Cow lease* 1626, *v.* cū, lǣs 'pasture'); Haywards Folly house (*v.* folie); Kingsham close; Lott mead (*Smartes Lott meade* 1639, *v.* hlot 'lot, share', mǣd, here as elsewhere denoting a meadow allocated or shared out by lot); Low Meer (*v.* mere 'pool'); Malthouse; Middle Gap; Ring furlong (*v.* hring, cf. Ranbury Ring *supra*).

(*b*) *Berrowes* 1626; *Biterham* 1250–75 (*v.* hamm 'water-meadow', the first el. possibly ME *bitter* 'water carrier', MED s.v.); *Brademor* 1250–75 (*v.* brād, mōr); *Bro(a)dmead(e)* c. 1603, 1637 (*v.* mǣd); *Brownesheye* c. 1603 (cf. *Brownesham* 53 *supra*, *v.* (ge)hæg 'enclosure'); *Calvecrofte* 1250–75; *pastur' voc' Clakkes* 1542; *le estfild* c. 1603; *Evesbrok* 1414 (the ME fem. pers.n. *Eve*, *v.* brōc); *Galehayes* 1626 (the local surname *Gale* (cf. *Galecrofte* 53 *supra*), *v.* (ge)hæg); *le Helmehouse* 1542 (*v.* helm 'shelter', hūs); *claus' voc' Lanes* c. 1603 (*v.* leyne); *Lyvsorsum heye* c. 1603 (*v.* (ge)hæg); *Londmede* 1250–75 (*v.* land, mǣd); *Milfielde* 1626; *Pinnes heye* c. 1603 (the ME surname *Pinne* (Reaney 252), *v.* (ge)hæg); *Pul(l)mead* c. 1603, 1637 (probably identical with *Pulmede* 50 *supra*, *v.* pull 'pool', mǣd); *Pultons Bridge* c. 1603 (named from Poulton 79 *infra*); *Thinlandes* c. 1603 (*v.* þynne 'thin, poor', land); *Verniforlong* 1250–75 (*v.* fearnig, furlang); *Warden hay* 1626; *le West fild* c. 1603.

Bagendon

BAGENDON (157–0106) ['bædʒəndən]

Benwedene 1086 DB

Bagindon', -yn- 1211–13 Fees, 1279 Episc, -*den(e)* 1291 Tax, 1327 SR *et freq* to 1442 FF, *Bagenden(e)* 1303 FA, 1334 Heref, 1535 VE

Bagingedon(e) 1216 ClR, 1236 Fees, -*den(a)* 1229 Bracton, 1248 Ass, 1291 Tax, -*ynge*- 1380 FF

Baggingeden' 1220 Fees, 1227 *FF*
Bachingedene 1226 ClR   *Bakyn(g)ton* 1316, 1335 Ipm
Bagginden(e) 1277 Heref, *-yn-* 1336 *FF*
Baggedene 1287 *Ass*
Badgendon 1577, 1610, 1648 M, 1813 PR 17
Badginton als. Bagingdon 1630 *FF*

'Valley of Bæcga's folk', *v.* -ingas, denu (often replaced by dūn 'hill'). The pers.n. is an OE *Bæcga*, an unrecorded variant of *Bacga*; it is found in Badg(e)worth (ii, 115 *infra*, So), Badgemore (O 65), and possibly in Badgworthy (D 59).

BAGENDON DOWNS, *the Downs* 1792 *EnclA*, *v.* dūn 'hill', cf. Ampney Downs (49 *supra*).   BURCOMBE LANE, *-field* 1792 *EnclA*, *Burkham bottom* 1777 M, *v.* būr 'cottage', cumb.   DYKE.   FIVE ACRE GROVE, *Five Acres* 1838 *TA*.   FORTY ACRE COPSE, *The Forty Acres* 1830 M.   MERCHANT'S DOWNS, *-Down* 1792 *EnclA*, probably from the surname *Merchant*, *v.* dūn 'hill'.   MOOR WOOD, 1792 *EnclA*, cf. *atte More* 1327 *SR* (p), *v.* mōr 'marsh, moor'.   PERROTT'S BROOK, 1830 M, formerly *Barrows brook* 1777 M, cf. Barrett's mead (*infra*).   PEWET'S COPSE, *Pewet hill* 1838 *TA*, from e.ModE *puwit* 'pewit'.

FIELD-NAMES

The principal forms in (*a*) are 1838 *TA* 15. Spellings dated 1779 are Rudder 258–9, 1792 *EnclA*.

(*a*) Bagendon grove (ib 1792, *v.* grāf); Barrett's breach, brook & mead (ib 1792, *Bearrotts bridge* 1702 *CirenP* 3, *Barrows-bridge* 1779, from the surname *Barrett*, *v.* brēc, brōc, mæd); Bear inn (*-bank* 1792); Bens Acre 1792; Birts ham 1792 (*v.* hamm); Black grove (ib 1792); Bonny mead (ib 1792); Centry ground (ib 1792); The Combs (1792, *v.* cumb); Coney garth (ib 1792, *v.* coning-erth 'rabbit-warren'); Dry Leaze 1792 (*v.* drÿge, læs 'meadow'); Football close (ib 1792); Great & Little hook (*the Hook* 1792, *v.* hōc, 'bend, angle'); Halfpenny hill (ib 1792); Hitchings (ib 1792, *v.* heccing 'part of a field sown'); Langet (*the Lanket* 1792, *v.* langet 'long strip'); the Lott mead (ib 1792, cf. Lott mead 55 *supra*); Millhams (*v.* myln, hamm); North field; Oyster well (ib 1792, possibly eowestre 'sheepfold', wella); Picked ground (ib 1792, cf. Picked Lease 40 *supra*); Pontons hill (ib 1792); the Pound; the Purlieu (ib 1792); Rack close 1792 (cf. Rack hill 140 *infra*); Round ham (ib 1792, *v.* hamm); Great & Little Several(s) (ib 1792, cf. Severals 28 *supra*); South field; Trinity mill (ib 1792); Wateringham (ib 1792, *v.* hamm); Whirlstone; Whitehays.

Baunton

BAUNTON (157–0104)

Bavdintvne, -tone 1086 DB

Baldinton 1208 Cur, 1221 *Ass*, Eyre, *FF*, *Baldington als. Bawding-ton* 1570 *FF*

Baudinton(e), -yn- 1215 ClR, 1220 Fees, 1221 *Ass* (p), 1241 *FF et passim* to 1442 *FF*, *Bawdynton* 1316 FA

Baudington, -yng- 1248, 1287 *Ass et freq* to 1409 Pat, *Bawdington, -yng-* 1535 VE, 1540 *AOMB*, c. 1560 *Surv*, (*als. Bawn-, Baunton*) 1539 *AOMB*, 1622 *FF*, 1626 Inq

Bawnton 1535 VE, 1623 *Rec*, *Baunton* 1682 PR 17

'Farmstead associated with Balda', from an OE pers.n. *Balda* (cf. Mawer, *Problems* 100), *v.* ing⁴, tūn. The form *Baud-* shows AN vocalisation of *-l-* (cf. IPN 113, Phonol. § 5). The late contraction of *Baudin-* to *Baun-* is to be noted.

BAUNTON DOWNS, 1830 M, *v.* dūn, cf. Ampney Downs (49 *supra*). DENTICE BUSHES, *-bush* 1849 *TA*, probably from the surname *Dainty*, ME *Deinte* (cf. Reaney 87), *v.* busc. ELDON WOOD, *Elden cross* 1849 *TA*. FIELD BARN, 1830 M, *New Barn* 1777 M, named from *Baunton Fields* 1777 M, *v.* feld. GALLEY HILL, 1849 *TA*, *v.* galga 'gallows', hyll. LYNCH BRAKE, *the Lynches* 1849 *TA*, *v.* hlinc 'ridge, an unploughed strip between fields'. WHITELANDS WOOD, 1849 *TA*, *v.* hwīt, land. WHITE WAY, the road from Cirencester to Andovers-ford (cf. 20 *supra*, Ridgeway *infra*).

FIELD-NAMES

The principal forms in (*a*) are 1849 *TA* 21.

(*a*) Barley stone; Brook hay; Claydon hull (*-hille* 1460 *CirenD* 19d, *v.* clǣg, dūn, hyll); Elms Quarr; Hitching hedge & knowl; Honey hams (*v.* hunig, hamm); Kaps ham; Lamburn hill; Mortar pitts; Ridgeway (another name for White Way *supra*, which is on the ridge east of the Churn); Rook hill; Sheep hill & house; Shooters clive (*v.* scēotere, clif); Whitecars hill.

(*b*) *maner' de Burges* 1535 VE, *Burges Bury* 1540 *MinAcct* (possibly this is to be identified with Barton Bury 66 *infra*); *Sturwold* 1327 *SR* (p) (*v.* wald).

South Cerney

SOUTH CERNEY (157–0497) [ˈsəːni, ˈsaʀni]

> loco...æt *Cyrne*, terra *Cyrne* 999 (13th) KCD 703, terra...apud
> *Cyrne* c. 1000 (13th) ib 1312
> *Cernei, -ey(e), -ai, -ay(a)* 1086 DB, 1138, 1144 Glouc, Hy 2 (1318)
>   Ch, 1166 RBE, l. 12 Berk, 1201 Cur, 1220 Fees, 1221 *Ass et freq*
>   to 1512 Comp, (*Sud-*) 1274 Episc, (*Suth-*) 1285 FA, (*South(e)-*)
>   1287 *Ass*, Ipm *et passim* to 1584 *Comm*, (*-Milon'*) 1291 Tax
> *Sarney(e)* 1286 Ipm, 1492 Comp, (*Suth-*) 1304 FF
> *Cerningg* 1289 Ch   *Serney* 1492 Comp

South and North Cerney (148 *infra*), which lie south and north of Cirencester respectively, are both on the R. Churn (5 *supra*), and all these names are related, Cirencester (60 *infra*) being the oldest recorded one. Cerney itself means 'the Churn stream' (from OE *ēa* 'stream, river') and the first element is possibly an old river-name formed from the same British root as that of the first el. of Cirencester or it is an early back-formation from the latter name. This problem is fully discussed by Ekwall, RN 78–9. As in Cirencester, initial *C-* [s] is due to French influence which is absent in Churn (cf. Phonol. § 32, IPN 100–2). The affix *-Milon'* refers to the tenure of the manor by *Milo* Fitzwalter, Earl of Hereford, son of Walter, the DB tenant.

CERNEY WICK

> *Cernewike* 1220 *FF*, *Cerneywyke, -wike* 1398 Berk, 1402 *FF*, Imp,
>   *-week(e)* 1628 *FF*, 1640 Inq
> la *Wyke* (de *Cerney*) 1240, 1248 *FF*, *Wyk* 1327 *SR*
> *Cerneyeswike* 1417 Berk, *Cerneyswyke* 1439 IpmR

'Outlying farmstead belonging to Cerney', *v.* wīc and cf. *The Wick* (51 *supra*); it is on the eastern boundary of the parish.

HAILSTONE BRIDGE, *Halgestane* Hy 1 Glouc, Hy 3, 1300 W, *Cerneya Helkestan* c. 1140 Glouc, *Halagheston* 1228, *Hal(e)weston* 1263, Ed 3 W, *Haghelstan* 1268 *Ass*, *Halstone* c. 1603 *TRMB*, *Halstonebridge* 1779 Rudder. Probably 'the holy stone', *v.* hālig (wk. *hālga*), stān. Hailstone itself is in Cricklade (W 43–4), but close to the county boundary. There has been an early confusion with OE *hagol-stān* 'hailstone'.

BARCLAYS HORNS.   BOW WOW.   BOXWELL SPRINGS & STREAM, *-hill* 1629 Inq, 'spring by the box-tree', *v.* box, wella, cf. Boxwell (iii, 25 *infra*). BROADWAY LANE, formerly *Dark Lane* 1777 M. CERNEYFIELD BARN, 1830 M, named from *the Vpper Field* 1653 GR 474, *Middle Field* 1863 *TA*, *v.* feld. CLARK'S HAY, 1863 *TA*, *la Haye* 1291 Tax, from the surname *Clark*, *v.* (ge)hæg 'enclosure'. CLAYMEADOW FM. CRANE FM, cf. *Crane mead* 1863 *TA*, *v.* cran 'heron', mæd. CROSSLANE COTTAGE, *-Lanes* 1830 M. HALES FM, great & little Hale 1863 *TA*, *v.* halh 'nook of land'. HAM LANE, great Ham, Ham ground 1863 *TA*, *v.* hamm 'water-meadow'. NORTHDOWN COPSE, *North Downe* 1628 Inq, *the Downes* 1653 GR 474, *v.* norð, dūn 'hill', cf. Ampney Downs (49 *supra*). NORTH-MOOR, 1863 *TA*, *the Moore* 1653 GR 474, *v.* norð, mōr 'marsh, moor'. PACKER'S LEAZE, 1863 *TA*, from the surname *Packer*, *v.* læs 'meadow, pasture'. UPPEROP, 1830 M, probably 'upper dependent farmstead', *v.* upp, þrop, cf. Upthorpe (ii, 217 *infra*). WILDMOORWAY LANE, 1863 *TA*, *Will-*, *Wildmore* 1653, 1669 GR 474, *v.* wilde, mōr, weg.

FIELD-NAMES

The principal forms in (*a*) are 1863 *TA* 41 and in (*b*) 999 KCD 703. Spellings dated 1425, 1463 are GR (D. 671), 1538 ib (D. 671), 1540 *MinAcct* 1240, 1622, 1653, 1669 GR (D. 474), 1628, 1629 Inq, 1675 GR (D. 1448), 1688 ib (D. 474), 1759, 1770 ib (D. 671, 474).

(*a*) Ashton Mead & Moor; Barleys hale; Black breach (*v.* brēc); Brasiers 1759 (*Mess' voc' Brasyers* 1463, 1538, the surname *Brasier*); Bridge ham (*v.* brycg, hamm); Brinklake (*Brinkelake* 1628 InqM, *Brincke-* 1653, the OE pers.n. *Brynca*, *v.* lacu 'stream'); Brockwell hale; Brownings hill; Butts (*v.* butte); Bye croft; Cats brain (*v.* cattes-braʒen); Cook's Mead (cf. *Cooks house* 1675); Corn mead; Cow leaze; Croft (*the Croft* 1653, *v.* croft); Dirt furlong; Dovey's leaze (cf. *Dovys piece* 1628); Downings; the Fearn; Fitchews Moor leaze; Foss leaze (named from the Fosse Way); Friday's gate; Furzy leaze; Gastons (*v.* gærs-tūn 'pasture'); Green ham (*v.* grēne[1], hamm); Gretton (OE grǣd-tūn 'stubble field'); Haden (*ea denn* 999, *v.* ēa, denn); Harding brook; the Hill; Howes mead; Hussey ham (*Huswives Ham* 1669, 'housewife's water-meadow', *v.* hamm); the Leap; Leonard; Lidbury hill (cf. *lide lace* 999); Littocks; long Dole (*Longdoles* 1770, *v.* dāl 'share'); Long Lands (*Longlandes* 1622, *v.* lang, land); Longshutt hall (dial. *shut* 'divisions of land'); Lot; Mead leaze (*the Meade lease* 1653; *v.* mæd, læs); Middleford (*motera ford*, *-lace* 999, *Muttleford* 1653, *v.* mōtere 'speaker', ford, lacu 'stream'); Mill ham (*v.* myln, hamm); Moor leaze (*Moore leaze* 1628, *v.* mōr, læs); Ox lease; Picked lamp; Piddle lake ('marsh stream', *v.* pidele, lacu); Pughill, -well; Sheams end (possibly identical with *mess' voc' Sher-*, *Shar-mannes* 1425, 1538, the surname *Sharman*); Shoulder of Mutton; Slamgate; Smoke acre; South ham; Tedmoor close; Thames furlong (ib 1628, 1688, 1770, named from R. Thames); Tucks moor leaze; Tween eyes (*Tweeny* 1653, '(land) between streams', *v.* betwēonan, ēa, cf. Twyning ii, 71 *infra*);

Weedings (*Widden* 1653, 'wide valley', *v.* **wid, denu**); West ham; Wick berry & hill (ib 1653, *v.* Cerney Wick *supra*, beorg 'hill', **hyll**); Wines ham (*Windsham* 1688, the ME byname *Wind*, *v.* hamm); Wine shore (perhaps the compound *windels-ōra* 'bank with a windlass'); Woodbridge.

(*b*) *Austill* 1653; *cattes stan* (*v.* **catt, stan**); (*the*) *Eastfield* 1628, 1629; *Flexlandes* 1622 (*v.* fleax 'flax', land); *haran stan* (*v.* **hār, stān**); *hean streat* (*v.* hēah, strǣt, Ermin Street i, 16); *hodes lace* (an OE pers.n. *Hod*, lacu 'stream'); *huredes mor* (probably OE hīred 'household', mōr); *nunnena pol* ('nuns' pool', *v.* nunne, pol); *oteres ham(me)* *v.* otere 'otter', hamm); *the Queeneway* 1629 (*v.* cwēn, weg); *Tweene Walls* 1653 ('between the walls', *v.* betwēonan, wall); *Walkney* 1669, *Winteney* 1584 *Comm* (the OE pers.ns. *Walca*, *Winta*, ēg 'island').

Cirencester

CIRENCESTER (157–0201) [ˈsairənˈsestə, ˈsɑiʀən, ˈzɑiʀnsestə, ˈsisitə]

Κορίνιον c. 150 Ptol   * Cironium* c. 650 (13th) RavGeog
[*Durocornovio* 4 (8th) AntIt] (*v.* Addenda)
Cirenceaster, æt, to Cirenceastre late 9 ASC (A), s.a. 577, 628, 879, 880, c. 1120 ASC (E), s.a. 879, 880
Cirrenceastre, Cairceri 894 Asser, *Cair Ceri* 11 Nennius
Cirneceastre c. 1120 ASC (E), s.a. 628, 999 (13th) KCD 703
æt Cyrenceastre e. 12 ASC (D), s.a. 1020
Cyrneceaster c. 1000 (13th) KCD 1312, *on Cyrnceastre* c. 1120 ASC (E), s.a. 1020
Cire, Cyrecestr(a)' 1086 DB, 1130–65 P (*freq*), 1221 *Ass*, 1315 Ipm, 1332–1413 Ch (*freq*)
Ciren-, Cyrencestr(e)' 12 *Tewk* 76d, 1156 RBE, 1174 Theok, 1190 f P, 13 Misc, 1211–13 Fees, Hy 3 *Surv*, 1220 Bracton, Cur-, 1221 Eyre, 1223 Abbr *et passim* to 1759 PR 2, (-*als. Ci*-, *Cycestr(e)*) 1562, 1566 FF, (-*als. Syssyter*) 1571 ib, (-*als. Ciciter*) 1577, 1690 M, (-*vulgo Cissiter*) 1675 Ogilby
Chiringecestre c. 1270 Gerv
Cycestre 1276 Misc, *Cicestre* 1453 Pat, (-*als. Cycyter*) 1570 FF
Cirncestre 1290 Ipm
Circestre 1317–46 Misc, 1400–64 Pat (*freq*), -*cetre* 1394 FF, 1406 Pat   *Sircestre* 1408 Pat
Surce(s)tre 1412–39 Pat (*freq*)   *Circetur* 1494 FF
Surencestre 1436 Pat, *Si-, Syrencestre* 1439, 1476 Pat, c. 1560 *Surv*, *Sironcester* 1716 PR 9
Cisetur 1453 Pat, *Cicet(t)er* c. 1490 ECP, 1718 PR 17, *Cyssetyr*, -*tur* 1491 Pat, 1563 FF, *Cyciter* 1587 FF
Sissetur c. 1500 ECP, *Sussetour* c. 1515 ib, *Sisator* 1685 PR 15

The name of Cirencester, like those of the R. Churn and South Cerney (58 *supra*) and North Cerney (148 *infra*), is connected with that of the great Roman station, *Durocornovio* in the Antonine Itinerary, and possibly that of the West Midland British tribe, the *Cornovii*, whose name is recorded in *Civitas Cornov(iorum)* on an inscription at Wroxeter, their chief town (Jackson 377 note). The Roman town of Cirencester was actually in the territory of the *Dobunni*; Ekwall (RN 79, EtymNotes 37) has suggested that either Cirencester was a colony of the *Cornovii* or that the *Dobunni* were a branch of the *Cornovii*. Neither of the oldest names, *Korinion* and *Durocornovio*, easily explains the OE forms in *Cyrn-* or *Cirn-* (with a palatalised initial consonant). The presence of the initial palatalised consonant is proved by its retention in the r.n. Churn and by the French substitution in Cirencester and Cerney of *c-* [ts], later [s], which does not take place with OE *c-* [k] (cf. IPN 100–2); this removes any possibility of a change of Brit **Corin-* to PrOE **curin-* and *cyren* by OE *i-*mutation. Stevenson (*Archaeologia* lxix, 200–2) and Förster (*Themse* 299) take Ptolemy's *Korinion* to be the correct form; Stevenson assumed that by British *i-*affection this would give a form *Cerin-*; Ekwall (RN lxviii ff) regards this particular PrWelsh change as probably too late in operation to have affected the British name of Cirencester, which was in Saxon hands by 577, and proposes that affection caused by *-j-*, *-ī-*, which was lost, could take place earlier than that caused by an *-i-* which was retained as in *Korinion*. He therefore assumes that *Korinion* is an error for *Kornion*, a shortened form of *Cornovion*, which would become PrWelsh **Cern-* early enough to account for OE *Ciren-*, etc. Jackson 613, 616 puts the period of internal *i-*affection after the 6th century in the north and after the early 8th in the south-west (cf. also Jackson 617 note). These various comments have of course assumed that with the Saxon capture of Cirencester in 577 an end was made of British speech in the region. Some doubt exists about Asser's *Caer Ceri* being strictly identical with the correct Welsh form of Cirencester; Ekwall thinks the name might have been confused with Kerry in Wales.

The meaning of the British name *Cor(i)nion* is uncertain. Ekwall suggested that it is from the tribal name *Cornovii*, which is to be connected with the root **korn-* 'horn, horn of land', as in Cornwall (cf. Holder s.n. *Cornovii*).

The PrOE form **Cern* (from **Cornion*) would by palatal influence give WSax **Ciern*, later OE *Cirn-*, *Cyrn-*, with a svarabhakti vowel developing in the form *Ciren-*; Ekwall (EtymNotes 38) cites a good parallel to this in OE *cyrin, cerin* 'churn' (a word which led, as he points out, to a curious Welsh mistranslation of Cirencester as *kaer vudei* 'fort of the churn' from Welsh *buddai* 'churn'). Alternatively if we have a PrWelsh **cerin-* (from *Corinium*) the nexus *e-i* (which did not exist in PrOE) would have the regular OE *i-i* substituted, giving OE *ciren-*, late OE *cyren-*. The OE compound with OE ceaster 'Roman camp or town' is a normal type with the names of Romano-British towns, as in Gloucester (ii, 123 *infra*).

It should be noted that the current local form of the name is a spelling-pronunciation; the reputed pronunciation [ˈsisitə] is not used nowadays, though it was a common form from the 14th century and still finds a place in some pronouncing dictionaries and hence in some non-local learned society.

CIRENCESTER STREET-NAMES

ABBOT ST. (lost), *Abbotstret(e)* 1460 *CirenD* 19, 1540 *AOMB, MinAcct, Abbotes street* 1545 *Rogers* 11, *Abbott Streete* 1676 *GR* 1130, *v.* abbat (here the Abbot of St Mary's, Cirencester), strǣt, cf. Coxwell St. *infra*.   BATTLE ST. (lost), *placeam de batail* (ib margin *Batailstrete, in vico bellico*) 14 *CirenD* 14, *Batelstrete*, 1460 ib 18d, 1540 *AOMB, Battlestreet als. St. Thomas Street* 1626 Inq, *v.* bataille 'battle, juridical dispute', but the allusion is unknown; it is now Thomas St. (*infra*).   BLACK JACK ST., 1779 Rudder 344, doubtless named from an inn; a *black jack* was a tarred leather jug for ale (cf. NED s.v. recorded from 1591).   BUTCHER ROW (lost), 1626 Inq, 1779 Rudder, *-Rowe* 1597 Inq, *Bocherrewe* 1460 *CirenD* 18, 'row of butchers' shops', ME *boucher, v.* rǣw.   CASTLE ST., *Castelstrete* 1311 *CirenD* 15d, 1320 *Ass* 12d, *-streete* 1550 *GR* 445, *Castellstret* 1540 *AOMB, v.* castel.   CECILY HILL, 1705 *CirenP* 3, *Seyntcecyly strete* 1460 *CirenD* 18d, *Sycilye streete* 1652 *ParlSurv*, named from the chapel of St Cecilia (Rudder 344).   CHIPPING ST. (lost), *Chepyngstret(e)* 1367 *CirenD* 10, 1414 Pat, 1460 *CirenD* 18, 1540 *AOMB, Chippenstret* c. 1560 *Surv, Chippinstreete als. Sheepingstreete* 1652 *ParlSurv*, 'market street', *v.* cēping, cf. The Chipping (110 *infra*); it was part of Dyer St. (*infra*).   CHURCH ST.   COXWELL ST., *Coxwell-street more antiently Abbat-street* 1779 Rudder, named from John *Coxwell*, who gave 20*s.* a year for two sermons (1607 Rudder 366); cf. *Abbot St. supra*.   CRICKLADE ST., 1629 Inq, *Crickeladestrete* 13, 1460 *CirenD* 7d, 18, *Crekeladestrete* 13 ib 7d, 1540 *MinAcct*, the street leading to Cricklade (W 42).   DOLLAR ST., 1779 Rudder, *Dolehalestrete* 1540 *AOMB, Dolehall strete* 1540 *MinAcct, Doller-street* 1626 Inq, 'street of the hall where charitable gifts were doled out', *v.* dāl, hall.   DYER ST., 1732 *Rogers* 11, *in vico tinctorum* (in margin *Dyarstret als. Chepyngstret*) 13 *CirenD* 2, *Dyer(e)strete* 13 ib 2d, 3d, *Dyers Street* c. 1560 *Surv, -streete* 1652 *ParlSurv, Dyar street* 1626 Inq, 'street where cloth-dyers worked', from ME *dyere, dighere* (Lat *tinctor*) 'dyer', a reference to the wool-trade of Cirencester; cf. Chipping St. (*supra*). GLOUCESTER ST., 1779 Rudder, leading to Gloucester (ii, 123 *infra*), formerly called St Lawrence St. (*infra*). GOSDITCH ST. (lost), 1626 Inq, 1709 *GR* 16, 1779 Rudder, *Gosedichestrete* 1540 *AOMB*, *MinAcct*, a street named from 'a ditch used by geese', *v.* gōs, dīc. GROVE LANE, 1830 M, *v.* grāf 'copse'. INCHTHROP LANE (lost), *Instrop lane* 1660 *Rogers* 11, named from *Inchthrop* (64 *infra*); it was in Cecily Hill. LEWIS LANE, *Leause-lane* 1779 Rudder 344, cf. *claus' voc' Lewes* 1540 *MinAcct*, named from Adam de *Lewes* who held land here from Margaret de Bohun in the 14th century. MARKET PLACE, *foro Cirenc'* 1276 RH, *le Markett place* 1540 *MinAcct*, *v.* market (Lat *forum*), place. NEW ST. (lost), *New(e)strete* 14, 1460 *CirenD* 16, 18, 1540 *AOMB*, *MinAcct*, *v.* nīwe, strǣt; it later became Querns Lane (*infra*). PARK ST., leading to Cirencester Park, formerly *Law-ditch-lane* (*infra*). QUERNS LANE, formerly called *New St.* (*supra*), leading to the Querns (65 *infra*). RATTEN ROW (lost), *Ratonrewe* 1460 *CirenD* 19, *le Rotton Rewe* 1540 *MinAcct*, a common street-name meaning 'rat-infested row of houses', *v.* raton, rǣw, rāw. ST LAWRENCE ST. (lost), *vico Sancti Laurentii* 1329 *CirenD* 1d, *Saynt-, Seyntlaurenstrete* 1384 ib 11, 1540 *AOMB*, -*Laurence*- 1540 *MinAcct*, *Lawrenstrete* 1460 *CirenD* 19, *St Lawrence street(e)* 1652 *ParlSurv*, named from the hospital of St Lawrence, now called Gloucester St. SHEEP ST., *Sheep-street-lane* 1779 Rudder, 'street where sheep were kept', *v.* scēap. SHOOTER ST. (lost), *Shoterstrete* 1460 *CirenD* 18d, 1540 *AOMB*, *MinAcct*, 'street where shooters lived or shooting was practised', *v.* scēotere 'shooter, archer', possibly identical with *Schyttestrete* Ed 2 BG xv (from OE *scytta* 'archer'). SILVER ST., 1700 *CirenP*, 1779 Rudder, a common street-name probably meaning 'silversmiths' street' (*v.* seolfor). SPITALGATE LANE, *Speringate lane* 1736 *CirenP* 27, *Spital-gate-lane corruptly called Spiringate-lane* 1779 Rudder, a lane within the town leading to Spital Gate (65 *infra*). THOMAS ST., 1779 Rudder, *St Thomas Street* 1626 Inq, named from the Hospital of St Thomas, formerly called *Battle St.* (*supra*), cf. BaddeleyC 206.

Amongst minor lost street-names are *Butler-, Butter Row* 1726 *CirenP* 9, 1779 Rudder ('row where butter was sold', *v.* butere, rāw); *Clementbrugge* 1460 *CirenD* 18d (*v.* brycg, named from St Clement); *the Corn-market* 1779 Rudder; *le Dakker yate* 1540 *MinAcct* (*v.* geat 'gate'); *(le) Gildenebrig(g)e, -bruggia* 13 *CirenD* 7, 1316 ib 15d ('bridge erected and maintained by a guild', *v.* gilda, brycg, cf. BaddeleyC 211); *Law-ditch-lane* 1779 Rudder, doubtless identical with *le Lawegutter* 1460 *CirenD* 18d (probably named from a ditch or gutter dividing two jurisdictions, doubtless the moat of the castle, now called Park St.); *Newbridge* 1540 *AOMB* (*v.* nīwe, brycg); *Ponder Lane* 1535 VE (probably pundere 'a pinder'); *Seynt Johns Brudgge* 1540 *MinAcct* (*v.* brycg, probably named from the Hospital (BaddeleyC 160), *hospic' Sci' Johannis Evangeliste* 1535 VE); *Shoe-lane* 1779 Rudder; *via lapidosa voc' Stone causewey* 1540 *MinAcct* (*v.* stān, caucie); *Swyne Brudge* 1540 *MinAcct* (*v.* swin, brycg, possibly replacing ford, as often in such names; it was in Dollar St.); *Tolhall street* 1545 *Rogers* 11 (*v.* toll 'toll', hall).

Buildings included *le Bothehall* 1535 VE, 1540 *AOMB*, *MinAcct* ('the town-hall'); *le gaole, Gaolam* 1540 *MinAcct* ('the prison'); *Trinyte house* c. 1560 *Surv*; and amongst many taverns were *le Angell* 1540 *MinAcct* ('the

Angel'), *le Antelopp* 1540 ib (which later became the Boothall, 1709 *GR* 16), *le Bell* 1540 *MinAcct*, 1709 *GR* 16, *le Bere* 1540 *MinAcct* ('the Bear'), *le Crowne, le Hartished* 1540 ib ('the hart's head'), *le Katheryn Whele* 1540 ib ('the Catherine Wheel', that is 'a wheel with spikes on its rim', cf. NED s.v.), *the Kings Head* 1709 *GR* 16, *le Lyon* 1540 *MinAcct, ye Pound of Candles* 1652 *ParlSurv, the Ramme* 1626 Inq, *le Swan* 1540 *MinAcct, the Talbott* ('a common inn') 1634 Inq; some of these (like the King's Head and the Talbot) survive. Cf. BaddeleyC 309–28 for notes on the streets, etc.

ARCHIBALDS (lost), *Archebaldes* 1434 *Knole* 19, *-baldys* 1512 FF, *Archbawdes* 1578 ib, *Archebaudes als. Erchenbawds* 1637 Inq; this was the manor house of the family of *Archibald* (*Erchembald* 1235 Fees, *Archebalde* 1251 Inq aqd, *Erchebaud* 1273 *FF*, etc.) and was said to have occupied a site in Dyer St. (cf. K. J. Beecham, *History of Cirencester*, 1886, BaddeleyC 93, 110, 141).

THE BARTON, *Barton* 1540 *MinAcct, Barton Feeldes* 1540 *AOMB, -Graunge* 1543 ib, *-Grange* 1544 LP, *v.* bere-tūn 'a grange' (of Cirencester Abbey); this word is often used of outlying granges of abbey and other estates (cf. Barton *passim*, esp. in the older towns like Tewkesbury, Gloucester, Bristol, etc.).

CHESTERTON

> *Cesterton(e)* 1086, 1139–48 Glouc, 1274 Ipm, (*-Bardolfi*) 13 Glouc
> *Cestrentone* 12 Glouc
> *Cestreton(a)* 1138, 1154–89 Glouc, 1220 Fees, 1221 Eyre (p), 1274 Cl, 1287 *Ass*
> *Chesterton(e)* 1327 *SR*, 1332 *CirenD* 12d *et freq* to c. 1560 *Surv*

'Farmstead belonging to or near to the town (of Cirencester)', *v.* ceaster, tūn; this interpretation is the most acceptable one as Chesterton itself was not the site of a *ceaster*; it lies on the southern outskirts of Cirencester (60 *supra*); a similar use of *ceaster* appears in the lost names *Cestreford* and *Chesterhemefeld* (67 *infra*).

INCHTHROP (lost), *Inchesthorpp* 1540 *AOMB, Inchthrop* 1540 *MinAcct*. The first el. may be a ME *enche* 'manorial tenant' (*v.* Addenda), *v.* prop 'outlying dependent farmstead'. It was near Cecily Hill to the south of the town (cf. *Inchthrop Lane* 63 *supra*).

OAKLEY WOOD

> *Achelie* 1086 DB, *bosc' de Acle* 1221 *Ass*
> *Ok-, Ocley(e)* 1343 Ch, 1460 *CirenD* 19d
> *Ockeleywode* 1539 *CirenR* 131

Okeley (-feld(es), -wd.) 1539, 1540, 1543 *AOMB*, 1547 Pat, 1577 M
'Oak glade or clearing', *v.* āc, lēah, a common p.n.

PORT FM, 1830 M, cf. also *Portfelde* 1460 *CirenD* 19d, *le Porteffeld*
1540 *MinAcct*; from OE port[2] 'a town, market-town', here referring
to Cirencester; *Portfeld* means 'the town common-field', *v.* feld.

THE QUERNS

> *Crondeles* 1292 *CirenD*, *Crundeles* 1315 Pat, 1316 Orig, *Crondles*
> *als. Cronnes* 1343 *CirenD*
> *Cornedes* 1543 *AOMB*, 1550 Pat, (*-als. Cornes*) 1539 *AOMB* 204,
> (*-als. Cornes als. Quernes*) 1544 LP
> *Quern(e)s* 1540 *AOMB*, *MinAcct*

The name refers to an area to the south-west of the town, where
are found the Bull Ring (*infra*), a Roman amphitheatre and cemetery,
tumuli, heaps of stones and old pits and earthworks (cf. BG ix, 324,
xv, 113–15, Rudder 349). It is undoubtedly OE crundel 'quarry,
chalk-pit' or the like (*v.* EPN i, 116–17). The development of its
form is curious, with metathesis and shortening to *Corn-* and then
confusion with *quern* (*v.* cweorn 'mill-stone'), an inversion of the
development in *Cornford* (35 *supra*), cf. Phonol. §§ 20, 42 (*b*), 46.

SPITAL GATE, *Spiringate als. Spytle Grange, Spyr-, Spitell-graunge*
1538, 1540 *AOMB*, *Spitle Gra(u)nge* 1540 *MinAcct*, 1543 *AOMB*,
Campo de Spyringe 1540 *MinAcct*, *Spytylgate* 1540 ib, *Spyryngate*
1543 *AOMB*, 1587 FF, (*-als. Spitle graunge*) 1543 *AOMB*. This was
without doubt a gate in the northern wall of the town and near
St John's Hospital (cf. *Seynt Johns Brudgge* 63 *supra*); *v.* spitel, geat.
The alternative name *Spiringate* is probably to be connected with
OE *spyrian* 'to interrogate, question', presumably used of a gate at
which interrogations were made of those entering the town; Rapsgate
and Kiftsgate (155, 261 *infra*) have somewhat similar connotations.

STRATTON

> *Stratone* 1086 DB, 1215 ClR
> *Stretton* 1200 Cur, 1220 Fees, 1221 *Ass*, (*-als. Stratton*) 1600 *FF*
> *Stratton(e)* 1221 *FF*, Eyre, 1241 *FF*, 1248 *Ass*, 1285 FA, 1287 *Ass*
> *et passim* to 1595 PR 17, (*-juxta Circetre*) 1394 *FF*

'Farmstead on the Roman road', *v.* strǣt, tūn. The road is Ermin
Street between Cirencester and Gloucester; the village is a mile
north-west of the former. Cf. Phonol. § 2.

5

THE ABBEY, 1709 Rudder 352, the site of Cirencester Abbey. ACOTT'S BARN, cf. *Agodeshalf* 1327 *SR*, *Aycott Lane* 1771 *EnclA*, the surn. *Godsafe* (Reaney 137). ALFRED'S HALL, 1779 Rudder 357, who describes it as having 'the semblance of great antiquity', built in memory of a tradition of King Alfred by Lord Bathurst in the 18th century. ALMERY GRANGE (lost), (*le*) *Almery(e) gra(u)nge* 1538 *AOMB* 238, 1540 *MinAcct*, *Almarygraungefelde* 1566 *FF*, ME, OFr *almarie* 'store, pantry', *v.* grange, here one providing for the ambry of Cirencester Abbey. BARTON BURY, 1830 M, *Burgesbury* 1543 *AOMB*, *Bridgbury* c. 1560 *Surv*, *v.* brycg, burh, cf. *Burges* 57 *supra*, Phonol. § 46; it was near Barton House. THE BEECHES, 1830 M. BRICK KILN PLANT., formerly *Brick Yard* 1830 M. BULL RING (lost), 1779 Rudder 349, near The Querns. CIRENCESTER PARK, *the Home Park* 1779 Rudder, *v.* park. CLEEVE HO. COLLEGE FM, formerly *Park Fm.* 1777 M. CRANHAMS, *-ham* 1838 *TA*, possibly 'heron-haunted water-meadow', *v.* cran, hamm, but it could be transferred from Cranham (157 *infra*). CROWTHORNE (lost), *Crawthorne* 14 CirenD 12, *v.* Crowthorne Hundred (47 *supra*). EWE PENS. GOLDEN FM, 1830 M. GOOSEACRE BRIDGE, *Gose Acre* 1540 *MinAcct*, *v.* gōs, æcer. GRISMOND'S TOWER, *Grosmund* 1460 WmWo, *Grismund* c. 1540 Leland, *Grisnams* 1540 *MinAcct*, a barrow, a Fr p.n. *Grosmunt* 'great hill'. GUMSTOOL BANK, *Groomstolebridge* 1779 Rudder 344, e.ModE *gum-stoole* 'cucking-stool', with the substitution of ME *grome* 'groom' for *gome* 'man'. HAINES ASH BOTTOM, 1830 M. HARE BUSHES, 1830 M. KINGSHILL QUARRY, formerly *Hill Fm.* 1777 M, cf. King's Hill (80 *infra*). PERRY MOOR, 1830 M. POPE'S SEAT, 1830 M. SWEETHILLS PLANT., *Sweethill* 1838 *TA*, *v.* swēte, hyll. TAR BARROW, 1830 M, *Thoreboruhe, -berowe* c. 1210 BaddeleyC, *Tarbury Barrow* 1777 M, a tumulus, ME *Thori* (ON *Þórir*), *v.* beorg. WATERMOOR, 1709 *GR* (D. 16), *v.* wæter, mōr. WOOD HO, 1830 M.

FIELD-NAMES

The principal forms in (*a*) are 1838 *TA*. Spellings dated 13, 1259 are *CirenD* 3d, 7d, 16d, 1241 *FF*, 14 *CirenD* 12, 17, 1327 *SR*, 1350, 1425 *CirenD* 13, 13d, 1460 ib 18d, 19d, 1535 VE, 1538–1543 *AOMB*, c. 1560 *Surv*, 1771 *EnclA*.

(*a*) Ashcroft (ib 1695 *GR* 16, *Ayshecroft* 1550 ib 445, *v.* æsc, croft); Bedwells ground; Broadmead 1771; Byrches Beeches; Court Hill 1771; Dagham Downs 1771; Dolemead 1771 (*Dolemeade Clyffe* 1540 *MinAcct*, *v.* dāl 'share', mǣd); the Downs (*v.* dūn); Drift Way 1771 (e.ModE. *drift* 'drove, herd', weg); Dry leaze (v. læs 'pasture'); the Foss field 1771 (v. Fosse Way 17 *supra*); Furnace hole; Green Downs (*Grandone* 1460, 'green hill', v. grēne¹, dūn); the Ham 1771 (v. hamm 'water meadow'); King's Mead (*Kyngesmede* 1538, 1540, the surname *King*, mǣd); Knockers Hole 1771; Longmead ford 1771; Mill hams, -way 1771 (v. myln, hamm, weg); Piddington bottom 1771; Peaked ground; Pitacres; Pool ground; Smoak Barn 1771; Step Stairs; Water Furrows 1771; Whittle Furlong 1771; Withy bed; the Woodfield 1771.

(b) *Abbodesmede* 1259 (v. abbod 'abbot' (of Cirencester), mǣd); *Adel(l)-me(a)de* 1539, 1540 (v. adela 'filthy place, sewer', mǣd); *Barnetes Closes* c. 1560; *Benetfeld* 13 Misc (v. beonet 'bent-grass' or the pers.n. *Bennet*, feld); *Bissemere* 1241 (the OE pers.n. *Bisa* as in Bisley 117 *infra*, v. mere 'pool', or possibly a nickname from OE *bismer* 'shame' as in *Bysmarerowe* YW ii, 111); *Bollewell* 1327 (possibly bolla 'bowl', wella); (*Moche*) *Brod(e)-bury* 1539, 1540 (v. micel 'great', brād, burh); *Brodenham, -yn-* 1538, 1540, *Bradnam* 1540 (v. brād, hamm); *Brod(e)ley* 1539, 1540 (v. brād, lēah); *Buckemede* 1539, 1540 (v. bucca 'he-goat', mǣd); le *Canell* 1540 *MinAcct* (ME, ONFr canel 'water-course, gutter'); *Carsslade* 1460 (v. cærse 'cress', slæd 'valley'); *Catebraynehulle* c. 1300 *GR* 1448 (an early example of cattes-braჳen 'cat's brain, rough clay mixed with stones', v. hyll); *Cestreford* 1248 *Ass, Chesterhemefeld* 13 (both elliptical forms of Chesterton *supra*, v. ford, hǣme 'dwellers', feld, cf. Weston Subedge 261 *infra*); *Clerke(s)mede* 1460, 1539, *Clarkemede* 1539 (v. clerc, mǣd); *Clerkesmille* 1460, *Clerkismyll als. Barton Milles* 1540 (v. prec., myln and The Barton *supra*); *Coc(k)merse* 13 Misc (v. cocc², mersc); le *Con(n)yger, -gar* 1539, 1540 (v. coninger 'rabbit-warren'); *Cornemede* 1540 *MinAcct* (v. corn¹, mǣd); *Cotamdene* 1460 (possibly 'valley of the men of Coates (68)', v. hǣme, denu); *Cotes Wey* 1460 (v. Coates 68 *infra*, weg); *Culuerhey, -hay* 1538, 1540 (v. culfre 'dove', (ge)hæg 'enclosure'); (*le*) *Do(w)ny lease* 1538, 1540; *Dungcartesclose* 1540 ('dung-cart enclosure'); *Estcot* 1327 (v. ēast, cot 'cottage'); *Estmede* 1543 (v. mǣd); *Garrolde(s) meade* 1539, 1540 (ME *Garold*, OG *Ger(w)ald*, v. mǣd); *Harethorn* 1241 ('grey or boundary thorn', v. hār, þorn); *Heysulle* 13 Misc; *Howneshille Pathe* 1460; *Invude* 13 Misc (v. in, wudu); *Lampehousse, Lampe-land* 1540 Chant (described op. cit. 288 as 'a tenement given...to finde and maynteigne in the said church oon lamp burnynge'); *Langeleyes mill* 1540 *MinAcct*; the *Leaჳ* 1539 (v. lēah); *Lucasplace* 1403 Ipm; *Mable mere* 1460 (v. mere 'pool'); *Macellshille* 1540; *Mayesmylle* 1535; *Merstable* 1350 ('mare's stable', v. mere², ME *stable*); *Morestall(es)* 1539, 1540 (v. mōr 'moor', stall); *Pulham(s)barne* 1538, *Pullens Barne* 1540 *MinAcct* (probably the surname *Pullen*, v. bere-ærn); *Rikkeslade* 13, *Rixlade(sforlong)* 1350, 1425, *Rikksladeswelle* 1460 (ME *rix*, a metathesised form of risc 'rush', slæd 'valley'); *Rokhulle* 13, *Rokehille* 1460 ('rook hill', v. hrōc, hyll); *Rusheymede* 1543 (v. risc, mǣd); *Seynte Johns Me(a)de* 1538, -*Ionys-* 1540 (cf. *Seynt Johns Brudgge* 63 *supra*); *Seynt Marymyll* 1540, 1542, *St Marie mill* c. 1560 (the Abbey mill); le *Saltewhich* 1540 *MinAcct* ('shed where salt was made or sold', v. salt, wīc); *Shalford* 1460 ('shallow ford', v. scealu, ford); *Shayles lond* 14, *Shaylyshille* 1460; (le *Hartes-, Olyuers*) *Shepehouse* 1538, 1540 (v.

scēap, hūs); *Somerbarowe* 1540 *MinAcct*, *Somerpasture* 1540 (*v.* sumor, beorg 'hill', pasture); *prat' de Southam, Southammede* 1538, 1543 (*v.* sūð, hamm 'water-meadow'); *le Stoke howse* 1540 *MinAcct* (*v.* stoc 'place', hūs); *le Thyrty acres* 1540 ib; *Whitteshouse* c. 1560; *le Wodecrois, -croys* 13, 1460 ('wooden cross'); *Wodeweye* 1425 (*v.* wudu, weg); *Wythebroc* 13 Misc ('withy brook', *v.* wiðig, brōc).

Coates

COATES (157–9800)

Cota 1175 P

Cotes 1220 Fees, 1221 *Ass*, 1223 Abbr, 1232 Bracton, 1248 *Ass*, 1285 FA *et passim* to 1584 *FF*, (*-Cokerel, -Randulfi*) 1236 Fees, *Cotys* 1546 *FF*

Cooteʒ 1466 AD ii, *Cootes* 1535 VE, 1595 *FF*

'The cottages', *v.* cot. It was held in 1236 by Elye *Cokerel* and *Ralph* Paganel (Fees i, 439).

TREWSBURY HO

Tvrsberie 1086 DB

Trussebur(i), -b'y, -bir', -byry 1211–13, 1220 Fees, 1222 *FF*, 1248 *Ass* (p), 1285 FA, 1287 QW, 1327 *SR*

Trusebury (*-iuxta Cotes*) 1307, 1369, 1474 *FF*

Trosbury 1327 *SR* (p)

Trouesbury 1349 GlR 348 (p)   *Trewesbury* 1475–80 ECP

Treuesbery 1483–5 *AOMB* 411, *-bury* 1483 IpmR

Trewsbery 1599 *FF*, *-bury* 1779 Rudder 392

Probably 'fortification overgrown with brushwood', *v.* trūs, burh. The earlier spellings of the first el. are similar to those of Trusley (Db 613), but the later ones *Troues-, Treues-, Trews-* appear to have been influenced by forms like *trow, trewe* for OE trēow 'tree' (cf. Phonol. § 29). There is some question of the vowel-length of OE *trūs* 'brushwood', but ME *trous(e)* suggests that it was long (cf. NED s.v. *trouse* and W. H. Stevenson, *Transactions of the Philological Society* (1898), 15). This is the site of an encampment with a double ditch, to which *burh* refers.

ASHWELL POOL, 1793 *EnclA*, *v.* æsc, wella.   COATESFIELD BRIDGE, *Cote Fields* 1777 M.   DOCKEM HO, *Dockam* 1626 Inq, 'dock meadow', *v.* docce, hamm.   HULLASEY BARN, 1793 *EnclA*, *v.* Hullasey (106 *infra*).

FIELD-NAMES

The principal forms in (a) are 1793 *EnclA*; they may include some for Rodmarton (107 *infra*); those in (b) are 1547 *AOMB* 411.

(a) Brown's Tyning (v. tȳning 'fence, enclosure'); Chapmore (*Chapmere* 1547); the Conygree (v. coninger 'warren'); Edgerley; Ewen Way (v. Ewen 76 *infra*); Foss Hill (named from Fosse Way 17 *supra*); Oxlease Way; Perrymore (v. pirige 'pear-tree', mōr); Port Way; the Setts; the Sleight (v. slæget 'sheep-pasture'); Span Acre Way; Thistley close.

(b) *Cheymestretrete* 1335 Ipm (v. strǣt); *Hilbrokes*; *Humbstens*; *Stantars*.

Daglingworth

DAGLINGWORTH (157–9905)

> *Daglingworth, -yng-, -wurth* c. 1150 Godstow, 1273 *FF*, 1323 *MinAcct*, 1324 Ipm *et freq* to 1535 VE, *Dagelingwurth, -yng-, -worth* 1248 *Ass*, 1268 Episc, 1287 *Ass*, 1291 Tax *et freq* to 1365 *FF*
> *Dalingworþe* c. 1150, c. 1200, c. 1220 Godstow, *Dalyngworth* 1322 Orig, *Dallingworth, -yng-* 1285 FA, 1287 *Ass*
> *Daglingeworth* 1200, 1587 *FF*, *Dag(g)elingew(o)rth, -ynge-* 1200 Fees, 1233 Cl, 1274 Episc, 1335 Ch
> *Dakelingwrth'* 1200 Cur   *Dachyngwrthe* 1291 Tax
> *Dagelingesworth'* 1200 Cur, *Daglinsworth* 1675 Ogilby
> *Dagelesworth* 1284 Episc (p)
> *Daulingeworth* 1291 Episc
> *Dogelyngworthe* 1316 FA
> *Daggelyn(g)worth(e)* 1413, 1493 Pat

'Enclosure of the people of Dæggel or Dæccel', v. -ingas (gen.plur. -inga), worð. The OE pers.n. *Dæggel* would be a derivative in -*el* of a hypocoristic form of some such pers.n. as *Dægbald*, *Dæghelm*, etc. (as that suggested for Dagnall in Bk 94), and *Dæccel* would be a similar -*el* derivative of the OE *Dæcca* suggested for Dagenham (Ess 91). Some p.ns. in *Dag*- have regular early spellings with *Dak*- (as Dagenham itself) which becomes *Dag*- with voicing of intervocalic -*k*- as in Bragenham (Bk 83) or Wigginton (YN 14). The spellings *Dakelingwrth'* and *Dachyngwrthe* suggest that this might be the case with Daglingworth. The name of this folk, the *Dæccelingas*, appears also in the surname of *Margaret de Dagelingstrete*

(GlR no. 382), who is also called *de Coueleg* (ib no. 378) from Cowley 6 miles north. Here the 'street' is Ermin Street (*v.* strǣt).

DAGLINGWORTH GROVE, 1830 M. DOWER'S LANE, *Dowers ground* 1837 *TA.* GROVE HILL, 1837 *TA.* ITLAY, *Hitterley* 1879 Glos Chron. LIGHTEND BARN. LONGHILL FM. OLDFIELD COTTAGES, *Old field* 1837 *TA.* OVERLEY WOOD, 1830 M. OYSTERWELL FM, 1830 M. WICKS (lost), *Wike close* 1592 *GR* (D. 22), *Daglingworth Wicks* 1830 M, *v.* wīc 'outlying farmstead'.

FIELD-NAMES

The principal forms in (*a*) are 1837 *TA* 63. Spellings dated c. 1350, 1462 are *GR* (D. 1448), 1540 *AOMB* 63, 1592, 1696 *GR* (D. 22), 1638 InqM.

(*a*) Bean hill; Bile shore (possibly identical with *Biwal* c. 1350, 'by the wall', *v.* bī, wall); Downs (*v.* dūn); Emplay piece; Foss ground (near the Roman road from Cirencester to Gloucester 16 *supra*); Gill hays; Green acre; Hitchen (*v.* heccing 'part of a field sown'); Langet (*v.* langet); Long Lands; Lushington field; Puck acre; Severals (cf. Severals 28 *supra*); Slat quar hill ('slate quarry hill'); Smoke acre (a common f.n. in W 446 and O 466, originally referring to land held by the payment of a money-tax (smoke-penny, smoke-silver) in place of tithewood); Snakes grove; Stankombe (*v.* stān, cumb); Take in; Twitching hill (*v.* twicene, cf. YW dial. *twitch(ing)* 'a short steep bend in a road'); Waines hill; Waterway; Well field (*le Welfeld* c. 1350, *v.* wella, feld); Withy acre; Wooden hill; Wood field (*le Wodefeld* c. 1350).

(*b*) *le abbottes lande* 1540 (named from the Abbot of Cirencester); *Archebawdes lande* 1462 (named from the Cirencester family of *Erchembald* (cf. *Archibalds* 64 *supra*), of whom Bartholomew *Erchebaud* made a grant of land in Daglingworth l. 13 *GR* D. 22, T. 4); *Barrowhouse* 1638, *the Barrowe* 1696 (*v.* beorg 'hill'); 'a barn called *Francklyns*' 1696 (named from the family of William *le Frankelyn* l. 13 *GR* D. 22, T. 4); *Haryomforlonge* c. 1350; *Hiscockes* 1638; *Kynggesmede* 1413 Pat; *le Rouforlang* c. 1350 (*v.* rūh 'rough', furlang); *Stretfeld* c. 1350 (*v.* strǣt, here the Roman road from Cirencester to Gloucester); *Wydoweclose* 1638.

Driffield

DRIFFIELD (157–0799)

> *Drifelle* 1086 DB, *-feud* 1248 *Ass*, *-feld* 1540 Monast, *Dryfielde* 1316 FA
> *Driffeld* 1190 P (p), 1221 *Ass*, Hy 3 *Surv*, 1287 *Ass*, 1289 Episc *et passim* to 1587 FF, *Dryffyld* 1571 ib

Probably 'stubble field', v. drīf, feld, but it could be 'dirt field' (v. drit) with an assimilation of -tf- to -ff- which Ekwall assumes for Driffield (YE 153, Ekwall, EtymNotes 43).

ARBOUR LEAZE. THE FOLLY. THE FOSS, *Foss Farm* 1830 M, named from Fosse Way (17 *supra*). HOOK CORNER, 1801 *EnclA*, v. hōc 'bend, angle'. OLD COPSE, 1830 M.

FIELD-NAMES

The principal forms in (a) are 1801 *EnclA*. Spellings dated 1540 are *MinAcct*, 1542 *AOMB* 447, 1639 Inq.

(a) Broad Hammocks (cf. *Hommuk* 205 *infra*); Broad Lane; Cullbrook Field; Flaxlands; Gastons (*the Gastons* 1639, v. gærs-tūn 'pasture'); Gatmore close; the Ham (v. hamm); the Hayles; Inn Mead (*the Inmeade* 1639, v. in, mǣd); Kingshams Mead; Lash Ford; the Layes; Littleworth Mead; Mill Holmes (*Milhame* 1540, -*hames* 1542, v. myln, hamm 'water-meadow'); Moor Leaze (v. mōr, lǣs); Spur Field; the Wallis; Westhams (*Westham* 1535 VE, 1540, v. hamm); the Wet Chessells (*Wett-* 1639, v. wēt, ceastel 'heap of stones'); Wren Leaze (*Wrens leaze* 1639).

(b) *terr' voc' Braynes* 1540; *mess' voc' Brightis* 1540; *Davys hey* 1540 (v. (ge)hæg); *the Dry ground* 1639; *Russhey* 1540, 1542 (v. risc, (ge)hæg); *Sheperdishousse* 1540; *Thyn(ne)mede* 1540, 1542 (v. þynne, mǣd).

Duntisbourne Abbots

DUNTISBOURNE ABBOTS (157–9607) ['dunzbɔRn]

> *Duntesburn(e)* 1055, 1138–1215 Glouc (*freq*) *et freq* to 1322 Pat, (*-Hotot*) 1220 Fees, 1313 *FF*, (*-Abbatis*) 1287 *Ass*, 1316 FA, (*-Abbatis Gloucestr'*) 1307 *FF*, (*Ouer-*) 1577 M
> *Dantesborne, -is-, Tantes-* 1086 DB, *Dantesburne* c. 1155 Godstow
> *Dvntes-, Duntesborn(e)* 1086 DB, 1221 *Ass*, 1322 Misc, 1354 Ch
> *Duntisburn'* 1236 Fees, 1285 FA
> *Duntesbourn(e)* 1291 Tax, 1303 Pat, 1471 *Talbot*, (*-Abbatis*) 1291 Tax, 1535 VE, (*-Houtert*) 1295 *FF*
> *Dontesbo(u)rn(e)* 1327 Ch, (*-Hotat, -ot*) 1303 FA, 1474 Pat, (*-Abbatis*) 1327 SR, (*-Abbots*) 1474 Pat, *Dontisburn* 1462 ib
> *Dountesborne Abbottes als. Regis* 1580 *FF*
> *Dunsburn, -born(e)* c. 1560 *Surv*, (*-Abbottes*) 1587 FF, (*-Abbots*) 1657 PR 16

'Dunt's stream', v. burna. An OE pers.n. *Dunt* is not recorded, but is assumed from Duntisbourne, Downstow (D 291), and Dunsfold

(Sr 234, where it is suggested that it would be cognate with OG *Tunzi, Tunza* and related to ON *Dynta, Dyntr*); etymologically it is also related to OE *dynt* 'a dint, a blow' and ModE dial. *dunt* 'a blow'. The affixes refer to the Abbot of St Peter's, Gloucester, who was given land here by Ermelina, wife of Walter de Laci (Glouc i, 258), and to the family of *Hotat* who had lands here (1237 ClR); cf. Duntisbourne Leer (foll.) and Duntisbourne Rouse (73 *infra*).

DUNTISBOURNE LEER, *Tantesborne* 1086 DB, *Duntesb(o)urn(e) Notebem* 1275 Glouc, *-Lyre* 1307 *FF*, 1327 SR, 1540 *AOMB*, *-Lyer* 1540 *MinAcct*, 1542 LP, *Dunsborne Lerr* 1795 PR 16, with other spellings as for Duntisbourne Abbots (prec.). It was held in 1086 (DB) by the Abbey of Lire in Normandy, to whom it had been given by Roger de Laci. The affix *-Notebem* refers to Nutbeam (*v.* foll.).

NUTBEAM FM, *Nutebeame* 1220 Fees, *Notebeme* 1275 Glouc, 1327 *SR* (p), *Nutbeme* 1535 VE, 1539 *CirenR* 132, *Nuttebeme* 1540, 1542 *AOMB*, LP. 'The nut-tree', OE *hnutbēam*, *v.* hnutu, bēam (the latter here having its older sense of 'tree').

BULL BANK, *Bullbank-leaze* 1659 Rudder 663, *v.* bula, banke. COTSWOLD FM, 1830 M, *v.* Cotswolds (2 *supra*). DUNTISBOURNE GROVE, *Duntsborn-* 1830 M. HOARSTONE, a long barrow, probably 'boundary stone', *v.* hār, stān. JACK BARROW, 1780 *EnclA*, *Chakborowe filde* 1575 *TRMB* 39, possibly an OE pers.n. *Ceacca*, and beorg 'hill, barrow'. LONG FURLONG BARN, 1780 *EnclA*. KNIGHTS WOOD, 1780 *EnclA*. THICK WOOD, *Thicke Woode* 1575 *TRMB* 39, 'dense wood', *v.* þicce², wudu.

FIELD-NAMES

The principal forms in (*a*) are 1780 *EnclA*, and in (*b*) 1575 *TRMB* 39. Spellings dated 1540, 1542 are *AOMB* 40, 447.

(*a*) Addlescomb; Bullridge; Burcombe Mead; Comb Field (*leʒ Combeʒ* 1540, 1542, *Commes Fild* 1575, *v.* cumb 'valley'); the Coniger (*v.* coninger 'warren'); Creephole ('a hole in a wall through which sheep could pass'); Ditch Acre; Ealy Hill; the Folley (*v.* folie); the Foss Field (*Fosfilde* 1575, named, like Foss ground 70 *supra*, from the Roman road from Cirencester to Gloucester 16); Halcomb; Hareland Slad (*v.* slæd); Hounshed; Innox (*v.* in-hoke 'land enclosed from fallow land for cultivation'); Knockhill Close; Ladyway; Lammas Common; the Leach Way; Meadleys; Tombs Green; Vale Hill.

(*b*) *Chereye heye* (*v.* chiri, (ge)hæg); *Hanscumb* (*v.* cumb); *Kichin heye*; *Newe Bridge*; *le Northefild*; *Tymber Combes* (*v.* timber, cumb); *le West feld*.

Duntisbourne Rouse

DUNTISBOURNE ROUSE (157–9806)

Dvntesborne 1086 DB, *Duntesb(o)urn(e)* 1268 Episc, 1285 FA, (*-Rus*) 1287 *Ass*, (*-Rous*) 1287, 1327 ib, 1327 *SR*, 1474 Pat, (*-Militis*) 1291 Tax, 1298 Episc, 1544 LP, *Dunsburn Rowse* 1533 *FF*, with other spellings and meaning as for Duntisbourne Abbots (71 *supra*). The affixes *Rous* and *Militis* 'knight' refer to the possession of this place by Sir Roger *le Rous* and other members of this family in the 13th century (FA ii, 242, 245, 1294 Ipm, 1327 *SR*).

PINBURY PARK

Pennebiria, -beria, -buri 1082 France, 1086 DB, 1246 Ch, 1287 QW, 1358–9 Ch, *Penebery* c. 1150 France
Panneberie Hy 2 France
Pendebery, -bir', -byr', -bur(i), -bury, -bure 1174–88 France, 1192 P, 1213 *FF*, 1221, 1248, 1287 *Ass*, 1287 QW *et freq* to 1327 *SR*
Penthebery 1192 France   *Pentebury* 1327 Ch
Pandebir(ia) 1221 *Ass*
Pyn-, Pintbury, -bere 1542 LP, 1544 Will, 1582 *AOMB*, 1687 PR 17, (*-Park*) 1695 M

'Penda's fortified place', *v.* burh. The pers.n. is OE *Penda* which is recorded only as that of the famous Mercian king (626–55); it could be a shortened form of such pers.ns. as *Pendhere, Pendræd* and the like which seem to have had an Anglian but more especially a Mercian provenance. In p.ns. it appears to be limited to the West Midlands as in Pinvin (Wo 223). Cf. Pimbury Park (87 *infra*), Phonol. § 14.

DARTLEY FM.   FRANCOMBE WOOD, *Frankcomb* 1780 *EnclA*, *Frankum* 1837 ib, probably 'valley of the Frome', *v.* R. Frome (1) 7 *supra*, cumb, with assimilation of -*m*- to -*n*- [ŋ] before -*c*-; the wood is by the upper course of the river.   LADY WELL.   PARK CORNER, 1830 M.   SCOTT'S BUSHES, 1837 *EnclA*.   SHADY WELL, 1837 *EnclA*. SLY'S WALL PLANT., *Slys* 1780 *EnclA*, from the local surname *Sly* (cf. John *Slye* 1579 PR 17, 48, Joanna *Sly* 1706 ib 51).   VOXHILLS FM, *Voxhill* 1837 *EnclA*, *v.* fox, hyll.

FIELD-NAMES

The principal forms in (a) are 1837 *EnclA*.

(a) Acrey; Bourne ground; the Brake (*v.* bræc[1] 'thicket'); Bryar furlong; Clapyatts (dial. *clap-gate* 'a gate that shuts on to either of two posts to allow people but not animals to pass'); Clinker Barrow; Foxbury Hill (*v.* fox, burg); Gulph Park Bottom 1777 M; the Langett (*v.* langet); Long Kiln; Mearly Bottom; Pennyworth of Cheese; Slatequar Hill; Townsend field.

(b) *atte Besthrop* 1327 *SR* (p) (*v.* þrop); *Kynemundestone* 14 *CirenD* 12d (the OE pers.n. *Cynemund, v.* stān); *North-, South Feild* 1652 *ParlSurv*.

Meysey Hampton

MEYSEY HAMPTON (157–1199)

Hantone 1086 DB

Hamtun 1185 Templar, *Hamtone Rogeri de M(o)eisi* 1221 *Ass*

Hampton(a) 1220, 1242 Fees, 1262 Ipm, (-*Meys(e)y, -Meisi*) 1243 Abbr, 1269 Episc, 1277 Heref, 1278 Abbr *et freq* to 1587 *FF*, (-*Mesy*) 1248 *Ass*, 1473 Pat, (-*Moi-, -Moysi, -y*) 1275 Episc, 1291 Tax, 1342 Ipm, (-*iuxta Heyworth'*) 1272 *FF*

Meseishampton 1287 QW, *Masi-* 1306 *Ass, Meyse(y)-* 1437 Pat, 1614 *Sloane* 91, *Mesyse-* 1574 *FF*

'The homestead', *v.* hām-tūn. The affix *Meysey* recalls the possession of this estate by the *Maisi, Moisi* family from the 12th century (Gaufrid *de Maisi* 1134 P, Robert *de Meisi* 1185 Templar 48, Roger *de Meisy* 1221 *Ass* 12d, John *de Meysey* 1243 Abbr 126, Robert *de Meysey* 1262 Ipm, etc.). *Heyworth* is Highworth (W 25), 7 miles to the south-east. *Heamtun* 1062–6 KCD 823 must be Hampnett (173 *infra*).

FIELD BARN, 1830 M, HAMPTON FIELDS, named from *feld of Est, feld of West* c. 1300 Godstow, *v.* feld 'common field'. HARTWELL FM, 1830 M, *v.* heorot, wella. SOUTH HILL FM, 1779 *EnclA*. SUNHILL, *Sundays hill* 1711 *GR* (D. 540), probably of the same origin as Sundayshill (iii, 108 *infra*).

FIELD-NAMES

The principal forms in (a) are 1779 *EnclA*. Spellings dated c. 1300 are Godstow, 1614 *Sloane* 91, 1639 Inq.

(a) Barnes; Bratchill close; Clandridge; Dead Moor; Foreshews Laines (*v.* leyne); Foxholes; Garston (*v.* gærs-tūn 'pasture'); Hawkes Ham (*Hawkes* (*mess'*) 1629 *GR* 540, 1639, the surname *Hawkes, v.* hamm); Horse

Croft; Howells Green (*Howells mess'* 1629 *GR* 540, *Howells (greene)* 1639, the surname *Howell*); the Laines (*v.* leyne 'arable strip'); the Leazes (*v.* l**æ**s 'meadow'); Lip Yat (*v.* hlïep-geat); Mucklands; Settle Thorn; Shadwell ('shady well', *v.* sceadu, wella); the Shire Ditch (*v.* scīr[1] 'shire', dīc; the parish is on the Wiltshire border); Street Way (*v.* str**æ**t, a reference to Welsh Way 20 *supra*).

(*b*) *Flexland* c. 1300 (*v.* fleax, land); *the Ham meadow* 1639 (*v.* hamm); *Heath close* 1614, *the Heath* 1639 (*v.* h**æ**ð); *Hill mead(e)* 1549 Pat, 1653 *GR* 185; *Market grove* 1614; *Nutt close* 1639; *the Overpadden* 1639 (cf. Paddington 78 *infra*); *Pit hay* 1639 (*v.* pytt, (ge)hæg); *Stockheyes* 1639 (*v.* stocc 'stump', (ge)hæg); *Stonemeadowe* 1639; *Whitewalles* 1614 (*v.* hwit, wall).

Harnhill

HARNHILL (157–0700)

Harehille 1086 DB, *Harhull* 1248 *Ass*, 1285 FA
Harnhill(a) 1177 P (p), 1287 *Ass*, 1406 Pat, 1454 FF, -*hull(e)* 1220
    Fees, 1221, 1248 *Ass*, 1303 FA *et passim* to 1421 Pat, -*ulle*
    1225–50 *CirenP*, -*helle* 1316 BM, -*yll* 1535 VE
Harenhull 1221 *Ass*, Eyre (p), 1225–50 *CirenP*, 1226 *FF*, 1269
    Episc (p), -*hill* 1420 AD i
Harnehull 1415 AD iii, 1494 Ipm, 1586 FF, -*hill* 1509 *MinAcct*

'The grey hill' or 'hares' hill', *v.* hār, hara, hyll, as suggested by the variation between the *har(e)*- and *har(e)n*- spellings.

FIELD BARN, named from *middle-, little Field* 1839 *TA*, *v.* feld 'common field'.

FIELD-NAMES

The principal forms in (*a*) are 1839 *TA* 99.

(*a*) Beggar furlong; Bushy hayes (*v.* (ge)hæg); the Hill; Mays ground; Old Gore (*v.* gāra 'gore of land'); Quar close; Shadwell mead, Stanks Shadwell (*v.* sceadu, wella, stank 'pool'); Stony croft; the Vens (*v.* fenn); Waterton, Winterton (*v.* wæter, winter, tūn).

(*b*) *le Dounfeld* 1381 *MinAcct* (*v.* dūn 'hill', feld); *Forfeldy* 1420 AD i (*v.* fore, feld).

Kemble

Kemble was formerly in Wiltshire and the names of this parish are included in W 60–1; they are therefore summarily dealt with here.

KEMBLE (157–9896)

C-, Kemele 682 (14th) BCS 63, 688 (14th) ib 70, 854 (14th) ib 470, 1065 (14th) KCD 817, 1180 P, 1327 *SR*, *Chemele* 1086 DB,

Kemel 1421 AD vi, *Kembyll* 1535 VE, *Kemble* 1613 *FF*. Probably a British p.n. from a word related to Welsh *cyfyl* 'border, brink, edge'. In BCS 63, 64 Kemble is described as a wood.

EWEN, at *Awilme, Awelm* 931 (14th) BCS 671, *Euulme* n.d. (14th) ib 673, *Ewulm* 937 (e. 12th) ib 719, *Ewelme* 1289 *Ass*, 1428 FA, *Ewen* 1621 *FF*, 1709 *GR* 225, *Yewelme* als. *Yewen* 1736 *Rec. v.* ǣ-welm 'spring, source', here referring to the source of the R. Thames, now called Thames Head (*infra*).

BEANFIELD PLANT. CLAYFURLONG FM, *Clay Furlong* 1772 *EnclA, v.* clǣg, furlang. GREAT BARN, 1830 M. JACKAMENTS BOTTOM, *Jockyman's ground* 1772 *EnclA, Jackmans* 1777 M, *Jackments Bottom* 1830 M, doubtless a pseudo-manorial name from the surname *Jackman*; it is unlikely to be from Akeman Street, as Rudder 349 suggested. KEMBLE WICK (1830 M, *Weeke* 1591 W) & WOOD (1830 M), *v.* wīc 'outlying farmstead'. LYDWELL, *Lydewelle* n.d. (14th) BCS 673, *Lidwell* (*peece*) 1650 *GR* 225, 1772 *EnclA*, 'the loud spring', *v.* hlȳde, wella. PARK LEAZE BARN, (*the*) *Park Leaze* 1650 *GR* 225, 1772 *EnclA, v.* park, lǣs 'meadow'. PEASTON LANE, *Perestone* n.d. (14th) BCS 673, *Pirrstone* 1650 *GR* 225, *Peereston* 1656 ib, *Pearston* 1709 ib, *Peastones* 1772 *EnclA*, possibly 'stone by the pear-tree', *v.* peru, stān. SMERRILL FM, *Smarrell foote* 1650 *GR* 225, *Smerehill* 1656 ib, *Smeerhill* 1709 ib, 'hill with rich fat-producing pasture', *v.* smeoru, hyll, cf. Smeril (32 *supra*). SWALLOW COPSE, cf. *the swallow furlong* 1650, 1709 *GR* 225. THAMES HEAD BRIDGE, 1777 M, the actual source of the Thames is nearby in Coates parish.

FIELD-NAMES

The principal forms in (*a*) are 1772 *EnclA* and in (*b*) 1639, 1650 *GR* 225. Spellings marked n.d. are (14th) BCS 673 and others dated without source are *GR* 225.

(*a*) Abbotts peice 1725; Benchwell 1710; Black Pitts; Breach hill 1710 (*v.* brēc); Brook Green (-*greene* 1639, *v.* brōc, grēne[2]); Burnhill (*Born(e)hill,* -*way* 1650, 1710, *Bourn*- 1709, *v.* burna 'stream'); Cheescake 1710; Ciseter feild 1710 (named from Cirencester); Coates Way (*Cotes*- 1650, named from Coates 68 *supra*); Crowthorne grounds (cf. Crowthorne 48 *supra*); Ditch Acre (cf. *la diche walle* n.d., *v.* dīc, wall 'embankment'); yᵉ Dry leaze 1710 (-*leasowe* 1660, *v.* lǣs 'meadow'); Fair Hill; the Folly; Furzen Leaze Way; Graft Thorne (*v.* graft 'ditch', þorn); yᵉ Green 1710; yᵉ Green ditch, hill & way 1710; the Ham (ib 1650, *v.* hamm); Hitching Field 1725 (*v.* heccing); Hoar stone 1713 (*la Hore stone* n.d., 'boundary stone', *v.* hār, stān); Ideover

1725 (*v.* ofer², cf. *Idmead infra*); Lamas mead 1725 ('pasture available at Lammas (1 August)', cf. O 456); Lanes Shermore; Lay Leaze; Long Chalketts 1725; Mill Acre; Nattocks (*v.* nattok); Picked ground (*-peice* 1710, cf. Picked lease 40 *supra*); the Purley (probably for *purlieu*); Ricks Lane (cf. *the Ricke peece* 1650); Risden (*v.* hrīs 'brushwood', denu); Rudges Leaze; Scotland; Several (*the Seueralles* 1639, *v.* Severals 28 *supra*); Shord Gate; Sidelonge 1709; Sowbrooke 1725 (*v.* sūð, brōc); Stean Hill 1725 (*Stonehill* 1650); Through Shoots 1709 (*the thorough shootes* 1650 (*v.* scīete 'strip of land'); Tilepitts Leaze 1725; Wampstone; Wickbridge Leaze (named from Kemble Wick *supra*).

(*b*) *Bikenhulle* n.d. (the OE pers.n. *Bica, v.* hyll); *the Buttes* 1656; *Ciceter way* ('the road to Cirencester'); *Clarkes hay* (the surname *Clark, v.* (ge)hæg); *Creehill*; *le estlakebrigge* n.d. (*v.* ēast, lacu 'stream'); *feor more* n.d. ('far moor'); *Heavens Haye* 1623; *heneofre* n.d., *Henriddens* (*v.* hēah 'high', ofer² 'slope', ryden 'clearing'); *le holde mulle dich* n.d. (*v.* ald, myln, dīc); *Holland Court*; *the Hollybush*; *Hookham Sladd* (*v.* slæd); *Horsley* (*v.* hors, lēah); *Idmead* (possibly the ME (OG) pers.n. *Ide*, which may also be found in *Ideover supra*); *Jervice quarr*; *Lytle Berwe* n.d. (*v.* bearu 'grove'); *litle more* n.d., *Lytmore* 1650 (*v.* lȳtel, mōr); *le Meredich* n.d. ('boundary ditch', *v.* (ge)mǣre, dīc); *le ofre* n.d. (*v.* ofer²); *Scefernus graue* n.d.; *the throate peece*; *Woe furlong* (*v.* wōh 'crooked'); *Woluecrundle* n.d. (*v.* wulf, crundel 'quarry'); *Ʒuuyte stone* n.d.

Minety

Minety was formerly a detached part of Gloucestershire in Wiltshire and is now in Wiltshire (cf. 47 *supra*); its names are dealt with in W 61–2 and given here summarily, as it once formed part of the Hundred of Crowthorne and Minety.

MINETY (157–0191) ['minti]

Mintig, -tih 844 (14th) BCS 444, *My-, Minti, -ty(e)* 844 (14th) ib 447, 1185, 1190 P, 1211–13 Fees, c. 1220 GlR, 1221, 1248 *Ass*, 1249 *FF et passim* to 1567 ib, *Minthi* Ric 1 (1423) Pat, c. 1220 GlR, 1221 *Ass*, 1232, 1413 Ch, *Minety* 1282 Cl, 1343 Ch. 'Water-meadow where wild mint grew', *v.* minte, ēg.

STERT FM, *la Stirte, la Styrte* 1248 *Ass*, *atte Steorte* 1327 *SR* (p), *the Sterte* 1540 MinAcct, 1542 AOMB, 1544 LP. *v.* steort 'a narrow pointed strip of land'.

BRANDIER, *Brandyres als. Branyrons* 1653 Ipm (W), *terr' voc' Brand-iron* 1681 W, doubtless a manorial name from an occupational surname *Brandier* 'one who uses a brandier or brandiron (i.e. a grid-iron)'. BRAYDON HALL, cf. *bosc' de Braydon* 1540 MinAcct, *Brayden*

1629 Inq, named from Braydon (W 41). BROWNOCKHILL PLANT., *Browning Oke* 1591 W, cf. also *prat' voc' Brownynges* 1540 *MinAcct*, from the surname *Browning, v.* āc 'oak'. BUCKSWELL FM, *Books Well* 1773 W, cf. *Bucks* 1839 *TA*. COOLES FM, 1830 M, cf. *Tomcoules Lane* 1629 Inq, a surname *Coole*, probably from a p.n. *Cowhill* or the like. GIBB'S FM, named from the family of Francis *Gibbs* (1670 PR). THE MANSELLS, cf. John *Mansell* (1689 PR). MOOR FM, (*le, the*) *Mores* 1538, 1542 *AOMB*, 1540 *MinAcct, v.* mōr. PLEYDELLS FM, 1839 *TA*, cf. Edward *Pleydell* (1611 W). SAMBOURN, *Sandeburne* 1196 Cur (p), *Sandbourn* 1839 *TA*, 'sandy stream', *v.* sand, burna. SAWYERS HILL, 1839 *TA, terr' voc' Sawyers* 1540 *MinAcct*, from the family name of Jacob *Sawyer* (1622 PR). TELLINGS FM, cf. Henry *Tellin* (1671 PR). WAITS WOOD, 1839 *TA*, cf. William *Waight* (1633 PR). WELLFIELD, cf. *Welmede* 1542 *AOMB, v.* wella, mǣd. WOODWARDS FM, cf. Mary *Woodward* (1716 PR).

FIELD-NAMES

The principal forms in (*a*) are 1839 *TA* 132, and in (*b*) 1540 *MinAcct* 1240. Spellings dated 1538 are *AOMB* 238, 1542 ib 447, 1561–1698 *GR* 80, 1629 Inq.

(*a*) Bean lands; Berry lands; Breaches (*v.* brēc); Brights (*claus' voc' Brightes* 1540, the surname *Bright*); Burnt patch; Chawcroft; Coal pit hill; Corn leaze; Court Goares (cf. *Courte close* 1538, *v.* court, gāra); Cow leaze; Cuckoo pen (cf. Cuckoo Pen 43 *supra*); Day close (*Deyclose* 1540, 1542, *v.* dey 'dairy'); Flistrage; Frog Hayes (*Froggehey* 1540, *v.* frogga, (ge)hæg); Furzen ground; Goose ham (*Goseham* 1540, *v.* gōs, hamm 'water-meadow'); Hell green; Herrings (*claus' voc' Heringis, Heringeshey* 1540, the surname *Herring, v.* (ge)hæg); Hilley (*Hyley* 1540, 1542, *v.* hyll, lēah); Honey ham (*v.* hunig, hamm); Horsepitt leaze; Hurdy (*Hurdehey* 1540), Hurdys (*Hurdesplace* 1540, the ME surname *Herd, Hurd, v.* hirde); Lammas mead (cf. Lamas mead 77 *supra*); Laycotts (*prat' voc' Lacockes* 1540, the surname from Lacock W 102); Laynes (*v.* leyne); Long Doles (*v.* dāl); Mathews (*cotag' voc' Mathewes* 1540); Middells (*mess' voc' Muddelles by the lane* 1540, possibly the surname *Middle*, Reaney 221); Oxwell's hay; Paddington (*Padingden* 1540, 'Pada's valley', from the OE pers.n. *Pada, v.* -ing[1], denu, cf. *Overpadden* 75 *supra*); Parkers (*claus' voc' Parkers* 1540); Picked ham (cf. Picked lease 40 *supra*); Purgatory; Purlieu; Pye End (cf. *Py(e)brech(e)* 1538, 1542, *Py- als. Pyenham* 1538, 1540, possibly OE pie, pēo (gen.pl. *pēona*), an insect, *v.* brēc, hamm); Ruddock(s) (*claus' voc' Ruddokes* 1540, the surname *Ruddock*); Rye close (*Rieclosse* 1540); Stall hangings; Stewards mead (*Stuardes mede* 1540, *v.* stīg-weard, mǣd); Swillbrook bridge (cf. Swill brook 12 *supra*); Toveys (*ten' voc' Tobyes* 1540, the surname *Tovey*); Towley; White hays; Whitings (*Whitings close* 1629).

(b) *le Acres* 1538; *le Balehull*; *Brodemede* 1538; *Bruggeham* (v. **brycg,** hamm); *Cromehey* 1540 (v. (ge)hæg); *Dry Leaze* 1628; *le Hamakers* (v. hamm, æcer); *the Hale* 1314 Pat (v. halh 'nook'); *Hanger* (v. hangra 'wooded slope'); *Haukesbroke, claus' voc' Haukes, Hawkesclose* 1629 (the surname *Hawkes*, v. brōc); *le Hawle house*; *le Marelease* 1538, *Mareslease* 1542 (v. mere² 'mare', lǣs); *Netherbury* (v. burh); *Northouse*; *atte Ok* 1314 Pat (p) (v. āc 'oak'); *Perryelands* 1629 (v. pirige 'pear-tree'); *Potters hill* 1561; *the Suthehale* 1327 SR (v. sūð, halh 'nook').

Poole Keynes

Poole Keynes was formerly in Wiltshire and its names are dealt with in W 64; they are summarised here.

POOLE KEYNES (157–9995) ['puːl 'keinz]

Pole n.d. (14th) BCS 673, 1086 DB, 1241 Cl, 1268 *Ass et freq* to 1315 Ipm, *Pole Canes* 1610 M. v. pōl 'a pool'. The daughter of John Maltravers (who held the manor in 1327) married Sir John *Keynes* (W 64); the family of Keynes (*Kahaines*) also held the nearby manors of Somerford Keynes (83 *infra*) and Ashton Keynes (W 40).

FLAGHAM BROOK, 1830 M, *Flaghams* 1613 GR 225, v. **flagge** 'reed, rush', hamm. MILL FM, *atte Mulle* 1327 SR (p), v. myln. OAK WELL, *Okewell hed* 1591 W, v. āc, wella. WESTEND FM, 1830 M.

FIELD-NAMES

The principal forms in (a) are 1772 *EnclA*, and in (b) 1613 GR 225.

(a) Blatts; Court Fields (*Court feild* 1613); Ditch Acre; Ellymoor; Goldages; Goose Hay (v. gōs, (ge)hæg); Kent's Mead; Peas Leaze (v. pise, lǣs); Quay Pool; Southfield; Tadpole Lane; Wood field.

(b) *Lordshore*; *Millmead*; *Norwood*; *Pillsmore* (cf. Pills Moor 84 *infra*); *Rideings* (v. rydding 'clearing'); *Well hey*; *Woodlandes*.

Poulton

Poulton was formerly a detached parish of Wiltshire.

POULTON (9157–1000)

æt Pultune 855 (11th) BCS 487, n.d. ib 1320, *Pultun, -ton(e)* 1100–35, 1125–54 Tewk 72, 73, 1185 Templar, 1242 Ipm, 1248 *Ass*, 1263 Ch *et freq* to 1577 M

Poulton 1221 Eyre (p), 1263 Ch *et freq* to 1654 PR 16, *Powlton* 1667 ib 17

Polton(e) by (juxta) Crecke-, Crekkelade 1316 Ipm, 1317 Fine

'Farmstead by the pool', *v.* pull 'pool' (which is often indistinguishable from pōl 'pool'), tūn. Cf. Poulton iii, 252 *infra.*

BETTY'S GRAVE, 1830 M, *-Grove* 1796 *EnclA.*   THE BUTTS, 1796 *EnclA, v.* butte 'an abutting strip in the common field'.   POULTON FIELD, *the upper, lower Field* 1796 *EnclA.*   READY TOKEN, 1796 *EnclA,* an inn where ready money was required.   THE VERGE.

FIELD-NAMES

The principal forms in (*a*) are 1796 *EnclA,* and in (*b*) 1544 LP.

(*a*) Cowdown Lane (*Cowdown* 1544, *v.* cū, dūn); the Downs; Hull Piece (*v* hulu 'shed'); Lid Furlong; Lisbrook (possibly OE lisc 'reedy marsh', brōc); the Lot Mead (*v.* hlot); Meadham Lake (*v.* mǣd, hamm, lacu 'stream'); Moor Leys; Oatlands furlong; Poulton Street; Stone Hill; Varnhills Lane (*v.* fearn, hyll).

(*b*) *Nether, Overbreche* (*v.* brēc); *Moreclyffe; le Parke.*

Preston

PRESTON (157–0400)

Prestitvne 1086 DB, *Preston* 1221, 1248 *Ass,* 1279 *FF,* 1291 Tax *et passim* to 1587 *FF,* (*-juxta Cyrenc'*) 1298 Episc, *Prestetone* 1540 Monast. 'The priests' farm', *v.* prēost, tūn, a common p.n.

KING'S HILL, *Kyngeshull'* 1287 *FF, Kingeshill* 1540 *MinAcct,* 1542 *AOMB,* 1545 LP. *v.* cyning 'king', hyll. Cf. King's Mead (*infra*).

NORCOTT

Nortcote 1086 DB   *Nordcote* 1204 P (p)
Norcot(e) 1086 DB, 1276 RH, 1582 *FF*
Northcot(e) 1221 *Ass* (p), 1274 RH, 1279 FF, 1287 QW *et passim*
    to 1540 *MinAcct,* (*-iuxta Cyrencestr'*) 1355 *FF*

'North cottage', *v.* norð, cot; it lies rather more than a mile north of Preston.

ERMIN FM, named from Ermin Street.   KING'S MEAD, 1771 *EnclA, v.* King's Hill (*supra*), mǣd.   MERRILL HILL, *Merry-hill* 1830 M, *v.* myrig 'pleasant', hyll.   PRESTON FORTY, 1830 M, *Forty Farm*

1771 *EnclA*, v. forð, ēg, cf. *Fortheye* (36 *supra*). SIDELANDS.
WITPIT COPSE, *Wygeput* 1327 *SR* (p), *Week Pitt* 1771 *EnclA*,
'Wicga's pit', from the OE pers.n. *Wicga* as in Wiggold (49 *supra*),
and pytt.

FIELD-NAMES

The principal forms in (*a*) are 1771 *EnclA*.

(*a*) the Coneygrees (*v.* coninger 'warren'); Dances Fancy; Dockhams
(*v.* docce, hamm); Forestall (*v.* fore-stall 'place in front of a farm'); Gallows
Quar; Hangman Stone; Knapps; Meer furlong; the Moor; Moor Cow-
gappen (probably from dial. *gap* 'gap in a fence or hedge'); Moorhill; Oak-
leaze; Oxhay (*v.* (ge)hæg); the Pinhills; Wanthill (ME *wante* 'mole'
or a surname from it); Watertarn.

(*b*) *Lotte Medowe* 1535 VE (cf. Lott mead 55 *supra*); *Sherstons Mylle*
1535 ib.

Siddington

SIDDINGTON (157–0399)

Svdi(n)tone 1086 DB

Svintone 1086 DB, *Suenton* 1145 France, *Suinthon* 1157 ib,
Swinton 1186 ib

Suthintun(a), *-ton(e)*, *-yn-* 1146 France, 1223 Abbr, 1226 *FF*, 1233
Cl *et freq* to 1409 Ipm, (*Nether-*) 1223 *FF*, (*-Lang(e)le*) 1274,
1280 Ipm, (*Ouer-*) 1310 *FF*, *Suthington(a)* 1221 Eyre, 1235
Bracton

Sudinton, *-yn-* 1201 Cur, 1220 Fees, 1221 *Ass*, 1272 Ipm *et freq*
to 1494 *MinAcct*, *-(Galfridi)* 1220 Fees, (*-Musard*) 1325 *MinAcct*,
(*Nether-*, *Over-*) 1395 *FF*, *Sudincton'* 1248 *Ass*, *Sudington*, *-yng-*
1248 *Ass*, 1327 Ch *et freq* to 1587 *FF*, (*Nether-*, *Over-*) 1503
Ipm, 1511 *FF*, (*-Mary(e)*) 1587, 1617 *FF*, *Nether Sudington als.*
Sudington Musard 1617 ib, *Sudington Peter als. Lower Sudington*,
Over Sudington als. Sydington Langley 1637 ib

(*Uuere*) *Suddington'* 1261 *FF*, c. 1560 *Surv*, (*Nether- als. -Langlie*)
1634 Inq

Sodinton, *-yn-* 1262 Ipm, 1274 RH, 1286 Episc (p) *et passim* to
1415 *FF*, (*-Langeley*, *-Musard*) 1303 FA, (*Over-*, *Ouere-*) 1306
FF, 1352 Ipm, (*Nether-*) 1330 FF *et freq* to 1375 Ipm, *Sodington*,
-yng- 1316 FA, 1325 Orig *et freq* to 1440 IpmR, (*-Langley*)
1409 Ipm, (*Over-*) 1434 Pat

Sotington 1285 FA   *Sothinton* 1327 *SR*

Sutton juxta Cicestre 1398 Ipm

Sydyngton, -ing- 1535 VE, 1540 *AOMB, (-Petri, -Beate Marie)*
1535 VE, *(-inferiore, -superiore)* 1575 *FF, Upper Siddington* 1742
PR 16

Siddington lies about a mile south of Cirencester and it might be
expected that the name referred to this fact. The village is not in fact
contiguous with Cirencester and the interpretation '(land) south in
the village' is here less likely than a similar interpretation for
Eastington (54 *supra*) which seems to have been the eastern part of
Ampney St Peter village, or Westington (239 *infra*) which is the
south-western part of Chipping Campden village. But '(land) south
in the township or district' would be appropriate, in this case of
Cirencester (*v.* sūð or sūðan, in, tūn); the spelling *Sutton juxta
Cicestre* is interesting in this respect. The earlier spellings *Svintone*,
etc. have AN loss of intervocalic -*th*- (cf. IPN 109). The development
of *u* to *i* before dentals which occurs in other p.ns. like Sinton (Wo
128), Diddington (Hu 254), Dinnington (YW i, 146) and probably
Hidcote (243 *infra*), is well established (cf. Phonol. § 29). The various
affixes refer to the two parts of Siddington: Lower or Nether Siddington, also distinguished as *St Peter* from the church of that
dedication and *Musard* from the family of *Musard* who held land
here from the time of DB to 1349 (Aid 280); Upper Siddington, also
called *St Mary* from the former church of St Mary, *Langley* from
the family of *Langeley* who had an estate here from the 13th century
(1285, 1303 FA, 1349 Aid 280, cf. the f.n. *Langley infra*), and *Galfridi*
from *Geoffrey de Langele*. In 1617 *FF* and 1634 Inq the affix *Langley* is
an alternative to *Nether*, but in 1637 *FF* to *Over-*; this was apparently
because the Langleys had later acquired land in Lower Siddington.

BARTON FM, *-ground* 1779 *EnclA, v.* bere-tūn. BOWLEY'S FM, 1830
M. DRYLEAZE FM, *Dryleaze* 1725 Will, *v.* drȳge, lǣs 'meadow'.
FURZEN LEAZE FM, *-leases* 1777 M, *-Leys* 1779 *EnclA, v.* fyrs(en),
lǣs. NOOKS, 1830 M. SANDY LANE FM, 1779 *EnclA*. SHELLS
GROVE, 1830 M. TUDMOOR, *-more* 1632 *FF*, 1779 *EnclA*, from the
OE pers.n. *Tud(d)a, v.* mōr. WORM'S FM, 1830 M.

FIELD-NAMES

The principal forms in (*a*) are 1779 *EnclA*. Spellings dated 1387–1503
are Ipm.

(*a*) Backslade Gate (*v.* slæd); Bear Way; Bidsmore; Blackpitts; Bradnam
(*v.* brād, hamm); Col Bath Mead; Fludyrs close; the Gastons (*v.* gærs-tūn);

the Ham (v. **hamm**); Kill(i)more; Littleworth; Newnham; Nigham (*Niham* 1639, 'near-by meadow', from OE *nēah*, hamm); the Old Lain's (v. **leyne**); Purley (e.ModE *purlieu* 'outskirts'); the Several (cf. Severals 28 *supra*); Sheer Hay; the West Field.

(b) *Barebasts* 1387, *-bascet* 1392; *le Calewall hill* 1490, *Calwell Hyll* 1503; *Ditchams* 1633 Inq; *Langley* 1587 *FF* (v. **lang**, **lēah**); *Marleis* 1490, *-leys* 1503; *Rowe Leasowe* 1616 *Rogers* 13 (v. **rūh**, **lǣs**).

Somerford Keynes

Somerford Keynes was formerly in Wiltshire; its names are dealt with in W 46–7 and are summarised here.

SOMERFORD KEYNES (157–0295) ['sumǝfǝd 'keinz]

Sumerford 685 (e. 12th) BCS 65, 931 (14th) ib 671, 1065 KCD 817, 1211 RBE, 1242 Fees, *Somerford* 1281 Ipm, 1299 AD vi, (*-C-*, *-Kaynes*) 1289 *Ass*, 1327 IpmR, 1321–8 Ipm (*freq*) *et freq* to 1547 Pat, (*-Keynes*) 1487 Ipm, 1535 VE. 'Ford usable in summer', v. **sumor**, **ford** (here one across the R. Thames). The affix is the surname of the feudal owners, *de Kaaines* (1215 ClR), *de Kaynes*, *de Kahaynes* (1281 Ipm), etc.; cf. Poole Keynes (79 *supra*).

SHORNCOTE ['ʃɑːŋkǝt]

S(c)hern(e)cote 1086 DB, 1221 *Ass*, 1249 *FF et freq* to 1492
    MinAcct, *Sernecote* 1262 Ipm
Scornecote 1221 *Ass* (p)   *Corncote* 1334 IpmR
Cern(e)cote 1296 IpmR, 1327 SR *et freq* to 1553 Pat
Sharnecote 1375 Ipm   *Sharcote* 1387, 1392 Ipm

'Cottage in a mucky spot or dung-hill', v. **scearn**, **cot**. The *Cerne-* spellings are doubtless due to the influence of South Cerney (58 *supra*).

HOWELL'S BARN, 1830 M. MILL FM, cf. *Mulleham* 1327 Ipm, *Mill Brook* 1807 *EnclA*, v. **myln**, **hamm**. NEIGH BRIDGE, *le Ebrigge* 1327 Ipm, *Ney bridge* 1591 W, *Nearbridge* 1807 *EnclA*, 'at the river-bridge', v. **atten**, **ēa**, **brycg**, cf. Phonol. § 45. POOL MILL, 1830 M. PURLIEU FM, *the Purlieu* 1807 *EnclA*, e.ModE *purlieu* 'the outskirts of a forest or other place' (cf. NED s.v.). SHOOTERS HILL BARN, 1830 M. SKILLINGS MILL, 1830 M. SOMERFORD HASK, probably *hassuc* 'clump of coarse grass', as in Hask(e) (D 419, 430). SPRATS-GATE LANE, 1830 M. WASHBURNS MILL, 1830 M.

FIELD-NAMES

The principal forms in (a) are 1807 *EnclA*.

(a) The Angles; Barrow Hill (*v.* beorg); Bickenham (probably the OE pers.n. *Bic(c)a* as in *Bikenhulle* 77 *supra*, *v.* hamm); Breaches (*v.* brēc); Greenditch; the Grove; Handgrove; Pills Moor (*Pillesmor* 1328 Misc, possibly the OE pers.n. *Pīl*, but more probably OE *pīl* 'pile, shaft', doubtless used of a stake used as a marshland land- or track-mark, as it occurs in the same compound several times (*Pillsmore* 79 *supra*, Pillsmore and *Pylewey* 88, *Pilles-*, *Pillismore* 101, 115 *infra*), *v.* mōr); Rickmoor Hay; Splash Bush; Stadham 1707 *GR* 81; Stradleham; the Whell Patch.

III. LONGTREE HUNDRED

Longtree Hundred is in the south of the county on the Wiltshire border west of Crowthorne Hundred. Ashley and Long Newnton were formerly in Wiltshire but were transferred to Gloucestershire in 1930. Rodmarton was in Cirencester Hundred in DB, but the Culkerton part of this parish was in Longtree.

LONGTREE HUNDRED

Langetrev hd', *Langetrewes hd'* 1086 DB, (*hundr' de*) *Langetre* 1169, 1174 P, 1221, 1248 *Ass*, 1263 Misc, 1285 FA *et freq* to 1535 VE, *Langetr'* 1220 Fees, 1221 *Ass et freq* to 1276 RH, *-tree* 1316 FA, 1587 *FF*, *Langtree* c. 1540 *AOMB*, 1559 *FF*, *Longtree* 1577 M. In 1400 the hundred-court was held on Chavenage Down (BG ix, 333), and the place from which the hundred is named is identified with Longtree Barn on Chavenage Down in Avening parish (87 *infra*); this is on the high ground on the road between Avening and Tetbury and centrally placed in the hundred.

Ashley

Ashley was formerly in Wiltshire; the names in this parish are dealt with in W 53, and are summarised here.

ASHLEY (157–9394)

Esselie 1086 DB, *-lega* 1196 Cur, 1198 Abbr, *Asseleye* Hy 3 BM, *Ayssele* 1268 *Ass*, *Assheleye* 1281 ib. 'Ash glade or clearing', *v.* æsc, lēah.

ASHLEY MARSH, cf. *Marsh House* 1830 M.

FIELD-NAMES

The principal forms in (*a*) are 1840 *TA*.

(*a*) Coneygre (*v.* coninger 'warren'); the Headen (*v.* hēafod 'headland'); Holly Bush Tyning (*v.* tȳning 'fence'); the Lains (*v.* leyne); Long Thong; Picked Piece (cf. Picked lease 40 *supra*); Rowdens (*Rowdowns hedge* 1591 W, *v.* rūh, dūn); the Slait (*v.* slæget 'sheep pasture'); Town Leaze (*v.* læs 'pasture').

Avening

AVENING (156–8897) [ˈeivniŋ]

to Æfeningum 896 (1560) BCS 574

Au-, Aveninge, -ynge 1086 DB, 1199, 1241, 1368 FF, 1433 Pat, 1463 Rent, 1587 FF, Auenyge 1327 SR, Avenyngge 1328 Banco

Havelinges 1103–12 France

Au-, Avelinges 12 Tewk 70d, 76, 1154–88, Hy 2, 1170 France, Avelingis 12 (1300) Ch, 12 (1496) Pat, Avelingnes 1246 Ch

Au-, Aveninges 1165–77 France, 1192 P, 1297 Cl, Avenigges 1287 QW, Auenynges 1325 MinAcct

Aveling(e) 1192 France, 1358 Ch

Eueninges 1221 Ass, Eyre

Eueninge 1221 Ass, FF, Deuening 1221 Eyre

Eueringes 1221 Ass

Avening, -yng 1291 Tax, 1305 Pat et passim to 1700 PR 5

Auning 1697 PR 2

In all probability Avening is an OE folk-name in -ingas (dat.plur. -ingum) denoting 'people who dwelt on the R. Avon'; Ekwall (RN 22) suggests that the nameless stream which runs through the village might formerly have been called Avon (OE Afon from Brit *abonā 'river'); it was simply referred to as riuulum 'stream' in 1443 MinAcct. There are three Avons in Gl (cf. R. Avon 2–3 supra) and the nearest of these is the Little Avon which rises in Newington Bagpath 5 miles south-west in another valley. The name Avening could refer to folk who had moved to Avening from one of the known Avons. Old Wennington (La 181), which is not on the R. Wenning (YW vii, 142), offers a parallel to this transferred use of a river-name. There are two other Avenings in Thornbury and Tortworth (iii, 16, 41 infra), both with no early material, but the latter is on the Little Avon R. The spellings with Avel- and Euer- are due to the AN interchange of unstressed -ne-, -le- and -re (cf. IPN 107–8). The last spelling Auning arises from the vocalisation of pre-consonantal -v- (cf. Phonol. § 34 (b), Jordan § 216), but the pronunciation [ˈɔːniŋ] is not now heard.

ASTON FM, Aston 1325, 1453 MinAcct, 1463 Rent, 1492 ib. 'East farmstead', v. ēast, tūn. It lies in a detached part of the parish to the east. Cf. Aston Down (96 infra).

HAZEL WOOD, 1830 M, appears to have been formerly called *Hasalholt* Hy 2 France, *Heselhold* 1329 *MinAcct*, *Hasselleholte* 1411 ib, *Haselholtis* 1443 ib, *-hold* 1449 ib. 'Hazel wood', *v.* hæsel, holt.

LONGTREE BARN, 1777 M, *æt Langa treo* 1052 (late 11th) ASC(D), *Longetr*' 1309 *MinAcct*, *Lang-*, *Longtree* 1379, 1453 ib. 'The tall tree', *v.* lang, trēow; cf. Langtree (D 95). This place gave its name to Longtree Hundred (85 *supra*). It was here that Earl Godwin, who had land in this hundred (DB fol. 164a), and his sons Swein and Harold gathered their armies to fight against King Edward in 1052.

LOWSMOOR FM

> *Louesmere* 1192 P   *Lovvesmere* 1418 *Rent*
> *Lowesmare* 1291 Tax, *-mere* 1309, 1329, 1474 *MinAcct*
> *Lowasmere* 1316 *MinAcct*
> *Lousmere* 1379 *MinAcct*, *Lousemere* 1411, 1453 ib, 1418 *Rent*
> *Losemore* 1542 *LP*, 1638 *FF*, 1779 Rudder

The first el. is uncertain; the spellings *Loues-*, *Lovves-* could represent an OE pers.n. *Lēof* but the persistent early *Lowes-* is unlikely to come from this, as *-w-* (which could also be represented by *-u-*, *-vv-*) seems to be original. We could therefore have OE hlēo (gen.sg. *hlēowes*) 'shelter', and the name would mean 'pool near the shelter', *v.* mere. OE hlōse 'pigsty' which we have in Lowesmoor (Wo 112) is improbable in view of the early *Lowes-* spellings.

PIMBURY PARK, probably named after *Richard Pinbury* 1724 PR 10, p. 17, whose name may be derived from Pinbury Park (73 *supra*). There is, however, some uncertainty about the identification of many spellings with this name or with Pinbury Park; they include *Pendebur* 1291 Tax, 1309 *MinAcct* 856, 17, 1325 ib 15, *Peendebury* 1380 ib, *Puyndebury* 1411 ib, *Pyndeburg* 1418 *Rent* 11, 240, *Pynbury* 1453 *MinAcct* 857, 11, *parco domine Pyndbury* 1483 ib, and seem to belong to the Avening–Minchinhampton area. It may of course be a manorial name derived from that of a family who came from Pinbury Park, but if not, it has a similar origin, 'Penda's fortified place', *v.* burh.

THE TINGLE STONE, 1838 *TA*, *Tangle-stone* 1779 Rudder 244. The name refers to a long barrow with a stone on top (156-882989); the first el. may be connected with ME *tingel* 'a nail' (from the root *teng-*, *ting-* 'fastening') or the e.ModE. vb. *tangle* 'to cover with something that obstructs' (NED s.v.), in either case referring to a stone which obstructs the entrance to the barrow.

BRANDHOUSE FM, 1838 *TA*, 'burnt house', *v.* brende, hūs. BROOK-SIDE HO, cf. *Brook acre* 1838 *TA*. CHURCH FM, *le Churchehouse* 1492 *Rent* 7, 65. COLD HARBOUR BARN, 1838 *TA*, 'cold inn', *v.* cald, here-beorg. COPSE HO, 1830 M. DANE HILL PLANT., 1730 M. FIELD BARN, 1830 M, named from *Avenyngfeld* 1492 *Rent*, *v.* feld. THE FOLLY. FOREST GREEN, 1775 Wills. GILLHAYS BOTTOM, *Gilling Hays* 1830 M, probably named from the family of John *Gills* or William *Gill* (1697, 1750 PR 10, 12, 22), *v.* (ge)hæg. HAMPTON HILL, *Hamptons* 1492 *Rent*, probably a surname from Minchinhampton (95 *infra*). HILL FM & HO, *Hullehous* 1438 *Rent* 11, 241, cf. also *Upehile* 1327 *SR* (p), *Hylemede* 1381 *MinAcct*, *v.* hyll. LINTON BARN, 1830 M, *broad-, long Linton* 1838 *TA*. LONGMAN'S BARN, *Longman* 1838 *TA*. NINE ACRE COVERT, *Nine acres* 1838 *TA*. OLDFIELD WOOD, *Oldefeld* 1379 *MinAcct*, *v.* ald, feld. PARKER'S HILL PLANT., 1838 *TA*, named from the family of Elizabeth *Parker* (1702 PR 10, 13). PICKETPIECE QUARRY, *Picked piece* 1838 *TA*, cf. Picked lease (40 *supra*). POUNDHILL, cf. *Pound piece* 1838 *TA*. RACKLEY BARN, 1830 M, probably named from the family of Elizabeth *Rachley* (1805 PR 10, 37). SANDFORD, 1838 *TA*, *v.* sand, ford. STAR FM, *-house* 1838 *TA*. STEPS LANE, *Steps* 1838 *TA*, *v.* stæpe 'step'. SUMMERWELL FM, 1830 M, *v.* sumor, wella. WARRENTUMP, 1838 *TA*. WASHPOUND. WESTFIELD BARN, *West field* 1838 *TA*. WOODHOUSE BARN, 1830 M.

FIELD-NAMES

The principal forms in (*a*) are 1838 *TA* 12. Spellings dated Hy 2 are France, 1379–1483 *MinAcct*, 1492 *Rent* 7, 65.

(*a*) Ash grove; Barrow tump (ib 1779 Rudder 244, *v.* beorg, dial. *tump*, here a tumulus); Bunting hill; Chavenage Sleight (*v.* Chavenage 91 *infra*, slæget 'sheep-pasture'); Claycomb; Cockshead; Cockpitts; Conegar (*v.* coninger 'warren'); Crow hill; Cuckoo pen (cf. Cuckoo Pen 43 *supra*); Darnott hill; Deer paddock; Enox (*v.* in-hoke); the Gastons (*Garston*' 1379, *v.* gærs-tūn 'pasture'); Green hill; Grove piece (cf. *West Grava* Hy 2, *v.* grāf); Hare brake; Hentall; Hole gores (*v.* gāra); Lagger (dial. *lagger* 'a narrow strip of land', cf. Lagger Hill 28 *supra*); Leys; Little down (*le Doun, Auenyngesdown* 1411, *v.* dūn 'hill'); Little tyning (*v.* tȳning 'fence'); Longsham; Moorlands, Moors (cf. *Ouermor* 1379); Norn (hill); Oat leaze; Ox leaze; Pillsmore (cf. *Pyleswey* 1381, *v.* pīl 'stake', mōr, *Pyleswey* doubtless being a marshland track marked by a stake, cf. Pills Moor 84 *supra*); Pool hay; Ridings (*v.* rydding); Rock hill; Rudgway (*v.* hrycg, weg); Shadwell (*v.* sceadu, wella); Shear hill (probably OE scearu 'share, boundary'); Shreeves acre (probably scīr-(ge)rēfa 'sheriff'); Far & Middle Sleight (*v.* slæget); Stone hill; Sundays hill (cf. Sundayshill iii, 108 *infra*); Tyning (*v.* tȳning 'fence'); Verney hill (*v.* fearnig 'ferny'); Whirl pitts (*v.* hwerfel 'circle'); White wall; Winter field (*Wynterfeld* 1381, *v.* winter, feld); Woodcroft (*Wodecrofte* 1492); Woodlands.

(*b*) *Berymore* 1453; *Bythewal* 1381 ('(land) by the wall'); *Brodemede* 1381; *Chapelhey* 1535 VE; *le Chirch style* 1443, *le Churchestile* 1455; *Doddyngesmede* 1381, *Dodyng-* 1492 (the OE pers.n. *Doding*); *Hardyngesmulle* 1379 (the OE pers.n. or ME surn. *Harding*); *Hatwell* 1381; *Haw-*, *Haukynslond(es)* 1443, 1467 (named from the family of Walter *Hawkyns* 1467 *MinAcct* 857, 25, 1492 *Rent*); *Hoggenhay* 1453 (*v.* hogga, (ge)hæg); *Holemede* 1381; *Husley* 1381 (*v.* hūs, lēah); *Martynesmede* 1379; *Oldelonde* 1492; (*le*) *Ouerley, -leghe* 1463, 1483; *le Quykefrith* 1453 ('wood with a quickset hedge', *v.* cwic, fyrhðe); *Rattingdane* Hy 2 (*v.* denu); *Siredesmulle* 1381 (the OE pers.n. *Sigerēd*); *Strongbowehey* 1379 (named from Will' *Strongbow*, *v.* (ge)hæg); *Upfeld* 1379; *Welleheyes* 1379; *Wynewaresegge* 1379 (the OE pers.n. *Winewaru*, as in *Winwareswik* 842 KCD vi, 227 (So), *v.* ecg).

Cherington

CHERINGTON (156–8998)

Cerintone 1086 DB

Chederintone 1166 RBE i, 293 (p)

Cherinton(a), -yn- 12 (1267) Ch, 13 Oseney, 1283 Cl, 1308 Ipm

Chiri-, Chyriton 1195 P, 1225 Pat, 1248, 1287 *Ass*, 1303 FA, 1305 Pat

Chirin-, Chyrynton, -tun(e) 13 HMC v, 336, 1220 Fees, 1221 *Ass*, 1283 Ipm, 1291 Tax *et freq* to 1455 FF, *Chirentone* 1346 Ipm

Chir-, Chyrington, -yng- 1234 Cl, 1285 FA, 1287 *Ass*, 1313 Pat, Ric 2 *Rent*

Schyrington' 1248 *Ass*, 1285 Abbr (p), *Shirynton* 1318 Ch

Cheryngton, -ing- c. 1300 Godstow, 1432 Pat, 1439 FF *et freq* to 1695 M, (*-als. Cheryton*) 1583 FF, *Cherrington* 1727 PR 4

Chir(e)ton 1305 Ipm, Orig, 1346 FA

Churneton 1360 Ipm, *Chirneton* 1382 ib

Cheri-, Cheryton 1577, 1610, 1646 M

'Village with a church', *v.* cirice, tūn. This type of p.n., Cheriton, Cherrington, of which nearly a dozen examples occur, has been discussed by Ekwall, Studies[1] 33 ff and in Wa 279; they mostly have the ME spellings *Chire-*, *Chiri(n)-*, *Cheri(n)-*, but Wallenberg (K 442) has noted the form *Ciricetune* for Cheriton, which usually has spellings like *Cire-*, *Ceri-*, *Cheri(n)-* and the like, and some similar confirmatory evidence is given for the name Cherrington (Wa 279). Ekwall (*op. cit.* 37) also provides evidence for the development of OE *cirice* to *chiri-* in other p.ns. where the *-c-* has been assimilated by the initial consonant of the following element and for the development of medial unstressed *-i-* to *-in-*, as in such names as Torrington (D 123) which must go back to OE *Toric-tūn* 'farm on the Torridge' or Cannington (So) from OE *Cantuc-tūn*. The single spelling *Chederintone*, if it is correctly identified with Cherington, might, however, point to the first el. being a reduced form of OE *cēodor* 'bag' or the like (used in a topographical sense as in Cheddar So); it would describe the deep valley at Cherrington; *v.* ing[4], tūn. But the name is of such a well-evidenced pattern that the first interpretation is the more likely. The first el. may be repeated in the f.n. *Chernbury* (*infra*).

WESTRIP FM, *Westrop*, *-opp(e)* 13 HMC v, 336, 1272, 1556, 1603 *FF*, *Westroope* c. 1300 Godstow (p), *Westrippe* 1500–15 ECP, *Westrip* 1777 M. 'West farmstead', *v.* west, þrop and cf. Westrip (ii, 178 *infra*). This place must be so named from its position in the west of Cherington parish.

FIELD BARN, named from *Est-*, *Westfeld* c. 1230 Hale, *Chirrington feildes* Jas 1 TRMB 157, *East*, *West Field* 1733 *EnclA*, *v.* feld. GROVE FM, *the Grove* 1733 *EnclA*. HAILSTONE BARN, 1830 M, *Halston* Jas 1 *TRMB*. LOCKSTONE BARN. MONTPELIER, 1830 M. POSTLET. TROUBLEHOUSE INN, 1777 M. TRULL HO, *Trill Fm.* 1777 M, cf. Trullwell (98 *infra*). WICKFIELD HO, *past' voc' Wikes* 1575 *TRMB*, *the Wickfield* 1733 *EnclA*, probably the surname *Wick*.

FIELD-NAMES

The principal forms in (*a*) are 1733 *EnclA*, and in (*b*) Jas 1 *TRMB* 157. Spellings dated c. 1230 are Hale, 1538, 1575 *TRMB*, c. 1580 *LRMB* 191, 1627 Inq.

(*a*) Avening Field (*-Feild* 1654 *Asht* 5, *v.* Avening 86 *supra*, feld); the Breach (*v.* brēc); Comb close (*Combe-* 1627, *v.* cumb); the Droveway; the Down (*Northdune* c. 1230, *Cherington downe* 1594 SurvTet, *the Downes* Jas 1, *v.* dūn); Gostin (possibly the same as *Garstun infra*); Meerway ('boundary road', *v.* (ge)mǣre); the Mill Dam & Hill; the Norm; Oxleaze (ib 1627, *v.* oxa, lǣs); the Park Wall; Passwell.

(b) *Appeshey* c. 1580; *Blakin grove* 1575; *Broke yate* 1575 (*v.* brōc, geat); *Canditch peece*; *Chernbury* c. 1230 (perhaps connected with Cherington); *Chirrington Barrowe* (*v.* beorg); *Churchheye* c. 1580; *the Clayfeilde* c. 1580; (*le*) *Conygar* 1536 Monast, 1538 (*v.* coninger 'warren'); *Copper Thornes Waye* (probably 'lopped thorn-tree', *v.* copped, þorn); *Cowne heyes* 1575 (*v.* cū, gen.plur. *cūna*, (ge)hæg); *Deys house*, 1575; *Dunneshinhoch* c. 1230 (the ME pers.n. *Dunn*, inhōke); *Garstun* c. 1230 (cf. Gostin *supra*, *v.* gærstūn); *Godineshull* c. 1230 (the ME, OFr pers.n. *Godin*, hyll); *Goldsmithes lane* 1575; *Grenehilles* c. 1580; *Grindudge peece*; *Hardnell* 1575; *le Hewersdone* 1575; *Hide meade* 1575; *the hill* c. 1580; *Holymore* c. 1580; *Homescrundle* c. 1230 (*v.* crundel); 'barne called *Kinges*' c. 1580; *Merchionis horne* 1575 (*v.* horn); *the Milking pathe*; *le North fild* 1575; *Pyttmede* c. 1580; *Portslade* c. 1230 (*v.* port[2] 'town', slæd); *the Sandfeilde* c. 1580; *Smalecumbe* 13 HMC v, 336 (*v.* smæl, cumb); *le Streat heyes* 1575 (*v.* strǣt, the O.S. marks a Roman road in the parish); *Sudeheye* 1575; *Thickinge groue*; *the Water peece*; *Well pool* 1575.

Horsley

Horsley (156–8497)

Horselei(a) 1086 DB, 1103–12 France, *-lega* 1176 P, *-ley* 1261 Ch, 1316 FA *et passim* to 1614 Rec, *-legh* 1327 Madox, 1335 Misc
Horsle 1221, 1248 Ass, *-leg'* 1221 ib, 1271 Episc, *-legh* 1221 Ass, 1293 MinAcct, 1327 SR, *-ley(a)* 1274 Episc *et freq* to 1644 PR 2

'Horse clearing', *v.* hors, lēah, cf. the f.n. Horsecroft (*infra*).

Bagley (lost), *Baggeley, -legh'* 1448, 1473 MinAcct, *Bagley* 1448 ib, a further example of this fairly common p.n. *v.* bagga (some kind of animal), lēah 'clearing' and cf. Bagpath (ii, 239 *infra*).

Barton End, *atte Bertonende* 1327 SR (p), *Bartonend* 1612 Asht 5, 1642 Misc, 1764 Kingsct 9, *Bartning* 1777 M. *v.* bere-tūn 'outlying grange, demesne farm', ende 'end of the village'. The *barton* is perhaps that referred to in *le Cowrte Berton* 1511 MinAcct. On the form with *-ing* cf. Downington (41 *supra*), Phonol. § 14.

Chavenage Ho

Chauenedisshe 1327 SR (p), *-edich'* 1332 MinAcct
Shauenedisshdoun 1369 MinAcct, *Chauenasshdown* 1370 ib, *Chaueneggedoune* 1371 ib, *-heggesdoune* 1411 ib, *-ayschdone* 1477 ib
Cheueneg(ge) 1371 MinAcct, 1385 Ass, *Cheuenassh* 1411 MinAcct, *Cheuenynche* 1459 ib

Chauenhegge 1477 *MinAcct*, *Chaveneage* 1638 Inq, *-edge* 1642 InqM

Probably 'Ceafa's enclosure', *v.* edisc. The first el. is not certain. An OE pers.n. *Ceafa* is not on record unless *Ciaba* (Redin 88) is a variant of it; it would be connected etymologically with OE *ceaf* 'chaff'. Dr Feilitzen regards *Ciaba* as a Kentish spelling of *Ceoba*, and not connected with *ceaf*. It is possible that Cheveridge (Wo 51) contains the same pers.n. The second el. has clearly been influenced by OE ecg 'edge, escarpment'. In some forms we have OE dūn 'down' added.

CRANMORE FM, *Cronmeresmed* 1369 *MinAcct*, *Cranemere(sfeld)* 1370 ib, *Cranmer(e)feld(e)*, *-mede* 1435, 1473, 1511 ib, *Cranmer* 1638 Inq. 'Pool haunted by herons', *v.* cran, mere, feld, mǣd 'meadow'.

HAY LANE, *Haydowne* 1435 *MinAcct*, *le Haye* 1458 ib, *laʒ Hay* 1511 ib, *High Lane* 1777 M. *v.* (ge)hæg 'fenced-in piece of ground, hunting enclosure', cf. also le, dūn.

LEDGEMORE BOTTOM & POND

Loddesmore 1327 Madox, 1327 *SR*
Luddesmore 1411 *MinAcct*, 1498 AD ii, *Ludsmore* 1617 *GR* 547a
Ledgemoore 1715 *GR* 547a

'Lud's marshland', *v.* mōr. The first el. is the OE pers.n. *Lud(d)*, a strong form of the OE *Luda* proposed for Ludworth (Db 143); a pers.n. of similar form may occur in *ludescumbe* 955–9 BCS 936 (in Olveston iii, 123 *infra*). On the assimilation to *Ledge-* cf. Phonol. § 44 (*b*).

NUPEND, 1723 *Kingsct* 6, *Upende* 1639 Inq, occurs several times in Gl (ii, 194, iii, 154, 193, 250 *infra*) and is clearly a shortened form of a ME *atten upp-ende* 'at the upper end (of the village, etc.)' in contrast to Downend (*infra*); *v.* atten, upp, end. Initial *n-* comes from a wrong analysis of the name as *atte nupp-end* (cf. Phonol. § 45).

BEDLAM, 1830 M, named from the famous *Bedlam* or *Bethlehem* Hospital in London.   BOSCOMBE HO, *Boxcombesmede* 1370 *MinAcct*, *Boscombe Hill* 1699 *Kingsct* 3, *v.* box 'box-tree', cumb.   CHAMBERS GROVE, *-Tyning* 1840 *TA*, *v.* tȳning 'fence'.   DOWNEND, *Downing* 1777 M, 'lower end', *v.* dūne, ende, cf. Nupend (*supra*).   ENOCH'S BARN, *Innocke* 1595 *Asht* 5, *Innox* 1639 Inq, *Innocks* 1840 *TA*, *v.*

in-hoke. Fooks. Hartley's Bridge, cf. *Harleyfield* 1676 *Asht* 5,
-head 1840 *TA*. Harvey's Grave, 1840 *TA*. Hazlecote Lane,
1840 *TA*, a lane leading to Hazlecote (ii, 238 *infra*). Hollingham,
Hellingham 1639 Inq, *Ollingham* 1830 M. Horsleyfield (*Horsleys-
felde* 1385 *Ass*) & Wood (1830 M), *v.* feld, wudu. Kilcombe, 1840
TA. Laggers Covert, *the Laggers* 1840 *TA*, dial. *lagger* 'narrow
strip', cf. Lagger Hill (28 *supra*). Lophorn, 1830 M. Luthe-
ridge Fm, 1840 *TA*, *Letheridge* 1777 M. Lutsome Cottage, *-field*
1840 *TA*, *Lutsom* 1830 M. Miry Brook, 1830 M. The Nelms.
Newnham, 1830 M. Park Wood, 1840 *TA*, cf. *Parkemede* 1411
MinAcct, *Litelparke* 1435 ib, *the Parke* 1639 Inq. The Peaked
Stone, 1830 M, *Picked stone field* 1840 *TA*, cf. Picked lease (40
supra). The Priory, cf. *Priorifeild* 1654 *Asht* 5, on Horsley Priory,
a cell of Trouarn and then of Bruton, cf. VCH ii, 91. Ragged Barn,
Ragged Smock 1777 M. Rockness Fm, *-Hill* 1830 *TA*, *Rocesnest*
1248 *Ass* (p), 'the rook's nest', *v.* hrōc, nest. Sandgrove, 1840 *TA*.
Sealey Wood, 1840 *TA*, *Sellywood* 1723 *Kingsct* 6, *Sally woods* 1788
ib 5, the surname *Sealey*, *Selley*. Short Wood, 1788 *Kingsct* 5.
Sleight Wood, *Sleight* 1840 *TA*, *v.* slæget 'sheep-pasture'.
Sugley Fm, 1830 M. Tickmorend, 1830 M, *Tich-* 1779 Rudder.
Tiltups End, 1830 M, cf. Tiltup (46 *supra*). The Tump, 1830 M,
dial. *tump* 'hill-top, barrow'. Twatley, 1830 M. Wallow
Green. Washpool, *-pond* 1777 M. Wood Leaze, 1840 *TA*.
Wormwood Hill.

FIELD-NAMES

The principal forms in (a) are 1840 *TA* 110. Spellings dated 1292–1515 are
MinAcct, 1595–1676 *Asht* 5, 1638, 1639 Inq, 1642 InqM, 1682–1764
Kingsct 2–9.

(a) Ashley Road (*Ashley* 1712, *v.* æsc, lēah); Axpills; Balls Tyning (the
surname *Ball*, *v.* tȳning 'fence'); Bannett-, Barnett Tree ground (e.ModE
bannenote-tre 'filbert', dial. *bannut-*, *barnut-tree* 'walnut-tree', occurring esp.
in WMidl from Ch to So); Barley Hill (ib 1595); Bennetts mead (cf. *Ben-
nettes grove* 1654, the surname *Bennett*); Bithern wood (*Bittorne* 1654);
Bittums (*v.* bytme 'bottom'); Brinkley; Church mead; Clarkes leaze (cf.
Clark(e)s meade 1639, *-Coombes* 1654, named from the family of William
Clarke, tenant (1654 *Asht* D. 5, 19), *v.* lǣs 'pasture', cumb); Clay leaze;
Coles Tyning; Combses (*Lokiers combeses* 1654); Coombes (*the Combs* 1723,
v. cumb); Coney ground (cf. *Conyngfeld* 1466, *v.* coning 'rabbit'); Conigre
(*the Cunyngerfield* 1595, *Conygree feild* 1638, (*the*) *Conigree* 1676, 1764, *v.*
coninger 'warren', cf. prec.); Copped Ash (*v.* copped, æsc); Cox's Tyning;
Fire Shovel (doubtless so called from its shape); Fishers (cf. *le Fysshweresplot*

1411, *Fishersleaze, -meade* 1639, 'plot near the fish weir', *v.* fisc, wer, splott); Folly; Frogmore (ib 1654 *Froggemore* 1370, *v.* frogga, mōr); Green Tyning (*v.* tȳning); Grove (*Westgrof* 1369, *le Westgrove* (1370); Grumbles Ash (a transferred name from Grumbald's Ash Hundred iii, 22 *infra*, cf. foll.); Hagg mead (*Eggemede* 1411, 1473, *Eggmeades* 1651, from the OE pers.n. *Ecga* as in Acton (ii, 228 *infra*), *v.* mǣd; the modern form of the name has been influenced by *Hagmead* Hundred iii, 23 *infra*); Hanging Hill (*v.* hangende 'steep'); Hanover; Harmers (*Horemeresfurlong* 1370, *Hormer* 1411, 'close called *Harmers*' 1595, *Harmers lane, -poole* 1654, 'filth pool', *v.* horu, mere); Hill paddock (cf. *la Hulle* 1293, *Hyllemede* 1435); Hilliers Hatherlings (*Haythlyng* 1411, *Hatherlin(ge)* 1638, 1642, *Hillers Hatherlins* 1654, the main theme is possibly a compound of hagu-þorn 'hawthorn' (often reduced to *Hather-*) and hlinc 'slope', and for *Hilliers* cf. also *Hillers grove* 1654, from the family name of Christopher *Hyller* to whom land was assigned here in 1629 *Asht* D. 5, 10); Horsecroft 1712 ((*leʒ*) *Horscroft(e)* 1417, 1639); Hove Pond; Kinney Hill; Long Mead (*Longemeade* 1369); Longridge Wood 1712; Maiden Hill; Markham (*Marecumbe* 1371, *Markham* 1654, 'mare valley', *v.* mere², cumb); Mill Ridings (*Millrideing* 1677 *GR* 185, *v.* myln, rydding 'clearing'); Necklace; Owls grove; Ox leaze; Penley; Pike (*v.* pīc 'hill-top'); Riddings (*Rydings* 1639, *v.* rydding); Ringley Grove; Roseley; Ruckley green; Rushmore (*Russhemore* 1458, *v.* risc, mōr); Sedgemore mead (*v.* secg, mōr); Shamble leaze; Sheppey Hays (*Schephay* 1369, *Shepheye* 1370, 'sheep enclosure', *v.* scēap, (ge)hæg); Shewbridge; Stanborough hill (*Stanburrow-(hill)* 1654, *v.* stān, burh); Standley grove (*Stoneleygrove* 1417, *v.* stān, lēah); Testament ground (doubtless from the rent being for the provision of testaments); Toothill (*v.* tōt-hyll 'look-out hill'); Tyning (*the New Tyning* 1675, *v.* tȳning); Waghill house; Wain croft; Webbs down & leaze; Weldon hay; Wickley wood (*Wykeley, -legh* 1448, 1472, 1511, *Wickley* 1639, *v.* wīc 'dairy-farm', lēah); Will mead (*-meade* 1595); Wimblebarrow (*-barowefeild* 1639, possibly OE *Winebald*, *v.* beorg); Woodmans hay.

(b) *Arkeley Bridge* 1639; *Barnes Hayes* 1654; *Beornbury* 1370, *Banbury* (*fielde*) 1595, *Byn-, Bynbury feild* 1629, 1654, *Ben-*, 1638, 1642 (*v.* burh); *le Bernhay* 1458 (*v.* bere-ærn 'barn', (ge)hæg); *le Brom* 1385 *Ass* (*v.* brōm 'broom'); *Bud-, Bydellesmed(e)* 1411, *Bedellesmede* 1417, *Biddlesmeade* 1639 (the ME occupational name *Bedel, Budel* 'beadle' (Reaney 26), *v.* mǣd); *Calcot* 1473 (probably the common p.n. 'cold cottage', *v.* cald, cot); *Caperonesclos* 1370 (the ME surname *Caperun*, Reaney 60); *Cockshoot piece* 1682 (*v.* cocc-scīete 'cock-shoot, glade where woodcock were netted'); *Cholenyngfeld* 1473; *Crayleygh* 1417; *la Hale* 1293 (*v.* halh 'nook'); *Hol(e)-croft(e)* 1369, 1370, *Hollow-* 1654 (*v.* hol¹, croft); *Horndmede* 1411; *Hudgemore* 1654; *Lepeghete* 1332 (*v.* hlīep-geat, cf. Lypiatt 119 *infra*); *Netherlegh*' 1371; *the Orcharde* 1595; *Pigeon house close* 1676 (so named from 'a dove-house standing thereon', *Asht* 5); *le Splot* 1417 (*v.* splott 'plot of land'); *Steuenes-croys* 1370 ('Stephen's cross', *v.* crois); *la Vorthey* 1370 (*v.* forð, ēg, cf. *Fortheye* 36 *supra*); *Whitelegh* 1411 (*v.* hwīt, lēah); *Wyt(e)hurst* 1292; *Withybare* 1435 ('willow grove', *v.* wīðig, bearu); *Wodemede* 1370.

Minchinhampton

MINCHINHAMPTON (156–8500)

Hantonia, -tone 1082, Hy 2, 1180–7, 1304 France, 1086 DB,
1358 Ch
Hamton(i)a 1154–89 Berk, 1246 Ch
Hampton(e) 1215 AD iii, 1220 Fees, 1221, 1248 *Ass*, 1276 RH
et passim to 1631 InqM
The affix takes the following forms:
-Monialium 1220–30 Berk, 1269 Ch, Episc *et freq* to 1553 *FF*
-Abbatisse 1221 *Ass*
Mun(e)chen(e)- 1221 *Ass*, 1215 AD iii, 1287 *FF*, 1291 Tax, 1294 Cl
et freq to 1416 Pat, *Mun(ne)chenne-* 1305, 1308 Ipm, *Munechyn-*
1371 ib, *Munchyn-, -chin-* 1411 Pat, 1609 *FF*
Min(e)chen-, Mynchen-, -in-, -yn- 1221 *Ass*, 1316 FA, 1320 Pat,
1368 Works, 1409 Pat *et passim* to 1756 PR 2, *Mynchon-* 1347
Rent, Mynchun- 1400 ib, 1405, 1417 Pat
Men(e)chene- 1282 Episc, 1287 *Ass*, *Moenchen-* 1313 Fine
Monechene 1308 Ipm, *Monchyn-* 1379 *MinAcct*
Michel-, Mychel- 1403, 1461 Pat, 1583 *FF*, *Muchel-* 1474 Pat,
Mitchell- 1598 *Comm*
Myncher- 1549 Pat
Minsing- 1672 PR 2, *Mincing-* 1675 Ogilby, *Mincen-* 1684 PR 2

'The high farmstead or village', *v.* hēah (weak obl. *hēan*), tūn,
so called from its high situation. The affixes are from Lat *monialis*
'nun', *abbatissa* 'abbess' and OE myncen (gen.pl. *myncena*) and refer
to the nuns of the Trinity at Caen in Normandy, to whom the manor
was granted c. 1080.

AMBERLEY

Unberleia 1166 RBE   *Omberleia* c. 1240 Berk
Ambresleg' 1248 *Ass* (p), *-ley* 1461 *MinAcct*
Amberley, -leie 1240–50 Spillm, 1307 MchCust, Ric 2 *Rent*, 1449,
1454 *MinAcct, -lea* 1659 GR 25
Aumberley 1411 *MinAcct*

The first el., as in Amberden (Ess), is probably OE amore, the
name of a bird (perhaps the bunting), but the two spellings with the
gen.sg. *-es* as well as the persistent *-b-* might link it with Ombersley
(Wo 268, *Ambreslege* 706 BCS 116), Amesbury (W 358, *Ambresbyrig*

c. 880 BCS 553), Ambrosden (O 161), and Amberley (He 5), which are from an OE pers.n. *Amber*, cognate with OG *Ambri* (*v*. Wo 268). 'Amber's clearing', *v*. lēah.

ASTON DOWN, 1777 M, *Astonesdoune* 1379 *MinAcct*, *le Doun* 1453 ib. Named from Aston (86 *supra*), which it adjoins. *v*. dūn 'a stretch of open hill-country'.

BESBURY FM, *Bessebour'*, *Besseburylond* Ric 2 *Rent*, *Bestberry* 1830 M. The first el. is possibly a pers.n. OE *B(e)assa* or *Be(o)ssa*. No such name is known but it could be a hypocoristic form of some OE dithematic name such as *Beadusige*, **Bēdsige*, etc. or indeed a mutated variant of the recorded *Bass(a)* (Redin 26, 84). Such a pers.n. is thought to occur in Besley (D 535) and possibly in *Besley* (Db 73), though the latter may contain ON *Bessi*. But it is also possible that the p.n. is from an OE *be ēastan byrig* '(land) to the east of the fortification' (*v*. be, ēastan, burh); Besbury Fm lies half a mile east of Burleigh and The Bulwarks (*infra*), which would be the *burh* referred to. Cf. Beastbrook (46 *supra*).

BOX, *Boʒ* 1234 Cl, *la Boxe* 1260 Ipm, 1307 MchCust, Ric 2 *Rent*, *ate Boxe* 1329 *MinAcct*, *Box* 1374 Ipm, *the Box* 1737 *GR* 25, 6; cf. also the local f.ns. *Boxaker*, *-hanger*, etc. (*infra*). *v*. box 'a box-tree', which occurs several times in Gl (cf. Box iii, 251, Boxbush iii, 193, Boxwell iii, 25 *infra*).

BURLEIGH, *Burley(e)* 1248 *Ass*, Ric 2 *Rent*, 1542 LP, *-lee* Ric 2 *Rent*, *Bourlee* 1307 MchCust, *Longford's Burley* 1779 Rudder 469. 'Clearing near the fortification', *v*. burh, lēah. Burleigh is just below the embanked earthworks on Minchinhampton Common called The Bulwarks (156–8601), which are also referred to in the names of Besbury (*supra*) and Bury Moor (foll.). For *Longfords* cf. Longfords Ho (*infra*).

BURY MOOR (lost), *la Burimor* 1306 *MinAcct*, *Burmor* 1309 ib, *Buri-*, *Burymor(e)* 1307 MchCust, 1379, 1400 ib, 1438 *Rent*, *-mores* 1438 ib, *Berymore* 1449 *MinAcct*, *Burymere* 1542 LP. *v*. burh, mōr. The *burh* or fortification is that referred to in Burleigh (prec.); cf. Burleigh Court (*infra*).

COWCOMBE HILL & WOOD

> *Colecumb(e)* 1221, 1248 *Ass*, 1307 MchCust, 1309 *MinAcct*, 1327 *SR* (p) *et freq* to 1411 *MinAcct*

Colcombe, -cumbe 1268 Episc, 1403 BG li, 1438 *Rent*, 1454 *MinAcct*,
  1465 Pat *et freq* to 1533 *FF*
Collcombeslone 1379 *MinAcct*
Cokcombe 1449 *MinAcct, Cocomb* 1777 M
Cowkeham 1594 *FF, Cowcombe* 1779 Rudder

Probably 'valley where charcoal was burnt', *v.* col, cumb. For
Cow- cf. Phonol. § 27. The little valley and hill-side are still well-
wooded. The word *cumb* is often used in the p.ns. of Stroud valley
to describe such side-valleys, as in Gatcombe (*infra*), Brimscombe
(141 *infra*), etc.

FORWOOD, *Forewud* 1241 *FF, -wode* 1270 Spillm, Ric 2, 1438 *Rent,
Fordwode* 1247–60 Spillm, *Forwode* 1287 *Ass* (p), 1327 *SR* (p), 1463
Rent, 1542 LP. 'The wood in front of the village' (*v.* fore, wudu);
the wood, long cleared, was below Minchinhampton on the south
side.

GATCOMBE

Catecumba l. 12 Berk (p), *-cumbe* 1309 *MinAcct*
Gatecumbe 1306, 1309 *MinAcct, -combe* Ric 2 *Rent,* 1411 *MinAcct
  et freq* to 1489 Pat
Gattecombeshed(e) 1347, 1438 *Rent,* 1456 *MinAcct*
Gatcombe 1441 *GR* 849, 1453 *MinAcct,* 1487 Pat, (*-combeshede*)
  1454 *MinAcct*
Yatcombe 1454 *MinAcct*

The name describes the deep valley running north from Gatcombe
Water to The Long Stone (156–8899), which makes a clear gap in
the hill-side between the wooded slopes, *v.* geat 'gap in the hills'
(as the last spelling *Yat-* indicates), cumb. Gatcombe (iii, 252 *infra*)
is probably of similar origin.

HYDE, *Hida* 1234 Cl, *la, le Hide, Hyde* 1248 *Ass,* 1287 *FF,* 1379
MinAcct et freq to 1438 *Rent, atte Hyde* 1327 *SR* (p), *Hyde* 1400
Rent, 1542 LP, 1699 Will. *v.* hīd 'a hide, an estate of one hide
extent'; the hide varied in size but was approximately 120 acres,
cf. Hyde (ii, 20, 110, iii, 198 *infra*) and other examples in Gl.

LONGFORDS HO, *Longeford* 1301 Ipm, Ric 2 *Rent, Langeford* (p) 1327
SR (p), *Langford place* 1463 *Rent.* The house is near Gatcombe
Water and doubtless by a river-crossing at 'the long ford' (*v.* lang,
ford). There was a family of *Langford* in the parish named from this
ford (cf. also Burleigh *supra*).

St Chloe ['siŋkli]

Sentodleag 716–43 (11th) BCS 164 (v.l. *Sengedleag*)
Sengetlege 896 (1560) BCS 574
Sanctleha 1220 Spillm, *Senctleie* 1230–50 ib
Seyntele(e) 1248 *Ass*, 1291 *Tetb* (p), 1295 *FF* (p), *Seyntle(y)* 1320
  Ass, 1322 *MinAcct*, 1438 *Rent*
Sentle(ye) c. 1250 Berk (p), Ric 2 *Rent*, (*Dure-*) Ric 2 ib
Seyncle(ie) 1322 *MinAcct*, Misc
Sencle 1322 Fine, Orig, Pat, 1417 IpmR
Seyn-, *Seincler(e)* 1322 Misc, 1368 Ipm, *Seytclere* (sic) 1476 *FF*,
  Senclerdesende 1411, 1474 *MinAcct*
Sa-, *Seintcleye* 1368 Cl, 1439 IpmR, *Seyncleye* 1389 Ipm
Sen(c)kley(e) 1400 *Rent*, 1688 GR 25, *Sainckley* als. *Seinckloe*
  1625 *FF*
Seynctley 1570 *FF*   *Silkeley* 1611 *FF*
Synckley als. *Seyntley* 1573 *FF*   *Seintkley* als. *Seyntloe*
  1612 FF
Sayntloe 1609 *FF*, *Santlo* 2777 M, *St Chloe* 1830 M

'Clearing made by burning', *v.* senget (or OE *senged* 'singed, burnt', pa.pt. of *sengan*), lēah; cf. Saintlow (iii, 219 *infra*), Syntley (Wo 36). The adaptations to the name of a St Chloe and that of St Clair is paralleled by St Clair's Barn (Wo 36).

Trullwell, *Trolwell(e)* 1240–50, 1270 Spillm, 1307 MchCust, *Trollewell(e)* 1400 *Rent*, 1411 *MinAcct*, *Trewell* (sic), *Trolwell* Ric 2 *Rent*. The first el. is ambiguous, but could be an early example of e.ModE *trolle*, *trulle*, a variant of ME *trowelle* 'trowel' in the sense of Lat *trulla* 'scoop' (used with OE **wella** 'well' in much the same way as was OE **byden** 'vessel' or **canne** 'can, cup') or preferably e.ModE *trowle*, *trulle* 'a trollop, a strumpet' (NED s.v. *trull*) used with *wella* to denote a well where such women were ducked; the latter seems more likely.

Ball's Green, 1839 *TA*, cf. *Ballesmede* 1438 *Rent* 11, 241, from the surname *Ball*.   Beechknapp, -*nap* 1784 Will, *v.* bēce[2], cnæpp 'hillock'.   Black Ditch.   Bubblewell, 1839 *TA*, 'bubbling spring'.   The Bulwarks, old earthworks, cf. Burleigh (*supra*). Burleigh Court, *Burycourt* 1438 *Rent*, cf. Burleigh, *Bury Moor* (*supra*), *v.* court.   Burnt Ash, 1830 M.   Camp Field.   Christow. Claycombe, 1839 *TA*, *v.* clæg, cumb.   The Close, 1839 *TA*.

CRACKSTONE, -*ston* 1830 M. CULVER HO, 1839 *TA*, *v.* culfre 'dove', hūs. DEANLEY, 1830 M, named from *le dene* Ric 2 *Rent* 11, 238, *v.* denu 'valley', lēah. THE DEVIL'S CHURCHYARD & ELBOW, cf. The Devil's Chapel (iii, 258 *infra*) and for folklore connected with it cf. BG liii, 259. DUNKERSPOOL, 1830 M, *Dunkirk house & mill* 1839 *TA*, named after the Siege of Dunkirk (1793). FIELD HO. THE FOLLY, 1777 M, *v.* folie. FROGMARSH, *Froggemore* 1381 *MinAcct*, *Frogmore Shard* 1777 M, *v.* frogga, mōr 'marshy moor', sceard 'gap'. GATCOMBE PARK (1779 Rudder 244) & WOOD (1839 *TA*). GILLHAYS COPSE, cf. Gillhays (88 *supra*). GOLDEN VALLEY, 1779 Rudder, *Golding* 1777 M, doubtless so called from the wealth that came from its industries. GYDYNAP LANE, *Giddy Knap* 1777 M, probably the surname *Giddy* (Reaney 134), *v.* cnæpp 'hillock'. HAMPTON FIELDS, *Hamptons feilde* 1569 *Comm*, *v.* feld. HEATH HO. HIGHCROFT. HOLLYBUSH FM. JACOB'S KNOWLE. THE KNAP, 1779 Rudder, *v.* cnæpp 'hillock'. KNAVE-IN-HOLE, *Knave-in-all* 1830 M, probably cnafa 'youth', halh. THE KNOLL, *Knowl* 1830 M, *v.* cnoll 'hill'. THE LAMMAS, *Lammas orchard* 1839 *TA*, cf. Lamas mead (77 *supra*), but the name may be an adaptation of *Delamers maner als. Lambards* 1475 Ipm, 'the manor of *Dalamere als. Lambertis*' 1485 Pat, from the ME surname *Lambert*. LITTLEWORTH, 1830 M, *v.* lȳtel, worð, a late name which occurs several times in Gl, probably in some cases meaning 'field of little value'. THE LONG STONE, 1779 Rudder, 244, described as a tumulus with a stone on top; for its folk-lore associations cf. BG liii, 257. MARLEY LANE. NEW BARN, 1830 M. PEACHES FM, *The Peaches* 1830 M, *Peaches farmhouse* 1839 *TA*, possibly identical with *Peckes* 1492 *Rent* 7, 65, from the ME surname *Peche*. PENNYHILL WOOD, 1830 M. QUARRY HILL, 1839 *TA*, *atte Quarren* 1400 *Rent*, *Quarrers, Rede-, Rodequarrey* 1474, 1480 *MinAcct*, *v.* quarriere 'quarry'. RAGGED COT. SCARHILL LANE, *Scar hill* 1839 *TA*. SPRIGGS WELL, 1830 M. THEESCOMBE, 1777 M, *Thieves Coomb* 1830 M, 'valley haunted by thieves', *v.* þēof, cumb. WALL'S QUARRY, -*Quarr* 1773 Will. WELL HILL GROVE, 1830 M, cf. *atte Well*' 1438 *Rent* (p), *v.* wella. WIMBERLEY MILL, 1839 *TA*, *Wyn-, Wymberle(y)* 1307 MchCust, Ric 2 *Rent*, *Wymburlegh*' 1400 ib, possibly the OE fem. pers.n. *Wynburh*, *v.* lēah. WHITFIELD'S TUMP, a long barrow. WOEFULDANE BOTTOM & FM, *Wulfham Dene* 14 BG liv, 311, *Dane Bottom* 1830 M; Rudder 468 has an unsubstantiated tale of the place being the site of 'a great battle between Wolphgang the Saxon and Uffa the Dane' but *Dane*

Bottom simply means 'valley bottom', *v.* denu, cf. Phonol. § 13; the first el. is 'wolf meadow', *v.* wulf, hamm; Woeful Lake (204 *infra*) is also an adaptation of an older p.n. WOOD HO, 1830 M.

FIELD-NAMES

The principal forms in (*a*) are 1839 *TA* 131, and in (*b*) Ric 2 *Rent* 11, 238. Spellings dated 1220–30 are Berk, 1235–45, 1270, 1291 Spillm, 1307 MchCust, 1347, 1400, 1438, 1463, 1492 *Rent* 11, 237–43, 1628 InqM, 1633–1766 *GR* (D. 25, 892), 1779 Rudder, and others dated without source are *MinAcct.* Some Nailsworth f.ns. are probably included.

(*a*) Abbey Close & Way 1737 (*Abbeys house* 1688); Alders tyning (*v.* tȳning 'fence'); Barcelona; Barley hill; Barn close (cf *Bernaker* 1235–45, *Bernehey* 1411, *v* bere-ærn, (ge)hæg); Bidneys 1777 M; Blackwells tyning (*Blakewell* Ric 2, *Blackwell* 1777 M, *v.* blæc, wella, tȳning); Brake (*v.* bræc[1] 'thicket'); Church hill (cf. *Chirchestyle* 1438, *Churchehous* 1474); Cocks leaze (*v.* læs); Coneygre (*v.* coninger 'warren'); Ditch yate (*v.* dīc, geat); Dryleaze 1760; Foxhill; Garston (*Gerston* 1235–40, *Garston*(*a*) Ric 2, 1400, 1438, *v.* gærs-tūn 'pasture'); Hagerly; Hampton down (*Dunā* 1311, *Hampton*(*e*)*s-doun*(*e*) 1379, 1467, *v.* dūn 'hill'); Heridens; Hilbore's-mead 1779; Horse hill; the Irons-mills 1779; the Lagger (ib 1628, dial. *lagger* 'narrow strip', *v.* Lagger Hill 28 *supra*); the Lots (*v.* hlot); Maddock land (*Matto*(*c*)*klond*(*e*), 1400, 1438, *Mattokes-* 1448, the Welsh pers.n. *Madog*, OWelsh *Matōc*); Mills mead (*ten' voc' Myles* 1400); Nailsworth (*Nail'* 1311, *Naylesworthes-mede* 1411, *crofte voc' Burynaylesworth'* 1438, named from the neighbouring Nailsworth (102 *infra*), for *Bury-* cf. *Bury Moor* (*supra*), Berry Wormington (ii, 23 *infra*), *v.* mæd); Pease leaze; Rack hill (cf. Rack hill 116 *infra*); Rattles; St Mary's-Mill 1779; Shailes (*terra Schail* 1316, Ric 2); Shoulder of Mutton (so called from its shape); Sideland; Slovens acre (ib 1779); Wakin hill; Well leaze 1760; Westend street 1766 (*Westende* 1235–45); Westfield (ib 1779); Withy bed.

(*b*) *Arneborghescroft* 1379 (the ME, OG pers.n. *Erneburg*); *Balderey* 1400 (the OE pers.n. *Baldhere*, ēg 'island'); *la Balenhall* 1307; *Bisshopestharwill* 1347, *Bysshopesacr'* 1411 (named from the family of Isabel *Bysshop* 1414 *MinAcct* 857, 2); *Boxaker, -hangere* 1241 FF (-*hunngre* 1307), -*el, -well* Ric 2, -*leaze* 1691 (*v.* Box *supra*, æcer, hangra 'wooded slope', hyll, wella); *Brechcumbe* 1307, *Brechage* (*v.* brēc, cumb, haga); *Brydlee* Ric 2, -*leys* 1438, *Burdeley* 1400 ('bird clearing', *v.* bridd, lēah); *Bussecumbe* (ib 1307, possibly the OE pers.n. *Busa, v.* cumb); *Butenhale* (ib 1307, '(land) outside the nook', *v.* būtan, halh); *Choldermed*(*e*); *Clive* 1235–45 (*v.* clif); *Coldwell* (*v.* cald, wella); *Coleley* 1235–45 (*v.* col[1], cumb, cf. Cowcombe *supra*); *Colgrave* 1448; *Cotriche place* 1463 (from the local family name *Cotriche*); *Credenhull* 1379 (the OE pers.n. *Creoda*); *Croysland* 1470 (cf. Robert atte *Croys* 1416, *v.* crois 'cross'); *Cuttenhale* 1270; *Daggincroft, Dagging-* 1307 (probably an OE pers.n. *Dægga*); *Dathcombe* 1235–40, *Dedesmonnesdike* 1270–80, *Dethesgate* 1235–40 (*v.* dēad, dēað); *Delehey* 1492 (*v.* dæl 'share', (ge)hæg);

Duddene 1307, *Dodden'* Ric 2, *Doddingmed* 1306, *Dodebrigge* Ric 2 (the OE pers.n. *Dudda*, v. denu, -ing⁴, mǣd, brycg); *le Dreghercombe*; *le Duppemor* 1220–30; *Estfeld* 1379; *ferundell terre* 1438 (v. fēorða, dǣl, 'quarter'); *Ferneheye* 1414 (v. fearn, (ge)hæg); *Ferry pool field* 1688; *le Fletscherde* 1438 ('stream gap', v. flēot, sceard); *Folewell*; *Garston* 1307 (v. gærs-tūn); *Gregorescroft* 1379 (from the local surname *Gregorys* 1347 *Rent* 11, 237); *Grenehilles*, *-hulle* 1347, 1400; *Hamptonrode* 1438 Pat (v. rōd² 'cross, gallows'); *le Hanwynge* 1270, *claus' de Haw(e)nynge* 1380 *MinAcct*, *lez Hawyn(ge)* 1400, 1438 *Rent*, *Haywynge* 1307; *Haregraue* 1316 ('hare wood', v. hara, grāf); *Heygrave* 1307, *Hay-*, *Heygroue(feld)* 1400, 1449 (v. (ge)hæg, grāf); *Hengestleye* 1235–45 (v. hengest 'stallion', lēah); *Hevedberiels* 1235–45, *Henetheburiestes* 1235–45 (probably an error for OE hǣðenan byrgelse 'the heathen burial-place'); *Hychecokesacre* 1400; *Hillous* 1347 (cf. *la Hull* 1307, Ric 2, v. hyll); *Hokedemed* 1235–45 ('pointed meadow' or 'meadow in which service was given on Hoke-day', the second Tuesday after Easter); *Hoggeshey* 1379, *Hogenhay* 1411 (v. hogga, (ge)hæg); *la Horston(e)* 1307, Ric 2, *Horestone* 1438 ('boundary stone', v. hār, stān); *Hundislonde* (the OE pers.n. *Hund*); *Jonetescroft* (ib 1307); *Johanne Felde* 1438; *la Kingweie* 1235–45; *Ki-*, *Kynnesmed(e)* 1306, 1379 (the OE pers.n. *Cyne* or the ME surname *Kinne*, cf. King's Court 104 *infra*); *Lymbury* 1307, 1379, 1400, (-*crofte*) 1414 (v. burh, the first el. may be līm 'lime' or līn 'flax'); *Linleye* 1235–45 (v. līn 'flax', lēah); *Locsti* 1235–45 (v. loc 'fold', stīg 'path'); *Melescumbe* (ib 1307); *la Mor(e)* 1307, 1309, *Morcroft* 1311 (cf. also Robert *atte More*, tenant of *Morecroftes* 1400 *Rent* 11, 239); *Newelond*; *Oldway* 1650; *Outmore* 1458 BG li, *le Outewode(s)* 1448, 1453 (v. ūt 'outer', mōr, wudu); *la Perle*; *Pyksmor* 1400, *Pikesput* Ric 2 *Rent* (the ME byname *Pike*); *Pyl(l)es-*, *Pil(l)esmor(e)* 1307, 1379, 1438, 1492 (cf. Pills Moor 84 *supra*); *Pynnokesacr'* 1411 (the ME byname from *pinnok* 'hedge-sparrow'); *Pool field* 1688; *le Qu* 1235–45 (probably OFr *cue*, e.ModE *queue* 'tail' used of a narrow strip of land as with steort); *Rebeyngtree* 1400; *Rippingcroft* (from OE *ripan*, ME *ripen* 'to reap'); *Rodequarrey* 1474; *Ra-*, *Rommyngerthe*, *-hurthe* 1400, 1438 (v. eorðe); *Schiremaresslade* (ib 1308, possibly an unrecorded OE pers.n. *Scīrmǣr*, but it may be the same as *Shircumslade* 1414, v. scīr², cumb, slæd); *Selegaresleye* 1235–45, 1291 (the OG pers.n. *Seliger*, lēah); *Sprullesrudinge* 1235–45 (v. rydding); *Tidolfsid* 1316, *Tideshyde* 1379 (the OE pers.n. *Tīdwulf*, v. hīd 'hide of land'); *Trywhey* 1483 (the ME byname *Trewe* 'faithful', v. (ge)hæg); *Tungerston* 1235–45 ('town pasture', v. tūn, gærs-tūn); *ten' voc' Vynynge* 1400 (v. fīning 'heap'); *Waddenesthorne* 1235–45; *Wellehey* 1400; *Westwod* 1309; *Whestoneswelle* 1400 (v. hwet-stān 'whetstone', wella); *Wylecroft* 1291 (the ME pers.n. *Wille*); *Wynelond* (-*land* 1307), *Wynworth* 1309 (the OE pers.n. *Wyna*, v. land, worð); *Wodecroft* 1220–30; *Wormenhull* 1379 (probably the OE pers.n. *Wurma* suggested for Worminghall (Bk 129), v. hyll).

Nailsworth

NAILSWORTH (156–8599)

Neilesw'nda (sic) c. 1170 France (p)
Nailleswurd 1196 P, *-wurðe* 1197 P, *-worth* 1327 *SR* (p)
Nai-, Nay-, Nei-, Neylesw(o)rth(e) 1220–30 Berk (p), 1248 *Ass* (p),
   1261 Berk (p), 1298 GlR (p), 1320 *Ass et passim* to 1434 Pat,
   -wurth 1241 *FF, -warde* c. 1250 Berk (p), *Naylysworth, -is-* 1371
   Ipm, 1420 Pat, *-wurthe* 1492 *Rental*
Nelesworth 1542 LP

'Nægl's enclosure', *v.* worð. The same OE pers.n. *Nægl*, cognate
with OG *Nagal*, is found in the nearby *negles leag* (f.n. *infra*) and
other p.ns. like Nailsbourne and Nailsea (So), as Ekwall notes
(DEPN).

ASH GROVE, 1830 M.   BUNTING HILL.   COLLIER'S WOOD, 1830 M,
Colyers 1492 *Rent* 7, 65, from the surname *Collier*.   FOREST GREEN,
1830 M.   HARLEY WOOD, *Hareley-* 1830 M, possibly identical with
heardan leag 716–43 (11th) BCS 164, *on Heardanlége* 896 (16th) ib
574, 'the hard clearing', *v.* heard, lēah.   HIGH WOOD, 1830 M.
HOLCOMBE HO, *Holecumbe, -combe* Ric 2 *Rent*, 1411 *MinAcct, How-
combe* 1691 *GR* 25, *Hal-, Hawcombe* 1779 Rudder, *v.* hol², cumb.
NEWMARKET.   PINFARTHING 1839 *TA* 131.   ROCKNESS HILL,
Rockners 1830 M, near to Rockness (93 *supra*).   ROWDEN.   RUG-
GERS GREEN BARN, 1830 M.   SHORTWOOD, 1640 *FF*.   TINKLEY FM.
WAGHILL.   WALKLEY WOOD.   WATLEDGE, 1830 M, *Wadenegg'*
Ric 2 *Rent, Wattle Hedge* 1777 M, 'Wada's scarp', from the OE
pers.n. *Wada, v.* ecg.   WHIPPLE, 1830 M, *Whiffle* 1777 M.   WHITE-
CROFT.   WINDSOREDGE, *Winworseg* 1329 *MinAcct, Wynwardhegge*
1414 ib, *Wenewordishegge* 1461 ib, *Winnisedge* 1777 M, possibly
'escarpment near *Wynworth*' (101 *supra*), *v.* ecg.   WORLEY, 1663
Will, *Wrocheley als. Wrotesley* 1549 Pat, an OE pers.n. *Wrott* suggested by Ekwall for Wrottesley (St), *v.* lēah.

FIELD-NAMES

Some Nailsworth f.ns. are included in those of Minchinhampton (100 *supra*).
The spellings are 716–43 (11th) BCS 164, 896 (16th) ib 574.

(b) *Dryganlég* 896 (*v.* drȳge, lēah); *negles leag* 716–43, *læssan nægleslége*
896 (*v.* Nailsworth *supra*, lēah).

Long Newnton

Long Newnton was formerly in Wiltshire and the names of the parish are dealt with in W 63; they are summarised here.

LONG NEWNTON (156–9192)

> *Niuentun* 681 (e. 12th) BCS 58   *le niwe heme wodeweye* 680 BCS 59
> *Newenton(e)*, *-tuna* 1065 KCD 817, 1086 DB, 1258 *Ass*, (*Lange-*)
> 1287 ib, (*Long-*) 1337 Cl, *Neweynton* 1437 Pat
> *Longnewnton* 1585 FF

'(At) the new farmstead', *v.* nīwe (wk. obl. *nīwan*), tūn. 'Long' refers possibly to the lane along which the houses of the hamlet are dispersed or to the length of the parish; *niwe heme* is 'Newton dwellers', *v.* hǣme.

ADDY'S FIRS, *Adey's Firs* 1830 M.   BOLDRIDGE BRAKE & FM, *Bowbridge Brake* 1830 M, *Boldridge* 1840 *TA*.   CHURCH FM, *atte Churche* 1327 *SR* (p).   THE FOLLY, *the Folly House* 1840 *TA*, *v.* folie. HAM BRAKE, 1840 *TA*, *v.* hamm.   LARKHILL FM, 1773 W, *v.* lāwerce 'lark'.   NEWNTON FIRS (1830 M) & MILL (*atte Mulle* 1332 *SR* (p)).   SLADS FM, 1830 M, *la Slade* 1279 *Ass* (p), *v.* slæd. WALLGUTTERS COVERT, *Wall Gutter* 1840 *TA*.

FIELD-NAMES

The forms in (*a*) are 1840 *TA*.

(*a*) Breach (*v.* brēc); Coneygre (*v.* coninger 'warren'); Lagger (cf. Lagger Hill 28 *supra*); Long Thong Tyning; the Plaish (*v.* plæsc 'pool'); Strodlands (*v.* strōd 'marsh').

Rodborough

RODBOROUGH (156–8403)

> *Roddan beorg* 716–43 (11th) BCS 164, *Roddanbeorg* 896 (c. 1560)
> BCS 574
> *Redeberg'* (sic for *Rode-*) 1199 FF, *Redebergh* 1221 *Ass* (p)
> *Rodeb'ge*, *-berg(e)*, *-bergh* 1207 Abbr (p), 1221 *Ass*, c. 1250 Berk
> (p), 1262 Misc (p), 1313 Pat, 1407 FF, *-burwe* 13 HMC v, 336,
> *-bure* 1220–30 Berk (p), *-ber(e)w(e)* 1220–43 ib (p), 1291 Tax,
> Ric 2 Rent, *-boeruwe* 1292 BM
> *Radeberwe* 1287 *Ass*, *Radburgh als. Redbarwe* 1420 Pat, *Radburgh*
> 1542 LP, *-borowe* 1559 FF

Rodbergh(e) 1294 Cl, 1306 *Ass*, 1414 Pat, *-berwe* 1368 *FF*, *-berugh*
1400 Ipm, *-burgh* 1417 Pat *et freq* to 1476 ib, *-borough(e)* 1569
Comm, *-borowgh* 1570 GlR, *-borowe* 1581 *FF*
Rudeburgh 1456 *MinAcct*   *Roddeburgh* 1492 *FF*

The OE form shows that this name, as Ekwall has suggested, may be
from an unrecorded OE *rodde* (gen.sg. *roddan*) corresponding to Norw
rodda 'an upright pole', or from an OE pers.n. *Rodda* (derived from
OE *rodd* 'rod, stick'); *v.* beorg 'hill', here denoting Rodborough Hill.

THE ARCHERS, *Achards* 1307 Cust, *Achard ten.* 1417 AD iii, *Achardes
manor* 1421 Ipm, (*the manor of*) *Achars* 1617 *FF*, 1640 InqM, *the
Arches* 1712 GR 67. This is a manorial name from that of the family
of John *Achard* who in 1216 witnessed a Minchinhampton deed
(AD iii), cf. also BG lxi, 70.

BAGPATH, 1830 M, cf. Bagpath (ii, 239 *infra*).   BOWNHAM (GRANGE),
Bownhams 1638 InqM.   BUTTER ROW, *the Butt(e)row(e)* 1638 InqM,
Buttrow 1639 ib, 1690 *GR* (D. 892), *v.* butt[2] 'archery butt', rāw.
THE BUTTS, 1830 M, *v.* prec.   CHURCHFIELD, cf. *le Churche Howse*
1569 *Comm*, *Church leaze* 1839 *TA*.   COOPER'S HILL, probably
identical with *Copeshall* 1637 InqM.   COTSMOOR.   THE FOLLY,
1830 M, *the Folly ground* 1793 *EnclA*, *v.* folie.   FROME HALL, 1830
M, *Froomhall* 1839 *TA*, *v.* R. Frome (1) 7 *supra*.   GRAVELHILL
COTTAGE, 1830 M.   GREYSTONES.   HOUNDSCROFT, 1830 M.
KING'S COURT, 1830 M, '(lordship of) *Kynnes*' 1463 *Rent*, *Kings* 1839
TA, a manorial name from the surname *Kinne* (cf. *Kynnesmede*
101 *supra*).   LIGHTPILL, 1724 Will, 1779 Rudder.   LITTLE BRITAIN
FM, *Britain ground* 1839 *TA*.   MONTSERRATT, *-Serat* 1839 *TA*,
Mount Surat 1830 M, probably a transferred name from Montserrat
in the Leeward Isles.   MUGMOOR FM, *Moggemore* Ric 2 *Rent*,
Mugmore 1839 *TA*, probably an OE pers.n. *Mucga* suggested for
Mugworthy (D 390) and Mugginton (Db 509), *v.* mōr.   RAVENS-
BERG.   ROOKSGROVE, ROOKSMOOR, *Rokismor(e)*, *-es-* 1306 *Ass*, 1449
MinAcct, 1492, 1596 *FF*, *Rocksmoores* 1659 *GR* 25, *v.* hrōc, grāf,
mōr.   SLATTER'S FM, *Slaughters (Barn)* 1830 M, 1839 *TA*.   SPIL-
MAN'S COURT, *Spyl-*, *Spil(l)-* 1438 *Rent*, 1631 InqM, 1638 *FF*, named
from the local family of *Spilemon* 1225 *MinAcct*, *Spylmon* 1400 *Rent*
11, 239.   STANFIELDS.   STOCKING BRIDGE.   STRINGER'S FM &
COURT.   SWELLSHILL, 1830 M, *Swelys* 1496 *FF*, from the local
surname *Swele* c. 1300 Cust.   WALLBRIDGE, 1703 Will, *v.* wall,
brycg.   WOODHOUSE, 1638 InqM.

FIELD-NAMES

The principal forms in (a) are 1839 *TA* 131. Spellings dated 1609 are *AOMB* 394, 1637, 1638 InqM, 1647–1777 *GR* (D. 24, 25), 1779 Rudder, 1793 *EnclA*.

(a) Ashley; Blackwells; Bowhill orchard; Bowhouse; Brake; Chapel hill; Cold Bath field 1777 (a well was sunk here, *GR* D. 25, 19); the Conygree 1793 (*v.* coninger 'warren'); Culkerdown, -ton 1793; Dunyards 1779; Earley (*Eardleye* 1235–45 Spillm, *Erdesleye* 1291 ib); Freezeland; Garston 1793 (*v.* gærs-tūn 'pasture'); Gastrells; Green wood croft; the Guinea; Harding mead; Haresdown Tining 1793 (*v* tȳning); Hescombs; Kirkbarton 1793; Lagger (*v.* Lagger Hill 28 *supra*); Lanes 1793 (*v.* leyne); Langhett (*v.* langet); Long Combs wood; Lord's Down; the Park; Pleck; Rack hill & leaze (ib 1647); Scarry bank; Sporkbury Tining 1793; Stone hill 1793; Wastings; Westhill 1793.

(b) *Brech(e)cumbesfrith* 1316 *MinAcct*, 1638, *Brechynfryth* 1484 *MinAcct* (*v* brēc, cumb, fyrhðe); *Bury St Lewis* 1647; *Butterlea meade* 1659 (*v.* butere, lēah); *Candlemascroft* 1609; *Ernescumb* 1250–70 Spillm (*v.* earn 'eagle', cumb); *Fishelot* 1659 (*v.* hlot); *atte Horstone* 1327 *SR* (p) ('boundary stone', *v.* hār, stān); *Mores* 1638; *Oldfield* 1659; *Oxonfolde* 1463 Rent (*v.* oxa, fald); *Picked leaze* (cf. 40 *supra*); *Rippull* 1673 (*v.* rip(p)el 'strip of land'); *the Roade* 1638; *Skorhill* 1609.

Rodmarton

RODMARTON (157–9497)

> *Redmertone* 1086 DB, 1301 Ch, -*mare*- 1227 *FF*, *Redemerton* 1287 Ass
>
> *Rodmarton(e)* 1220 Fees, 1221, 1248 *Ass*, 1328 Banco
>
> *Rodmereston'* 1221 *Ass* (p)
>
> *Rodmerton*, -*tun* 1227 FF, 1234, c. 1250 Berk (p), 1261 Ipm *et passim* to 1587 *FF*, *Rode*- 1303 FA, 1378 Oseney

Rodmarton, Didmarton, and Tormarton (iii, 28, 56 *infra*) are all on the Wiltshire border and it is probable that the second el. in each case is OE *mǣr-tūn* 'farmstead on the boundary' (*v.* (ge)mǣre, tūn), a well-evidenced p.n. The first el. of Rodmarton is, as the variation between *Red*- and *Rod*- shows, OE hrēod 'reed'.

CULKERTON

> *Cvlcortone*, -*torne* 1086 DB *Culchertona* 1137 *Lanth*[2] 15d
>
> C-, *Kulkerton(a)*, -*tune* 12 HMC v, 334, 1185 Templar, 1204 Cur, 1220 Fees, 1221 *Ass* (p), 1224 Bracton *et passim* to 1587 *FF*, (-*als. Cukerton*) 1559 ib

Culc-, Culkrinton 1195 P, 1292 *FF*
Culcretun(e), -ton 13 Berk (*freq*), 1232 HMC v, 336, 1236 *FF*
Colkerton 1287, 1320, 1398 *Ass*
Colcretone, -k- 1287 QW, 1301 Ch
Cullerton 1535 VE

The first el. of this difficult name is obscure; but it could be an OE pers.n. **Culcere*; no such name is known, but a nickname based on a *nomen agentis* in -ere from **kulk-* (as in OE *cylcan* 'belch', Napier, *Old English Glosses* 20²) would be possible; it would mean 'the belcher'. OE *cylcan* itself is clearly related to ME *colken*, which has been associated with G *kolken* 'to swallow up', Dan *kulka* 'to gulp', etc. (cf. NED s.v. *colkin*). It must be admitted that such names are rare until later Middle English, though Hilcot (187 *infra*) points to a parallel usage. 'Culcere's farmstead', *v.* ing⁴, tūn; cf. also *Culker-brugge* (*infra*). *v.* Addenda.

HAZLETON FM

Hesedene 1086 DB, *Heselden(e)* 12 (1267) Ch, 13 Oseney
Haselden(e) 1248, 1287 *Ass*, 1291 Tax *et freq* to Hy 8 *Rent*
Hasulton 1466 AD ii, *Hazleton als. Hasleden* 1639 *GR* 872
Hasynden 1515–29 ECP   *Hasidon* 1535 VE

'Hazel valley', *v.* hæsel, denu.

HULLASEY HO

Hvnlafesed 1086 DB, *Hunlaueseta, Hunleueshyd* Hy 2 (1268) Ch, *-heda* 1192 P, *Vnlaueshid* 1204 *FF*, *Hundlausyde* 1287 *Ass*, *Hunlaueseye* 1306 ib, *Hunlansyde* 1349 Pap
Hundalaside 1287 *Ass*   *Hunlaicyde* 1327 *SR* (p)
Hulaicide 1327 *SR*   *Houlasith* 1328 Banco
Hunlacy 1540 AOMB, MinAcct, (*-als. Honlacy*) 1542 LP
Hullasy 1543 AOMB, *Hullacy als. Hulladye* 1606 Rec, *Hullacye als. Hullacide* 1617 *FF*

'Hūnlāf's hide of land', *v.* hīd. The pers.n. is OE *Hūnlāf*. Ekwall's derivation from OE *hȳð* 'landing-place' is not possible on topographical grounds; the place is on high ground (500 ft) at the north end of Tarlton and there is no river in the vicinity.

TARLTON

Torentvne, Tornentone 1086 DB
Torleton 1204 *FF*, 1287 *Ass*, 1291 Tax *et freq* to 1590 Camd

Thorleton 1287 *Ass,* c. 1433 BM
Torlton 1327 *SR*

The DB spellings suggest that Tarlton is the common p.n. OE
þorn-tūn 'farmstead amongst the thorns', but the persistent replace-
ment of -*n*- by -*l*-, due to AN influence (cf. IPN 106–7), would be
unusual in one example of such a frequent compound. We may
therefore have an older p.n. *þorn-lēah* 'thorn clearing' as the first el.,
with loss of -*n*- before -*l*- which we have in names like Thorley
(Hrt 204), Hullasey (prec.), cf. Phonol. § 37 (*b*). *v.* þorn, lēah, tūn.
The modern form with *Tarl*- is dialectal (Phonol. § 26).

HARESDOWN BARN, 1830 M, *Erresdon* 1287 *Ass, v.* dūn; the first el.
is possibly a pers.n. contracted from a name in *Here*- (*Hererǣd,
-wulf,* etc.). HOCBERRY, 1636 Rudder, the site of a long barrow and
Roman villa. LORDS DOWN. OATHILL BARN, 1830 M. OXLEAZ
RD., (*the*) *Oxe leaze* (*waye*) Jas 1 *TRMB* 157, *v.* oxa, lǣs. PURLEY
COVERT, *The Purley* 1830 M, probably e.ModE *purlieu* 'outskirts'.
SANDPOOL BARN, 1830 M. STONEHILL BARN, *Stanhulle, Stan-,
Stonhulle* 13 BG lxxiii, 167, *Stone hill* Jas 1 *TRMB.* TARLTON
DOWN (cf. *Estdon* 1287 *Ass, Littledun(e)* 13 HMC v, 336, *v.* dūn)
& WOOD, 1830 M. WESTEND HO.

FIELD-NAMES

The principal forms in (*b*) are Jas 1 *TRMB* 157. Spellings dated 13, 1239
are BG lxxiii, 167, 1253 HMC v, 336, 1319, 1350 BG (l.c.), 1537 Hale.

(*b*) *Annesdene* 1350 (*v.* denu); *Aschemerseye* 1350 (the OE pers.n. *Æscmēr,*
ēg or (ge)hæg); *Barlyng-, Barlychhulle* 1319, 1350 (*v.* bærlic 'barley');
Barrettes hill; *the Beache* (*v.* bēce² 'beech-tree'); *Beetesnest* 1319 (*v.* nest);
Beysley 1538 *TRMB*; *Boswell*; *la Brech* 1350 (*v.* brēc); *la Butine* (sic) 13
(*v.* bytme 'bottom'); *the Butterway*; *Culkerbrugge* 1319 (*v.* Culkerton *supra,*
brycg); *Cunyger meade* (*v.* coninger 'warren'); *the Downe gate* (cf. Tarlton
Down *supra*); *Driuers Gutteracre* (ME *guter* 'water-course'); *the Droue end,
the Drouewaye* (ModE *drove* 'drove of cattle', *drove-way* 'a road on which
cattle are driven to the fields'); *Ellecrundle* 13 Hale (the OE pers.n. *Ella,*
crundel 'pit'); *Fernham thorne* 1319 (*v.* fearn, hamm, þorn); *le Gores* 1350
(*v.* gāra); *the Groue end*; *Hasyldyn* 1537 (*v.* hæsel, denu); *Heydich* c. 1250
Berk (*v.* (ge)hæg, dīc); *Hordeston* 1350; *the Horse leaze*; *Horsell* (*foote*);
Inhokis 1253 (*v.* inhōke); *Inlande* (*v.* in-land); *Langleys* 1564 *GR* 52 (*v.* lang,
lēah); *Launsyngesland* 1350; *the Leyes*; *Lynche* 1350 (*v.* hlinc); *le Lippiette*
1239 (*v.* hlīep-geat); *London waye* ('the London road'); *Mixenhull* 1350
(*v.* mixen 'dung-hill'); *great Parke feilde, the Parke lynch* (*v.* hlinc 'slope');
Pigion howse leaze; *le Quarer* 1350 (*v.* quarriere 'quarry'); *le Rythie* 1350
(*v.* rīðig 'stream'); *Rotherewey* 1319 (*v.* hrīðer 'ox', weg); *Saltharperweie*

-weye 1340 BG xxii, 1350 ('salt way', *v.* salt, herepæð, **weg**); *Sandputtes* 1350; *Siluer slade*; *Smal(t)thorne* 13, 1350; *Smytheswey* 1350 (*v.* smið, **weg**); *Stanmereswei* 13 (named from *Stanmere* 1350, *v.* stān, mere 'pool', **weg**); *Stepnell bush* (*Stepenhull* 1350, 'steep hill', *v.* stēap, hyll); *Swetenhullested* 1350 (*v.* swēte 'sweet', hyll); *Templers quarer* 1350 (*v.* quarriere 'quarry'); *Thistlye leaze*; *Titburywaye* ('the road to Tetbury'); *Wadberewe* 1319 ('woad hill', *v.* wād, **beorg**); *the Warrengate*; *le Wawes* 1350 (*v.* wāg 'wall'); *Wickefeilde, -hill* (*v.* wīc 'dairy-farm'); *Wodemannesthorne* 1350 (*v.* wudumann, þorn); *Wokemeweye* 1350 ('road of the dwellers in Oaksey (W 63)', *v.* hǣme, **weg**); *W(o)uldon hill*.

Shipton Moyne

SHIPTON MOYNE (156–8989)

> *Scipetone* 1086 DB, *Scipton(e)* 1086 DB, 1200 Abbr, (*-Moygne*) 1295 Ipm
>
> *Sippeton'* 1220 Fees
>
> *Schip-, Schypton(e)* 1221, 1248, 1287 *Ass*, 1291 Tax, (*-Moigne*) 1340 AD iii, 1462 IpmR
>
> *Ship-, Shypton* 1221, 1248 *Ass*, 1304 Pat, (*-Moi-, -Moygne*) 1287 *Ass*, 1307 FF, 1314 Ipm *et freq* to 1375 ib, (*-Moin(e), -Moyn(e)*) 1308 FF, 1316 FA *et freq* to 1728 PR 7
>
> *Shupton Moigne, -Moy-* 1306, 1329 *FF*
>
> *Shepton Moy(g)ne* 1495 Ipm, 1544 *FF*

'Sheep farm', *v.* scēap, tūn. The normal ME form would be *Shep-*, but *Ship-* and *Shup-* in this and names like Shipton Oliffe or Shipton Solers (180, 181 *infra*) are from a late WSax *scȳp, scī(e)p*, which is probably an *i*-mutated form of *scēap* (cf. EPN ii, 100–1). The manor was held by the family of *Moygne* from the 13th century (Radulfus *le Moine* 1221 Eyre 19, Will' *le Moyne* 1248 *Ass* 4d, 1295 Ipm, 1303, 1316 FA ii, 248, 272, etc.).

SHIPTON DOVEL, *S(c)hepton Douffeld* 1541 FF, *-Dowfyld* 1570 Will, *Shipton Dovel(l)* 1576, 1587 *FF*, *-Doffeld* 1579 ib, *-Dowell* 1667 Will, *Shipton Dovell als. Shipton Estcourte* 1637 *FF*. *v.* prec. *Dovel*, which is apparently a feudal affix, has not been traced; it may be from a local p.n. *Dowfield*, named from the family of William *de Ou* (DB) or *Dow* in FA (*Nomina Villarum*). The *Estcourt* family had an estate here from the 15th century (cf. Estcourt *infra*).

CLAYFIELD FM, 1830 M.   CRANMORE FM, *Cranmore* 1839 *TA*, 'crane-haunted marsh', *v.* cran, mōr.   ESTCOURT HO, *Estcourt(e)*

1327 *SR* (p), 1474 IpmR, *v.* ēast, court; it gave its name to the *Estcourt* family, and their property was also known as *Shipton Est-courte* 1637 *Rec.* Foss BRIDGE, 1777 M, a bridge carrying Fosse Way. HEDGEDITCH LANE, 1839 *TA*. HILL COURT, 1830 M, *Hullecourt(e)* 1375, 1462 Ipm, *Hulcourte or Hulcrofte* 1495 ib, *v.* hyll 'hill', cf. Phil' *atte Hulle* 1306 *Ass* 6. TUGWELL'S GORSE. WESTEND FM, *Weston field* 1839 *TA*. WORMWELL LANE, cf. *Wormhill* 1839 *TA*, *v.* wyrm 'snake', hyll.

FIELD-NAMES

The principal forms in (*a*) are 1839 *TA* 175. Spellings dated without source are Ipm.

(*a*) All Muxon; Ayle; Blacklands; Bursenhills; Chalkhill; Clay hill & leaze; Crab hay; Dean mead; the Down; Drift way; Hallowell; Heavens burrow (possibly for an OE *hǣðenan byrgelse* or the like 'heathen burial-place', *v.* hǣðen); Holly Well (*v.* hālig, wella); the Lains (*v.* leyne); the Lindoles (*v.* līn 'flax', dāl); Long Chiswell; Pool head; Quabb mead (*v.* cwabba 'marsh'); Rockborough; Sheep slait (*v.* slæget 'sheep-pasture'); Stanbridge; Stockwell (*v.* stocc 'stump', wella); Tyning (*v.* tȳning); Vine-yards.

(*b*) *le Abbottes lande* 1542 *AOMB*; *Pedeworthys* 1463 Cl, *Pedworthisplace*, *-es-* 1486, 1495; *Wockesyesplace*, (*W*)*okysyes-* 1375, 1486, 1494 (a surname from Oaksey W 63).

Tetbury

TETBURY (156–8993)

Tettan-, *Tectan monasterium* 681 (late 14th) BCS 58–9
to *Tettan byrg* 872–915 (11th) BCS 582, *Tettan byrig* n.d. (11th) ib 1320
Teteberie 1086 DB, 1165–77 France, *-bir* 1221 *Ass*
Tetteberia c. 1170 Monast, *-bur(y)*, *-bir(e)*, *-biria*, *-buri* 13 AD i, 1219 ClR, 1220 Fees, c. 1220 *Tetb* 1, 1220–30 Berk (p), 1221 *FF*, 1234 Cl *et passim* to 1499 *FF*
Totteberia c. 1170 Monast, *-bir'* 1211–13 Fees, *-bury* 1316 FA (p)
Tuttesbire 1212 ClR   *Tuttebury* 1459 *MinAcct*
Tettesbir(e), *-byr* 1214 ClR, 1221 *Ass*, 1285 Abbr, *-bury* 1303 FA
Tetesbir' 1221 *Ass*   *Thettebur'* 1287 *Ass*
Tetbery 1288 Abbr, *-bury* 1438, 1460 Pat *et passim* to 1675 Ogilby
Tedburie, *-bury* c. 1300 Godstow, 1455 *FF*, 1486 Ipm *et freq* to 1700 PR 2

'Tette's fortified place', *v.* burh. The *burh* was no doubt the encampment just south of the parish church. The OE fem. pers.n. *Tette* is recorded only as that of a sister of King Ine of Wessex who founded Wimborne Abbey (c. 700) and of the mother of St Guthlac (c. 670) (cf. Searle s.n.). An OE masc. name *Tetta* has been proposed for Tedburn (D 14, 451), *on Tettan burnan* 739 (11th) BCS 1331, but this could equally well be from the fem. *Tette*. Tetbury was, judging by the oldest spellings, a monastic foundation and was near the land granted by the Mercian king Æthelred to Malmesbury Abbey in 681, but we do not know the identity of the lady who gave her name to *Tettan monasterium*; the locality does not favour Guthlac's mother, but if the hazy chronology of Ine's sister Tette can be extended backwards a little she might well be the founder, in view of Ine's interest in organising the church in Wessex and her own activities at Wimborne.

TETBURY STREET-NAMES

BLACK HORSE HILL. THE CHIPPING, CHIPPING LANE, *the Chipping* 1639 *Tetb*, *Chipping lane* 1732 ib, cf. also *Chipping Crofte (Lane)* 1594 SurvTet, 1633 *Tetb*, *v.* cēping, 'a market, market-place'. CHURCH ST., *Churche-stre(e)te* 1470 *FF*, 1533 *Rent* 714, 1594 SurvTet, leading to the parish church. CIRENCESTER RD., *Cissetors strete* 1533 *Rent*, *Ciciter street* 1676 Tetb, the road to Cirencester (60 *supra*); part of it was formerly called *Gumstool St.* (*infra*). COMBER'S MEAD. COTTON'S LANE. FOX HILL. THE GREEN, 1727 *Tetb*, *v.* grēne[2]. GUMSTOOL ST. (lost), *Gomstolestrete* 1533 *Rent*, *Cicester Streete als. Gumstalle Streete* 1594 SurvTet, *Gumsto(o)le street* 1607 *Tetb* 2, 1682 *GR* 875, from e.ModE *gum-stool* 'a ducking-stool for scolds' (first recorded in NED s.v. *gumble-stool* from 1623 and also in Tewkesbury (ii, 69 *infra*) from 1487); the street was part of Cirencester Rd, cf. also Gumstool Bank (66 *supra*). HAMPTON ST. HARPER ST. LONG ST. MARKET PLACE, cf. *the Cheese Markett house* 1667 *Tetb*, distinct from The Chipping (*supra*). SILVER ST., 1818 *GR* 875, *v.* seolfor 'silver'. WEST ST. (lost), 1628 *Tetb*, *le Westrete* 1397 ib, *Weststrete* 1460 Cl, 1533 *Rent*, *v.* west, strǣt. Other names include *Arthers stret* Hy 8 *Rent*, *the Long Bridge* 1739 *Tetb*; tenements are *the Dungeon (house)* 1633 *Tetb*, *the Tolzey or Markett house* 1633 ib (ME *toll-sell* 'custom-house, borough court-house'), and amongst inns are *the Boot Inn* 1797 *Tetb*, *the Horse Shooe* 1726 ib, *the Lyon* 1594 *SurvTet*, *the Mitre* 1667 ib, *the Salutation or Bear* 1754 ib, *the Swane* 1594 SurvTet, *the Swann* 1784 *Tetb*, *the White Harte* 1594 SurvTet, *the White Lyon* 1707 *Tetb*.

THE BARTONS, *Bertone* 1296 Ipm, *v.* bere-tūn 'grange'. BATH BRIDGE, 1837 *Tetb* 2, 23, a bridge leading to Bath (So). CUTWELL HILL, *-lane* 1635 *WstCt*, 1794 *Tetb* 2, 19, *v.* cut 'water-channel', wella. HORSE GARSTON, *-gastons* 1838 *TA*, 'horse-pasture', *v.* hors, gærs-tūn. THE GREEN, 1838 *TA*. THE KNAPP, cf. *Cuckolds Nap*

1812 *Tetb* 2, 22, *v.* cnæpp 'hill'.   NORTHAY (lost), *Northhay* 1291 *Tetb* 1, *Northey* 1296 Inq, *the North Hayes als. the Warren* 1633 *Tetb* 1, 'north enclosure', *v.* (ge)hæg, cf. *Southay* (foll.).   SOUTHAY (lost), *Suthehey(e)*, *-hay* 1248 *FF*, 1296 Inq, 14 HMC v, 337, *South-heyes als. Suddyheyes* 1629 *FF*, 'south enclosure', cf. *Northay* (prec.). THE SPLASH.

FIELD-NAMES for Tetbury and Tetbury Upton are dealt with 113 *infra*.

Tetbury Upton

TETBURY UPTON (156–8895)

Upton(e), *-tune* 1086 DB, 13 AD i, 1221 *FF*, 1221 *Ass* (p), 1232 HMC v, 335 *et passim* to 1587 *FF*, (*-juxta Tettbury*) 1418 IpmR, *Opton* c. 1220 *Tetb* 1 (p), 1236 Fees, *Vpton* 1494 *MinAcct*, c. 1560 *Surv*. 'Higher farmstead', *v.* upp, tūn, probably so-called from its loftier position in relation to Tetbury (109 *supra*) itself.

CHARLTON HO

    Cherleton(e), *-tune* 13 HMC v, 336, 13 AD i, 1221 *FF*, 1287 *Ass*,   1301 Ch, 1494 *MinAcct*, (*-juxta Tettebury*) 1360 Ipm, *Cherlton(e)*   1327 *SR*, 1346 Ipm
    Chorlton 1282 Ipm, 1447 *MinAcct*, 1461 Pat, *Chorleton* 1382 Ipm,   1459, 1494 *MinAcct*
    Cherlington, *-yng-* 1305 Ipm, Orig, Pat
    Charleton iuxta Tetbury 1470 *FF*, *Tedburies Charleton* 1584 *FF*
    Charlton juxta Tedbury 1486 Ipm   *Charrelton* 1587 *FF*

'Peasants' farmstead', *v.* ceorl, tūn; the same *churls* doubtless gave their name to *Cherleford* (f.n. *infra*). A *ceorl* was originally one of the lower classes of freemen, but later the word denoted a peasant. It is possible that a *ceorla-tūn* was land recovered from waste on the edges of an estate for the use of peasants, since many are located on the outskirts of more important towns, like Charlton Abbots near Winchcomb (ii, 5 *infra*) or Charlton Kings near Cheltenham (ii, 96 *infra*); cf. EPN i, 89. *Cherlington* is an interesting secondary form in its use of -ing[4] to denote an association.

DOUGHTON ['dɑutən]

    æt Ductune 775–8 (11th) BCS 226, *Ductun(e)*, *-ton* 13 BG lxxiii,   167, 1236 1241 Berk (p)

Duchtune 13 HMC v, 336, 1220–30, 1241 Berk (p), *Duhtton* 1248
   Ass (p), *Dughton(e)* 1287 *Ass*, 1301 Ch, 1305 Cl, Misc
Dutton 1221 *FF*, 1398 RBBr   *Douton* 1298 Ipm
Doughton 1327 *SR*, 1328 Banco, 1335 FF *et passim* to 1641 *FF*,
   Dowghton c. 1560 *Surv*
Dogthone 1415 BM   *Doghton* 1443 *Rent* 817
Dovton 1499 *FF*   *Dowton* 1506 *FF*
Duf(f)ton (*als. Doughton*) 1641 *FF*, 1647 Will, 1654 PR 8

'Duck farmstead', *v.* dūce, tūn. The change of -*ct*- to -*ght*- is a
common phenomenon in p.ns. like the numerous Broughtons,
Leightons, etc.; that of ME -*gh*- to -*f*- in *Dufton* is dialectal (cf.
Phonol. §§ 32, 36).

ELMESTREE

Æþelmodes treow 962 (late 11th) ASChart xxxiv (BCS 1086)
Ermundestre, -is- 1189 France, J BM
Elmondestreo 1201 BM, (*H*)*elmundestre* 1287 *Ass*, 1301 Ch, 1415 Cl
Eylmundestre 1226 Monast, 1263 *FF*, 1287 *Ass*, 1413 Pat, *Heil-*
   13 BG lxxiii, 167, *Ail-, Ayl(e)mondestre* 1535 VE, 1544 *Asht* 1,
   LP, 1570 *FF*
Almundestre 1327 *SR*
Aylmynstre als. Elmystre 1464 Pat
Elm(e)stree 1587 *FF*, 169 PR 10, *Elmestrie* 1594 SurvTet

'Æthelmund's or Æthelmōd's tree', *v.* trēow. The identification
of the OE form is not certain. On OE *Æþel-* becoming ME *Ail-,
Eyl-*, etc., cf. Feilitzen 102–6.

BLIND LANE.   CHARLTONDOWN, 1830 M.   COLLY FM, *Colly Muxen
Cottage* 1830 M, *v.* mixen 'dung-hill'.   CUTWELL, *v.* Cutwell Hill
(110 *supra*).   DOWN FM, *far, near Down* 1838 *TA*.   THE FOLLY,
1838 *TA*.   GRANGE FM, 1830 M, *Tedbury Grange* 1630 *FF*, *v.*
grange.   HEDGEPEAK FM, 1830 M.   THE HERMITAGE, HERMIT'S
CAVE.   HIGHFIELD FM, *old Highfield* 1838 *TA*.   HIGH GROVE, 1830
TA.   HILLSOME FM, 1830 M.   HOOKSHOUSE, 1830 M.   LONG-
FURLONG FM, 1830 M.   LOWFIELD FM, *Low Field* 1830 M.   NORTH-
FIELD, 1838 *TA*.   NORTHLAND, *Norteland* c. 1560 *Surv*.   STARVEALL,
1830 M.   STREET FM.   TWELVE ACRES, 1838 *TA*.   UPTON GROVE,
1830 M.   WELL HO, cf. *Well down* 1838 *TA*.   WOR WELL, *Worrall
ground* 1838 *TA*, the source of the Avon.

FIELD-NAMES

The f.ns. for this parish and Tetbury (109 *supra*) are included here. The principal forms in (*a*) are 1838 *TA* 194, and in (*b*) 13 HMC v, 336. Spellings dated 775 are 775–8 (11th) BCS 226, 13 BG lxxiii, 167 (ib xxii, 183–5), 1248 *FF*, 1296 Inq, 1443 *Rent* 817, 1594 SurvTet, 1630–5 Inq, 1779 Rudder. The spellings for the bounds of Doughton and Eisey (W) in BCS 226 are included here, but only *bedewellan* and possibly *mægðan wyllan* can be located in the area.

(*a*) Arundells (*great, Little Arundell* 1550 Pat, 1635); Barn field & *tyning* (*Barnehay* 1635, *-ground* 1676 *Tetb* 2); Bennett hayes (*v.* (ge)hæg); Botton; Burgage (ME *burgage* 'freehold property in a borough'); Cockham slads; Cold bath ground; Cold comfort; Coneygre (*the Coniger* 1594, *Conigree* 1690 *Probyn* 33, *v.* coninger 'warren'); Cow leaze (*the Cowlease* 1635, *v.* læs 'pasture'); Cuckoo pen (*v.* Cuckoo Pen 43 *supra*); Deans end (*Danes End* 1779, possibly identical with *to ðære dene* 775, *v.* denu); Elm hayes; Ewe down; Ferney leaze (*the Fearnye lease* 1635); Grove mead (*the Grove* 1635); the Harp (*the Harpe*, a close 1635, doubtless so called from its shape); Henroods; Horse Pool 1788 *Tetb* 2, 18; Hurd; Lagger (cf. Lagger Hill 28 *supra*); Langett (*v.* langet); Lislads; Maddock; Magdalene mead well (at grid 156–893937, *Mawdelen mede* 1496 *Tetb* 1, 5, possibly identical with *into mægðan wyllan* 775, *v.* mægð 'maiden' or preferably, in view of the wk decl. *mægðan*, mægðe 'may-weed', wella); Nettlebeds; Ox leaze (*-leas* 1630); Park (*le Park* 1248); Picked Harp (cf. the Harp (*supra*) and Picked Lease 40); Redmoor; Sheep stall (*Sepestalle* 13 HMC, *v.* scēap, stall); Stoke lays; Tugwell; Warren mead (*warenna de Tettebury* 1398 *Ass*, *Tedbury Warren* 1594, *Tedburies Warren* 1608 *FF*, *the Warren* 1633 *Tetb* 1, *v.* wareine); Westletts hill; Wheat hill.

(*b*) *Abbewei* 13 (the OE pers.n. *Abba*, weg); *to Ægan stane* 775; *Bartylotescrofte* 1443 (the surname *Bartlett*); *on bedewillan, of bedewellan* 775; *Bidwell* 1630 ('well with a vessel', *v.* byden, wella); *Beidunesslade* 13 (*v.* dūn, slæd); *Blackengrove* 1630 (*Blakingroue* 13); *on brádan beorh* 775 (*v.* brād, beorg); *Brodesierd* (the surname *Broad*, geard 'yard'); *Buledene* (*v.* bula, denu); *Bushie Leaze* 1594; *Carnetecrundle* (*Curtenecrundle* 13, *v.* crundel 'pit, quarry'); *Cherleford* 1248 (*v.* ceorl, ford, cf. Charlton *supra*); *Cleihulle* (*v.* clǣg, hyll); *the Courtes Courtfield* 1594; *on ðone ellenstub* 775 (*v.* ellern 'elder', stubb); *Froggaputtesforlong* (*v.* frogga, pytt); *Garstone* (*v.* gærs-tūn); *Gretethorn* 13 ('great thorn'); *Hadenhulle* (*Haldenhulle* 13); *Hareburne*; *Hiwoldesdene* 13 (*Hewlsdeane hill* 1594, the OE pers.n. *Hygewald*, *v.* denu); *Horemaredoune* 13, *Harmer Downe* 1633; *on hrisweg* 775 (*v.* hrīs 'brushwood', weg); *Huns-, Hus(e)don* 1630; *on mærweg* 775 ('boundary road', *v.* (ge)mǣre); *Meddene* 13 (*v.* mǣd, denu); *Myreford*; *Neddreswelleslade* ('adderstream valley', *v.* nǣddre, wella, slæd); *Ochoure* 13 ('oak bank', *v.* āc, ofer[2]); *Olledene* (an OE pers.n. *Olla*, *v.* denu); *Ophemedoune* 1296 ('the down of the men of Upton (*supra*)', an elliptical formation with hǣme, *v.* dūn); *Ouerwyke* 1443 (*v.* wīc 'dairy-farm'); *Pereshull* 1443 (the ME pers.n. *Per(s)*); *the Picked lease* 1635; *Prusteland* 13 (*v.* prēost 'priest'); *on Pumere* 775 (*v.* mere 'pool');

8

on Puttan crundell 775 (the OE pers.n. *Putta, v.* crundel 'quarry'); *Rixwell* 13 ('rush well', *v.* risc (*rix*), wella); *the Sheephouse* 1635; *Stenethulle* 13 ('stony hill', *v.* stæniht, hyll); *Stueslond* 1443; *the Velletts* 1635 (*v.* fellet 'a clump of felled trees, clearing'); *Vertone* 1296; *Wensierd* (*v.* geard, with the OE pers.n. *Wynsige*); *Wick Lease* 1594 (*v.* wīc, lǣs); *on winterburnan* 775 (*v.* winter, burna); *on ðone ýfemestan hangran* ('the uppermost wooded slope', *v.* hangra).

Weston Birt

WESTON BIRT (156–8589)

Weston(e) 1086 DB, 1215 ClR, 1220 Fees *et passim* to 1749 PR 5, with the affix *Brette-* 1309 *FF*, *-Brut(t)* 1322, 1324 *MinAcct*, 1331 Ipm *et freq* to 1392 ib, *-Britt(e)*, *-y-* 1324 *MinAcct*, 1427 IpmR *et freq* to 1501 *FF*, *-Bruyte* 1327 *SR*, *-Birt(e)*, *-y-* 1535 VE, 1553 Pat *et freq* to 1717 PR 5, *-Burt* 1749 ib. 'West farmstead', *v.* west, tūn; it lies west of Tetbury. Richard *le Bret* held the manor in 1242 (Fees) and the heir of John *le Bret* in 1285 (FA ii, 244).

LASBOROUGH

Lesseberg(e) 1086 DB, 1242 Fees, 1248 *Ass*, *-beruwe, -burg* 1248 ib, *-ber(e)we* 1260 Ipm (p), 1285 FA
Lasseberg(e), -bergh(e) Steph (1318) Ch, c. 1260 GlR (p), *et freq* to 1354 Ch, *-berwe* c. 1220 GlR, 1255 *FF*, 1287 *Ass*, *-bur(e)* 1282, 1307 Ipm, *-bury* 1283 Cl
Lasceberwe 1292 Ipm
Lasshebarowe als. *Lasbarowe* 1532, 1557 *FF*, *Lasheboroughe* als. *Laseboroughe* 1589 FF
Lasbarowe 1522 *FF*, *-borough* 1535 VE, 1540 *AOMB*

This referred to the tumulus just east of the village (156–824942); a much larger one lies a mile south-east in Tump Covert in Beverston (156–840935), so that Lasborough may well mean 'the lesser barrow', from OE *lǣssa* 'smaller' and beorg. Lassington (iii, 160), nearly 18 miles to the north across the Severn, has similar forms for the first el.

BOWLDOWN FM, *-field* 1779 Rudder, *v.* the nearby Bowldown Wood (iii, 26 *infra*). CASTLERAG BARN, *Castle-rag-* 1830 M. THE DOWNS. ELMLEAZE BARN, *le little Elmes leases* 1635 WstCrt, *v.* elm, lǣs. RUSHMORE COVERT.

FIELD-NAMES

The principal forms in (a) are 1839, 1849 *TA* 119, 217. Spellings dated 1575 are *TRMB*, 1579–1688 *WstCt*, 1602, 1613 *GR* 246, c. 1603 *TRMB*.

(a) Birds (*terr' voc' Birdes* 1575, *-Byrdes* 1579, the surname *Bird*); Black Pits (*-pittes* 1633); Buckle Moor (ib 1575); Clay Garson (*Cley-*, *Claygaston* 1575, 1667, *v.* clǣg, gærs-tūn 'pasture'); Clay leaze; Deer Park; Goose leaze; Haverstone hill; Hitching (*v.* heccing); Horse leaze; the Shade; Great, Little & Sheep Slait (*v.* slæget 'sheep-pasture'); Sourmead; Stock well (*Stockwelles gate* 1635, *v.* stocc, wella); Thornhill piece (*Thornewell leaze* 1650, *v.* þorn, wella); Wabley (ib 1667); Wigmore Bottom (*Wigmores bottom* 1635); Willow bed.

(b) *le Beuerstons bushe* 1635 (Beverston ii, 213 *infra* is an adjoining parish, *v.* busc); *Bristoll Waye* 1635; *Brodwaye furlonge* 1633; *Deane bottom* 1579 (*v.* denu); *le Grimestones waye* 1575, *the Grindstones way* 1667 (ME *grin-stone* 'grindstone', weg); *le Grove* (*lane*) 1575, 1635; *Long Elme* 1667; *Longemeade* 1602; *the Millpath* 1667; *Newe wall* 1635; *le Northefi(e)ld* 1575, 1602; *Pillismore* 1575 (cf. Pills Moor 84 *supra*); *the Pound* 1579; *Smal(e)croft(e)* 1575, 1579; (*le*) *Southfi(e)ld* 1575, 1602; *Stanwelles bottom* 1688; *Stone hill* 1635; *the Swallow pitt* 1667 (*v.* swalg 'pit, pool', pytt); *Westbarne* 1575; *Whaddon Brudge* c. 1603; *Willesley feild* 1688; *Wy-*, *Wisheley* 1575, 1613 (*v.* wisc 'marshy meadow', lēah).

Woodchester

WOODCHESTER (156–8402)

Uuduceastir (v.l. *-cester*) 716–43 (11th) BCS 164

Wuduceaster, ceaster setna 896 (16th) BCS 574

Widecestre 1086 DB, *Wydechestre* 1380 FF, 1408 Ipm, *Witchester* 1635 Will

Vdecestre 1086 DB, *Wdecestre* 1216 ClR, 1221 *Ass*

Wudecestr' 1221, 1248 *Ass*

Wodecestr(e) 1220 Fees, 1221, 1248 *Ass et freq* to 1376 Ipm, *-chestr(e)* 1297 ib, 1313, 1338 FF, 1421, 1435 Ipm, 1436 Pat

Wodcestre 1287 QW, *-chestre*, *-er* 1465 Pat, 1535 VE

Wychestre, *-er* 1416, 1420 Pat, 1455 FF, 1533–8 ECP, 1553 FF

Woodchester 1584 *Comm*, (*-als. Wychester*) 1602 FF, 1634 InqM

If OE ceaster 'camp' refers here to a Roman settlement, as it usually does, the first el. must be OE wudu in the sense 'woodland' as any wooden structures of the Roman period are unlikely to have survived to produce an OE name indicating the materials of their construction; 'Roman camp in the wood' is therefore the likely meaning. Remains of a Roman villa and tessellated pavement have been found just north of the village. The DB form *Wide-* is probably a vestige of OE *widu*, the archaic form of *wudu*; on the later *Wyde-* forms cf. Phonol. § 29. For *ceaster setna*, *v.* sǣte 'dwellers'.

LAGGAR LANE, *Lagger* 1838 *TA*. The word *lagger* appears frequently in Gl minor names and f.ns. and was reported as a Gl term for 'a narrow strip of unenclosed land uniting two parts of a farm, a broad green lane' (EDD s.v.). Its origin is not known.

ATCOMBE FM, *Hatcombe leaze* c. 1700 *GR* 677, *Attcombe House* 1830 M.   BENWELL HO.   BOWN HILL, 1830 M.   COLEPARK WOOD, *Cold Park-* 1830 M.   DARK WOOD, 1830 M.   DINGLE WOOD, 1830 M, *v.* dingle 'deep dell'.   HONEYWELL POND.   INCHBROOK, 1777 M, cf. also *Inchcombe Grove* 1819 *GR* 677, cf. Incham (ii, 111 *infra*, a former name of the R. Chelt 5 *supra*).   OAKLEY HO, *-leaze* 1819 *GR* 677, *v.* āc, lēah.   THE PRIORY, *-house* 1838 *TA*.   SELSEYHILL FM, *Selsly great park* 1838 *TA*.   SUMMERWELL HO.   WOODCHESTER PARK 1634 Inq.

FIELD-NAMES

The principal forms in (*a*) are 1838 *TA* 228. Spellings dated 716–43 are (11th) BCS 164, 896 EHD xiv, 1606 *GR* 445, 1640 Inq, 1708 *GR* 25, 1693, 1700, 1800, 1819 *GR* 677.

(*a*) Bean Acre; Berry Moor; Birds Hill 1800; Boorely Croft 1700; Cock pits; Coneygre (*v.* coninger 'warren'); Daniels leazes 1708; Devil's Bowling Green; Dog wood; Folly Orchard; Frith 1819 (*v.* fyrhðe); Frogmarsh 1700, 1800; Hampstead 1800 (*v.* hām-stede); Harkley 1800; Kings Field (ib 1819, *King's Stead* 1819); Ox Leaze; Perry leaze 1819; Pud hill (ib 1751 *GR* 892, 1779 Rudder, *v.* puddel 'pool'); Rack Hill (cf. *the Rackeclose* 1640, e.ModE *rack* 'a rack for drying or stretching cloth', cf. Rackhill 140 *infra*); the Road grove 1800; the Salt Box (dial *salt-box* 'a lean-to shed'); Sheppards leaze 1819; Shortcomb; Shoulder of Mutton Grove 1819 (so called from its shape); Upper & Lower Slade 1800 (*v.* slæd); Sour Well 1819; Stankcombe (*v.* stān, cumb); Walls Hill; Woodlands ground (ib 1819).

(*b*) *to Æþelferðes londe* 896; *Carlesleage* 716–43 (v.l. *Ceorles*, *v.* ceorl; lēah); *Dyerslade* 1498 Ct (the surn. *Dyer*, *v.* slæd); *Eatelands* 1640 ('grazing land', *v.* ete, land); *haboccumb* 716–43 (v.l. *hauoc-*, *heafoccumb*, 'hawk valley', *v.* hafoc, cumb); *hæslburg* 716–43 (v.l. *hælsburg*, 'fort by the hazel', *v.* hæsel, burh); *Hanging Acre* 1693 (*v.* hangende 'steep', æcer); *iemyðleag* 716–43, *gemyðleag* 896 ('clearing near the river-confluence', *v.* (ge)mȳðe, lēah); *Knappes Hall* 1606; *Maple Thorne* 1640; *Millmead* 1640; *the Moore* 1640; *Smiececumb* 716–43, *on Smececumbe* 896 (OE *smēc* 'smoke', *v.* cumb); *Walhweg* 716–43 ('the Welshman road', *v.* walh, weg, cf. Welsh Way 20 *supra*); *Wellsteeds Meade* 1642 InqM; *uuidancumb* 716–43 ('wide valley', *v.* wid, cumb).

IV. BISLEY HUNDRED

Bisley Hundred is approximately as it was in DB, but there have been some adjustments, especially in the case of Stroud parish, parts of which were in 1894 made into the separate civil parishes of Cainscross (in Lower Whitstone Hundred), Whiteshill (in Upper Whitstone Hundred), Thrupp and Uplands. Cainscross and Uplands have now become wards in Stroud Urban District. The hundred lies to the west of the southern Cotswolds north of Longtree Hundred (85 *supra*), between the upper R. Frome and Stroud Water.

BISLEY HUNDRED

Biselege hvnd' 1086 DB, *Bise-, Bysel', -le(a), -leg, -ley(a) Hund'* 1168–95 P (*freq*), 1220 Fees, 1221 Eyre, 1248 *Ass et passim* to 1378 Works, *Hund' de Bis-, Byslegh, -ley(e)* 1221 *Ass*, 1274 RH *et freq* to 1587 FF, (*hundr' de*) *Bi-, Bysseley* 1501 Pat, 1535 VE. The hundred is named from Bisley (*infra*) at its centre. The exact meeting-place is not known, but a suggestion made by the late Mr F. T. S. Houghton is The Wittantree (121 *infra*), a mile north of Bisley at the highest point just west of the Calf Way (156–902074).

Bisley

BISLEY (156–9005)

to Bislege 986 (16th) BCS 574
Bise-, Byseleg(e), -lei(a), -l(e)', -legh(e), -ley(e) 1086 DB, 1130 P, 1175 BM, 1220 Fees, 1221 Eyre, 1236 Fees *et passim* to 1424 IpmR
Bisse-, Byssele(g), -ley(a) 1204 P, 1209 Fees, 1295 Episc, 1378 Works *et freq* to 1598 *Comm*, *Bissley* 1535 VE
Bis-, Bysle(y), -legh 1211–13 Fees, 1221 *Ass*, 1243 HMC v, 336, 1280 Episc, 1360 Ipm, 1377–99 Works *et passim* to 1600 FF
Bisileye 1351 BM   *Biesley* 1621 FF
Beseley 1555 FF, *Beeseleyghe* 1590 ib, *Beesley* 1618 ib

'Bisa's glade or clearing', *v.* lēah. The OE pers.n. *Bisi*, or preferably an unrecorded weak form *Bisa* corresponding to OG *Biso*, is also found in neighbouring names, Bismore (*infra*), Bussage, *Bisendune* and Biscombe (127, 139, 147 *infra*), and the same man may have given his name to all five places.

BATTLESCOMBE, *Battlescomb(e)* 1609 *AOMB* 394, 1830 M, *Battlefrome field* (sic for -*scome*-) 1702 *GR* 892. Probably 'Bæd(d)el's valley', *v.* cumb. This OE pers.n., which is not on record but is a normal derivative of OE *Bada*, has a similar change in other p.ns. like Battle Bridge (242), Battledown (ii, 97 *infra*) and Battlesden (Bd 115).

BISMORE BRIDGE, *Bismore* 1609 *AOMB* 394. 'Bisa's marshy ground', *v.* mōr. The pers.n. is doubtless that of the OE *Bisa* who gave his name to Bisley (*supra*).

BOURNES GREEN, 1830 M, *Bourne in parochia de Biseleye* 1394 *Ass*, *the Borne* 1638 Inq, *Bourne* 1647 *FF*, cf. also *Burnemede* 1459, 1494 *MinAcct*, *Bornegrove* 1609 *AOMB*. *v.* burna 'stream', here one running into the Frome between Oakridge and Chalford; it is distinct from Bourne (140 *infra*) in Thrupp.

CALFWAY FM & WOOD, 1830 M, (*semita que tendit versus*) *Calphaye* 1255–90 *CirenR*, *Galfehagh* 1459 *MinAcct*, *Calfehagh'* 1461 ib, *wood* ...*Cawpho* 1599 *Comm*, *Calfee* 1609 *AOMB* 394. 'Calf enclosure', *v.* calf, haga. The change in the second el. to -*way* is paralleled by Northway (ii, 54 *infra*, cf. Phonol. § 42 *c*). Calfway Fm is ¼ mile from a lane from Bisley to Cheltenham which is now called Calf Way, doubtless because of the development of the p.n. to that form.

CATSWOOD, 1738 Will, *Catewode* 1459 *MinAcct*, *Catteswode*, -*wood* 1468, 1494 ib, 1599 *Comm*, 1609 *AOMB* 394. 'Wood haunted by wild cats', *v.* catt, wudu.

DAGNISH WOOD, *Tagonhegge* 1448 *MinAcct*, *Dagenhege*, *wood*... *Cagnishe* (sic for *Tag*-) 1599 *Comm*, *Dagnes* 1609 *AOMB* 394. Probably in view of 1448 and 1599 spellings a compound of OE tacca or tagga 'teg, young sheep', and ecg 'edge, escarpment' or hecg 'hedge'. The change to *Dag*- is unusual (cf. Phonol. § 44*d*).

DANEWAY, *Denneway* 1397 Ipm, 1401 Cl, *Denwey*, -*way(e)* 1562, 1647 *FF*, *Daneway* 1779 Rudder 292. 'Road through the valley' (*v.* denu, weg), referring to a lane leading up a small valley on the north side of the Frome. Cf. Phonol. § 13.

FRITH FM & WOOD, *del Friht'* 1248 *Ass* (p), (*la*, *leʒ*) *Frith(e)* 1327 *SR* (p), 1494 *MinAcct*, 16 *Rent*, 1540 *AOMB*, *le Ferth(e)* 1459 *MinAcct*, *Frithhouse* 1632 *Rogers* 10. *v.* fyrhð(e) 'wood, woodland', a common term in this well-wooded parish.

LITTERIDGE WOOD

> *Litterigge* 1287 *FF*, *-ridge* 1609 *AOMB* 1394, *wood...Littaridge*
> 1599 *Comm*
> *Lutterugge* 1327 *SR* (p), *Luteruge* 1448, 1461, 1494 *MinAcct*

The spellings *Litte-*, *Lutte-* suggest an OE pers.n. *Lytta*, a mutated variant of the *Lutta* which lies behind OE *Lutting* (Redin 174); it would be from the root of *lȳt* and *lȳtel* 'small', the latter being also apparently used as a pers.n. in Lidlington (Bd 79) and other p.ns. The earlier forms are against a derivation from OE *lȳt* itself. *v.* hrycg.

LYPIATT (MIDDLE)

> *Lup(e)iate* 1207 ChR, c. 1250 Berk (p), *Lup(e)yat(e)* 1287 *Ass*, 1324
>   Ipm *et freq* to 1584 *Comm*, (*Ouer-*) 1321, 1520 *FF*, (*-sup'*) 1327
>   *SR*, *Lupieyte* 1328 Banco
> *Lopegate* 1220 Fees   *Lupegate* (*superiori*) 1303 FA, 1349 Aid
> *Lepiet* 1221 *FF*, *Lep(e)yat(e)* 1325, 1455 *FF*, (*Ouer-*) 1338 ib, 1378
>   Works, *Lep(e)gate* 1255–90 *CirenR*
> *Li-*, *Lyp(p)egat(e)* 1220 Fees, 1248, 1287 *Ass*, (*-magna, -parua*)
>   1287 ib
> *Lippehiete* c. 1238 Berk, *Lipp(e)yate* 1248 *Ass*, (*Ouer-*) 1497
>   *AOMB*, *Overlypeyate* 1395 Ipm, *Middle Lypiat* 1830 M

v. hlīep-geat 'a gate in an enclosure fence which deer can leap over but which restrains other animals'. It is a term found chiefly in the woodlands and old parks of south-western England. There are two other local examples including Lypiatt in Miserden and Lower Lypiatt in Thrupp (131, 141 *infra*); the spellings for these names are not easily separated. Cf. Phonol. § 16.

OAKRIDGE, OAKRIDGE LYNCH, *Okerigge* 1459 *MinAcct*, *-rinch* 1509 Ipm, *-ruge* 1535 VE, 1540 *MinAcct*, *-rudge* 1540 *AOMB*, *-ryge* 1549 *FF*, *-ridge* 1609 ib, *Oakridge Linch* 1775 Will. 'Oak-tree ridge', *v.* āc, hrycg, and hlinc 'ridge, bank'.

ROOK WOOD, *Roc-*, *Rokwude* 1190 *FF*, 1248 *Ass*, *-wde* 1243 HMC, v, 336, *-wode* 1327 *SR* (p), *la Rockwod* 1287 *Ass*, *Rookewood* 1621 *FF*. 'Rook wood', *v.* hrōc, wudu.

STEAN BRIDGE

> *Stewenebrige* 1248 *Ass*
> *Stevenebrugge* 1315 Glouc, *Steuenesbrugge* 1459 *MinAcct*, *Steven-*
>   *brug* 1461 ib, *-bridge* 1609 *AOMB*, *Stevens bridge* 1598 *Comm*

Stenynbrug' 1377–99 Works
Stenesbrugge 1408 *FF*
Stenbridge 1562, 1605 *FF*, 1608 Will, 1609 *AOMB*
Steanebridge 1638 *Rec*, 1639 InqM

'Stephen's bridge', *v.* brycg. The first el. is the ME pers.n. or surname *Steven, Stephen*; there was a Thomas *Stevens* locally as late as 1598 (*Comm*), and the name also appears in the local p.n. *Stevenes-hill, Steneshille* 1459, 1461 *MinAcct* and the f.n. Stevens's (*infra*). The reduction of *Steven-* to *Sten-* is paralleled by such ME forms as *sen* for *seven* and the spellings of Sevenhampton 177 *infra* (cf. Jordan § 216, 2, Phonol. § 34*b*).

STONEBRIDGE (lost), *Stonebruge* 1327 SR (p), 1449 *MinAcct*, *-brigge* 1494 ib, *Stanbrygge* 1546 *FF*. 'Stone-built bridge', *v.* stān, brycg. Its location in the parish has not been determined; it is possibly simply a variant of Stean Bridge (prec.), where ME *sten-* was regarded as from stǣnen 'made of stone' and so could be replaced by *stān, stone.*

THROUGHAM ['þrufəm, 'drufəm]

    Troham 1086 DB, 1200 Abbr, 13 WinchLB (p), 1201 Cur, 1220
        Fees *et freq* to 1327 *SR*   *Trouham* l. 13 BG li
    Truham 1190 P (p), 1208 Cur, 1221 *Ass*, 1221 Eyre (p)
    Throham 1255–90 CirenR   *Throgham* 1378 *Ass*
    Trug-, Trogham 1287 *Ass*   *Truchham* 1287 *Ass*
    Thurgham 1313 Pat (p)
    Throughham 1318 *FF*, *Throuham* 1378 Works, *Througham* 1477
        Pat, 1535 VE, 1544 LP, 1629 *Asht* 5
    Drowham 1377–99 Works
    Thoroweham 1448 *FF*
    Thruffham 1549 *FF*   *Druffham* 1830 M

The spellings favour derivation from OE þrūh 'conduit' rather than OE trog 'trough, valley', though doubtless there has been some confusion (cf. EPN ii, 187, 217). OE *þrūh* meant 'water-pipe, conduit, coffin' and may here refer to the water-course in the deep-cut valley of Holy Brook, a semantic development paralleled by the topographical sense 'hollow, valley' which OE *trog* developed from 'trough'. The latest form *Druffham* is dialectal (cf. Phonol. §§ 36, 41 *a*). The second el. is OE hām or hamm. Cf. Ðruhham BCS 180 (Ha).

TUNLEY

Tunleg', -lee, -leye 1220 Fees, 1248, 1287 *Ass*, 1587 *FF*
Thonleya 1248 *Ass*   *Tolneye* 1287 *Ass*
Tonley 1303 FA, 1338 *FF et freq* to 1475–80 ECP
Toueley (sic) 1483 IpmR

This isolated place in the east of this large parish is hardly likely
to be OE *tūn-lēah* 'the clearing belonging to the village', but it could
denote 'a fenced-in clearing' from tūn in its older sense; *v.* lēah.
The spellings do not favour the OE pers.n. *Tunna*.

THE WITTANTREE, *Wittingtree quarrs* 1841 *TA*, which from its situation might have been the meeting-place of Bisley Hundred (117 *supra*),
possibly represents an OE *witena-trēow* 'tree of the councillors, tree
where the councillors met' in allusion to some such assembly as that
of the hundred; *v.* wita, trēow, and cf. Longtree (85 *supra*) for
another hundred named from a tree. But the evidence for the name
is so late that it may equally well be from OE *hwīting-trēow* 'whitten
tree, water elder, wild guelder-rose', as Professor Arngart suggests
(Anderson 28). For *quarrs*, *v.* quarriere 'quarry'.

ABBEY FM & WOOD, cf. *murum clausi domini abbatis* c. 1255–90
CirenR, named from Cirencester Abbey. ANSTEADS FM, *Hanstead-*
1830 M, *-steeds* 1779 Rudder.

BAKER'S BARN, *Bakers Wilbraham* 1777 M. BARNAGE WOOD,
Barn(e)hegge 1448 *MinAcct*, *-age* 1468 ib, *-idge* 1599 *Comm*, 'scarp
near the barn', *v.* bere-ærn, ecg; it denotes the steep hillside overlooking the R. Frome. BLACK FIRS, *Blac(k)frith(e)* 1448 *MinAcct*,
1599 *Comm*, 1609 *AOMB*, *Blakefrith* 1461 *MinAcct*, 'black wood',
v. blæc, fyrhðe. BLANCHE'S BANK. BOUNCE HORN, 1841 *TA*.
BOYS' WOOD. BRISTLEY HILL WOOD. BUTTS COPPICE, 1841 *TA*,
named from *the Butts* 1841 ib, *v.* butte 'abutting strip in the common
field'.

CALVES MEAD, 1841 *TA*, *v.* calf, mǣd. THE CHANTRY, cf. *the
Chauntrie hill* 1609 *AOMB*, *Chantry thicket* 1841 *TA*. THE
CHEQUERS. COLLIER'S PLANT., *mess' voc' Collyars* 1609 *AOMB*,
from the surname *Collier*. CONIGAR, *the Conyngar*, *-ig-* 16 *Rent* 7,
70, *v.* coninger 'rabbit-warren'. CONYGRE WOOD, *the Coneygree*
1841 *TA*, *v.* prec. COPSEGROVE FM, *Coppiche groue* 1327 *SR*, *Copsgroue*
1609 *AOMB*, *v.* copeiz 'coppice', grāf. CRICKETTY MILL, 1830 M.
CUTHAM'S STILE.

DANIEL'S FM, -*ground* 1841 *TA*. DAW'S LANE, cf. *Dawes piece* 1841 *TA*, from the surname *Dawe*. DUNKITE HILL.

EASTCOMBE, *E*(*a*)*stcomb*(*e*)*s* 1633 Inq, 1763 Will, *v.* ēast, cumb. ELCOMBE, 1841 *TA*, *Eltham* 1609 *AOMB*, *Hellcomb* 1830 M, cf. Elcombe (ii, 254 *infra*), *v.* ellern 'elder', cumb.

FENNELL'S FM, 1830 M, from the surname *Fennel*. FERRIS COURT, 1830 M, *Ferrys Courte* 1562 *FF*, -*es*- 1600 ib, from the surname *Ferris*, which occurs in Gl in the 17th century, *v.* court. FIDGES LANE, cf. *toft' voc' Figges* 1609 *AOMB*, from the ME surname *Fig*(*g*)*e*, a variant of *Fitch* (Reaney 120–1). FIELD HO, named from *the feilde* 1609 *AOMB*, cf. also *Inthefelde* 1327 *SR* (p), *v.* feld 'common field'. THE FOLLY, 1841 *TA*, *v.* folie. FURNER'S FM, cf. *Ferners mead* 1841 *TA*.

GAT WOOD, *Gatt*- 1841 *TA*, *Gatewode* 1461 *MinAcct*, *v.* geat 'gate', wudu. THE GIANT'S STONE, *Giant stone tyning* 1841 *TA*, the name of an ancient burial chamber. THE GREYS, *Grays* 1747 Will, from the surname *Gray*.

HAWKLEY WOOD, *Hawkeleyswode* 1461, 1468 *MinAcct*, 'hawk glade or clearing', *v.* hafoc, lēah. HAYHEDGE LANE, *Hay edge* 1841 *TA*, *v.* (ge)hæg, ecg. HEN WOOD, 1777 M, *v.* henn, wudu. HIGH-MEADS WOOD, *High mead* 1841 *TA*. HILL HO, *la* (*atte*) *Hull*(*e*) 1255–90 *CirenR*, 1327 *SR* (p), *le Hill*(*e*) 1459 *MinAcct*, 1609 *AOMB*, *v.* hyll. HOGLEY, *Hoggeleye*, *Hoggesleyeshull'* 1255–90 *CirenR*, 'hog clearing', *v.* hogg, lēah. HOLLOWAY, -*mead* 1841 *TA*, *v.* hol², weg. HOPYARD WOOD, *Hop yard* 1841 *TA*. THE HORNS, 1777 M, *Horn hill* 1841 *TA*, *v.* horn 'nook'.

ILE'S GREEN, *Iles piece* 1841 *TA*.

JAYNES COURT, cf. *Jones*-, *Janescrofte* 1459, 1494 *MinAcct*, from the ME surname *Janes*, a variant of *Johns*.

KEENSGROVE WOOD. KILMINSTER FM. KING'S HO, cf. *Kingesplace* 1609 *AOMB*, *Kings ground* 1841 *TA*, from the surname *King*. KITLYE, -*ley* 1609 *AOMB*, 'kite glade', *v.* cȳta, lēah. KNAPP FM, *Knap* 1777 M, *v.* cnæpp 'hillock'.

LAINES GROVE, *the Leynes* 1609 *AOMB*, *v.* leyne 'arable strip'. LILLYHORN FM, 1830 M. LIMBRICK'S FM, *Limericks ground* 1841 *TA*, cf. *Lymerykes* (159 *infra*). THE LIMEKILNS, -*kiln* 1841 *TA*. LONGDON HILL, 1841 *TA*, *Langedeneshegge* 1255–90 *CirenR*, *Longedon* 1295 Episc, 'the long hill', *v.* lang, dūn. LYPIATT PARK, *Lipiat parke* 1609 *AOMB*.

MONEY TUMP, 1841 *TA*, a tumulus.

NASH END, *Nashend(e)* 1609 *AOMB*, 1611 *FF*, 1631 Will, 'the end (of an estate) near the ash-tree', *v.* atten, æsc, ende.
PARK FM, *the Park* 1841 *TA*.   PEN FM, *-ground* 1841 *TA*, *v.* penn² 'enclosure'.   PENNY GROVE, cf. *Penycrofte* 1546 *FF*, Pennymead (*infra*), 'grove, etc. paying a penny rent', *v.* pening.   PERROTRY, *Perrety* 1841 *TA*, possibly for 'pear-tree', *v.* pirige, trēow.
PEST HO, 1841 *TA*, 'house for infectious diseases', usually a lazaretto for plague-stricken persons (cf. O 461).   PEYTON'S GROVE.   PIEDMONT, 1830 M, a transferred name from Piedmont, Italy.   PONTINGSHILL PLANT.   PROUD GROVE.   PUCK MILL, 1830 M.

QUANLEY GROVE, *Quanley* 1609 *AOMB*, *Quonley* 1841 *TA*.

REDDING WOOD, *Riddinge, the Readinges* 1609 *AOMB*, *v.* rydding 'clearing'.

SHEEPHOUSE FM, *le shepe howse(medd)* 16 *Rent* 7, 70, 1609 *AOMB*, *v.* scēap, hūs.   SICCARIDGE WOOD, *Seckaridge, Seckerige* 1599 *Comm*, *Seckridge* 1609 *AOMB*, 'secure, safe ridge', from ME *siker, seker* (OE *sicor*, Lat *securus*), but perhaps also used as a byname, hrycg.
SLADE LANE, SLAD GROVE, *Slade* 1546 *FF*, *Slad(d)* 1605, 1620 *FF*, *Sladde* 1616 *FF*, *v.* slæd 'valley', here Stroud Slad (*infra*).   SMART'S FM, *-orchard* 1841 *TA*.   SNAKESHOLE.   THE SNUBBS, cf. dial. *snub* 'to check the growth, to nip off the top, to crop closely'.   SOUTHMEAD FM, *Suthmed(e)* 1248 *Ass*, 1255–90 *CirenR*, *v.* sūð, mǣd 'meadow'.   STANCOMBE FM, *Stancomb(e)* 1327 *SR* (p), (*-Cross*) 1777 M, *Stankcombe feilde* 1609 *AOMB*, 'stony valley', *v.* stān, cumb, a p.n. which occurs several times in Gl.   STOCKS END, *Stokesend* 1360, 1424 Ipm, cf. *Stockelond* 1448 *MinAcct*, *Stokelonde* 1459 ib, *Stoke furlong* 1841 *TA*; one-third of the tithes of this parish were appropriated to the College of Stoke by Clare (Sf), cf. Rudder 292.
STROUD SLAD FM, the valley of Slad Brook which runs through Stroud (cf. *Strodehous, -mylle(s)* 1448, 1494 *MinAcct*), *v.* Slade Ho (140 *infra*).   SWILLEY GROVE, ib, *the Swilley* 1841 *TA*, dial. *swilly* 'whirlpool, gutter' (cf. swelg or swille, ēa 'stream', and Swilgate 12 *supra*).   SYDENHAM'S FM, *Sidenham* 1830 M, *v.* sīd, hamm.

TAUT COTTAGES, *-ground* 1841 *TA*.   THROUGHAM SLAD FM, 1841 *TA*, *Druffham Slade* 1777 M, *v.* Througham (*supra*), slæd.   TOADSMOOR WOOD, *Toad(s)moor* 1841 *TA*, named from Toadsmoor (127 *infra*).   THE TRENCH, ME *trenche* 'a path cut through a wood, a ditch'.   TRILLIS, *past' voc' Tri-, Trylles* 1540 *MinAcct*, 1542 *AOMB*, 1544 LP, a surname *Trylle, Trill*, cf. Trul's Piece (204 *infra*).

THE VATCH, *Vacchemylle, molend' aq'* 1459 *MinAcct, Vetch croft* 1841 *TA*, a southern variant of ME *fecche* (ONFr *veche*) 'vetch'; here the p.n. originally denoted a mill grinding vetches. VELLATTS, *Waletes-, Valettesplace* 1448, 1459 *MinAcct, Walettes-* 1494 ib, *Vellets* 1841 *TA, v.* fellet 'a clump of stumps, a clearing', but more probably the surname *Vallet*.

THE WARREN, 1841 *TA, v.* wareine. WATERCOMBE HO, *Watercombes* 1609 *AOMB, v.* wæter, cumb. WATER LANE, 1830 M. WEAR FM, *The Whyrr* 1777 M. WHITEHALL BRIDGE, 1830 M.

FIELD-NAMES

The principal forms in (*a*) are 1841 *TA* 25, which also includes some from Chalford (128 *infra*). Spellings dated 1255–90 are *CirenR*, 1448–68 *MinAcct*, 1486, c. 1490 ECP, 1494 *MinAcct*, 1540, 1542 *AOMB*, 1543, 1544 LP, 1546 *FF*, 1598, 1599 *Comm*, 1609 *AOMB* 394, 1628, 1638 InqM, 1633 Inq, 1779 Rudder.

(*a*) Ashey close (*the Ashy close* 1609); Auger stone piece.

Baldwin's grove; Barn close (*the Barneclose* 1609); Barn hill & wood; Beech wood; Berry mead (cf. *Berenbrigge* 1459, *Boroughbrigge* 1494); Bidmeads tyning (*v.* tȳning 'fence'); Bidwell piece (*v.* byden, wella); Birkham tyning (*Byrchecumb* 1248 *Ass, v.* birce, cumb); Bitcomb; Blackwells grove; Broad leaze & mead (*Broadmeade* 1609); Broadway; Bunnage.

Calves leaze; Camp hill; Candlemas croft; Chessells (*v.* ceastel 'heap of stones'); Chesswells (*Chec-, Chacwell* 1255–90); Chestergate piece; Churchway piece (*Chircheweye* 1255–90); Clay pits (*Cleyputte* 1255–90); Broad & long close (cf. *crofti que vocatur le Clos* 1255–90, *v.* clos); Cockshoot(s) (*v.* cocc-sciete); the Combs (*v.* cumb); Counter meadow (*the Counte meade* 1609); Cow leaze (*the Cowleaze* 1609); Cox(land); Cuckolds corner.

the Dane (cf. *Deane meade* 1609, *v.* denu 'valley', cf. Phonol. § 13 and Daneway *supra*); Deer park; Downs; Drought ground (cf. Draught 131 *infra*).

Flagghay (-*meadow* 1638, *v.* flagge 'reed, rush', (ge)hæg); Fox lane; Friars lane (cf. *Freremede* 1459, named from Roger *Frere*).

Garstones (*v.* gærs-tūn 'meadow'); the Green; Greensward.

Hairy hill; Handkerchief ground (a name usually applied to a small plot); Harp acres (so called from its shape); the Hitching (*v.* heccing); Hoar stone (*Harestan'* 1255–90, 'boundary stone', *v.* hār, stān); Honkits 1777 M; Horsepool ground; the Hulks (*v.* hulc 'shed'); Hyde bottom.

the Inacre; the Inake (*le Inhok(e)* 1449, 1494, *Innokes* 1609, *v.* in-hoke).

Key hill; Knights tyning.

Lady mead; the Lagger (dial. *lagger* 'narrow strip'); Ley grove; Longstone; Lot mead (*v.* hlot 'allotment').

the Mead (cf. *Little meade* 1609); Miles field (cf. *Myles wood* 1598); little Mill, Mill mead (cf. *Milstrete* 1459); Mundanes.

New tyning (*v.* tȳning); Night stile; Nip slade (*Nubbesslade* 1255–90, if

-ss- is an error for *-s-* the first el. is possibly OE *hnybba* 'point, peak' as in North Nibley ii, 240 *infra*, *v.* slæd 'valley'); Norcott corner.

Oakley (*v.* āc, lēah); Oaklands (*Ote-*, *Wootelande* 1599, *Otesland* 1609, *v.* āte 'oats', land, cf. Phonol. § 42 *a*).

Park field (cf. *the Parke closes* 1628); the Patch; Pear gate & horn ('gate and nook by the pear-tree', *v.* geat, horn); Picked patch & piece (cf. *the Picket close* 1609 Picked Lease 40 *supra*); Pier hill; Pike piece; Pimperwell; Priests acre & tyning (*Preestes* 1628 *v.* prēost, tȳning).

Rack hill (cf. Rackhill 140 *infra*); the Rails (ME *raile* 'fence'); Redmead (*-meade* 1609); Reids (*terr' voc' Reades* 1609, the surname *Read*); Rodborough wood (*Rowberue* 1255–90, 'rough grove', *v.* rūh, bearu, influenced by the nearby Rodborough 103 *supra*); Roman camp piece; Row leaze (*the Rough leaze* 1609, *v.* rūh, lǣs).

Shermers ground (*Shermans* 1448, *terr' voc' Shermandes* 1694, *Shermans place* 1609, the surname *Sherman*); Shirt mead; Skeveralls orchard (*cot' et terr' voc' Skeverells* 1609); Smokeham (*v.* Smoke Acre 70 *supra*, hamm); Soaphouse ground; Soot house piece; Sour mead; Starwell; Sterts (*v.* steort 'tail of land'); Stevens's (tyning) (*Stony Stevyns* 1546, *v.* stānig, a manorial name from the surname *Stevens*, cf. Stean Bridge *supra*); Stonedge.

Thicketts hill (*claus' voc' Thickets* 1609); Thorn piece & row (cf. *la Thorne* 1255–90, *v.* þorn); Tidmore; Timbercomb ground (*Ti-*, *Tymbercomb(e)* 1448, 1468, 1494, 1609, cf. *Tymberhill* 1448, *v.* timber, cumb, described by Rudder 279 as 'intirely separated from the rest of the world by thick surrounding woods', cf. Timbercombe ii, 98 *infra*); Tump ground; Twizzle stone ('twisting stone', from dial. *twizzle* 'spin, turn'); the Tyning (*v.* tȳning 'fence').

Washpool ground; Webbs ground (cf. *Weblegh* 1448, *v.* webba 'weaver', doubtless as a surname, lēah); Well mead (*-meade* 1609); Wheat leaze; Whitmore (*Wydimor* 1255–90, *v.* wīd 'broad', mōr); Wigley; the Wineyards; Withy bedd.

(*b*) *Andrewescroft* 1494; *Archardesinhechinge, le Inhechyng Petri Achard* 1255–90 (*v.* in, heccing, cf. in-heche); *le Aldcote* 1255–90 (*v.* ald, cot 'cottage'); *Auterescroft* 1448 (ME *au(l)ter* 'altar', *v.* croft).

Bachemylle 1494 (*v.* bece[1] 'stream', myln); *Balsale(mede)* 1448, 1494; *Bannuttree close* 1609 (cf. Bannet Tree 93 *supra*); *Bertramesgroue* 1255–90 (the ME, OG pers.n. *Bertram*, *v.* grāf); *Bigges place* 1628; *Bisly woode* 1599 (*bosc' de Bislegh'* 1221 *Ass*); *Blakemeresegg'* 1255–90 (named from a tenant called *Blake*, *v.* (ge)mǣre 'boundary', ecg); *Bli-*, *Blykerugge, -rigg* 1255–90, (probably an OE pers.n. *Blīca*, connected with OE *blīcan* 'glitter, shine' and the OE *Blicla* suggested for Blickling Nf, *v.* hrycg); *Brad(e)croft(e)* 1459, 1461, 1494 (*v.* brād, croft); *Bullenfrith* 1599, 1609 (the ME surname *Bulein*, *v.* fyrhðe 'wood'); *Buriscombe* 1609; *Burleyfrith(e)* 1461, 1494 (*v.* burh, lēah, fyrhðe); *Bushieleaze* 1609.

Calforth, -ford 1459, 1494 (*v.* calf, ford); *Carlesclose* 1461; *Chalkput* 1255–90 (*v.* cealc, pytt); *le Chapel(l) pece* 1540, 1544 (named from *le Chappell* 1540 *MinAcct*); *le Comynwell* 1494; *Cowmore* 1633; (*spinetum de*) *Crund(e)les* 1255–90, 1315 Pat (*v.* crundel 'quarry'); *Custome woode* 1609.

Dichescomb(e) 1250–90 (*v.* dīc, cumb).

the Eies 1609 (*v.* ēg 'island, water-meadow'); *Elyattys* 1486, *-es* c. 1490 (the surname *Elliot*); *Etwell place* 1609.

Firen howse 1609; *curs' aq' voc' le(z) Fleme* 1459, 1494 (*v.* flēama 'stream'); *lez Flodeyates* 1448 ('the flood-gates'); *Foxhall meade* 1638.

Galshagh 1448 (probably 'gallows enclosure', *v.* galga, haga); *Gigge mill, -y-* 1628, 1633 (e.ModE *gigge-mill* 'a mill for teazling cloth'); *le Grenewey* 1540; *the Groue* 1609.

Hadmeresthorn 1255–90 (the ME, OG pers.n. *Hademar, v.* þorn); *the Hale* 1638 (*v.* halh); *Hallecroft(e)* 1459, 1494 (*v.* hall, croft); *Harlanggesforlongge* 1255–90 (probably the ME, OG pers.n. *Herling*); *Hasell meade* 1628; *Higgen(s)frith* 1599, 1609 (the ME surname *Higgin, v.* fyrhðe); *Hobesweyesheuede* 1255–90 (the ME pers.n. *Hobbe, v.* weg, hēafod).

Inelandesfrith 1609 (*v.* in-land, fyrhðe); *Iscombes.*

Jubeslade 1255–90 (the ME pers.n. *Jubbe* (Reaney 183), *v.* slæd).

Kyngestones 1557 *GR* 445.

Lady(e)smore(s)mille, -mylle 1448, 1494; *Larkeberue* 1255–90 ('lark grove', *v.* lāwerce, bearu); *Lyleberue* 1255–90 (the OE pers.n. *Lil(l)a, v.* bearu).

Mayes-, Meysmed(e) 1459, 1494, *Maismershfrith* 1609 (the ME surname *Mey(s)* (Reaney 218), *v.* mǣd, mersc, fyrhðe); *Marshes* 1609; *Miforde* 1546 (possibly (ge)mȳðe 'confluence', ford); *Mistland* 1609; *the Moore* 1609; *Mossiehill* 1609 ('boggy hill', cf. mos).

Olderygge 1448.

Palemeade 1609; *Peyntours-, Peynter(s)-, Paintersfrith* 1448, 1468, 1494, 1599 (the surname *Painter, v.* fyrhðe); *le Pynyon* 1540; *the Pooleys* 1609; *Portweye* 1255–90 ('town road', *v.* port², weg); *Posthernehete* 1609 ('postern gate').

the Ridge 1609; *Rollescroft* 1628 (the surname *Roll(es), v.* croft); *Roweforlong'* 1255–90, *-mede* 1459, *Roughmede* 1494, *Rowmeadowe* 1633 (*v.* rūh, mǣd); *(le) Rudg(e)hull, -hill* 1540, 1542, 1544 (*v.* hrycg, hyll).

Seyntmarybrigge 1494 (probably named from St Mary's Chapel in Chalford); *Sheppelese* 1609 (*v.* scēap, lǣs); *Shortecombesgeate, Sortecumb* 1255–90 ('short valley', *v.* sceort, cumb, geat 'gate'); *Sinderhill* 1633 (*v.* sinder, hyll); *Smithes hill* 1609, *Smythstead* 1625 (*the Berwe Rogeri Fabri* 1255–90, *v.* smið, bearu, stede); *Stalland* 1448 (*v.* stall, land); *la Stanbench* 1255–90 ('the stone bench'); *Stapelweye* 1255–90 (*v.* stapol, weg); *Stenen(e)gate, -yate* 1255–90 ('stone gate', *v.* stǣnen, geat); *Stonie hall* 1609; *Stonehyll* 1494; *le Strete* 1448, 1494 (*v.* strǣt); *Stubbyng* 1459, 1494 (*v.* stubbing 'clearing').

Uppingland 1628.

Walkebruge 1448, *-brigge* 1494 (*v.* walc 'cloth-dressing', brycg); *Walkeleyswode* 1494 (*v.* prec., lēah); *Warinesinheching* 1255–90 (the ME surname *Waren, v.* in, heccing); *aq' voc' Water Tye* 1546 (cf. Devon, Cornwall dial. *tye* 'a trench from which peat is dug, a pit, a drain', probably from OE *wætertige* 'canal'); *Weycumbmed* 1255–90 (*v.* weg, cumb, mǣd); *Wellebrigge* 1494; *Westfeld* 1609; *Westrode* 1543 (*v.* west, rōd 'rood'); *Wymbres(h)egg(e)* 1255–90 (probably the OE pers.n. *Winebeorht, v.* ecg); *le Wodecourte* 1494; *Wolriche, -ryche* 1448, 1459.

Chalford

CHALFORD (156–9002)

Chalford(e) c. 1250 Berk (p), 1300 Episc, 1327 *SR*, 1347 *Rent et passim* to 1598 *Comm*
Chelkeford l. 13 BG li
Chalkford l. 13 BG li, 14 ECP   *Chaleford* Ric 2 *Rent* (p)
Chawlforde 1589 *Dep*   *Chawford* 1634 *FF*, 1643 BM

'Chalk or limestone ford', *v.* **cealc, ford**, and cf. Chalford (O 102, 348) for similar names. Chalford is on the Oolite beds.

ABNASH FM, AVENIS GREEN

Abbenesse 1243 HMC v, 336 (p), 1544 LP, -*asse* 1540 *MinAcct*, -*ash* 1609 *AOMB* 394
Habenasse 1270 GlR   *Vynnysse* 1442 BG li
Abenasse 1573, 1586 *FF*
Abnes 1576 *MonLand* 4, -*nash(e)* 1622 *FF*
Avenes 1604, 1622 *FF*, -*ishe* 1609 Will, -*iss* 1764 ib

'Abba's ashtree', from the OE pers.n. *Abba* and æsc. The change of *Ab-* to *Av-* is late and unusual, but occurs occasionally in dial. (cf. EDGr § 276, Phonol. § 31).

BUSSAGE, *Bis-, Bysrugg(e)* 1287 *FF*, 1287, 1320 *Ass*, l. 13 BG li, -*ruge* 1327 SR (p), *Boseryge* 1448 *MinAcct*, -*rigge* 1459 ib, *Busheridge* 1609 *AOMB* 394, *Busage* 1777 M. 'Bisa's ridge', *v.* **hrycg**. The pers.n. is the OE *Bisa* found in Bisley (117 *supra*), 2 miles north-east, and it may well be that the same man gave his name to these places.

RACK HILL, *the Rackhill* 1609 *AOMB* 394, the f.ns. Rackhill (140 *infra*) and Rack ground (ii, 243 *infra*) show that we have ME *rakke* 'rack' used of a tenter-frame.

TOADSMOOR, *Tudde(s)mere* 1250–90 *CirenR*, *Todgmore or Todesmore-bottom* 1779 Rudder 290. The first el. is probably an OE *Tudd*, a strong form of the recorded *Tud(d)a* (Redin 71). *v.* **mere** 'pool'.

ASHMEADS MILL, *Essemed'* 1255–90 *CirenR*, *Ashmeads* 1841 *TA*, *v.* **æsc, mæd**. BLACKNESS. BROWN'S HILL, 1830 M, *Browneshill* 1609 *AOMB* 394, from the surname *Brown*. CHALFORD LYNCH, 1830 M, *the Linches* 1779 Rudder, *v.* **hlinc** 'ridge, bank'. CORDERRIES.

DIMMEL'S DALE, *Dimmelds dale* 1841 *TA*, possibly an adaptation or transference of such p.ns. as Dimin Dale (Db 169), Dimsdale (St) or *Dimingdale* (YW vi, 108), which may be from an OE *dimmung* 'darkness' and *dæl* 'valley', 'valley of darkness'.   FIRWOOD HO.
FRANCE LYNCH, 1779 Will, cf. *France ground* 1841 *TA*, the surname *France(s)*, *v.* hlinc 'ridge'.   FRITH WOOD, *Frythlond* l. 13 BG li, *Freth hous* 1361 ib, *The Frith* 1830 M, *v.* fyrhðe 'wood'.   MARLE HILL.   OLDHILLS WOOD, *Old(e)hill(es)* 1609 *AOMB*, *v.* ald, hyll.
OLD NEIGHBOURING.   RIDINGS FM, *Ridings* 1841 *TA*, *v.* rydding 'clearing'.   SKAITESHILL HO, *Skates Hill* 1824 M.

FIELD-NAMES

The principal forms in (*a*) are 1841 *TA* 25, and in (*b*) 1609 *AOMB* 394, but others may be included in those of Bisley (124 *supra*).

(*a*) the Bottom (*Chalford-bottom* 1779 Rudder); Boultons Mead (*Bultyngis* 1540 *MinAcct*, *Bou-*, *Bowltings* 1544 LP, 1609, doubtless a surname *Bolting*); Fulcomb mead (*Fulcombe* 1609, 'dirty valley', *v.* fūl, cumb); the Hams (*the Holmes* 1609, *v.* hamm); Hopyard (*le Hoppyarde* 1609); the Leys (*the Lies* 1609, *v.* lēah); Maplethorn (ib 1609, probably an adaptation of OE mapuldor 'maple-tree'); Mowley (*Morley* 1609, *v.* mōr, lēah); Wheat close (*Wheatclose* 1609, 1628 InqM).

(*b*) *Bakers hill*; *Blankets mill*; *Brissell hill*; 'wood called *Chalfordes*' 1465 Pat; *Copes, Great-, litle Coops*; *Fernecroft*; *claus' voc' Maines*; *Mill meade*; *Pathcombe* 1361 BG li (*v.* pæð, cumb); *Rudyborne* 13 ib (*v.* hrēodig 'reedy', burna); *le Sowe-, le Stonyrudyng(g)e* 1395 ib (*v.* sugu 'sow', stānig, rydding); *Westleye* 13 ib (*v.* west, lēah).

Edgeworth

EDGEWORTH (157–9405)

Egesworde, Egeiswurde 1086 DB, *Egesw(u)rth(e)* 1222–8 *Hopt* 21 (p), 1225–9 GlR (p), 1248 *Ass*, 1270 Pat (p), 1285 FA

Egewurð, -w(u)rth 1138 AC, 1221 *Ass* (p), 1236 Fees, *-worth* 1232 Cl (p), 1535 VE

Eggew(u)rth(e), -worth(e) 1220 Fees, c. 1230 *GlCh* (p), 1236 Fees, c. 1238 Berk (p), 1248 *Ass et passim* to 1509 *FF*

Eggelewrde (for *Eggese-*) 1221 *Ass* (p)

Eggesw(u)rth, -worth(e) c. 1230 GlR, 1241 Berk (p), 1271, 1284 Episc *et passim* to 1427 *FF*

Egeswurthin 1255 Cl

Edg(e)worth 1539 FF, (*-als. Egworth als. Eggisworth*) 1602 ib

The village is on one of the steep slopes of the upper Frome valley and the first el. of the name could be OE ecg 'edge' (in the gen.sg. *ecges*). But we may have to derive this name from the OE pers.n. *Ecgi*, which is perhaps to be preferred because of the genitival form and because OE *worð* is most often combined with personal names. 'Ecgi's enclosure', *v*. worð. It has clearly been associated with *ecg*, as it has in Edge Hill (*infra*). The single spelling with -*wurthin* (*v*. worðign) is one of the most southerly instances of the WMidl word (cf. Introd.).

ASHCOMBE. BRIERY BANK. THE CLOSES, *lower, upper Close* 1839 *TA*. COURSE COPSE, -*coppice* 1839 *TA*. EASTHILL WOOD, *East hill* 1839 *TA*. EDGE HILL, *Edgeworth hill* 1839 *TA*. EIGHT ACRE PLANT., *Eight acres* 1839 *TA*. FEWSTERS GROVE, *Fosters Wood* 1839 *TA*. FOUR ACRES, 1839 *TA*. FOX WOOD, 1839 *TA*. GLOUCESTER BEECHES, cf. *Gloucester Thorns* 1839 *TA*. GREEN RIDGE, -*rudge* 1839 *TA*. HORSE PASTURES, 1839 *TA*. JACK ACRE, 1839 *TA*. KITCROFT GROVE, *Kit croft* 1839 *TA*. MONSELL WOOD, cf. *Monkills* 1777 M, *Mansels hill* 1839 *TA*. RESTING HILL. RUSCOMBE PLANT., -*piece* 1839 *TA*. SLUT WOOD. TUMP BELT, -*field* 1839 *TA*. WESTWOOD HO, *Westwod(e)*, -*wodd* 1291 Tax, 1327 *SR* (p), 1540 *MinAcct*, *v*. west, wudu.

FIELD-NAMES

The principal forms in (*a*) are 1839 *TA* 78.

(*a*) Broad mead; Capes hill; Chill mead; Dane hill; Hanging hill (*v*. hangende 'steep'); Hascomb; Hudgmoor hill; Innock (*v*. in-hoke); Laggett; Lords lains (*v*. leyne); Ox slade (*v*. oxa, slæd); Tumbrells land (*terr' voc' Tymbrells* 1542 *MinAcct*); White cross.

(*b*) *Chysewelle* 1327 *SR* (p) (*v*. cis 'gravel', wella); *Netherley* 1465 Pat; *Oxecroft* 14 AD i.

Miserden

MISERDEN (157–9309) [ˈmizədin]

Musardera 1186, 1190 P, (*la*) *Musarder'* 1211–13, 1220 Fees, 1255–9 *CirenR*, 1272 Ipm *et freq* to 1351 AD ii, (-*als. Misarden*) 1614 FF, (*la, le*) *Musardere* 1248 *Ass*, 1269 Episc, 1272 Fine, 1287 *Ass et passim* to 1461 Pat, (-*als. Grenehamstede*) 1297 AD i, *la Musardyre*, -*ire* 1264 Ipm, 1285 FA

9

La Musarde' 1233 Cl   *La Musardye* 1248 *Ass*
(*la*) *Mussarder*(*e*) 1291 Tax, 1415 *FF*, 1492 Pat
Musardrie 1322 Cl
Mi-, Myserder(*e*) 1535 VE, 1546 BM, (*-als. Myserdeane*) 1592 FF
Musarden(*e*), *-erd-* 1291 Tax, 1378 Works *et freq* to 1628 GlCorp
Mussarden 1447, 1449 *MinAcct, Muzarden* 1672 PR 16
Mesirden 1480 Pat
My-, Miserden 1488 Pat, 1567 *FF*, 1610 M, *Mysterdeane* 1602
AOMB 411, *Mizerdine* 1702 PR 7

The manor of *Greenhampstead* (*infra*) was held in 1086 by Hascoit
Musard and continued to be held by the *Musard* family till the 14th
century (cf. 1211–13 Fees i, 50, 1269 Episc, 1272–88 Ipm, 1285 FA,
1310 *FF* 22, etc.); on this name (from OFr *musard* 'stupid') cf.
Tengvik 352. *Musardere, -drie* is a p.n. formed from this OFr surname with the addition of the OFr p.n. suffixes -(*i*)*ere, -erie* (from
Lat *-aria*), of which Vincent § 701 gives many examples formed from
such family names. The later form of the name with *-den* (*v.* **denu**
'valley') is an adaptation to a common English p.n. type, no doubt
because the place is in the deep upper valley of the R. Frome. On
the change of *Mus-* [mys] to *Mis-* cf. Phonol. § 30.

BIDFIELD

Budevilla 1191 P, *Budefeld*(*e*) 1220 Fees, 1247, 1287 *Ass*, 1287 *FF*,
1303 FA *et freq* to 1476 Pat, *Budfeld* 1509 *MinAcct, Buddefeld
als. Bidfield* 1595 *FF*
Bidefeld 1248, 1287 *Ass*, Bid-, *Bydfe*(*i*)*ld* 1501 Pat, 1556 *FF*, 1576
MonLand
Bedyfeld 1377–99 Works, *Bedefeld* 1378 *Ass*

'Byda's piece of open countryside', from the OE pers.n. *Byda* and
feld.

GREENHAMPSTEAD (lost), *Gren*(*e*)*hã-, -hamstede* 1086 DB, 12 *Tewk* 75,
1221 *Ass*, 1297 AD i, 1310 FF, ('by some called *La Musardere*') 1301
AD i, *Grenhamstude* 1165–77 France (p). 'The green homestead',
v. **grēne**[1], **hām-stede, -styde**. This was the original English name of
the manor which became Miserden (*supra*).

SUDGROVE

Sodgraue 1248 *Ass*   *Suthgrave* 1307 AD i
Sudgraue 1494 *MinAcct*, -*grove* 1620, 1622 *FF*
Suttgrove 1611 *FF*

'The south wood', *v.* sūð, grāf; it lies in the south of the parish. A similar name is Sutgrove (ii, 141 *infra*).

WISHANGER

> *Wis-, Wychang(e)re, -er* 1221 *Ass*, 1318 Ch, 1322 Cl *et freq* to 1622
> *FF, Wysehanger* 1287 *Ass, Wishunger* 1327 *SR*
> *Wis-, Wysangr(e), -er* 1221 *Ass*, 1287 FF, 1387 Works, 1567 *FF,*
> *Wysongr'* 1377–99 Works, *Wyssangr'* 1507 *Rent* 831
> *Whyshangre* 1287 *Ass, Whissanger* 1535 VE, *Wysshehanger* 1556 *FF*

'Wooded hill-side near a wet meadow', *v.* wisc, wisse, hangra. The first el. is not certain, but its spellings are similar to those of Wisley (Sr 155); OE *wisse* itself occurs in Westley (153 *infra*) and is the more likely here. It refers to a farm by the stream called Holy Brook. On the form *-hunger* cf. Phonol. § 5.

BARN WOOD, 1830 M. THE CAMP, 1779 Rudder, *-field* 1838 *TA*, lying north of two long barrows. CASTLE MOUND, *-hill* 1779 Rudder, the remains of a castle mound and moat. CONIGAR, *v.* coninger 'warren'. DILLAY, *the Tilley* 1838 *TA*. DOWN FM & HILL, 1830 M, *v.* dūn 'down, hill'. DRAUGHT, 1830 M, from ME *draht* 'draught' in one of its later senses such as 'a bowshot', 'a stream course', 'a cesspool' or the like (cf. NED s.v.). FAMISH HILL. FISHCOMBE BANK. FOSTON'S ASH GROVE, *Forsters Ash* 1830 M. FRANCOMBE, named from the R. Frome (1), *v.* cumb 'valley', cf. Francombe (73 *supra*). GOLDWELL WOOD, *-field* 1838 *TA*, *v.* golde 'marigold', wella. HAZLE HO, *Haselhowse* 1595, 1602 FF, cf. *atte Hasele* 1327 *SR* (p), *v.* hæsel 'hazel-tree'. HENLEY, 1838 *TA*, *-leye* 1248 *Ass* (p), 'high clearing', *v.* hēah, lēah. HIGH WOOD, 1830 M. HONEYCOMBE FM, 1779 Rudder. LAMPHILL WOOD, 1838 *TA*, cf. *Lampe meade* 1668 *GR* (D. 892), doubtless denoting land the rent of which maintained a lamp in the church. LYPIATT, *Lyppiat* 1838 *TA*, formerly *Miserden Gate* 1830 M, cf. Lypiatt (119 *supra*). MISERDEN PARK, 1830 M. NEW SEAL WOOD, 1838 *TA*. PARSON'S HILL, 1838 *TA*. SNOW'S FM. STEANBRIDGE FM, *v.* Stean Bridge (119 *supra*). VENDRES, 1830 M, from the surname *Vender* (Reaney 335). WHITEWAY, cf. Saltway (20 *supra*).

FIELD-NAMES

The principal forms in (*a*) are 1838 *TA* 134. Spellings dated 1448–1494 are *MinAcct*, 1507 *Rent* 83, 1879 (f.ns. from C. T. Davis).

   (*a*) Arling grove; Ban-, Benley (*v.* bēan, lēah); Barrow field; Bushy Beech;

Church hill; Clay piece 1879; Clements Barrow; Deerpark; the Green; Hay Bank 1879; Horsecombs; Innock (*v.* in-hoke); Knapp ground (*v.* cnæpp hill'); Lagger (dial. *lagger* 'narrow strip'); Langet (*v.* langet); the Laynes (*v.* leyne); Littleworth; the Lyes; Mill hill & leaze (cf. *Millecroft* 1459); Nim Slad 1879; Nitcomb; Norcott; Northfield 1879; Oatle corner; Penniverland 1879; Pit acre; Ragwell (*v.* ragge 'moss'); Sharlcomb; Slad (1779 Rudder, *v.* slæd); Tining (*v.* tȳning); Wash pool ground.

(*b*) *Depcombe* 1448 ('deep valley'); *atte Fortheye* 1327 *SR* (p), *Fortheys* 1507 (*v.* forð, ēg); *Jamesplace* 1459; *Scalendurscrofte* 1459; *Smabryche* 1448, *breche* 1459, *Smabridge* als. *Smalerugg* 1623 *FF* ('narrow piece of broken-up and', *v.* smæl, brēc); *le Waterhacche* 1494 ('water gate', *v.* wæter, hæcc); *Wrythe-*, *Wrethele* 1448, 1449 (*v.* wrīð 'bush', lēah).

Painswick

PAINSWICK (156–8609)

> *Wiche* 1086 DB, *Wik(a)*, *Wyk(e)* 13 AD iii, ClR *et freq* to 1255 Cl, *Wicha* 1211–13 Fees, *Wyca*, *Wycke* 1220 ib
> *Painswik(e)*, *-wyk(e)*, *-wick(e)* 1237 *FF*, 1276 RH, 1287 *Ass*, 1291 Tax *et passim* to 1602 PR 7, *-weke* c. 1560 *Surv*
> *Payndeswike* 1285 FA   *Payngwyk'* 1306 *Ass*
> *Peyneswick*, *-wick* 1302 BM, 1331 Ipm
> *Paneswyk(e)* 1494 *FF*, 1508 Pat
> *Pens(e)wyke* 1527 *FF*, 1550 Pat   *Painsik* 1708 PR 10

v. wīc 'dairy-farm'. The first el. is the name of *Pain* Fitzjohn, lord of the manor, who died in 1137; cf. also Paganhill (139 *infra*).

CLISSOLD FM

> *Cliues-*, *Clyueshale* 1241, 1318 *FF*, 1255–90 *CirenR*, *Clyveshale* 1327 *SR* (p)
> *Clyfsale* 1255–90 *CirenR*, *Clyffeshale* 1448 *FF*, *Clyffsall* 1507 *Rent* 831, *Clifsale* 1540 *MinAcct*, *Cliffissale* 1544 LP
> *Clyssale* 1477 Pat, *-ole* 1549 *FF*, *-all* 1556 *FF*

'Nook of land on the steep bank', *v.* clif (gen.sg. *clifes*), halh.

DUTCHCOMBE, *Dud(d)escombe*, *-cumbe* 1400 Rudder 594, 1543 *MinAcct*, c. 1560 *Surv*, *Duds-*, *Dutchcomb* 1839 *TA*. 'Dud(d)'s valley', from the OE pers.n. *Dud(d)* and cumb. For the assimilation to *Dutch-* cf. Phonol. § 44 (*b*).

EBWORTH HO, *Ebbesworth* e. 13, c. 1270 BG li, *Ebbew(o)rth* 1291 Tax, 1327 *SR* (p), *Ebworth* 1354 Ch. 'Ebba's enclosure', *v.* worð. The pers.n. is OE *Ebba* or its strong form *Ebbi*.

EDGE, EDGEHILL FM, (*la*) *Egge* 1300 Ipm, 1324 *FF*, (*-in Payneswyk*) 1360 Ipm, *Vnderrege* Hy 8 *Rent*, *Edge* 1539, 1593 *FF*, (*-als. Rudge*) 1779 Rudder 595, *Rugge* 1328 Banco, *Rudghill* 1544 LP. *v.* ecg 'escarpment'. The secondary form *Rudge*, is doubtless due to a wrong analysis of such expressions as 'under edge', and association with hrycg 'ridge' (cf. Phonol. § 45).

HOLCOMBE FM, *Hollecumbe* (v.l. *Hole-*) 1166 RBE (p), *Holecumb(e)* Hy 3 Ipm (p), 1221 Eyre (p), *Howcombe* 1638 Will, 1795 *M*. 'Hollow valley', *v.* hol², cumb.

KIMSBURY

> *Kynemaresburia*, *-bury* 12, 13, 1263–84 Glouc, 1303, 1314 Pat
> *Kynnaresbur'*, *Kymmasbir'* 1287 *Ass* (p)
> *Kynemesbury* 1529 GlR   *Kimsbery-Castle* 1779 Rudder 592

'Cynemǣr's fortification', *v.* burh. The OE pers.n. *Cynemǣr* occurs also in Kempsford (38 *supra*). The name refers to an ancient encampment on the highest point in the district. Cf. also Castle Godwyn (*infra*).

SHEEPSCOMBE [ˈʃepskəm], *Sepescumb'* 1248 *Ass*, *Sebbescumbe* 1262 Ipm, *Shep(e)scombe* 1276 *FF*, 1396 *Ass et freq* to 1740 GR 849, *-is-* 1446 Pat, 1535 VE, *Sheppiscombe* 1592 FF. 'Sheep's valley', *v.* scēap, cumb.

SPOONBED, SPOONBED HILL, *Sponbedde* 1327 *SR* (p), *Sponebed* 1400 Rudder 594, 1540 LP, 1585 *GR* 445, 1592 FF, *Spoonebedd* 1636 ib, *the great hill Sponebed* 1779 Rudder 592. *v.* spōn, bedd; OE *spōn* was used in the sense 'chip, shaving' and in ME it also came to be used (like ON *spánn*) of a roofing shingle. In p.ns. like Spoonbed or Spoonley (ii, 27 *infra*) it no doubt refers to the chips or shavings made in the felling and preparation of timber, and Spoonbed itself would denote 'a bed or pile of such chippings'. Since OE *bedd* is used in p.ns. chiefly to denote 'a bed of growing plants', *spoon* in this p.n. is possibly figurative with some meaning which we cannot determine.

TOCKNELLS HO & COURT, *atte Tochale* 1327 *SR* (p), *Tokynhale* 1368 Ipm, 1439 Ipm, *Tucknall* 1593 FF, *Tocknells* 1707 Will, *Totnalls* 1777 M. 'Toca's nook of land', *v.* halh. An OE pers.n. *Toc(c)a* is not independently recorded, but can be assumed from such p.ns. as Tockenham (W272), Tockington or Tutnalls (iii, 121, 260 *infra*). Tock-

nell Ho and Court may be directly derived from a surname from the
older p.n.; a family of *Tocknell* lived in Painswick in the 17th century
(cf. Grace and Alice *Tocknell* 1600 PR 8, p. 13, Walter *Tocknell* 1609
ib, p. 16).

BACK EDGE, 1830 M.   BAYLIS MILL, *Baylis's Mill* 1830 M, cf.
Bayleys mead 1839 *TA*, named from the local family of *Baylye, Bailey*
or *Baylis* (1582, 1701, 1793 PR 8, pp. 8, 34, 76, etc.).   BEECH FM,
cf. *Beech close* 1839 *TA*.   BLAKEWELL, 1839 TA.   BROOK HO, 1830
M.   BROOKLANDS, 1795 *M*.   BROWN'S GATE & HILL, *Bromeshill*
1540 *MinAcct, Brown hill* 1785 Will, named from the family of
Browne (1569, 1573, 1581 PR 8, pp. 5, 6, 8).   BUDDING GROVE, *-ings-*
1839 *TA*, from the surname *Budding*.   BULL CROSS, 1830 M.
BUNNAGE, *-field* 1839 *TA, Bunadge* 1598 *FF*, from the OE pers.n.
Buna, v. ecg.   BUTLER'S GROVE, 1839 *TA*, named from the family
of Thomas *Butler* 1757 PR 8, 53.
    CAP MILL, 1830 M.   CASTLE GODWYN, 1779 Rudder, cf. *atte
Castle* 1327 *SR* (p), *v.* castel, here an ancient encampment, *v.* Kimsbury (*supra*).   CASTLE HALE, 1839 *TA, v.* prec., halh 'nook'.
CATSBRAIN TUMP, *v.* cattes-braȝen.   CLATTERGROVE, 1830 M, *v.*
clater 'heap of stones'.   COCKSHOOT, 1839 *TA, Cockshoute launde*
1400 Rudder, *v.* cocc-scīete 'glade where woodcock were netted'.
COMB HO, *Cumbe* 1287 *Ass* (p), *in the Combe* 1327 *SR* (p), *Comehouse*
1576 *MonLand* 27, *Combehowse* 1639 Inq, *v.* cumb 'valley'.   COX'S
MILL, 1830 M, named from the family of Obadia *Cox*, Thomas *Cox*,
etc. (1656, 1739 PR 8, pp. 23, 45).   CUD WELL.   THE CULLS,
Culls farm 1839 *TA*.
    DAMSELLS, *Damsel(l)s* 1400 Rudder, 1694 PR 8, p. 33, *Damysel-
lond(es)* 1419, 1454 IpmR, from the surname *Damsell* (Reaney 88),
as in Peter *Damysel* (13 BG vii).   DAY HILL, 1830 M, *Days ground*
1839 M, from the surname *Day*.   DELL FM, *Dell field* 1631 Inq,
Dell (house) 1839 *TA, v.* dell 'pit, dell', possibly as a surname.
DETCOMBE, 1839 *TA*.   DOREYS, *Daurers Mill, Doories* 1879 (Davis).
    EASTCOT, 1830 M, *Estcote* 1327 *SR* (p), *v.* ēast, cot.   ELDER HILL,
1839 *TA*.
    THE FOLLY, 1839 *TA, v.* folie.   THE FRITH, *Frith wood* 1839 *TA*,
v. fyrhðe 'wood'.
    GOODHURST GROVE, *Goodhouse grove* 1839 *TA*.   THE GRANGE,
-barn 1839 *TA*.   GRAVEL HILL, *Gravel pit field* 1839 *TA*.   GREEN-
HOUSE COURT, *-lane* 1839 *TA*.   THE GROVE, *la Graue* 1248 *Ass* (p),

v. grāf. GYDE'S FM, *Gydes* 1839 *TA*, named from the local family of *Gyde* (1607, 1676, 1704 PR 8, pp. 15, 28, 35, etc.).

HALEBOURNE, *the hale ground* 1694 *M*, *Hale* 1839 *TA*, *v.* halh 'nook', burna 'stream'. HAM BUTTS, *-buts* 1694 *M*, *v.* hamm, butte. HAMFIELD, 1839 *TA*, *v.* prec. HAMMONDS FM, 1830 M, named from the family of Elionor or John *Ham(m)ond(s)* 1665, 1679 PR 8, pp. 26, 29. HEART WOOD. HIGH CROFT, 1839 *TA*. HIGH FOLD, 1839 *TA*. HIGHGROVE, 1400 Rudder. HILL FM, 1830 M. HOLY WELL. THE HORSE POOLS, 1715 Will, *-pool* 1777 M. HUDDINKNOLL HILL, 1830 M, *Huddinalls Hill* (sic) 1400 Rudder, probably from the OE pers.n. *Hud(d)a*, *v.* cnoll 'hillock'.

JACKS GREEN, 1830 M, named from the local family of *Jaques* (1567–1666 PR 8, pp. 5, 9, 26) or *Jeacks* (1725 ib 41). JENKINS FM, 1830 M.

KING'S MILL HO, cf. *King's Piece* 1795 *M*, *Kings* (*leaze*) 1839 *TA*, from the surname *King*. KNAPP BANK, *the Knaps* 1694 *M*, *v.* cnæpp 'hill-top'. LADY'S WOOD. LILLYHORN, 1839 *TA*.

LONGRIDGE FM, *on Longanhrycge* 896 (16th) EHD xiv, *Longridge* 1400 Rudder, (*-howse*) 1627 Inq, *Lonckridge* 1636 ib, *v.* lang, hrycg. LORD'S WOOD, *-mead* 1839 *TA*. LOVEDAY'S MILL, 1830 M, named from the local family of *Loveday* (1584–1672 PR 8, 8–27). LULLINGWORTH, 1739 *TA*, cf. *Lully wells* 1694 *M*. LYNCOMBE, *Lincombs* 1839 *TA*.

MASON'S MILL, 1830 M, named from the family of Richard or William *Mason* (1562, 1569 PR 8, 4–5). MOORLANDS, cf. *the Moors* 1839 *TA*.

OLIVERS, 1830 M, from the local family of Thomas or Margaret *Olyver* (1574, 1585 PR 8, 6–9).

PACKHURST. PAINSWICK HILL (1795 *M*), Ho (1830 M), LODGE (1740 *GR* 849), MILL (*Mill close* 1694 *M*) & SLAD (1839 *TA*). PARADISE, 1779 Rudder ('a handsome seat'), *Paradys* 1327 *SR* (p), a usual name for a pleasant house or place. THE PARK, *the parke* 1400 Rudder. PAULIN'S MILL, 1830 M, named from the family of John *Pawlinge*, Edward *Pawlin*, William *Pauling*, etc. (1579, 1678, 1700 PR 8, pp. 7, 28, 34). PILL HO, *Pilhowse* 1654 PR 8, 21, probably from the surname *Pill* (Reaney 252). PINCOT HO, *Pinketts* 1839 *TA*. PODGEWELL, *Podgell* 1839 *TA*. POULTRY COURT.

QUARRY BARNS, *Qwarre pyttes* 1507 Rent, *Quarr head* 1839 *TA*, *v.* quarriere.

SALTBOX, dial. *salt-box* 'a lean-to shed'. SEAGRIMS, *Zeagrims* 1839

TA, possibly from the family name of Samuel *Segrey* (1655 PR 8, 22) or the ME pers.n. *Segrim*. SHEEPHOUSE, *le Schipehowsemedd* 16 *Rent*, *Shepehowse* 1593 ib, *v.* scēap, hūs. SKINNER'S MILL FM, named from the family of William *Skinner* (1747 PR 8, 48). THE SKIPPETS, *Skippet ground* 1839 *TA*. SLAD, *the Slad* 1779 Rudder, *v.* slæd. STROUD END, *Strode als. Strode End* 1539 *FF*, *Strowde ende* 1592, 1642 FF, 'the end of the manor towards Stroud (139 *infra*)'.

TICKLESTONE, 1839 *TA*, 'unstable stone', from ME *tikil* 'unstable, easily upset, balancing', *v.* stān. TRILLGATE FM, 1830 M, *Thrill Gate* 1824 M, probably from þyrel 'hole, gap', and geat. THE TUMP. TWYNING'S GROVE, *Twinnings* 1839 *TA*, named from the local family of *Twynynge*, *Twining* (1548–1750 PR 8, pp. 2, 3, 25, 40, etc.).

VERLANDS. VINER'S WOOD, named from the family of William or Mary *Viner* (1654, 1804 PR 8, pp. 20, 85).

WASH BROOK, *le Washebrooke* 1647 *FF*, *v.* wæsc, brōc. WELL FM, 1839 *TA*, named from *ye Well* 1654 PR 8, 20, *Well leaze* 1795 *M*, *v.* wella. WICKRIDGE HILL (*Wykeryge* 1540 *FF*), WICK STREET (*Wickstreete* 1611 *FF*), named from the older form of Painswick, *v.* hrycg, strǣt (the road from Painswick to Stroud below Wickridge Hill). WITHYBED FM, *Withy bed* 1839 *TA*. WOODSIDE, cf. *attewode* 1327 *SR* (p), *v.* atte, wudu. WORGAN'S WOOD, *Worgans* 1839 *TA*, named from the local family of *Organ* (1563, 1667, 1758 PR 8, pp. 2, 26, 53).

FIELD-NAMES

The principal forms in (*a*) are 1839 *TA* 153. Spellings dated 1291 are Tax, 1400 Rudder 594 n, c. 1500 *GR* (D. 849), 1507 *Rent* 831, 1543 *MinAcct*, c. 1560 *Surv*, 1590 *GR* (D. 547), 1631 Inq, 1695 *M*, 1740 *GR* (D. 849), 1762 ib (D. 185), 1779 Rudder, 1795 *M*, 1879 (*ex inf.* C. T. Davis).

(*a*) Aldrick; Badger grove; Bar croft (*v.* bere 'barley'); Bar(n)pins; Batch Field 1879 (*v.* bece[1] 'stream'); Batcomb; Ben hill & Stiles; Blackmoor; the Bladders; Bow croft; Briar lands; Brimps; Broad Ham (-*home* 1694, *v.* hamm); Broad Riddings (*v.* rydding); Clay pit close; Colwell close; Coneygre (*v.* coninger 'warren'); Cow leaze; Crow wells; Cuckoo pen (ib 1795, *v.* Cuckoo Pen 43 *supra*); Cuff Horn; Culverwell (*v.* culfre 'dove'); Curdwick; Cut croft; Dead mead 1740; Dear Lips ('deer leap', *v.* dēor, hlēp); Dodsgrove; Doveholes 1879; Dry leaze; Durndale field 1879; Edgemundstone (the OE pers.n. *Ecgmund*, stān); Fishpond ground 1879 (ib 1795); Foxpenhale; Gallows-lands 1779; Golden acre; Half moon (so called from its shape); Hangman's Acre 1779; Hawkwell (*Hawkell* 1795, *v.* hafoc, wella); Hay Knaps; Hazle End & house; Hazlelonger mead (*the Haselingermead* 1740, 'hazel wood', *v.* hæsel, hangra); Helbridge; the Lagger (dial. *lagger* 'narrow strip'); Landsmoor; Langhett (v. langet); Longford; the Lots (v. hlot); Mill mead & pond (Millmead, -eight 1740, v. myln, mǣd, ēgeð 'island, ait'); Moreswood 1631; Nash; Osley; Owls nest; Packurst field 1879; Paddock (ib 1740 Probyn 27); the Pen; Penny croft (v. pening); Pig hay; Rack hill (ib 1762, v. Rack Hill 127 supra); the Redding (v. rydding); Rixmores (v. risc, mōr); Rounham (v. rūh, hamm); Santer(s) Ridding; Scanty (ib 1795); Shadwell ('shady well', v. sceadu, wella); Shear Riddings (v. scearu 'share, boundary', rydding); Shedding tree; Splash meadow; the Stirts (v. steort 'tail of land'); Sytches (v. sīc 'stream'); Thicket wood; Tinding (v. tēonde 'tenth, tithing'); Tithingmans acre; Trunch hill; Tyning (v. tӯning); Whindle; Whitcomb; Winmead; Wolley.

(b) Arnegrove 1400 (v. earn 'eagle'); Brasse hill 1631; Bushie launde 1400 (v. launde 'glade'); Crochen, Crocheland 1400; the Culverhouse-hill 'with a culverhouse decayed' 1400 (v. culfre 'dove'); Frerenclose 1507 (v. frere 'friar'); Hawking hill 1400; la Hide 1291 (v. hīd 'hide of land'); Lady Lande vel St Marie Land 1575 Comm (belonging to the Chapel of St Mary in Painswick); Mundies ground 1400, Mundays landes c. 1500 (cf. Sundayshill iii, 108 infra); Nettlebeds 1400 (v. netele, bedd); le Node 1543, c. 1560 (v. atten, ād 'ash heap'); le Smythes close 1507; Steanbridge slade 1590 (v. Stean Bridge 119 supra, slæd); Swayneford 1400; 'landes called the thretten', Threttenes farendelles c. 1500 ('the thirteen (quarters)', v. fēorða, dæl); Westwell c. 1560, Westwelles hame 1543; Whitelond 1694; Wodameslese 1372 Inq (v. wudu, hamm, lǣs); Wykefrod 1291 (cf. Wick Street supra, ford).

Sapperton

SAPPERTON (157–9503)

Sapertun(e) c. 1075 (1367) Monast, -ton' 1211–13 Fees, 1216 ClR, 1221 Ass, 1236 Fees et passim to 1602 FF

Sapletorne 1086 DB   Cappartona 1220 Fees

Saberton 1248 Ass, 1305 FF

Seperton 1285 FA, 1546 FF

Sapurton 1378 Works, 1389 Ipm, 1399 Pat, 1466 AD ii

Cold Sapperton 1728 PR 15

'Soap-maker's farmstead', v. sāpere, tūn. Cf. also Saberton (ii, 43 infra).

FRAMPTON MANSELL

Frantune, -tone c. 1075 (1367) Monast, 1086 DB, 1240–55 Spillm

Frompton(a) 1211–13, 1220 Fees, 1287 Ass, 1327 SR, (-Maunsel) 1368 FF, 1377–99 Works

Framton' 1221 Ass, 1236 Fees

Fromton 1248 Ass, 1285 FA, 1293 FF

Frampton 1540 *MinAcct, (iuxta Saberton')* 1305 *FF, (Moysyl-)* 1463
Rent 242, (*-Mauncell*) 1466 AD ii, 1587 *FF*

'Farmstead on the R. Frome', *v.* Frome (1) (7 *supra*), tūn, distinguished as 'Mansell' from Frampton on Severn (ii, 196 *infra*) on the
same river and Frampton Cotterell (iii, 116 *infra*) on the Bristol Frome,
because it was held in the 13th and 14th centuries by the *Maunsel*
family (John *Mansell* 1285 FA ii, 236, William *Mauncell* 1303 ib ii,
251). On the variation between *Fram-* and *From-* cf. Frampton on
Severn (ii, 196 *infra*), Phonol. § 6.

HAILEY FM & WOOD, *Haile, Haylegh* 1327 *SR* (p), *Haley* 1623 *FF,
Hayley* 1794 *GR* 892. 'Clearing used for hay', *v.* hēg, lēah, but there
is nearly always some ambiguity in the first el. in such names between
'hay' and (ge)hæg 'hunting enclosure'. Hailey Wood is a very
extensive continuation of the great Oakley Wood in Cirencester
(64 *supra*).

TYNING VILLA, *the Tyning* 1833 *Downs*. The dial. word *tining* is used
in some south-western counties (Wo, Gl, W, So) to denote either
'a fence of wood, brushwood or quickset' or 'an enclosure with such
a fence' (EDD s.v. *tine* vb²), and it often occurs in later minor names
and f.ns. in Gl. The word is first recorded c. 1440 in the sense 'dry
hedge' (NED s.v.) and is from OE *tȳnan* 'to enclose' (*v.* tȳning,
a derivative of tūn in its original sense of 'enclosure').

ASH HILL, 1830 M.   BEACON FM, *-field* 1779 Rudder.   BLISS
DOWN GROVE, 1830 M.   CARSEY WELL, CASSEYWELL BOTTOM.
CHURNHILL BARN, 1830 M, *Chiridoneslides* 1250–60 Spellm, prob-
ably similar to Churchdown (ii, 119 *supra*), *v.* crūc¹, dūn.   THE
COOMBES, *Combes* 1830 M, *v.* cumb.   CRANHILL BARN, 1830 M,
v. cran 'crane', hyll.   DORVELL HO.   THE DOWNS, *Downs farm*
1839 *Downs, v.* dūn 'down, hill'.   HARGROVE, *spinet' de Haregraue*
1287 *Ass*, 'hare wood', *v.* hara, grāf.   LARKHILL FM, *-Bush* 1830 M,
Lark's Bush 1779 Rudder.   THE LEASOWES, 1830 M, *v.* lǣs 'pasture'.
SAPPERTON PARK, 1830 M.   TUMBLEDOWN.   WESTLEY FM, *le
Westley* 1417 *MinAcct, v.* west, lēah 'clearing'.

FIELD-NAMES

The principal forms in (*a*) are 1842 *TA* 172, and in (*b*) 1250–60 Spillm.

(*a*) Barn close; Calves croft; Halfacre 1824; Long wall piece; Ox leaze;
Pound piece; Sayers Firth 1833 (*v.* fyrhðe).

(b) *Bisendune* (cf. Bisley 117 *supra*, v. dūn); *Blakethurne* (v. blæc-þorn, -þyrne 'sloe'); *Brecthurne*; *Heselea* (v. hæsel, lēah); *Pilehulle* (v. pīl 'shaft, post', hyll); *Wildeneweye* (probably an error for *Vildene-*, 'road of the dwellers in the open country', v. filde², weg, cf. *Fielden Way* 16 *supra*).

Stroud

STROUD (156–8505) [strɑud]

(*la*) *Strode* 13 AD iii (p), 1200 ChR, 1221 *Ass* (p), 1243 HMC v, Ed 1 BM, 1287 *Ass et passim* to 1540 *MinAcct*, *Strod(a)* 1232 Cl, 1248 *Ass* (p)

Strowde 1542 LP, c. 1560 *Surv et freq* to 1698 PR 2, *Stroud(e)* 1652 *ParlSurv*, 1694 PR 2

Strood(e) 1561 *FF*, 1592 PR 8

'Marshy land overgrown with brushwood', v. strōd, and for the modern form, which is a spelling-pronunciation based on the form *Strowde*, cf. EPN ii, 164, Phonol. § 28. The name doubtless referred to a plot of marshy ground near the confluence of the R. Frome and Stroud Water.

PAGANHILL

Paggehull c. 1195 Cur   *Pagehull'* 1287 *Ass*

Pagenhull(e), *-hul* 1218 ClR, 1248 *Ass*, 1269 *FF*, c. 1280 GlR, 1303 FA *et passim* to 1538 *FF*, *-hill* 1354 Ch, *Pagynhull* 1491 Pat

Paganhull(e) 1287 *Rent* 245, 1292 Ipm, *-hill* 1509 *MinAcct*, *Pagonhull'* 1378 Works

Pakenhull 1287 *Ass*, 1614 Will, *-ell* 1377–99 Works, 1654 PR 8, (*-als. Paganhall*) 1639 InqM, *Pakynhyll* 1542 FF, *Pakenhyll*, *-hill* 1587 FF, (*-als. Pagnell*) 1566 ib

Packunhull 1574 FF, *Packenell* 1631 InqM

'Paga(n)'s hill', v. hyll. The first el. might be the ME pers.n. *Pagan*, which is from the MedLat form *Paganus* of the OFr name *Paien* 'the heathen' (cf. Tengvik 193, 223, Reaney 239), possibly the Latinised form of the name of the *Pain Fitzjohn* who gave his name to Painswick (132 *supra*), 3 miles north-east. But in the absence of some spellings with gen. *-es* or some in *Pain*, it is more likely to be the OE *Pæcga* suggested for Pagham (Sx 92), though the [pæg-] form of that name has been explained as a spelling-pronunciation (cf. also Pegglesworth 169 *infra*). The first spelling *Pagge-* certainly suggests such a possibility for Paganhill.

Bowbridge, 1673 *GR* (38 A), 1697 Will, 'arch bridge', *v.* boga, brycg. Bringfield Rd. Callowell, *Collowell Leaze* 1639 InqM, *Caliwell* 1830 M, possibly 'well in bare ground', *v.* calu (as a sb.), wella, referring to a spring below the hamlet; the area is lacking in woodland and this fact may be recorded in the name; the early *Collow-* suggests some confusion with e.ModE *collow* 'coal-dust, grime'. The Castle. Cull's Fm, 1830 M. Downfield, *Downefeld* 1641 Inq, *v.* dūne, feld. Enfield. Farm Hill, 1830 M. The Fields, *Inthefeld* 1374 Ipm, *The Field* 1779 Rudder, *v.* feld 'common field'. Gainey's Well, 1779 Rudder. Gannicox, *-cocks* 1779 Rudder. Hill Place, 1830 M. Horns Fm. Lodge-more. New Mills Court, *the New Mills* 1779 Rudder. The Plain, 1831 M, *v.* plain 'flat meadowland'. Rock Mill, 1830 M. Salmon's Spring, *-Mill* 1830 M. Slad Brook, Slade Ho, cf. *the Slade-water* 1779 Rudder, named from Stroud Slad (123 *supra*). Stratford Park, *Stretford* 1779 Rudder, *v.* strǣt, ford, a crossing of Painswick Brook. Weyhouse Cottage, *Wayehouse* 1607 *Rogers* 10, *the Wayhouse hill* c. 1690 *GR* 1756, cf. *Weyesplace* 1507 *Rent* 831, *v.* weg 'way' (or the surname from it), hūs, place.

FIELD-NAMES

Spellings dated 1641 are Inq, c. 1690 *GR* (1756), 1779 Rudder.

(a) the Bottoms 1779; Griffin's Mill 1779 (the residence of Thomas *Griffin*); Hemlocks Well 1779; the Knapp 1721 *GR* (D. 914) (*v.* cnæpp 'hill'); Mansel's Mead 1779; Rackhill 'where the tenters and racks stand' 1801 *GR* (D. 892) (*the Racke close* 1590 ib 547, cf. Rack Hill 116 *infra*); Silver Street 1724 *GR* 919.

(b) *Amon crofte* 1641; *the Brimes* c. 1690; *the Bunnett hey* 1641; *atte Chircheheye* 1328 Banco (p) (*v.* (ge)hæg); *Cockshoat* 1673 *GR* 38A (*v.* cocc-sciete); *Coneger* c. 1690 (*v.* coninger 'warren'); *Courte orchard* 1641; *the Lagger* 1682 *GR* 892 (dial. *lagger* 'narrow strip'); *Moorefield* 1641; *Pridyhay* 1638 InqM.

Thrupp

Thrupp (156–8603)

Trop' 1261 *FF*, *Throp(e)* 1393 Ipm, 1407, 1594 *FF*, *Throppe* 1547 *AOMB* 411, 1581 *FF*, *Throupe* 1594, 1597 *FF*, *Thorpe* 1639 Inq, *the Thrup* 1779 Rudder. *v.* þrop 'an outlying secondary farmstead'.

Lower & Upper Bourne, Bourne Bridge, *Bourne* 1715 Will, named from a small stream running from Toadsmoor into Stroud Water, which was called *Burnewater* 1448, 1459, 1494 *MinAcct*, cf. also *Bourne bridge* 1609 *AOMB* 394. *v.* burna 'stream', brycg. This place is not connected with Bournes Green (118 *supra*).

BRIMSCOMBE

> *Bremescumbe* 1306 *MinAcct*, Ric 2 *Rent* 238, *-combe* 1327 *SR* (p),
>   *Brem'cumbe* 1316 *MinAcct*
> *Brym(m)escombe* 1394 *Ass*, 1496 *FF*
> *Brymsc'* 1507 *Rent* 831, *Brymscombe* 1586 *FF*
> *Brynkescombe* 1542 LP

'Brēme's valley', *v.* cumb. The OE pers.n. *Brēme* (as in Bromsgrove Wo 336) possibly occurs also in Brimpsfield (144 *infra*). OE, ME *brēme* 'famous, fierce' (with which the pers.n. is ultimately connected) frequently becomes *brim(m)e* from the 13th century.

LOWER LYPIATT, *Lipgate parua* 1287 *Ass*, *Lupeyate Inf'* 1327 *SR*, *Netherlupʒate* 1368 *FF*, *Nether-*, *Nyderlep(e)yate* 1377–99, 1378 Works, *Netherlypyate* 1407 *Ass*, *Nethur Lyppeyate* 1507 *Rent* 831. *v.* hlīep-geat and cf. Lypiatt (119 *supra*), from which it is distinguished as 'Nether'.

STAFFORD MILLS, *Sta-*, *Stoford* Ric 2 *Rent* 238, *Stonford* 1546 *FF*. 'Stone ford', *v.* stān, ford. The loss of *-n-* before labials occurs in other p.ns. like Stafford's Bridge (32 *supra*), Stover (iii, 44), Stowell (182) and Stowick (iii, 138 *infra*); cf. Phonol. § 37 (*c*) and EPN ii, 143.

CLAYPITS FM. DRYHILL WOOD. GUSSAGE FM, *-Mill* 1830 M. HALE'S GROVE. THE HEAVENS, 1830 M. MACKHOUSE. PARK WOOD, 1830 M, cf. *Parkelandes* 1507 *Rent* 831, *v.* park. QUARHOUSE, 1687 Will, *v.* quarriere 'quarry'. WOOD THORPE.

FIELD-NAMES

The principal forms in (*b*) are 1507 *Rent* 831. Some modern f.ns. may be included in those of Bisley (124 *supra*).

(*b*) *le Badcockes* (the surname *Badcock*); *bosc' voc' Combes* 1576 *MonLand* 23; *Freremede* (*v.* frere 'friar', mǣd); *le Hame* (*v.* hamm); *Hathmores*; *Heedleeʒ* (*v.* hēafod, lǣs); *leʒ Hylles*; *Kaymbruges*; *Sethcombe*; *Southwelles flodde*, *Sudwells* 1638 InqM (*v.* sūð, wella, flōde 'gutter').

Uplands

UPLANDS (156–8505)

A modern civil parish formed out of Stroud and now a ward in Stroud Urban District.

BADBROOK, *Badbrook(e)* 1609 *AOMB*, 1788 Will, the OE pers.n. *Bada*, v. brōc. DIRLETON HO. THE GRANGE. HILL PLACE, *Hulplace* 1547 Pat, v. hyll, place. NORTHFIELD. PEGHOUSE FM, 1839 *TA* 153, *Pygas plase* 1485–1500 ECP, *Piggas als. Pigghouse* 1762 *GR* (D. 185), the first el. is possibly the Fr surname *Pigasse* (Reaney 251). WOODLANDS.

Winstone

WINSTONE (157–9609)

> *Winestan(e)* 1086 DB, 1178 P, *Wynestan* 1221, 1248 *Ass*, 1303 AD i
> *Wenestan* 1191 P
> *Wunnestan* 1211–13 Fees, *-ston* 1265 Misc
> *Winstane* 1216 ClR, 1277 Heref
> *Wonestan'* 1220, 1236 Fees, *-ston* 1287 *Ass*
> *Wi-, Wyneston(e)* 1264 Ipm, 1277 *FF*, 1286–7 Glouc, 1301 AD iii *et freq* to 1327 *SR*
> *Wynneston(e)* 1287 *Ass*, 1292 *FF*, 1298 Episc
> *Wi-, Wynston* 1291 Tax, 1311 Ch *et passim* to 1742 PR 16

'Wynna's stone', from the OE pers.n. *Wyn(n)a* and stān. The spellings for this name and Winson (185 *infra*) are not easily kept apart.

BULL BANK, *Bulbanks* 1622 *FF*, *-banck* 1647 ib, v. bula 'bull', banke. FOSSE FM, cf. *Foss Feilds* 1652 ParlSurv, v. foss[1] 'ditch', referring to the Roman road from Cirencester to Gloucester (16 *supra*). GASKILL'S FM. THE GROVE. SALTER'S HILL BARN, 1830 M, v. saltere, hyll; it is on a lane from Cheltenham to Sapperton, which may have been an old saltway (cf. 20 *supra*). WASHBROOK, (*le*) *Washebrooke* 1622, 1647 *FF*, v. wæsce '(sheep-)washing', brōc.

FIELD-NAMES

The principal forms in (*a*) are 1842 *TA* 226. Spellings dated 1414–94 are *MinAcct*, 1652 *ParlSurv* 22.

(*a*) Bunkham; Candle Hill; Dockham (*v.* docce, hamm); Dry leaze; Greensward Dancers (probably a place for country dancing); Innox (*v.* in-hoke); Kite meadow; Laines Leaze (*v.* leyne, lǣs); Langett (*v.* langet); Ockwells piece; Park field (*Parke Feild* 1652); Pendon; Playwells piece; Pully ground; Sanbury Knapp (*v.* cnæpp 'hill'); the Slade (*v.* slæd); Webb Hay.

(*b*) *Bernehey* 1414, 1448 (*v.* bere-ærn, (ge)hæg); *Church lane* 1652; *Fodrynghey* 1494 ('foddering enclosure', *v.* fōdring, (ge)hæg); *Hokesplace* 1414 (the surname *Hook*); *Mil(le)croft* 1447, 1494; *Newelond* 1414; *Skallerdescroft* 1414 (named from John *Skallard* ib 850, 25).

V. RAPSGATE HUNDRED

Rapsgate Hundred remained unchanged from the time of DB. It lies to the north of Crowthorne and Bisley Hundreds towards the west of the Cotswolds at the head of the Churn valley. It was one of the Seven Hundreds of Cirencester.

RAPSGATE HUNDRED

> *Respegete hundredum* 11 Heming
> *Respiget(e), Respiet hvnd'* 1086 DB
> *Respiate hdr'* 1168 P, (*hundred' de*) *Respezat(e)* 13 Glouc, *-gate* 1221
>   *Ass*, 1276 RH, 1285 FA *et passim* to 1587 *FF*
> *Resperegate* 1220 Fees
> *Repsgate* 1221 *Ass, Reppesgate* 1316 FA, *Rapesgate* 1535 VE
> *Resputte* (sic) 1248 *Ass*   *Ryspegete* 1276 RH

The hundred takes its name from Rapsgate in Colesborne 155 *infra* (grid 144–994110); in 1400 the hundred court was held at a bush near Marsden which is close to Rapsgate (cf. BG ix, 333).

Brimpsfield

BRIMPSFIELD (144–9312) ['brimzfi:ld]

> *Bri-, Brymesfeld(e)* 1086 DB, 1221 Eyre, 1275 Episc, 1280 Cl
>   *et freq* to 1496 GlR, *-feud* 1227 *FF*
> *Brumesfeld* c. 1180 GlR, 1211–13 Fees, 1221 *Ass*, c. 1230 GlR,
>   1281 Ch, 1291 Tax, 1299 Ipm, c. 1300 RGl
> *Bremlesfeld* 1221 *Ass*
> *Brummresfeld* 1221 Eyre   *Brummesfeld* 1285 FA
> *Brunnesfeld'* 1221 *Ass*, 1290 GlR, 1291 Tax
> *Bremesfeld'* 1221, 1248 *Ass*, 1280 Ipm, 1289 Episc, 1316 Glouc,
>   *Bremefeld* Ed 1, BM, *Bremmesfeld* c. 1300 RGl, 1481 Pat
> *Brinnesfeld* c. 1230 GlR
> *Brimfeud* 1248 *Ass, Brymfeld* 1450 *MinAcct*, 1488 Pat, *Brymefeld*
>   1535 VE
> *Bri-, Brymmesfeud* 1255 FF, *-feld(e)* 1279 Cl, 1299 Ipm, 1303 FA
>   *et passim* to 1492 Pat
> *Bromesfeld* 1262 GlR, *Bromfeld* 1287 *Ass, Bromsfeld* c. 1540
>   GlR
> *Broumesfielde* 1316 FA   *Bermesfeld* 1460 Pat

Brymsfeld 1494 Ipm, 1535 VE, 1537 *Rent*, 1577 M, *Brimps-* 1760 M

Names of this type often present difficult phonological problems in the variety of ME forms in *Brimes-*, *Bremes-*, *Bromes-*, *Brunnes-*, etc. In a few like Bromsgrove (Wo 336) or Bromsberrow (iii, 166 *infra*) which have a similar variation to Brimpsfield, OE spellings make it clear that we have to start with OE *brem-* or *brym-*. But this variation between *Brem-* and *Brom-* is not as a rule found with names that go back to OE *brōm-*. A possible explanation is that the *Brim-* spellings are due to an early raising of OE *ē* to *ī* (with subsequent shortening as in *Brimm-*) and the *Brom-*, *Broum-* spellings arise by the analogical substitution of OE **brōm** 'broom' (as compared with its derivative **brēmel** 'bramble'); such a substitution is certainly true of Bremhill (W 86) from OE *brēmel* with occasional ME spellings like *Bromel*. The first el. in some of these names is probably the OE pers.n. *Brēme*, as in Brimscombe (141 *supra*), and this could hold for Brimpsfield and Bromsberrow, or **Bryme(le)*, corresponding to OG *Brumi* and *Brumilo*. But the two forms *Bremles-* and *Brummres-* suggest that in Brimpsfield we may have OE **brēmel** 'bramble' (gen.sg. *brēmles*) or possibly **brēmer** 'bramble thicket', which would be reduced to *bremes-* by dissimilation (cf. IPN 113). The name would be paralleled in sense by Brimfield (He 28), *Bromefeld* 1086, *Bremelfelda* 1123. 'Brēme's or Bryme(le)'s stretch of open country' or 'such a piece of land amongst the brambles', *v.* **feld**.

BUCKLE WOOD, *Boc-*, *Bokholt(e)* 1340 Misc, 1380 *MinAcct*, (*-in Brymmesfeld*) 1338 Ipm, *Buc-*, *Bukholt(e)* 1448, 1494 *MinAcct*, *-helde* 1474 Pat, *-holt*, *-wold* 1477 Pat, *-hold* 1481 ib, *-olde* 1549 *FF*. 'Beech wood', *v.* **bōc**, **holt**; it was described as 'a beech wood called *Bocholte*' in 1338 Inq 275. This is the Brimpsfield part of the extensive Buckholt Wood in Cranham (158 *infra*).

CAUDLE GREEN

    Cald(e)well(a), *-welle* 1155 (1331) Ch, 1269 Ipm, 1327 *SR* (p), 1494 Ipm, 1529 *FF*, *-wall* 1269 Ipm
    Coldewelle(mor) 1380 *MinAcct*
    Cawdwall 1608 *FF*, *-well* 1638 ib, *Cawdell Greene* 1622 ib, *Cau-*, *Cawdle* 1662, 1671 Will

'Cold spring', *v.* **cald**, **wella** (Merc *wælla* giving the *-wall* forms). There are several springs in the immediate neighbourhood.

Eddington

Hedington' 1241 *FF*
Edyngton 1303 Episc, *Eddington* 1777 M
Edyndon(e) 1359 *FF*, 1361 Ipm

Probably 'Ēada's farmstead or hill', *v.* ing⁴, tūn, dūn. The pers.n. is OE *Ēada*.

Hazel Hanger Wood, *Hasel-, Hasulhunger* 1261 Misc, 1380 *MinAcct*, *Haselhonger* 1299 Ipm, *-angre, -er* 1380, 1448 *MinAcct, Hasylhonger* 1547 Pat. 'Steep slope wooded with hazels', *v.* hæsel, hangra. For *-hunger* cf. Phonol. § 6.

Beechwood Cottage, cf. Buckle Wood (*supra*). Birtlands Grove, *Bordlondes* 1494 *MinAcct, Birtlings grove* 1837 *TA*, ME *bord-land* 'land held by a bordar'. Blacklains, *-laines* 1837 *TA*, possibly identical with *Blakelond* 1380 *MinAcct, v.* blæc, leyne 'arable strip', land. Briery Hill Copse, *Briary-* 1830 M. Brimpsfield Park, *Brymsfeild Park* 1641 Inq. Buck's Head, *Bockes* 1537 *Rent*, from the surname *Buck*. Calley Wood, 1837 *TA, Kalvelegh* 1300 AD i, 1310 ib iv, 'calf clearing', *v.* calf, lēah. Castle, Castle Mound, *atte Castle* 1327 SR, *Castle hill* 1837 *TA*, the site of a castle (*castr' de Brymmesfeld* 1330, 1352 *FF*), cf. BG xx, 233 ff., *v.* castel. Gloucester Beeches, 1830 M. Gowanlea Fm. Groveridge Hill, 1837 *TA, Grofrug(g)e* 1230, 1262 GlR, *v.* grāf, hrycg. Ham Cottages, *the Ham* 1837 *TA, v.* hamm. Hawcote Copse, *-cott-* 1837 *TA*. The Knapp. Moor Ho, *Morehouse* 1556 *FF*, cf. *Moore end* 1622 ib. Morcombe, 1380 *MinAcct, More-* 1413, 1459 ib, *v.* mōr, cumb. Nettleton, *Nettlecomb* 1777, 1830 M, *v.* netele, cumb. Ostrich Wood, 1837 *TA*. Park Wood, 1830 M. Poston Wood, *Pastons copse* 1837 *TA*. The Quarry, *Quarry* 1837 *TA*. Sidelands, *Sidelongs* 1837 *TA*. Starveall. Stoney Hill, *Stony hill* 1830 M. Syde Wood, *Side-* 1830 M, *v.* Syde (162 *infra*). Watercombe 1837 *TA*. West Tump, a long barrow, cf. BG v, 201. Woodfield Ho, *Wadfield* 1837 *TA, v.* wād 'woad', feld. Wood Ho.

FIELD-NAMES

The principal forms in (*a*) are 1837 *TA* 32. Spellings dated 1299 are Inq, 1327 Ipm, 1380–1494 *MinAcct*, 1537 *Rent*, 1622 *FF*, 1641 Inq.

(*a*) Ashwells grove; Ashmoor orchard; Ban croft (*Bencroft* 1380, *v.* bēan 'bean', croft); Barnshill; Beggars bush; Bilbarrow (*Beldebergh* 1380, *v.*

beorg); Biscombe bottom (*Biscombe, Biscombesslade* 1380, the OE pers.n. *Bisa* as in Bisley (117 *supra*), *v.* cumb, slæd); Bitter coombe; Bittoms (*v.* bytme 'bottom'); Blackbush piece; Blawcot; the Bog; Brake; Brinkland; Bull land; Cocks piece (*past' de Cokkes* 1380); long & far Doles (*v.* dāl); Drawker; Eldern slad; Fern hill; Fogwells hill; the Forty (*v.* forð, ēg); Fryers pan; Gibridings; the Grove; Hill house; Hop yard; Hounsell paddock; the Knowl; Lamphooks hill; Langett (*v.* langet); Lawn; Limbricks hill (*Lynregge* 1380 'flax ridge', *v.* līn, hrycg); Littleworth; Manless town (*Manlestowne* 1622, possibly *Marlestone* 1641, from a manorial name *Mandelynes* 1475 Pat, *v.* tūn); Marks mead; Muckly; Munley; the Muzzards (*Meseford* 1299, *Moseford* 1380, 'ford in the bog', *v.* mēos, ford); Old mead (*Oldemed* 1380, *v.* mǣd); Parkers ground (*Parkers* 1537); Pennyless pinch; Plumb hay; Ridding mead (*Rudyng'* 1494, *v.* rydding 'clearing'); Rowble; Rye mead; Slaite (*v.* slæget 'sheep-pasture'); Stockwell Steps (*Stockewelle* 1641, *v.* stocc, wella); Sundays hill (cf. Sundayshill iii, 108 *infra*); Toveys leap (*Tobys* 1537, the Gl surname *Tovey*); Washbrook meadow; Whites hill; White wergs (*v.* Wregs *infra*); Whorestone ('boundary stone', *v.* hār, stān); Withy mead (*Wethemede* 1299, *v.* wīðig 'willow', mǣd); Wregs (dial. (obs.) *werg* 'willow', cf. NED s.v.).

(b) *Aldelcombe* 1494 (possibly the OE pers.n. *Aldhelm, v.* cumb); *Ashrugg* 1262 GlR, *Asshrugge* 1380 (*v.* æsc, hrycg); *Bulbankes Side* 1641 (cf. Bull Bank 142 *supra*); *Chatterley* 1641; *Chymmage* 1494 (possibly an OE pers.n. *Ceomma* as in Chimney (O 302), *v.* ecg); 'a cotage called *Compehouse*' 1537 (*v.* camp 'enclosed field', hūs); *Greneham* 1494 (*v.* grēne[1], hamm); *Holemed, Holmedesshrubbes* 1380 (*v.* hol[1], mǣd, scrubb); *Holrudyng'* 1380 (*v.* hol[1], rydding); *Hullet-, Hulittemed* 1225–9 GlR (the ME surname *Hulot*, later *Hewlett*); *Hillemede* 1496 ib; *Inhechyng'* 1380 (*v.* in, heccing); *Joppes* 1641; *Loddesleysiat* 1547 Pat (an OE pers.n. *Lod(d)* as in Lodsworth (Sx 26), *v.* lēah, geat 'gate'); *Longefeld(e)* 1287 Ass, 1299, 1380; *Monesdeieslond* 1299 (cf. Sundayshill iii, 108 *infra*); *Morsplot* 1380 (*v.* mōr, splott 'plot of land'); *Nashley* 1641 (*v.* atten, æsc, lēah); *Noblecombe* 1380 (ME *noble* as a byname, cumb); *Prestecomb'* 1380 (*v.* prēost, cumb); *past' de Puttes* 1380; *Reggeweyfurlond* 1380 (*v.* hrycg, weg); *Rouberghslade, Roucombe(slade)* 1380 (*v.* rūh 'rough', beorg, cumb, slæd); *Symondesplace* 1494; *Smokacre* 1380 (cf. Smoke Acre 70 *supra*); *Throkkouere* 1380 (*v.* þroc, possibly in some such sense as 'covered drain', ofer[2] 'slope'); *Urr(y)esmede* 1413, 1448, *Vrres-* 1494 (the ME surname *Urri*, cf. Reaney 174); *Vernhale* 1380 (*v.* fearn 'fern', halh); the *Washepoole* 1641 (*v.* wæsce, pōl); *Watersladd* 1641 (*v.* wæter, slæd); *Welhouse* 1494, 1537; *Wertwolde* 1299, *Wortewolde* 1327, 1380 (probably OE wyrt (wurt) 'plant, vegetable, crop', wald 'wold'); *Weverdesmede* 1299 (the OE pers.n. *Wīgfrið*, mǣd); *Worthymed* 1380 (*v.* worðig).

North Cerney

NORTH CERNEY (157–0207)

into Cyrnea 852 (13th) BCS 466, *Cernei, -ey(a), -eye, -ay(a)* 1086 DB, 1125–89 Glouc (*freq*), 1220 Fees, (*Nort-*) 1269 Episc, (*North(e)-*) 1277 WinchLB, 1279 *FF et passim* to 1564 *FF, Cyrneia* 1209 *FF, Northserneye* 1311 ib, *Sareney* 1387 Ipm, *Sarney(e)* 1392 ib, (*North-*) 1421, 1570 ib, *North Cherney* 1646 *FF*, with other forms and meanings as for South Cerney (58 *supra*). It is 4 miles north of Cirencester on the R. Churn.

BARFORD (lost), *on bereford(a)* 852 (13th) BCS 466, *pont' Beroford* (sic) 1531 Monast, *Barfford Bridge* 1552 Pat. 'Ford used during the harvesting of barley', *v.* bere, ford. The location is not known; Grundy 56 thought the ford would be a crossing of the R. Churn in the south of the parish.

CALMSDEN

Kalemundes-, to Calmundesdene 852 (13th) BCS 466
Calemundesdene 12 WinchLB (p), 1190 AD iv, 1220 Fees, 1231 Cl, c. 1320 *GlCh* (p), 1327 *SR, Calamondesdene* 13 *CirenD* 3d, *Calmondesden(e)* 1220 Fees, 1287 QW *et freq* to 1403 *FF, Chalmundesden'* 1287 *Ass*
Calemdesdene 1221 WinchLB
Calemonden' 1287 *Ass*
Calmesden(e) 1379 *GlCh* ii, 17, 1434 Monast, 1439 Pat *et passim* to 1584 *Comm*

'Calumund's valley', *v.* denu. The OE spelling makes it probable that we have, as Ekwall suggests, an OE pers.n. *Calumund* from a name-theme OE *calu* 'bald', not otherwise found in dithematic pers.ns. except in *Calunōð* in Candleshoe (L, Ekwall), and the common theme *-mund*. The only other evidence for such a pers.n. is in the local surname of John de *Calmundecote* of Cirencester (1248 *Ass* 1d).

WOODMANCOTE ['wudmǝkǝt]

Wodemancote, -kot 12 Monast, 1279 WinchLB *et freq* to 1429 ib, *Wude-* 13 AD v, *Wod-* 1277 WinchLB, 1497 *AOMB et freq* to 1533 *MinAcct*
Wodemanecota, -cote 1220 Fees, *Wude-* 1232 Ch, *-mone-* 1233 *FF, -manne-* 1279, 1311 ib

Wodemonescote 1314 Ch

Woodmacote 1632 *FF*   *Woodmurkot* 1683 PR 5

'The woodmen's cottage or shed', *v.* wudu-mann (gen.pl. -*manna*), cot. The name is repeated in Cleeve and Dursley (ii, 94, 222 *infra*).

BROADBRIDGE. CHALKHILL WOOD, *Chalk hill* 1837 *TA*, *v.* cealc, hyll. COTSWOLD PARK, -*House* 1830 M, formerly *Winters Grounds* 1777 M. CUTHAM LANE. DOWNS FM, *Down Ho.* 1777 M, *the Downs* 1837 *TA*, *v.* dūn. FOLLY BARN, *Foley ground* 1837 *TA*, *v.* folie. GOOSEHAM BARN, *Goose Ham* 1731 *GR* 475, *v.* gōs, hamm. HAMMERTONS, *Hamerton* 1837 *TA*. LODGE FM, 1830 M. NORDOWN, *North Down* 1830 M. NORTH CERNEY DOWNS, 1830 M. OLD GORE, *Old Goore* 1490 ECP, *Oldgor(e)* 1507 *Rent*, 1553 Pat, 1571, 1624 *FF*, *v.* ald, gāra 'gore of land'. OLD GORE BARN, formerly *Aldon Barn* 1777 M, *Allgrove Barn* 1830 M, *Old grove* 1837 *TA*. OLD PARK, 1830 M. SCRUBDITCH, 1773 *GR* 475, *v.* scrubb 'brushwood', dīc, which here refers to old earthworks. SHEWEL WOOD, 1830 M, dial. *shewel* 'scarecrow'. SLADBOTTOM COPSE, cf. *Slade hill* 1837 *TA*, *v.* slæd 'valley'. STAND PLANT., -*ground* 1837 *TA*. WINTERWELL (lost), 1837 *TA*, *on winter wellan* 852 (13th) BCS 466, *v.* winter, wella; it is at grid 157–049075.

FIELD-NAMES

The principal forms in (*a*) are 1837 *TA* 40. Spellings dated 852 are (13th) BCS 466, 13 AD v, 1692, 1695 *GR* (D. 16), 1731 ib (D. 475).

(*a*) Barley slaite (*v.* slæget); Barrow field (*v.* beorg); Beckstone (at grid 157–029090, identified by Grundy 56 with *on ðone stane* 852 BCS 466); Bittom (*v.* bytme 'bottom'); Black barrow (ib 1777 M, *v.* blæc, beorg); Bloody hill; Bond hay; Broken gore (*v.* gāra); Burcombe hill; Claypits; Cockpits; Coneygree (*v.* coninger 'warren'); Cowleaze; Crampool; Floodgate folly; Friars mead (*Freremede* 1507 *Rent* 831, *Fryars mead* 1692, *v.* frere 'friar', mǣd); Furze downs; Hackpenny bottom; the Ham (*v.* hamm); Hanley wood; Hooks bush; Langett (*v.* langet); Larks slade (*v.* slæd); the Leaze (*v.* lǣs); Lincomb ground; Long down; Mill Hays 1731 (*v.* myln, (ge)hæg); Moorcombs (*Morcumb* 13, *v.* mōr, cumb); Old ditch; Pipers hay (ib 1731); Pound hay; Sandford bush; Severalls (cf. Severals 28 *supra*): Shabley; Slaite (*v.* slæget 'sheep-pasture'); Townsend; Turks bottom; Waterstiles; Westlake barn; the Zetts.

(*b*) *Botterug* 13; *on brihtinc broc* 852 (an OE stream-name *brihting* 'the bright one' (*v.* beorht, -ing[2]) or the OE pers.n. *Beorht, Briht, v.* -ing[4], brōc); *Burkeling* 13; *on ebbel dic* 852; *Fildeneweye* 13 ('the field-dwellers' road', *v.* filde[2], weg, a term used of old roads in open country, in this case Fosse

Way); *Heynesthorn* 13 (*v.* hægen 'enclosure', þorn, but the first el. could be ME *heyne* 'niggard' used as a byname); *on hnices ðorn* 852 (possibly an OE pers.n. *Hnic*, related to OE *hnīgan* 'to bow', G *nicken* 'to nod', *v.* þorn); *on hrindan broc* 852 (*v.* Rendcomb 160 *infra*); *St Foyne ground* 1685 (ModE *sainfoin*, cattle herbage); *on swiftan beorh* 852 (an OE pers.n. *Swifta*, a weak form of *Swift, v.* beorg 'hill'); *on ðeofan dene* 852 ('thieves' valley', *v.* þēof, denu, but the ending *-an* may indicate an OE pers.n. *Þēofa*, cf. OG *Thiepo*); *on willan dic* 852 (the OE pers.n. *Willa, v.* dīc).

Chedworth

CHEDWORTH (144–0511)

æt Ceddanwryde (sic) 862 (l. 13th) BCS 535
Cedeorde 1086 DB   *Chedeorda* Hy 2 Monast
Cheddewrda, -wurðe, -w(u)rth(a), -worth(e) 1194, 1195 P, 13 CirenD
  3d, 1211–13, 1220 Fees, 1221 *Ass*, 1226 *FF*, 1242 Ipm *et passim*
  to Hy 8 *Surv*
Cheddesworde, -worth(e) 13 Glouc, c. 1230 GlR (p), 1233 Cl, 1279
  FF, 1287 *Ass*, 1359 WinchLB
Chedewurth, -w(o)rth 1221 *Ass*, 1236 *FF*, 1248 *Ass*, 1251 Ch, 1487
  MinAcct
Chadewrth 1248 *Ass*, *Chadworth* 1488, 1495 Pat
Ched(d)worth(e) 1276 RH, 1283 Ipm *et freq* to 1712 PR 14
Chyddeworth 1320 *Ass*, *Chidworth* 1646 *Rec*

'Cedda's enclosure', from the OE pers.n. *Cedda* and worð. The surname forms *Chedeleswrde, -wrthe* (12, 1183–94 WinchLB) and *Cheddreword* (1160 RBE) probably belong to Chaddleworth (Brk).

HUTNAGE, *Hodockenasshe* 1327 *SR* (p), *Hutnash* 1777 M. The first el. is probably a form of the ME pers.n. *Huddekin*, a diminutive of ME *Hodde* or *Hudde*, as in the surname *Hodkin* (Reaney 166). *v.* æsc 'ash-tree'.

POSTCOMBE, *on posecumbes heafdon* c. 800 (11th) BCS 299, *Puscombe* 1824 M. The first el. may be a form of the rare OE *posa, pusa* 'bag' used in some figurative sense to describe a hollow. *v.* cumb 'valley', hēafod 'head'.

WOODLANDS, *Wodelond* 1402 Inq aqd, *Woddelande* Hy 8 *Surv*, *Wod-landes* 1527 *Rent*, *Woodland(s)* 1554, 1564 *FF*, *Chedworth Woodlandes* 1636 *Guise* 8. *v.* wudu, land.

ASHWELL 1377 GlR, *Aswell'* 1287 *Ass* (p), *v.* æsc, wella. BLEAK-
MOOR, *Blackmoor* 1830 M, 1842 *TA*, *v.* blæc, mōr. BOY'S GROVE,
1842 *TA*, named from the family of *de Boys* 1327 *SR* (p), *v.* bois
'wood'. BURFORD'S GROVE, 1842 *TA*. CALVES HILL, 1842 *TA*,
Calfs Hill 1830 M. THE CASTLE, cf. *Castle ground* 1842 *TA*, *v.*
castel 'dwelling'; it is near Chedworth Beacon. CHEAP ST., 1830
M, 'market street', *v.* cēap. CHEDWORTH BEACON (1830 M),
LAINES (-*Lines* 1777 M, *v.* leyne 'arable strip') & WOODS (1830 M,
atte Wode 1327 *SR*). COULSTY BARN, *Colstray* 1811 Auct 5, *Coltstay
patch* 1842 *TA*, possibly 'colt path', *v.* colt, stīg. COWSLAIT GROVE,
Cows slade 1842 *TA*. FIELDS FM, *Chedworth Field* 1777 M, *the
Fields* 1830 M, *v.* feld. GREEN LANE, 1830 M. HARTSHILL.
HEDGELEY GROVE, *Edgley fields* 1793 *GR* (D. 1350), *Hedgly* 1830 M,
cf. *atte Hegge* 1327 *SR* (p), *v.* hecg 'hedge', lēah. HILL FM, *Hill
close* 1842 *TA*. LISTERCOMBE BOTTOM, 1779 Rudder, *Lustercumb*
1226 *FF*, *v.* litestere 'dyer', cumb. LONGFURLONG, 1735 *GR* (D.
1350), 1777 M. MONKHAM WOOD, 1842 *TA*, *Monkscombe-* 1830 M,
v. munuc, cumb. NEW BARN, 1830 M. NEWMAN'S COVERT,
named from the family of John *Newman* 1764 PR 2, 139. NEWPORT,
1830 M. PINKWELL, 1830 M, -*hall* 1777 M, 'finch well', *v.* pinca,
wella. PINSWELL, *v.* Pinswell (154 *infra*). THE PYKE, *Pike piece*
1842 *TA*, probably ModE dial. *pike* 'pointed plot of land in a ploughed
field'. RAYBROOK BARN, -*meadow* 1842 *TA*. ST JOHN'S CHURCH
(site), cf. *S(c)t Ions as(s)hes* 1577, 1610 M, *St Johns Ashe* 1777 M,
v. æsc 'ash-tree'. TUNWAY GATE. WELL HILL, 1830 M. WOOD
BARROW, a tumulus, 1777 M, *v.* wudu, beorg.

FIELD-NAMES

The principal forms in (*a*) are 1842 *TA* 46. Spellings dated 13, 1221–75 are
WinchLB, 14, 1398 AD i, vi, 1527 *Rent* 4, 1793 *GR* (D. 1350), 1811 Auct 5.

(*a*) the Almstones; Barnwell; Barrow; Black Scrubbs; Blakewells (*Blackwell Hill* 1811); the Breach (*the Breaches* 1811, *v.* brēc); Cadwallader's Barn;
Chatterpie grove (dial. *chatter-pie* 'magpie'); Chestells ground (*v.* ceastel
'heap of stones'); Chiddle grove; Claypitts; Cockshoot (*v.* cocc-scīete);
Coneygree 1811; the Coombs (ib 1811); the Coner; Crowdell; Cute hill;
Deans wood (*Dean-lands* 1779 Rudder, so called from its being held in trust
of the Dean of Leicester for the hospital there, Rudder 333); Deep lands;
the Downs (ib 1811); Draw Laines (*v.* leyne); Dry Bottom 1777 M; Falkham;
the Folly (*v.* folie); Foxbury, Foxley (*v.* fox, burg 'burrow', lēah); Gad-
bridge; Gastons (*v.* gærs-tūn 'pasture'); Grove Laines (*v.* leyne); Ham
grove (*v.* hamm); Hanhill 1811; Hay hill; Haystall; Hempland; Hitchells

(*Hitchill Coppice* 1811); Hollywell hill (ib 1811, *v.* hālig, wella); Kemplands 1793; Laines ground 1811 (*v.* leyne); Langett (*v.* langet); Linch (*v.* hlinc 'ridge'); the Lotts (*v.* hlot); Louse hill; Mob Hay; the Moor; Mudging Ham; Mumpasses ground; North field (*campo de North* 1221); Peaseley 1811 (*v.* pisu 'pease', lēah); Pleck (*v.* plek 'small plot'); Portway; Radwell; Ratcomb 1811; the Ridings (*v.* rydding 'clearing'); Scummington hill; the Several 1811 (*v.* Severals 28 *supra*); Shaddle; Shawswell bottom; Sigden ground; Sunday hill (cf. Sundayshill iii, 108 *infra*); the Take In; Till barn; Twiney Walls 1811; Wadley; Wheatley 1811; White walls (ib 1793); Wickswell 1811; Willey Wood 1811; Wisnell (ib 1811).

(*b*) *Alvinewelle* 14 (the OE pers.n. *Ælfwine*); *Conyng* 1398 (probably for coninger 'warren'); *Edric(h)esmede* 1265, *pratum Eadrici* 1275 (the OE pers.n. *Eadrīc*, *v.* mǣd); *Godhurst* 13, *Gothu(e)rst(e)* 1260, 1261, 1265, 1398, (*-Mill*) 14, *Gottrismylle* 1527 ('goat wood', *v.* gāt, hyrst); *Sortendich* 1221 (*v.* sceort 'short', dīc); *campo del Suth* 1221; *Stayresty* 1398 ('path with stairs', *v.* stǣger, stīg); *Stoke-, Stockslade* 13, 1260 ('stump valley', *v.* stocc, slæd).

Coberley

COBERLEY (144–9616) [ˈkubəli]

Culberlege, Coberlie 1086 DB

Cuthbrithleya 1148–79, 1200, 1215 Glouc, *Codbricleye* 1285 FA, *Cobrighteleye* 1291 Tax, *Cutbryhtleye* 1295 Ipm

Cuthberleya, -leg' 1182 Glouc, 1220 Fees, *Cutberl(eg)'* 12 Flax (p), 1270 FF, 1287 Ass, *Cudburlegh* 1287 ib

Cuberley(a), -leg(e), -lei(a) 12 Glouc, 1221 Ass, FF, 1265 Ch, 1275 Cl, *Cuburleye* p. 1412 GloucHist

Cubberleg(e), -ley(e), -le(gh) 1221 Plea, 1270, 1274 Episc, 1316 Glouc *et freq* to 1760 M, (*Upper-*) 1622 FF, *Cubbyrlay* 1453 Pat

Coberley(a), -le(ye), -legh 13 Glouc, 1270 Pat, 1294 Episc, 1301 BM *et freq* to 1610 M, (*North-*) 1328 Banco, *Coburley(e)* 1350 Ipm, 1515 Glouc

Cobberley(e) 1272 Ipm, 1327 *SR et freq* to 1374 Ipm, *Cobburley* 1480 *MinAcct*

Couberle 1301 Ipm, *Cowberley* 1571 FF, (*Nether-*) 1622 ib

Cow Berkeley 1540 Leland

'Cuthbert's glade or clearing', *v.* lēah. The pers.n. is OE *Cūþbeorht*. 'Nether' and 'North' in relation to Upper Coberley (*infra*).

HARTLEY FM & HILL, *Hurtelegh'* 1221 Ass (p), *Harteley* 1605 Comm, *Hartley hill* 1605 ib, *Hartle Hill* 1777 M. 'The harts' glade', *v.* heorot, lēah.

Wistley Hill, *Uuisleag* 759 (orig.) BCS 187, *Wistley Hill* 1777 M. This is a piece of marshy land at the highest local spot on the Thames–Severn watershed (144–977182), and there can be little doubt that it means 'clearing near a swampy meadow', *v.* wisse, lēah; OE *wisse* may also occur in Wishanger (131 *supra*).

Barrow Piece, *the Barrow* 1838 *TA*, near a long barrow, *v.* beorg 'barrow'. Chatcombe Wood, 1838 *TA*, *Chalcombe Wd.* (sic) 1777 M, 'Ceatta's valley' from the OE pers.n. *Ceatta*, *v.* cumb. Clerk's Patch, 1838 *TA*. Coberley Court, *Court* 1830 M. Upper Coberley, *U. Cubberley* 1777 M. Crickley Hill, 1777 M, the same hill as Crickley (ii, 115 *infra*). Cuckoopen Barn, *Cuckoo pen* 1838 *TA*, *v.* Cuckoo Pen (43 *supra*). Dowman's Fm, *Dowmans field* 1838 *TA*. Far Hills Langet, *Far hill* 1838 *TA*, *v.* langet 'long strip'. Hill Barn, 1830 M. Leaden Wells. Monday's Hill, 1838 *TA*, cf. *Mondaies Landes* 1598 *Dep*, *v.* Sundayshill (iii, 108 *infra*). Neatley (lost), 1838 *TA*, probably identical with *to nataleahes æsce* c. 800 (11th) BCS 299, 'wet clearing', *v.* nǣt, lēah; it is at grid 144–978168; the name is probably the first el. of the nearby Needlehole (189 *infra*). Niggerley. Poolpiece Langet, *Pool Piece* 1838 *TA*. Salterley Grange, *Salterley* 1691 *AddR*, *Solterley banks* 1838 *TA*, *v.* saltere 'salt-dealer', lēah, cf. Saltway (20 *supra*). The Scrubbs, 1838 *TA*, *v.* scrubb 'brushwood'. Seven Springs, *Seven Wells Head or Thames Head* 1760 M, *Seven wells* 1777 M, these springs are the source of the R. Churn, but are sometimes regarded locally as the source of the Thames; the latter is, however, in Coates near Cirencester just west of Thames Head Bridge. Short Wood, 1830 M, possibly an adaptation of *Shorteford* 1450 GlR, *v.* sceort, ford, wudu. Town End, *Townsend* 1838 *TA*. Ullenwood, *Ullen Fm.* 1777 M, *Ullen Farm & Wood* 1830 M, perhaps 'owls' wood', *v.* ūle (gen.pl. *ūlena*), wudu.

FIELD-NAMES

The principal forms in (*a*) are 1838 *TA* 62. Spellings dated 1619 are Sherb.

(*a*) Black hedge; the Bogs; Chestcombes (*Chesscombes* 1619, part of Chescombe 154 *infra*); Coneygree (*v.* coninger 'warren'); Fatting close (ib 1619, 'a close for fattening animals'); Furze brake; Goldwell bank; Halling wood (*Hollynwood Leazes* 1619 'holly wood', *v.* holegn); the Hamlines; Honey acre; Langet; Picked patch (dial. *picked* 'pointed,' 'cleared of weeds'); Rack hill (cf. Rack Hill 127 *supra*); Stoneway piece; Ten days math; White lands (*-land* 1619).

(b) *terr' voc' Chaundelors* 1542 *MinAcct*; *the Chauntrys* 1619; *Conyers* 161; *the Crowe* 1619; G̶u̶d̶r̶i̶d̶g̶e̶ *close* 1619; *Horse Leaze* 1619; *Sharps Leaz* 1619; *Thefstlo* 1139–48 Glouc (perhaps an error for *Thefstie*, 'thief's path', v. þēof, stīg); *Wellham* 1619 (v. wella, hamm); *Wlpitta id est fossa luporum* 1139–48 Glouc, *Wolfputtes* 1287 *Ass* ('pits for snaring wolves', v. wulf, pytt, perhaps identical with Woolpits 157 *infra*).

Colesborne

COLESBORNE (144–9913)

> *to Colesburnan forda* 800 (11th) BCS 299
> *æt Collesburnan* c. 802 (11th) BCS 304, *æt Colesburnan* n.d. (11th) BCS 1320
> *Colesborne* 1086 DB, c. 1430 GlR, *-burn(e)*, *-burn(i)a* 1086 DB, Hy 2 Madox, BM, 1199 *FF*, 13 WinchLB *et passim* to 1372 Ch, *-bourn* 1291 Tax, 1328 Banco, 1331 *FF*, *Colisburn'* 1260 *FF*
> *Collesburn(e)* 1171–83 AC, 1221 *Ass* (p), 1301 GlR *et freq* to 1529 GlR, *-bourne* 1303 FA, 1398 *Ass et freq* to 1535 VE
> *Col(l)eburne* 1227 *FF*, 1535 VE   *Colnsbourne* 1366 Ch
> *Cowlesbo(u)rne* 1540, 1587, 1621 *FF*, 1577, 1648 M

'Col's stream', v. burna. The pers.n. is an unrecorded OE *Col* which seems to occur in some OE and later p.ns. (cf. Coleshill Bk 227) and would be connected etymologically with col 'coal'. The stream is the headwater of the Churn, and the ford mentioned in the OE charter was probably a crossing of the R. Churn near its junction with Hilcot Brook south of the church.

CHESCOMBE BOTTOM, *Chescumbe* 1227 *FF*, *-combe* 1839 *TA*. This name (with Chestcombes 153 *supra* and Chescombe in Wapley iii, 57 *infra*) possibly denoted 'valley where cheese was produced' (v. cēse, cumb), but they may possibly be from some other word such as OE ceas or ceastel 'heap' (Chescombe Bottom stands just below the great escarpment of Norbury Camp), or cēast 'dispute, strife' (since the places are on the parish boundaries). Cf. also Chesley Hill (iii, 71 *infra*).

PINSWELL

> *æt Pindeswilla* 680 (15th) Glouc
> *æt Pindewillan* 862 (late 13th) BCS 535
> *Pi-*, *Pyndeswell* 15 Glouc, 1542 *MinAcct*, 1606 *FF*

The first el. is probably the rare OE word **pynd** which may have had some such sense as 'pond' in the Riming Poem 49; it certainly has this meaning in ME p.ns. (cf. EPN ii, 75), and the related verb OE (*ge*)*pyndan* means 'to dam up'. Pinswell would mean 'spring belonging to a pool where the water was impounded', *v.* **wella** (**wielle**).

RAPSGATE, 1824 M. This place gave its name to the hundred (144 *supra*). The earlier forms of the latter suggest an OE *resp-ʒeat*. The first el. would appear to be OE *resp, reps* which is recorded only in the sense of 'response' (in the Church service), but related words like OE *repsan, repsung* and (*ge*)*resp* extend its meaning to 'reprove, blame, convict'; OHG *refsan* meant 'argue', and OIcel *refsa* 'punish' and also 'inquire', whilst MSwed *räfsta-þing* denoted a kind of public meeting or court for the administration of the law (cf. Söderwall ii, 276–7 s.v. *räfst*). It is very probable that some such sense as 'public inquiry, public court of law' would pertain also to OE *resp*, a sense appropriate in the name of a hundred meeting-place. Rapsgate is on the hillside rising to the prominent Pen Hill and there is no topographical feature such as a gap in the hills which would be described by OE **geat**; the latter must here be used of 'a gate', no doubt one on the lane from North Cerney to Colesbourne which gave access to Rapsgate; for the use of *geat* cf. also Spital Gate (65 *supra*), Kiftsgate (261 *infra*).

BALBURROW WOOD, *Bolleberuestret* 13 WinchLB, *Bowberrow* 1839 *TA*, 'grove of tree-trunks', *v.* **bola, bearu**, similar in meaning to Stockwood (*infra*); for the modern form cf. Phonol. § 26. COCKLER PLANT., 1839 *TA*. FORTY ACRE PLANT., *Forty acres* 1839 *TA*. GATCOMBE PLANT., -*head* 1839 *TA*, 'gate or gap valley', *v.* **geat, cumb**. LINCOMBE INCLOSURE. LYDE COTTAGE, *green-, upper Lyde* 1839 *TA*, doubtless an old name of Hilcot Brook, from OE **hlȳde** 'the loud one'; the same stream is referred to in Lyde Bank (189 *infra*). NORBURY CAMP, *Norberry* 1839 *TA*, 'north encampment', *v.* **norð, burh** (here an ancient embanked enclosure), cf. Southbury (*infra*). PEN HILL, 1830 M, *Colesbourne-pen* 1779 Rudder, doubtless originally a British name, *v.* **penno-** 'hill', **hyll**. POWER'S WOOD, 1830 M, named from the family of *Power*; Hugh *le Po*(*h*)*er* held the manor (Taylor, DB 152). SLATESFIELD BARN, *Slaites, Sleight field* 1839 *TA*, *v.* **slæget** 'sheep-pasture'. SOUTHBURY, 1830 M, *Soncheberi* (sic for *Southe-*) 1306 Ipm, 'south barrow', *v.* **sūð, beorg** (a barrow is nearby) or '(land) south of the encampment' (at Norbury *supra*, *v.* **burh**).   STOCKWOOD, 1839 *TA*, 'stump wood', *v.* **stocc**, **wudu**. WESTEDGE WOOD, *western edge wood* 1830 M.

FIELD-NAMES

The principal forms in (*a*) are 1839 *TA* 53.

(*a*) Ashley Hall; Between Wood; Bittum (*v.* **bytme** 'bottom'); Cads moor; Clay butts; Counham (doubtless OE *cūna*, gen.pl. of **cū**, **hamm**); Cowhill; Crowhill; Foxes den; Green hay (*v.* (ge)**hæg** 'enclosure'); Henley nap; Isle of Wight; Langett (*v.* **langet**); Millers ham; Mortar pits; Nesseltons (*Nesteldena* 13 Madox, the first el. perhaps the p.n. *Nasteley* (157 *infra*), *v.* **denu** 'valley'); Oakley Hall; Sedcombe banks; Skittle banks; Smerrells; Tining (*v.* **tȳning**); Tyefield; Yew Yaw.

(*b*) *Longestona* 13 Madox (*v.* **lang**, **stān**); *Tikewell* 1227 *FF* (the OE pers.n. *Tica*, **wella**).

Cowley

COWLEY (144–9614)

> *Kulege* 1086 DB, *Culeg*(*a*), -*ley*(*e*) Hy 3 AD ii, c. 1240 GlR, 1248 *Ass*, *Gulege* c. 1260 Monast
>
> *Kauleg* 1251 Ch
>
> *Couley*(*e*), -*legh* 1253 AD iii, 1287 QW, 1291 Tax, 1295 Misc *et passim* to 1357 Monast, *Koulege* 1287 QW
>
> *Coueley*(*e*), -*le* 1279 Episc, 1287 *Ass*, 1322 Cl, 1325 Ipm
>
> *Coweley* 1488 FF, *Cowley* 1535 VE, 1540 *FF*, c. 1560 *Surv*

'Cow clearing', *v.* **cū**, **lēah**. Some other spellings for Cowley cannot be distinguished from those of Coaley (ii, 219 *infra*).

BIRDLIP

> *Bri-*, *Brydelep*(*e*) 1221, 1287 *Ass*, 1376 GlR (p), 1480 *MinAcct*
>
> *Bredelepe* 1288 Cl
>
> *Brudelep* 1240 GlR, 1295 Ipm
>
> *Bri-*, *Brydlep*(*e*) 1295 Misc, 1423 GlR, 1494 *MinAcct*, -*lipp*(*e*), -*lyppe* 1494 Ipm, 1529 FF
>
> *Briddelep* 1327 SR (p)
>
> *Bi-*, *Byrd*(*e*)*lyp*(*pe*), -*lipe* 1537 *Rent*, 1575 FF, 1637 PR 7
>
> *Burlip* 1675 Ogilby, 1682 PR 3

This describes a very steep declivity at the top of the Cotswold escarpment, and the second el. is OE **hlēp** 'leap' used in the sense 'a steep place'. The first el. could be OE **bridd** 'bird', the compound describing a prodigious leap which only a flying bird could make. But some of the earlier forms (*Brude-*) point rather to OE **brȳd** 'bride' shortened in the compound; the incident or folk-tale from which such a combination as 'bride's leap' could arise is, however, completely lost. Cf. Wintour's Leap (iii, 267 *infra*).

STOCKWELL, *Stok(e)-, Stoc-, Stockewell(e)* 1248 *Ass*, 1296 *MinAcct*, 1327 *SR*, 1357 Monast *et passim* to 1558 PR 16. 'Well or spring near a tree-stump' or 'a well in which the bucket is raised by a pole pivoted in a stump', *v.* **stocc, wella**, a common type of name.

BARROW WAKE. CALLY HILL PLANT., *Callow hill* 1841 *TA*, 'bare hill', *v.* **calu, hyll**. COLDWELL BOTTOM, *Cald(e)well* 1494 Ipm, 1537 *Rent*, 'cold spring', *v.* **cald, wella**. COWLEY MANOR, *maner' de Cowley* 1584 *Comm*. CUCKOO PEN, *v.* Cuckoo Pen (43 *supra*). HARCOMBE BOTTOM. NETTLETON PLANT., *Little Nettleton* 1841 *TA*. PINKHAM. SHAB HILL.

FIELD-NAMES

The principal forms in (*a*) are 1841 *TA* 59. Spellings dated c. 1240 are GIR, 1296, 1480 *MinAcct*, 1537 *Rent* 1022.

(*a*) Baghots hill; Church hill; Crowswell; Culverhay ('dove enclosure', *v.* culfre, (ge)hæg); lower & upper Down; Gold hill; Hasperley; Hitchings (*v.* heccing); Hurdletown field; the Moors; Nettleton laines (*v.* leyne); North field; Nothill; Row field (*Rochfeld* c. 1240, *v.* rūh 'rough', feld); Shermans peak (*land called Shermans* 1537, *v.* pēac); South field; Stony hill; Whirlpit ground; Whitehurst; Witherhongers (*v.* hangra 'wooded slope'); Woolpits Common (cf. *Wolfputtes* 154 *supra*).

(*b*) *Bradeweye* 1296 (*v.* brād, weg); *la Brodgrave* Hy 3 AD ii (*v.* brād, grāf); *Burned place* 1537; *ten' voc' Cokers* 1480; *mease called Fayreaunters* 1537 ('fair adventures', as a surname); *Nasteley* 1537 (possibly for *atten Asteley* 'at the east clearing', *v.* ēast, lēah); *Rydynges* 1537 (*v.* rydding 'clearing'); *Tichengraue* c. 1240 ('kid copse', *v.* ticcen, grāf).

Cranham

CRANHAM (144–8912)

> *Craneham* 1148–79 Glouc, 1281 Misc, 1291 Tax *et freq* to 1544 LP, *Cranaham* 1221 *Ass* (p), *Cranham* 1327 *SR*, 1537 *Rent*, 1584 Comm, *Crannam* 1567 FF
> *Croneham* 12 Glouc, 1429 Pat, 1535 VE, *Cronham* 1189 P, 1241 FF, 1598 *Dep*
> *Crunham* 1287 *Ass*

'Homestead or meadow haunted by herons', *v.* **cran, hām, hamm.** On the forms *Cron-,* and *Crun-* cf. Phonol. § 6.

BROTHERIDGE, *Braderugge* 1266 Glouc, 1327 *SR* (p), *Broadridge* 1838 *TA.* 'The broad ridge', *v.* **brād, hrycg**; it describes the ridge between Cranham and Witcombe where it broadens out towards the Cotswold escarpment.

THE BUCKHOLT, BUCKHOLT WOOD

> (*la*) *Bocholt*(*a*) 1121–1413 Glouc (*freq*), c. 1250 *GlCh* i, 16, 1380 *MinAcct, Bokholt* 1324 Misc
> (*la*) *Bokeholt*(*e*) 1148–79, 1343 Glouc, *-hold* 1529 GlR 428 *Buck*(*h*)*olde* 1549 *FF*, 1629 Inq

'Beech wood', *v.* **bōc**[1], **holt**. This wood extends as Buckle Wood (145 *supra*) into Brimpsfield.

CLIMPERWELL

> *Cli-, Clymperwell*(*e*) 13 Flax, 1287 *Ass*, 1291 Tax *et freq* to 1622 *FF*
> *Climpwell* 1221 *Ass* (p)   *Crimpewell* 1221 Plea (p)
> *Clomperwelle* 1306 *Ass*
> *Cl*(*e*)*ympourwel*(*le*) 1448, 1494 *MinAcct,* (*-pole*) 1449 ib

This spring is the source of the R. Frome. It seems to be a compound of OE **clympre** 'a lump of metal' and **wella**, but its significance is not known; *clympre* survives as dial. *clumper* 'a clod, a clot, a lump or mass' and as the verb *clumper* 'to clot, congeal'. The pool or *stagnum* referred to in 1449 still remains below the spring.

LADLECOMBE, *Ledecome* 1121 Glouc, *Ledencome* p. 1412 GloucHist, *Ladelcombe* 1537 *Rent, Laddlecombe* 1838 *TA. v.* **cumb** 'valley'; the spellings are too varied for certainty; topographically OE *hlædel* 'ladle' might be used here figuratively for the small deep valley which opens out west of Cranham to form a spoon-shaped hollow.

BATCH FM, 1830 M, *v.* **bece**[1] 'stream'.   CRANHAM COMMON (1830 M) & WOOD (1838 *TA*).   CRAYFIELD, *Crowfield* 1838 *TA.*   EBWORTH LODGE, *Elworth wood* (sic) 1848 *TA*, named from Ebworth (132 *supra*).   GREEN HILL.   THE HACKET, probably a derivative of *hack* 'to hack, clear'.   HAREGROVE.   HILLCOT, 1838 *TA.*   THE KNOLL.   MAN'S COURT.   MANY WELLS SPRINGS.   MONKS DITCH, *Monkenedych* 1380 *MinAcct, v.* **munuc, dīc**.   OVERTOWN, *Over* 1459 *MinAcct, Hill overtown Fm.* 1777 M, *v.* **ofer**[2] 'bank', **tūn**.   SALT-

RIDGE HILL, -*Wood* 1830 M, *Solridge wood* 1838 *TA*. SIMMONDS HALL, -*Farm* 1830 M. WATEREDGE. WELLMEAD, *Well ground* 1838 *TA*. YEWRICKS.

FIELD-NAMES

The principal forms in (*a*) are 1838 *TA* 60. Spellings dated 1121–79, 15 are Glouc, 1537 *Rent* 1022, 1540 *MinAcct*, 1639 Inq.

(*a*) Acrey; Ashcroft; Ashlers Knop; Barrow ground; Bodnams; Broad moor; Cheese lands; Cold bath; the Combs; the Crib (OE, ME *crib* 'crib, hovel'); Danley; Dead man's coppice; Downes; Elsely copse; Fostons hill (*Foxtons Knapp* 1627, *v.* cnæpp 'hill'); Glidewell; the Grattons (*v.* græd-tūn 'stubble field'); the Grove; the Hales (*v.* halh 'nook'); Haw field (ib 1777 M, *Hawe* 1627, *v.* haga 'enclosure'); Hen mead; Hitchings (*v.* heccing); Horsely (ham) (*Horsley ham* 1627, *v.* hors, lēah, hamm); the Langett (*v.* langet); Lawless downs (the same place as Lawliss down 160 *infra*); Nutwells; the Patch; Perry field & mead; Rack hill (cf. Rack Hill 140 *supra*); the Reddings (*v.* rydding); Slad acre; South leaze (*Sowdley more* 1627, cf. the local surname *Sudley* 1537 *Rent*); Stoney close (ib 1627); the Tyning (*v.* tȳning 'fence'); broad & deep Whitley.

(*b*) *Alchamsede* 1121; *Aldeberne* 1148–79 (*v.* ald, bere-ærn); *Alrecumbe* 1148–79 ('alder valley', *v.* alor, cumb); *Clarkes croft* 1639 Inq; *Haselshouse* 1540; *Lymerykes* 1537 (named from Thomas *Limerick*, a freeholder, the same surname doubtless being found in Limbrick's Fm 122 *supra*); *Mondesland* 1537 (cf. Sundayshill iii, 108 *infra*); *the Overhowse* 1627; *Salcombesbroc* 15; *Shephowse hey* 1627; *Thisley close* 1627 (*v.* þistel, lēah); *Westrowde* 1584 Comm (*v.* rōd 'rood'); *Woddtrehedge* 1540 (*v.* wudu, trēow, possibly identical with Wateredge *supra*).

Elkstone

ELKSTONE (144–9612)

Elchestane 1086 DB   *Elcustan* 1221 *Ass*
Helkestan 1125–5 Glouc, -*ston* 1287 *Ass*, *Hilkeston* 1285 FA
Elkestan(e) 1177 P, 1220 Fees, 1221 *Ass*, 1264 Ipm, 1291 Heref
Alkestan Hy 2 Madox, -*stone* 1235 Fees
Elkeston 1291 Tax, 1299 WinchLB *et passim* to 1580 *FF*
Elston 1540 *FF*, 1542 LP *et freq* to 1675 Ogilby

For this name, Elkesley (Nt 78), Elkington (L) and Elkstone (St), Ekwall has suggested the OE pers.n. *Ēanlāc*, first reduced to *Ēalāc*. But *Ēalāc* occurs independently in LVD (cf. Feilitzen, NoB xxxiii, 79). 'Ēalāc's stone', *v.* stān.

COCKLEFORD, *Coc(k)leford* 1327 SR (p), 1727 Will. 'Ford where darnel or tares grow', *v.* coccel, ford. But it is possible that the first el. is the ME surname *Cotel* as in the earlier forms of Comb End (*v.* foll.).

COMB END, *Cumb(e)* 1220 Cur, 1221 *Ass*, 1222 Bracton, *Cotelescomb(e)* 1287 *Ass*, 1334, 1346 *FF*, (*-als. Combe Cotell'*) 1460 ib, (*-als. Combend als. Combescottell*) 1542 ib, *Combe Cotele* 1433 ib, *Combes Ende* 1592 ib, *Combend* 1797 *GR* 1386. *v.* cumb 'valley'. *Cotel* is the name of a family who held land here in 1220 Cur, 1225, 1324 *FF* and 1287 *Ass* 31d.

BROMSLEY WOOD, *Bromsley* 1841 *TA*.　BUBB'S HILL, 1841 *TA*. BUTLER'S FM, cf. *Butlers field* 1609 *Craw* 36.　DAMSON GROVE, 1841 *TA*.　HAILER'S WOOD, *-mead* 1841 *TA*.　HIGH CROSS, 1777 M. HIGHGATE, 1766 *Crav* 51.　HILLCLOSE GROVE, *Hill close* 1841 *TA*. SPARROWTHORN.　WARD'S WOOD, 1841 *TA*, cf. *Ward's Hay* 1775 *GR* 184.　WATERCOMBE, *-combs* 1841 *TA*, *v.* wæter, cumb.

FIELD-NAMES

The principal forms in (*a*) are 1841 *TA* 80. Spellings dated 1529–1691 are *Crav* 35–50, 1775 *GR* 184, 1837 *Crav* 53.

(*a*) Barrow field (ib 1775, *v.* beorg); Blackbush piece (ib 1775); the Bogs; the Breach (*v.* brēc); Brimpits Stone Quarry 1775 (*Brimpitts Quarr* 1607, possibly ME *brimme* 'brim, border', pytt); Broad hill; Broken cross (ib 1775); Changeables; Cocklane close (ib 1775); Farthing meadow; Gosditch (*v.* gōs, dīc); Great slait (*v.* slæget 'sheep-pasture'); Home Slait (ib 1775); the Itching (*-Hitch-* 1775, *v.* heccing); Irksum close 1775; Lane (ib 1837); Lawliss down (*Lawless Downs* 1775); Nipes; the North field 1837; North slait(e) (ib 1775, *v.* slæget); (Clay, Green) Oldbury ('a sheephouse called *Oldbury*' 1537, *v.* ald, burh); Parshaws close (*Perssys* 1529); Reads close ('pasture called *Reads*' 1691); Ring meadow (ib 1775); the Seal (probably sele[2] 'willow copse'); Shawcombe (cf. *Shaw acre* 1775); Sling; South field; Stone pit & quar; Uncombe (ib 1775); the Vernal (cf. *Vernhale* 147 *supra*); Walling slait (ib 1775); Wash brook 1775 (ib 1612, *v.* wæsce, brōc); Well hazle; Wood laines (*v.* leyne); Yearcombe.

(*b*) *Badnam milles* 1549; *the Churchowse* 1589; *Long Lease* 1596 (*v.* lǣs); *Roche* 1542 (*v.* roche[1] 'rock').

Rendcomb

RENDCOMB (157–0209)

Rindecome, -cvmbe 1086 DB, *Ri-, Ryndecumb(e), -comb(e)* 12 AD ii, 1189–99 *Guise* 3, 1220 Fees, 1248 *Ass*, 1254 Theok *et passim* to 1372 Ipm, (*Vuer(e)-*) Hy 2 BM, 1171–83 AC, (*Ouer-*) 1255 *FF*, (*Nethere-*) 1311 ib, *Rindcumbe, -combe* 13 AD ii, 1392 Ipm *Rundecumba* Hy 2 Madox　*Reindecumbe* 1248 *FF*

Rendecumb(e), *-comb(e)* 1261 Ipm, 1275 Cl (p), 1285 FA *et freq* to
    1533 *MinAcct*, *(Nether-)* 1277 WinchLB, *(Neor(r)e-)* 1429 ib
Rencomb(e) 1460 Pat, 1752 PR 7
Rancombe 1535 VE, 1646 *Rec*

The first el. is that of the stream-name *on hrindan broc* 852 (13th)
BCS 466 (150 *supra*), and the name denotes 'the valley through which
the *Hrinde*-stream flows', *v.* cumb. The stream-name *Hrinde* has been
connected by Ekwall (RN 339) with the rare OE *hrindan* 'to push,
thrust' and means 'the pusher'. OE *Rindburna* (171 *infra*) is of
different origin and refers to a different stream on the west boundary
of Andoversford. On the spellings with *Rend-* cf. Phonol. § 24.

CLIFFERDINE WOOD, 1830 M, *boscum de Cliffordeham* 1171–83 AC,
Cliffordeam Ric 1 (1372) Ch, *Cliffordham* J Monast. 'Homestead or
meadow near *Clifford*, that is, 'ford near the bank', *v.* clif, ford, hām
or hamm. There is still a ford across the Churn below the steep bank
of Clifferdine Wood (144–014113).

EYCOTFIELD, *Aicote*, *-a* 1086 DB, 1199 *RBB*, 1209 Fees, *Eicot(ia)*
Hy 2 Madox, 1221 *Ass*, *Eykote* 1215 Glouc, 1287 *Ass*, *-cot(e)* 1221
Ass, 1241, 1273 FF, 1277 WinchLB *et passim* to 1588 FF, *Eacott*
1732 *Guise* 10. This farm now stands on high ground ½ mile west of
the Churn, but if *Eycot* itself was near the river the name would
mean 'cottage near the island or water-meadow', *v.* ēg, cot. The
course of the river was affected by the construction of the fishpond
in Rendcomb Park but there is still a small island ¼ mile south of
the pond.

MARSDEN HILL

Marisden Hy 2 BM, 1537 LP, *(-als. Marilden als. Marsh(e)dean)*
    1537 ib, 1635 *FF*, *Maresden* 1328 Banco
Mersdena Ric 1 (1372) Ch, J Monast, *Meresden* 13 AD ii
Marsden 1306 *Ass*, 1366 Ch

'Boundary valley', *v.* (ge)mǣre (gen.sg. (ge)mǣres), denu. This
small valley is on the north-western boundary of the parish.

CHITTLE GROVE, 1830 M.   CONIGREE WOOD, *Cunnigar Wood* 1830
M, *v.* coninger 'rabbit warren'.   GALLEY HILL COPSE, *Gally wood*
1837 *TA*, *v.* galga 'gallows'.   THE GROVE.   HACKPENNY WOOD,
Hackpenny (bottom) 1837 *TA*.   HOLLY BUSH, 1830 M.   IFFCOMB

WOOD, *Ybicumbe* 13 AD ii, *Ifcombe* 1830 M, 'ivy valley', *v.* īfig, cumb.
SHAWSWELL, 1830 M, *Sharshall* 1732 *Guise* 10.   SOUTHMORE GROVE,
1837 *TA*.

FIELD-NAMES

The principal forms in (*a*) are 1837 *TA* 165. Spellings dated 13 are AD ii,
1639 Inq.

(*a*) the Clive; Cow leaze; Cuckoo pen (*v.* Cuckoo Pen 43 *supra*); Dry
leaze; Hull piece; Langett (*v.* langet); North Moore; Ox leaze; Park wall;
Pluff hill; Ruff hill.

(*b*) *Berecrofta* 1171–83 AC (*v.* bere 'barley', croft); *croftam Brihtwoldi*
Ric I (1372) Ch (the OE pers.n. *Beorhtwald*); *Cleywey* 13 (*v.* clǣg, weg);
Greenes farme 1639; *Oxespath* 13 (*v.* oxa, pæð); *Rugwey* 13 ('ridge-way',
v. hrycg, weg); *Shokereswell'* 1236 *FF* (the ME byname *Schokere* 'one who
stooks corn' (Thuresson 39), *v.* wella); *Viners farme* 1639; *bosc' voc' Wethies*
1509 *MinAcct* (*v.* wiðig 'willow').

Syde

SYDE (144–9510)

Side 1086 DB, *Sid'* 1211–13 Fees, *Side, -y-* c. 1220 GlR (p), 1221
Ass, 1227 *FF*, 1232 Cl *et passim* to 1698 PR 8, *Sythe* 1279 *FF*, *Sydene*
1287 *Ass*, *Cide* 1303 FA. *v.* sīde 'hillside, slope'.

CALLEY WOOD, 1838 *TA*.   HARCOMBE BARN, 1830 M.   HIGH
CROFT, 1830 M, *Haycroft linch* 1838 *TA*.   LONGMEAD WOOD, 1838
TA.   SMITH'S CROSS, 1775 *GR* 184.   WOODLEAZE GROVE, 1838 *TA*.

FIELD-NAMES

The principal forms in (*a*) are 1838 *TA* 192.

(*a*) Ham lye close; How mead; Middle Slade; Morgan hill & mead;
Prince well; Severals (cf. Severals 28 *supra*); Wad leaze; Whiting.

(*b*) *Newell* 1291 Tax (*v.* nīwe, wella).

VI. BRADLEY HUNDRED

Bradley Hundred includes the Domesday hundreds of Bradley (the eastern part) and *Waclescombe* (the western part), which were united as Bradley Hundred by the 13th century; *Waclescombe* contained the manors of Aston Blank, Dowdeswell, Hampen, Notgrove, Sevenhampton, Shipton, Whittington and Withington, and Bradley the remaining ones, as well as 1 hide (Little Coberley) in Coberley (152 *supra*). Coln St Denis included here was a detached part of the Hundred of Upper Deerhurst. Bradley Hundred is in the middle of the Cotswolds, north of Brightwell's Barrow and Rapsgate hundreds, and provides the head-waters of the Leach and the Coln. It was one of the Seven Hundreds of Cirencester.

BRADLEY HUNDRED

Bradeleg(e), *-lei hd'* 1086 DB, *Bradesleah*, *-lawe* 1168, 1169 P, *Bradeleg(e)*, *-l'*, *-legh*, *-ley(e)* 1184, 1204 P, 1220 Fees, 1221, 1248 *Ass*, 1274 RH *et freq* to 1378 *Ass*, Bradley 1535 VE, 1540 *AOMB* 242, 1587 *FF*. 'The broad clearing', v. brād, lēah; *Bradley* from which the hundred is named has not been identified. The hundred is called 'the hundred of *Whytyngton*' in 1478 Pat, doubtless because it met there at that period, and there is a lost *Bradeleye* (188 *infra*) which seems to be in Withington (cf. also *Bradley* in Sevenhampton and the nearby *Spellhonger* 179, 180 *infra*). But these places were in *Waclescombe* hundred in DB; we should expect the lost *Bradley* to be in the eastern half of the combined hundred and it might well have been in the neighbourhood of the Fosse Way; in 1400 a meeting of the hundred-court was held near Stowell where the Salt Way crosses the Fosse Way (BG ix, 333).

WACLESCOMBE HUNDRED (lost)

Wacrescymbe hundredum 11 Heming, *Wacrescvmbe hd'* 1086 DB, cf. *waclescumbe* (190 *infra*). 'Wacol's valley', v. cumb. The pers.n. is an unrecorded OE *Wacol*, a variant form of the *Wæcel* which lies behind such names as *Wæclingaceaster*, the old name of St Albans (Hrt 86), Watling Street (Bd 5), Watlington (O 94), etc.; it would be formed from OE *wacol* 'watchful, vigilant'. The DB *Wacres-* shows the common AN interchange of unstressed *-le-*, *-re-* (cf. IPN 107). The site of the place can be approximately determined from the bounds of the Withington charter (BCS 299) by which it would appear to be the small valley east of the Coln between Andoversford and Withington (approximately 144–037170).

Aston Blank

ASTON BLANK or COLD ASTON (144-1319)

æt Eastunæ 716-43 (11th) BCS 165
in Easttune 1033-8 ASChart lxxxvii
Eston(e), *-tona* 1086 DB, 1184-94 WinchLB, 1208 Abbr, 1209
   Fees, (*Cold-*) 1255, 1286 *FF*, 1287 *Ass*
Hestonia 1127 P
Aston(e) 1184-95 WinchLB, 1285 FA, 1287 *Ass et passim*, (*Cold(e)-*)
   1184-94 WinchLB, 1287 *Ass*, 1309 Ipm *et passim* to 1675 Ogilby,
   (*-frigida*) 1275 BM, 1289 Episc, (*Coldi-*) 1303 FA, 1616 *FF*,
   (*Cowlde-*) 1586 ib
Aston Magna 1291 Tax, *Colde Aston als. Little Aston* 1590 *FF*
Aston Blan(c)k(e) 1685 PR 14, (*-als. Coldaston*) 1535 VE, 1627 FF
Aston Longchampe 1548 *FF*

'East farmstead', *v.* ēast, tūn, doubtless so called because it lies
in the east of the hundred or because it faces the east. The affixes
cold, *coldi* (*v.* cald) and Lat *frigida* refer to its cold exposed situation
nearly 700 ft. above sea level, *Longchampe* to its tenure by that family
from the 13th century (BG xxxvi, 133), and *Blank* possibly also to
its 'bareness' or poor vegetation (*v.* OFr blanc 'white, bare'), since
no family of that name occurs locally, though the Fr surname *Blanc*
is possible as a feudal affix. The spellings are sometimes difficult to
distinguish from those of Cold Ashton (iii, 62 *infra*).

ASTON GROVE, 1830 M.   BELHAM'S GORE, *Bellam's* 1796 *EnclA*,
v. gāra.   CAMP FM, *-piece* 1796 *EnclA*, a long barrow and entrenchments (Rudder 238), possibly the site of *þa cæstello* 963 BCS 1105
(*v.* ceastel 'heap of stones').   DRYGROUND BARN, *the Dry grounds*
1796 *EnclA*.   GROVE FM, *Grove Hill* 1796 *EnclA*.   NUTTING BANK.
VINTHILL BARN, *Vinthill common* 1796 *EnclA*.

FIELD-NAMES

The principal forms in (*a*) are 1796 *EnclA*. Spellings dated 963 are (11th)
BCS 1105, 1684-1719 *GR* 75, 1779 Rudder.

(*a*) Blackmoor furlong; Bourton Way (possibly identical with *on burghæma
weg* 963 (11th) BCS 1105, 'the road of the dwellers at Bourton on the Water',
(195 *infra*), *v.* hǣme (cf. Weston Subedge 261 *infra*), weg); Brook Hill;
Church Mead; Coldmoor furlong (cf. Coldmoor Coppice 175 *infra*, possibly
identical with *on colomores sic* 963, *v.* col 'charcoal', mōr, sīc); the Conygrees

(*Connygree* 1684, *v.* coninger 'warren'); Court hill; Foxberry Coppice; Freesland piece; Gate furlong (*v.* geat); Gore furlong (*v.* gāra); Grove hill & wood (ib 1719); High Meers; Hockersdean meadow; Holford Hedge; Hore Stone ground ('boundary stone', *v.* hār, stān); Hull furlong; Little Aston Farm (ib 1779); Meer Slade furlong (perhaps identical with *on mæres slæd* 963, 'boundary valley', *v.* (ge)mǣre, slæd); Morrow Leazow; Townwell Lays; Yew Pen.

(*b*) Baies leaze 1699; *Bowman Hay* 1684; *East field* 1656 *Rogers* 31.

Coln Rogers

COLN ROGERS (157–0809)

Culna(*m*), *Culne* 1100–1284 Glouc (*freq*), (-*Sancti Andreæ*) 1138 ib, (-*Roger*(*i*)) 13, 1200 ib, 1221, 1248 *Ass*, 1281 Episc *et freq* to 1354 Ch, (-*Rogers*) 1328 Banco, 1535 VE, (-*Roggers*) 1331 *Ass*, *Colne Roger*(*s*) 1287, 1331 *Ass*, 1577 M, *Cowln Rogers* 1695 M, with other spellings and meaning as for Coln St Aldwyn (29 *supra*). It was called 'St Andrew' from the original church dedication (Rudder 386), and 'Rogers' from *Roger* de Gloucester, who gave the manor to St Peter's, Gloucester, c. 1100 (cf. Glouc i, 350).

PINDRUP FM, *Pynthrop* 1266 Glouc, 1287 *Ass* (p), 1288 *GlCh* vi, 19, 1310 ib 11, *Pindrop or Pendrop* 1779 Rudder. OE pinn 'peg', some-times apparently denoting a structure held together by pegs (cf. EPN ii, 65), or an OE pers.n. *Pinna* suggested for Pinden (K 43). *v.* þrop 'outlying farmstead', cf. Hatherop (36 *supra*).

COLNPEN COPSE, -*grove* 1830 M, *v.* penn² 'enclosure'.   FOSS CROSS, 1830 M, on the Fosse Way.

FIELD-NAMES

The principal forms in (*a*) are 1839 *TA* 54.

(*a*) the Acre; Candle pill; Candleton hill; the Church-land 1779 Rudder (2 acres given to provide bell-ropes); Felder hill; Fern hill; the Folly (*v.* folie); the Garsons (*v.* gærs-tūn 'pasture'); the Ham (*v.* hamm); Harp hill; the Hitching (*v.* heccing); Long Hay (*v.* (ge)hæg); far & hither Lynch (*v.* hlinc 'ridge'); Ox lait (*v.* oxa, slæget 'pasture'); Postna piece; Sigden gound; Simmonds mead; the Splash; the Take in; Vineyards; the Whales.

(*b*) (*le*) *Culne Doune* 14 *GlCh* ii, 17, vi, 8 (*v.* dūn 'down, hill'); *le Spyne de Culne* 1379 ib (*v.* spinney).

Coln St Denis

COLN ST DENIS (144–0810)

Colne 1086 DB, 1287 *Ass*, (-*Sci' Dionis'*, -*isi*) 1287 ib, 1291 Tax, 1316 FA, (-*Seint Denys*) 1287 *Ass*, (-*denyes*) 1584 *FF*, *Culn(e)* 1191–9 WinchLB, 13 Misc, 1284 *Ass*, (*Sci' Dion'*, -*Dionis'*, -*isii*) 1244 *FF*, 1248, 1287 *Ass et freq* to 1610 *Rec*, (-*St Dynis'*) 1286 Episc, (-*S(t)*. *Denys*, -*is*) 1379 *GlCh* ii, 17, 1467 Pat, 1535 VE, (-*deins*) 1627 Inq, with other forms and meaning as for Coln St Aldwyn (29 *supra*). It was amongst the lands in Deerhurst Hundred given by the king to the church of St Denis (St Dionisius) of Paris in 1069; this also accounts for its inclusion in Deerhurst Hundred (163 *supra*).

CALCOT, *Caldecot(e)* 1086 DB, 1327 *SR*, 1328 Banco, -*cotes* 1306 *Ass*, *Caldycote*, -*i*- 1379 *GlCh* ii, 17, 1583 *FF*, *Calcot(t)e* 1540 *AOMB*, 1540 *MinAcct*, *Calcott* als. *Caldicot(t)* 1587 *FF*, 1627 Inq. 'Cold cottage', probably one offering shelter from the cold or (more probably) a cold, cheerless one, *v.* cald, cot; it is a common p.n. and other Gl examples are Coldicote (220, 251), *Coldicote* (ii, 18) and Calcot (ii, 239 *infra*).

ARRAS WOOD. BRATCH COPSE, *Coln Breach* 1777 M, *v.* brēc 'land broken up for cultivation'. DUDLEY POOL, cf. *Dudley's close* 1798 *EnclA*. FOSS BRIDGE, 1779 Rudder, a bridge carrying the Fosse Way over the Coln. GREENHILL, *Davis's Green Hill* 1798 *EnclA*. THE GROVE, 1798 *EnclA*. LEIGHTERTON BARN, *Leighterton* 1798 *EnclA*, *v.* leahtric 'lettuce', tūn. SALTWAY BARN, 1830 M, *v.* Saltway (20 *supra*). SPLASH COTTAGE, *Mesplush* 1777 M.

FIELD-NAMES

The principal forms in (*a*) are 1798 *EnclA*.

(*a*) Amadines; Barrow Field; Butts Hill; Calcot Street; Canbarrow Hill; Colndean Field 1777 M; the Conigrees (*v.* coninger 'warren'); Cuckoo Pen (*v.* Cuckoo Pen 43 *supra*); the Foss Field & Hill (near the Fosse Way); Kegley; the Lotts (*v.* hlot); the Maple 1779 Rudder; Rye Slade; Swain's Bridge (ib 1777 M); the Tyning (*v.* tȳning).

(*b*) *Clyff* 1540 *AOMB* (*v.* clif).

Compton Abdale

COMPTON ABDALE (144–0616)

Contone 1086 DB   *Cumton'* 1221 *Ass*, 1285 FA
Cumpton(a) 1221–32 WinchLB, 1248 *Ass*, 1267 Pat, 1283 Ch
Compton 1291 Tax, 1303 FA *et passim*, (*parva-*) 1291 Tax,
   (*Magna-*)1327 *SR*, (*Apdale-*) 1504 *FF*, (*-Abdale*) 1535 VE, 1543
   AOMB et passim to 1783 PR 4

'Valley farmstead', *v.* cumb, tūn, called *Abdale* to distinguish it
from Cassey Compton (187 *infra*) and other Comptons (Wa 299), etc.
Ap-, Abdale has not yet been identified with any p.n. or local family
name, unless it be a surname from Apedale (Sa), Apedale (St),
Apedal 1278 Misc, or the f.n. *Apedale* in Henbury (iii, 136 *infra*).

CALDRINGTON PLANT., *Coultangton hill* 1842 *TA*.   COMPTON
GROVE, SCRUBS & WOOD, 1830 M, *v.* scrubb 'brushwood'.   DOWNS
PLANT., *Compton Downs* 1811 Auct 5, *the Downs* 1842 *TA*, *v.* dūn
'hill'.   GROVE COTTAGE, *-wood* 1842 *TA*.   HAWKHILL BARN.
HOLLYBUSH PLANT., *-piece* 1842 *TA*.   SMALLHOPES COTTAGES, *-bank*
1842 *TA*.   STANCOMBE WOOD, 1830 M, 'stony valley', *v.* stān,
cumb.   STAR WOOD, 1811 Auct 5.

FIELD-NAMES

The principal forms in (*a*) are 1842 *TA* 55. Spellings dated 1811 are Auct 5.

(*a*) Arkell; Ashmore ditch; Boar acres; Brandon; Bury mead 1811; Butts;
Chalkwell 1811; Church hill; Compton field (1777 M), hill & park (ib 1777
M); Farm coomb; Fatcombe 1811; Fleet go (*Flintgoe Corner* 1777 M);
Grafton; Green hill; Harps hill; the Hitching 1811 (*v.* heccing); Hunter
horn; Landen; Langet (*v.* langet); Larkall; Long breach (*v.* brēc); Mead
hill; Measden hill; the Moors; Priesdown (*v.* prēost, dūn); Ridgeway; Rooks
hill; Shippy bank (*v.* scēap, (ge)hæg); Stoney bank; Tatcomb; Tately; West
field; Womans Go.

Dowdeswell

DOWDESWELL (144–0019)

Dogodeswellan, Dogedes wyllan, 781–98 (11th) BCS 283
Dodesuuelle 1086 DB, *Doddeswell* 1221 *Ass*, 1226 ClR, *Dodeswell*
   1225, 1529, 1571 *FF*, *Dodiswell* 1535 VE
Doudeswell(a), *-welle* 12 WinchLB (p), 1221 *Ass*, 1227 ClR, c. 1240
   GlR (p), 1248 *Ass et passim* to 1458 *FF*, (*Over-*) 1440 Pat

Dowdeswell(e) 1185 Templar (p), 1284 Episc, 1316 FA *et freq* to
1691 PR 4, *Dowdiswell* 1559 *FF*
Dud(d)eswell' 1221, 1287 *Ass*
Douteswell 1303 FA   *Dowcewall* 1576 *MonLand* 10
Dowedeswelle 1412 *Ass*

The OE spellings are from a reliable manuscript, and the first el.
would therefore appear to be an OE pers.n. *Dogod, Doged*; this would
normally appear as ME *Doud-* (with vocalisation of the OE fricative
-*g*-). But the pers.n. is otherwise unknown; Ekwall has suggested it
would be etymologically connected with OE *dugan* 'to avail, to be
strong, virtuous' with the suffix -*od* (of which no examples occur,
however, in pers.n. formation in OE); Dr Melville Richards reports
that there was an OWelsh pers.n. and saint's name *Doged* (from a
root **doc-*) but this should have had an OE form like *Doced*, for
PrWelsh -*g*- which arose by lenition of Brit -*c*- (in Brit **Doceto-*)
normally has OE -*c*- [k] substituted, as OE did not have the stop -*g*-
[g] in such positions (cf. Jackson p. 251 n, § 137); it would seem
therefore that this pers.n. is unlikely on phonological grounds.
v. **wella**, 'well, spring'. There are two springs and streams here
which unite to form the R. Chelt.

ANDOVERSFORD [ˈandəvəzˈfɔːRd]

Onnan ford, æt Onnanforda 759 (orig.) BCS 187
of ánna forda, in annanford c. 800 (11th) BCS 299
Aneforde 1185 Templar, *Anneford* c. 1243 *GlCh* i, 31 (p), 1274
RH (p), 1287 *Ass*, (*Temple-*) 1354 Inq, *Annesford* 1327 *SR* (p)
Temple Annford(e) 1287 QW
Andovere 1266, 1275 Glouc
Andford 1586 *Comm*, *Andiford* 1779 Rudder 414
Anfords Bridge lying at Anford 1580 Dowd 147
Anfordes forde 1586 *Comm*
Andoversford 1777 M

'Anna's ford', *v.* **ford**; the ford crossed the R. Coln. The OE
pers.n. *Anna*, without doubt that of the same man, occurs in other
p.ns. in the vicinity, *Onnanduun* 759 BCS 187, *æt Onnandune* 781–98
(11th) ib 283, *on annandune* c. 800 (11th) ib 299 (*v.* **dūn** 'hill, down',
identical with the f.n. Hannington *infra*) and *into annan crundele*
c. 800 (11th) ib 299 (*v.* **crundel** 'pit, quarry', referring to one of
several old quarries to the north of the village); if the identification
of *Andovere* is correct, it would also seem to be found in a third

(*v.* ofer² 'bank, hill'), but this may be an error for *Andford.* The forms *Anfordes forde* and later *Andiford*, which were subsequently influenced by Andover (Ha) or the local p.n. *Andovere*, referred more particularly to the ford at a time when the older name *An(d)ford* had come to be used of the village. *Temple-* from the Knights Templars who had land here (1185 Templar, cf. Templefield *infra*).

LINEOVER WOOD, *to lind ofres heafdan* c. 800 (11th) BCS 299, *Lyndover coppice* 1575 *TRMB*, *Lindover* 1641 Inq, *Lineover Wood* 1777 M. 'Lime-tree bank', *v.* lind, ofer², hēafod 'head, hill-top'. The boundary point in BCS 299 must be at the south end of the wood at the top of the steep bank on the Gloucester–Andoversford road (grid 144– 986186).

PEGGLESWORTH

> *wæcgleswyrðe* (sic for *P*-) 981 KCD 631.
> *Peclesurde* 1086 DB, *-wurdin* 1221 *Ass*, *-wurth* 1248 ib
> *Pechelesworth* 1182 *RBB*
> *Pekeleswrd* 1221 *Ass*, *-worth* 1287 *FF*, 1362, 1433 *FF*, *Pekelisworthe* 1535 VE, *Pekilswoorth* 1559 AD v, *Pecklesworth* 1648 *Rec*
> *Petheswrth* (sic) 1287 QW   *Pecchesworth* 1299 *RBB*
> *Pegkeleswrth'* 1287 *Ass*, *Peg(e)les-*, *Pegglesworth* 1327 *SR* (p), 1591 AD v, 1608 *FF*   *Petteleswoorthe* 1354 Inq

'Peccel's enclosure', *v.* worð, the single spelling in *-wurdin* being the Merc derivative worðign. The pers.n. is OE *Peccel*, a form of *Pæccel* suggested for Patchway (Sx 309) and Paglesham (Ess 189). We should, of course, have expected a palatalised form *Pech-* from this pers.n. (as we have in fact in Patchway), but non-palatalised forms occur as in Paglesham, which also has the common voicing of *-k(l)-* (cf. Daglingworth 69 *supra* for a similar voicing of *-k(l)-*). A shortened form of an OE pers.n. like *Peohtel*, a diminutive of some such name as *Peohtgils*, *Peohthelm*, etc. which Ekwall assumes for Peckleton (Lei), would avoid some of the phonological as well as the etymological problems of OE *Peccel*.

ROSSLEY MANOR

> *Rosteleie*, *-ley(e)* 1260 *FF*, 1327 *SR* (p), 1333, 1501 Ipm, 1539 *AOMB* 238   *Rasteley* 1576 *MonLand*
> *Rostley(e)* 14 AD iv, 1504 *Rogers* 1, 1540 *MinAcct*
> *Rosseley* 1554, 1591 AD v, *Rosley* 1576 *MonLand*

'Wood or glade where rafters or beams were got', *v.* hrōst, lēah.

CAMP, *the Camps* 1838 *TA*, an ancient encampment east of Dowdeswell Court. CASTLE BARN, *-piece, the Castles* 1779 Rudder 414, *the Castles* 1671, *v.* castel, here an ancient encampment south of Dowdeswell Court. COLD COMFORT, 1779 Rudder, 1814 *Rogers*, *-Hill* 1689 Dowd 204, formerly *Cold Common* 1777 M, 'so called from its exposed situation' (Rudder 414). DOWDESWELL COURT, Ho (1792 *Rogers*) & WOOD (1830 M). LITTLE GROVE, 1830 M. MATTSHILL WOOD, *Matts hill* 1838 *TA*. OLDBURY (lost), 1779 Rudder 414, *Aldeburhe* 1185 Templar, *v.* ald, burh. RATSHILL BANK. ROUGH HILL BANK, 1838 *TA*. ST PAUL'S EPISTLE, 1830 M, *Paul Aposd.* 1777 M, cf. *Epistle patch* 1838 *TA*, a mound on the south-east boundary of the parish, probably where an Epistle of St Paul was read on the beating of the bounds, cf. names like Gospel Oak, Gospel Thorn, etc., where the Gospel was read. SANDYWELL PARK, *Sandiwell* 1631 PR 15, p. 120, 1674 *GR* 444, *v.* sandig, wella. SCOBB GROVE, *-Lane* 1577 Dowd 142, *-field* 1838 *TA*, *the Scobb* 1663 Dowd 182. WOODLANDS, *(the-)* 1673 Dowd 203, 1777 M.

FIELD-NAMES

The principal forms in (*a*) are 1838 *TA* 69. Spellings dated 759 are BCS 187, 781–98 (11th) ib 283, c. 800 (11th) ib 299, 1562–1809 *Rogers*, 1632, 1641 Inq; others dated without source are Dowd.

(*a*) the Acre; Acres grove; Ayles wood (ib 1641, *Alles wood or grove* 1632); Ball Hays (*Ballheyes* 1596, *-peece, -hayes* 1663, the surname *Ball, v.* (ge)hæg 'enclosure'); Bowsing ground (dial. *bowsen* 'cowshed'); Burnt turf; Chatcombe piece; Churchill; Cockshead; middle & great Comb (*South Combes* 1562, *v.* cumb); Cow leaze (*v.* lǣs 'pasture'); Crawthorn (ib 1664, *Crothorne* 1654, *v.* crāwe, þorn, cf. Crowthorne 47 *supra*); the Dean (*the Deane* 1562, *Deane feild* 1577, *v.* denu 'valley'); Dowdeswell comb (*-Combe* 1724, *the Combes* 1611, *v.* cumb); Four days math ('four days' mowing', *v.* mǣð); Gastons (*v.* gærs-tūn 'pasture'); Grindles (*the Grindalls* 1632); Hannington (probably identical with OE *Onnanduun*, etc., mentioned s.n. Andoversford *supra*, it is at grid 144–029197 east of Andoversford); Hawkridge (ib 1632, *v.* hafoc, hrycg); *the Hogsleasow* 1671; Horse combs & plat (*v.* plat[2] 'plot of ground'); Hunger platt (*v.* hungor, plat[2]); Kat's hill (possibly connected with *catteshlinc infra*); Lanes close (*Laines closes* 1790, *v.* leyne 'arable strip'); Langet (*v.* langet); Nine days math (*v.* mǣð 'mowing'); Oakey Combs; little Orchard (*the Orchard* 1622); Ox leaze (*the Oxe leasewe* 1632, *-lease* 1669, *v.* oxa, lǣs); Park; Parsons acre; the Pens (*v.* penn[2]); Red wood (*Redd-* 1599); Shaw hill; Sheep slaight (*v.* slæget 'sheep-pasture'); Templands, Temple field (*Old Temple* 1577, *Temple* 1588, *Temple cowe leasowe, Temple mead(e)* 1578, 1632, named from the Knights Templars; cf. Andoversford *supra* and *Temple Greene infra*); Town piece (cf. *Town close* 1790); Washpool orchard; Withy bed (cf. *le Withee orchard* 1599, *v.* wiðig 'willow').

(*b*) *to alre wyllan* c. 800 (*v.* Arle Grove i, 185 *infra*); *into annan crundele* (v.l. *onnan-*) c. 800 (*v.* Andoversford *supra*); *to byrcsies heale* (v.l. *bircsiges hale*) c. 800 (the OE pers.n. *Beorhtsige, v.* halh); *les* (*the*) *Breach* 1599, 1632 (*v.* brēc); *Broadfeild* 1649, *Brodfield* 1641; *in catteshlinc* c. 800 (*v.* catt 'wild-cat', hlinc 'ridge'); *Church hey* 1618; *the Colledge ground* 1664 (named from Corpus Christi College, Oxford); *the Colt meade* 1632; *the Connigree* 1632 (*v.* coninger 'warren'); *Cutts Lone* 1577; *the Downe* 1632 (*v.* dūn); *the Driehurst* 1632 (*v.* drȳge, hyrst); *the Dry hill* 1649; *to þære ealdan dic* c. 800 (*v.* ald, dīc); *the Furzen hill* 1654; *Gaiteslede* 1221 Eyre (*v.* slæd); *the Gravill pitt* 1654; *the Grene diche* 1562; *le Greene end* 1577 (cf. *Temple Greene infra*); *on þone grenan weg* c. 800 (*the Greene way* 1588, *v.* grēne, weg); *the Hitchings* 1632 (*v.* heccing); *ofer huni burnan* c. 800 (*v.* hunig, burna, cf. Honeybourne 245 *infra*); *les Laundes* 1577 (*v.* launde); *Lott meade* 1577 (*v.* hlot, mǣd); *Lyllygate slade* 1562; *innan mærbroc, to mærforda* c. 800 (*v.* (ge)mǣre 'boundary', brōc, ford); *Meosglegeo* (v.l. *meosgeleo*) 759 (*v.* mēos 'moss, bog', the second el. uncertain but Forsberg 76 notes other examples, *rah gelega* 849 BCS 455 (Wo) and *grim gelege* 871–99 ib 565 (Brk) and suggests it is an OE *gelǣge, and Löfvenberg 116 an OE *gelegu* with some such meaning as 'tract of land, layer'); *in þone mylen pol* (v.l. *myln-*) c. 800 ('mill pond', *v.* myln, pōl); *Dowdeswells Mill* 1588; *Moore Lane* 1577, *Moore leasowe* 1632 (*v.* mōr, lane, lǣs); *the newe Tynings* 1632 (*v.* tȳning 'fence'); *the paddocke* 1632; *to pican stapele* (v.l. *-stapole*) c. 800 (possibly 'Pica's staple or post' from an OE weak pers.n. *Pīca*, corresponding to the OE byname *Pīc, v.* stapol); *to þære port stræte* c. 800 (*v.* port[2], strǣt, here the Cotswold Ridgeway); *the Quarre* 1594 (*v.* quarriere); *Rindburna* 759 (on the west boundary of Andoversford, *v.* rinde 'hill, ridge', burna); *Salt Lane* 1666 (an unidentified saltway); *to sceapan ecge* c. 800 (possibly an error for *scearpan ecge*, 'the sharp edge or escarpment', *v.* scearp, ecg); *Shacom hill* 1649; *the Sheep haie* 1632 (*v.* scēap, (ge)hæg 'enclosure'); *Sheephouse close* 1632; *on stanihtan weg* c. 800 ('the stony road', *v.* stāniht, weg, cf. Stantway iii, 204 *infra*); *Temple Greene* 1577 (named from the Knights Templars, *v.* grēne[2]); *to þam þorne* c. 800; *Trinsgroue* 1654; *the Tyte lane* 1667; *Woodacre lot meade* 1562 (*v.* hlot).

Eastington

EASTINGTON (144–1313)

Estinton(e), *-yn-* 1119 Glouc, 1227 *FF*, 1231 Cl, 1263–84 Glouc *et freq* to 1328 Banco, (*-iuxta Northlech'*) 1385 *Ass*, *Estington*, *-yng-* 1529 *FF*, 1535 VE, *Essington* 1605 *FF*, with the same meaning as Eastington (54 *supra*); it lies 1 mile south-east of Northleach.

BLACKHILL BARN, *-Bush* 1777 M. BROADFIELD FM, *Brodfeld* c. 1540 *AOMB*. CATS ABBEY BARN, 1830 M, doubtless an old barn infested

with cats.   CRICKLEY BARROW, 1830 M, a long barrow, cf. Crickley
(ii, 115 *infra*).   HELEN'S DITCH, 1830 M, *Ellins Ditch* 1783 *EnclA*.
HILL HO, cf. *Upethehulle* 1327 *SR* (p).   MIDDLE END.   NORBURY
CAMP, 1777 M, *Norbury* 1621 Inq, an ancient encampment, *v.* norð,
burh.   NORTHLEACH DOWNS, *Northleache Downe* 1627 *FF*, *v.* dūn.
NOSTLE FM.   SEVEN SPRINGS, 1830 M.   TROWELHEAD.   WINTER-
WELL FM, -*ground* 1783 *EnclA*, *v.* winter, wella.

FIELD-NAMES

The principal forms in (*a*) are 1783 *EnclA* (which also includes those of
Northleach 175 *infra*).   Spellings dated c. 1540 are *AOMB* 242, 1542
MinAcct, 1575, c. 1603 *TRMB* 39.

   (*a*) Brach Hill (*v.* brēc); Clayhill Lane; Cockman Down; Cockerup
Green; the Ham (*v.* hamm); Hill Leys; the Lammas Mead; the Langet
(*v.* langet); Larcot Hill; Maze Hill; Nosewell closes; the Park; Ripley
Barrow; Saltway (cf. Saltway 20 *supra*); Treadwell Spring; the West Field
(*Westfeld* c. 1540).

   (*b*) *Easte ende* 1575; *Estington meade* c. 1540; *the Fosse end* 1575; *terr' voc'*
Gayes 1542; *mess' voc' le Georges Inne* 1429 *FF*; *Gresecher* 13 Glouc (*v.* gærs,
æcer); *the Hycross* 1577 BG vii, 96; *the Lamp House* 1549 Sherb; *Longmedowe*
1542, *Longmeade* c. 1603; *the Market Place* 1575; *Okeholt* 1542 ('oak wood',
v. āc, holt); *the South ende* 1575; *la Stone meads* 1599 Sherb; *le Wyneyarde*
1542 (*v.* wīn-geard 'vineyard', cf. Vineyard Bridge ii, 36).

Farmington

FARMINGTON (144–1315)

Tormentone 1086 DB
Tormerton(*a*) 1182, 13 WinchLB, 1211–13 Fees, 1287 *Ass*, 1300
   Episc, (-*als. Thormarton als. Fermyngton*) 1573 *FF*
Tormarton(*a*) 1220 Fees, 1291 Tax, (-*als. Farmyngton*) 1566 *FF*
Thormerton 1236 Fees, 1248 *Ass*, 1278 Ipm *et passim* to 1621 Inq,
   (-*als. Fermynton*) 1554 *FF*
Thurmerton 1273 *FF*
Thormarton 1287 *Ass*, 1351 *FF*
Thermerton 1327 *SR*, 1462 Pat
Farmynton 1577 M, *Farmington* 1632 *FF*, 1719 PR 14

'Farmstead near the thorn-pool', *v.* þorn (which often loses -*n*-
in compounds, cf. Phonol. § 37*b*), mere, tūn (Ekwall); no pool is to
be seen today, but there is mention of a *stagnum molendini* or mill-pool

in 1182 WinchLB i, 197. The change of initial *th-* to *f-* is dialectal (Phonol. § 41 *b*). The earlier spellings of this p.n. are difficult to keep apart from those of Tormarton (iii, 56 *infra*).

BAUBLE'S BARROW, 1707 *Encl*, cf. *Hollowbarrowe* 1621 Inq, *v.* hol², **beorg**. BEDWELL FM. BITTAM COPSE, *Bittam hill* 1621 Inq, *v.* **bytme** 'bottom'. CAMP FM, *Under-camp Farm* 1830 M. EMPS-HILL FM, 1621 Inq, *Emshill* 1714 *EnclA, Hempshill* 1777 M. FOLLY FM, formerly *Newhouse* 1777 M. GROVE FM, *The Grove* 1714 *Encl*. THE LAWN. STARVEALL COPPICE, *-Farm* 1830 M. STONEBERRY PLANT., *-Hill* 1707 *Encl, Stoneborowe hill* 1621 Inq, *v.* stān, **beorg**.

FIELD-NAMES

The principal forms in (*a*) are 1707, 1714 *Encl*, and in (*b*) 1621, 1639 Inq. Spellings dated 1182 are WinchLB.

(*a*) Atcombe (hill) (ib 1621); Balls Hay (cf. Ball Hays 170); Burywell Green; Cap hill; Caudwell Head (*Cawdewell-* 1621, 'cold spring', *v.* **cald, wella**); Chadwell corner; Church slad (*v.* **slæd**); Cony Hill (ib, *Conybushe* 1621, *v.* **coni** 'rabbit'); Courthay (*-grove* 1621); Crabtree Leys (*the Crabtree* 1621); the Diggins; the Downs (*the Downe bottom* 1621); the Force Way (denoting Fosse Way); Gastons (*the Stable-, North Gaston* 1621, *v.* **gærs-tūn** 'pasture'); Hawkham Hill (*Hawkcombe* 1777 M); Mill path; Oakers Ash (*Okers Ashe* 1621); Oat Hill (*Otehill* 1621, *v.* **āte, hyll**); Oxmoor (*Oxemoore* 1621); Skeggs (*Skegghey* 1639); Smear hill (*Smyrehill* 1621, *v.* **smeoru** 'fat', **hyll**); Southley; Titewell Bottom; Wickstone (*-ton* 1621); the Willows.

(*b*) *The Benches; Bicknedge; the Breaches* (*v.* **brēc**); *Clift bancks; Floxe poole; Fortie yate* (*v.* **forð, ēg, geat**); *Gosborough; Horeston Hill* ('boundary hill', *v.* **hār, stān**); *Lutherne, -thorne; the Moores; Munnedge hill; Pighay* (*v.* **pigga, (ge)hæg**); *Ramden hill; Ridge-, Rudgeway; the Rowle; Roxhey* als. *Rokyshey; Sandpitt piece; Sherehay; Skuseacre; Southorne moore; Swellshay; the over-, the neather Swilly* (*v.* **swelg** 'pit, whirlpool'); *Three Bushes; the Whiteway* (cf. White Way 20 *supra*); *Witcombe bottom*.

Hampnett

HAMPNETT (144–1015)

> *Heamtun* 1061 KCD 823
> *Hanton(e)* 1086 DB, 12 (1267) Ch, *Hampton(a)* e. 12 OxfCh, 1274 RH, 1330 Ch
> *Hamtonet(t)* 1211–13 Fees, 1227 Ch, 1282 Ipm
> *Hamptonet(t)* 1212 ClR, 1220 Fees, 1263 *FF*, c. 1270 Oseney, Ed 1 BM *et passim* to 1500 ECP

Hamptenet(te) 1287 *FF*, 1290 Episc, 1360 Ipm
Hampenet 1458, 1529 *FF*
Hampnet(t) 1447 *MinAcct*, 1454 *FF et freq* to 1714 PR 4

'(At) the high farmstead', *v.* hēah (wk.dat. *hēan*), tūn. As with the two Hampnetts in Sx 67, 78, the French diminutive suffix *-et* was added by the 13th century.

FURZENHILL BARN, *Furz(e)y hill* 1811 Auct 5, 1842 *TA*.   THE MINE. OLDHILL.

FIELD-NAMES

The principal forms in (*a*) are 1842 *TA* 95.

(*a*) Barrow hill; Hampnett down; Hangmans stone down (*-stone* 1811 Auct 5); Hovel; the Patch; Townland.

(*b*) *atte Fortheye* 1327 *SR* (p) (*v.* forð, ēg).

Hazleton

HAZLETON (144–0818)

Hasedene 1086 DB, *Heseldene* e. 12 OxfCh, *Haselden* 1587 *FF*
Haselton(a) 12–1404 WinchLB (*freq*), 1174 France, 1195 P (p),
    1221, 1248 *Ass et freq* to 1327 *SR*, *Hasilton(a)*, *-yl-* 1313
    WinchLB, 1535 VE *et freq* to 1733 PR 14
Heselton(a) 13, 1201 WinchLB, 1251 Ch

'Farmstead near the hazels', *v.* hæsel, tūn. Some earlier forms point to an original or alternative 'hazel valley', *v.* denu.

PUESDOWN, *Peulesdon'* 1236 *FF*, *Piwelesdon* 1302 GlCorp (p), *Pewelesdon* 1322 Fine (p), *Puesden* 1777 M, *Pewsdown* 1830 M. 'Pe(o)fel's down or hill', *v.* dūn. The first el. seems to be either an OE pers.n. *Pēofel* suggested by Ekwall for Pilson (Sa), a diminutive of OE *Peuf(a)*, or an otherwise unrecorded OE pers.n. **Pefel*, which would be a similar diminutive of the OE *Pefi* in Pewsey (W 350); cf. also Pevensey (Sx 443), Pamington (ii, 54 *infra*). The same pers.n. may be found in *Peuellesbroke* (iii, 119 *infra*). The vocalisation of OE pre-consonantal *-f-* to *-u-*, *-w-* is common (Phonol. § 34*b*).

THE DOWNS BREAK, 1830 M.   HAZLETON GROVE, *Hasilton groue* 1530 *MinAcct*.   PRIORY FM.

Northleach

NORTHLEACH (144–1114)

Lecce 1086 DB

Lecch(e) 1086–1181 Glouc (*freq*), 1100–35 *Tewk* 72, (*North-*) 1200 Glouc, 1287 *Ass*, 1290 Episc, 1330 Misc

Lech(e) 12 WinchLB, 1213 Abbr, 1220 Fees, (*North-*) 12–13 Glouc (*freq*), 1221 *Ass*, 1268 Episc (p) *et freq* to 1514 *FF*, (*Nort-*) 1227 ClR, 1269 Episc, (*Nor-*) 1274 RH

Licchiam c. 1127 AC

Nortletche 1219 ClR, *North-* 1535 VE, 1542 *MinAcct*

Nordlegh 1227 Ch, *Nortlegg'* 1274 RH, *Norlegh* 1276 ib

Northlucche 1306 *Ass*   *Nor(th)leich* 1327 SR

Northlacche 1429 Pat, *-lache* 1492 *MinAcct*, 1546 *FF*, c. 1650 Surv, *Norlache* 1587 *FF*

Northlatche 1535 VE, 1543 *MinAcct*, 1552 Pat

Northleach(e) 1627 *FF*, 1641 PR 14, *Norleech* 1714 ib 4

This is a place on the R. Leach (10 *supra*) and is called 'North' to distinguish it from Eastleach (31, 33 *supra*).

MILL END, 1742 Will, *the Mille ende* 1757 *TRMB*, *v.* myln, ende.

Notgrove

NOTGROVE (144–1120)

ad Natangrafum 716–43 (11th) BCS 165

Nategraua, -grava, -grave 1086 DB, 1209 Fees, 1220 WinchLB, 1234, 1268 *FF et passim* to 1407 ib

Nattegraue, -grave 1230 Cl, 1248 *Ass*, 1469 *FF*

Nutgrave 1285 *FA*, *Nuttegroue* 1482 *FF*

Natesgrave 1315 Ipm   *Natgrave* 1393 Ipm

Notgrove 1535 VE, 1587 *FF*, 1616 *Dep*, 1695 PR 4

'The wet grove', *v.* næt (wk.dat. *natan*), grāf, but an OE pers.n. *Nata*, cognate with OG *Nato, Nazo*, is also possible, cf. Natton (ii, 53 *infra*). The change to *Not-* is late and may be an inversion after the dialectal change of *-o-* to *-a-* had taken place when *-o-* could become a spelling for the vowel *-a-* as well as *-o-* (Phonol. § 26). The *Nut-* forms are due to popular etymology.

THE BUCKLEAP. COLDMOOR COPPICE, *Coldmoor* 1771 *EnclA*, cf. Coldmoor furlong (164 *supra*). FOLLY FM, 1771 *EnclA*, *Notgrove Folly* 1777 M, *v.* folie. KITEHILL BARN. KITTS KNOB, *Kites Nobb* 1771 *EnclA*. PEMMINGTON COPPICE, *Pembertons close* 1771 *EnclA*. POWNTWELL, *Pountwell* 1771 *EnclA*, cf. Poultmoor (25 *supra*). SHEWHILL COPPICE, *Shewhill* 1771 *EnclA*, probably dial. *shewell* 'scarecrow'. SHRUBS COPPICE, *Shrubs close* 1771 *EnclA*, *v.* scrubb 'brushwood'. STANBOROUGH LANE, *Stamberrow Down & lane* 1771 *EnclA*, 'stone barrow', *v.* stān, beorg, denoting the remains of a long barrow 1 mile north-west of Notgrove; the lane was called *stræt* in 716–32 BCS 165.

FIELD-NAMES

The principal forms in (a) are 1771 *EnclA*. The spellings in (b) are 716–43 (11th) BCS 165.

(a) Ashway; Bushey Shrubs; Clamford piece; Colley croft; Coomhill ground; the Coney Gree (*v.* coninger 'warren'); Copperknowles; Cow leaze; Doghillock; the East Field; Freecroft; Hulk ground (*v.* hulc 'shed'); Langate (*v.* langet); Nattocks copse (*v.* nattok); Newhill; Notgrove downs; the Several (*v.* Severals 28 *supra*); Thorney grove; Wain Way.

(b) *on Cynelmesstan* (the OE pers.n. *Cynehelm*, *v.* stān); *on Turcanwyllas heafod* (*v.* Turkdean 183 *infra*).

Salperton

SALPERTON (144–0720)

   Salpretvne 1086 DB, *-tone* 1287 QW

   Salpertune, -ton(e) 1169 P, 1185 Templar, 1195 P, c. 1210 Monast,   1221 *Ass* (p), 1236 Fees, 1241 *FF et passim* to 1535 VE

   Salpartona 1220 Fees   *Salportona* 1321 WinchLB

This difficult name is probably one in which the first el. is a much reduced form. Ekwall has suggested that it is from an OE *sealh-burna* 'willow stream'. But since the village is near the Saltway (20 *supra*) we might well have OE *salt-herepæð* as the starting point; the compound *salt-herepæð* 'salt road' (that is, one used by salt-merchants) occurs only in a charter as *salt herpað* (KCD 645) and in *Salt-harperweie* (107 *supra*); *v.* tūn 'farmstead'.

CROW'S CASTLE. DOWN'S PLANT., *to þære ealdan dune, andlang dune* 816 (11th) BCS 356, *le(3) Downes* 1540, 1542 *AOMB*, *the Old Dun*

1712 *Rogers*, *Old Down* 1780 *EnclA*, *v.* ald, dūn 'hill'. FARHILL
FM, *the Hills*, *the Furr-Hills* 1735 *M.* LAMP ACRE, *Lampe Acre*
piece 1735 *M*, 1780 *EnclA*, 'an acre of which the rent provided for
a lamp', cf. *Lampehousse* (67 *supra*). SALPERTON PARK, *the Park*
piece 1741 M

FIELD-NAMES

The principal forms in (*a*) are 1780 *EnclA*, and in (*b*) 1540, 1542 *AOMB* 45,
447. Spellings dated 816 are (11th) BCS 356, 1712, 1752 *Rogers*, 1735,
1741 *M.*

(*a*) Alwalls Hill 1735; Ashey closs 1735; Bann Furlong 1741 (*v.* bēan
'bean'); the Barrow 1741 (*v.* beorg); Bees; Coppins Close (-*ings*- 1752, *claus'*
voc' Coppynges 1540 *MinAcct*, 1542, the surname *Copping*); Eastwell Spring;
the Furze Hills 1741; the Garstons (*the Gastons* 1741, *v.* gærs-tūn 'pasture');
Gidnells (*Gidnell* 1741); the Gores 1741 (*v.* gāra); Greenhill (ib 1741);
Upper & Lower Haies 1741 (*v.* (ge)hæg); Hails Hill; Harp hatch 1735;
Littleton Hill; the Lot meadows (*v.* hlot); Mickley Hill (ib 1741, *Mickle Hill*
1712); Lower & Upper Nattuck (*prat' voc' Nattokes* 1540 *MinAcct*, 1542,
the Nattocks 1735, *v.* nattok); Nutcroft (ib 1540, 1735); Penhill (ib 1735,
v. penno- 'hill' or penn²); Pool Hill (*the Pool* 1735, *v.* pōl); Round Hill
(ib 1712); St John's Green 1712; Shetwell Furlong 1741; Vatt Croft 1735;
Waterton (*Waterdown* 1741, *v.* wæter, dūn); Westgores (ib 1712, *v.* gāra).

(*b*) *of þam crum dæle* 816 (*v.* crundel 'quarry', an old quarry at grid
144-063207, Finb p. 189); *Frogmershe* 1535 VE (*v.* frogga, mersc); *le lordes*
meade; *Salperton meade*; *Stuble Feldes*; *leʒ Tenne Acres.*

Sevenhampton

SEVENHAMPTON (144-0321)

Sevenhamton(e) 1086 DB, 1216 ClR, 1291 Tax, c. 1560 *Surv*
Seuen-, *Sevenhampton* e. 13 WinchLB, 1248 *Ass*, 1274 RH, 1285
FA *et passim* to 1698 PR 7
Seuehamton 1221 Eyre (p), *Sevehampton* 1241 Ch, 1535 VE
Seues-, *Sevezhampton* 1327 SR
Sevanton 1437, 1454 Pat
Senhampton 1506 BM, 1610 M, (*-als. Sen(n)yngton*) 1575 *FF*, 1614
Rec
Semynton 1577 M   *Seynhampton* 1604 *FF*

This name, which finds parallels in the neighbouring counties of
Worcester (Sevenhampton, Wo 107), Wiltshire (Sevenhampton,
Sevington, W 27, 107), and Somerset (Seavington, *Seofenempton*

c. 1025 DEPN), appears to be a compound of OE seofon 'seven', hām 'homestead' or hǣme 'dwellers' and tūn 'farmstead, village' (v. hǣma-tūn, hām-tūn in EPN). In Wo 35 and W 107 the interpretation is discussed and the conclusion drawn that such a name denoted 'a village with seven homesteads', and a parallel is found for the type in Syrencot (W 366) 'cottages with six homesteads'. It is also pointed out that in Nt in DB a thane with 6 manors or less paid 3 marks of silver to the sheriff but a thane possessed of more than 6 manors paid a relief of 8 pounds to the king; though late, the allusion suggests that seven units of property was the point at which much heavier fiscal burdens came into operation. OE hǣme 'dwellers' is frequently used in compounds with topographical words (as in Brockhampton infra) or with contracted forms of older p.ns. (cf. EPN i, 216, 217), and Ekwall has therefore proposed that these names embody some older p.n. such as seofon wyllas 'seven wells' (184 infra). But the last named, which is some 3 or 4 miles away was never a settlement site and therefore unlikely to have had inhabitants to give their name to Sevenhampton. On the whole, the evidence would rather favour a name denoting 'a village of 7 homesteads' forming a single community which because of its size carried a special burden of taxation. For the reduced form Sen-, cf. Phonol. § 34(b).

BROCKHAMPTON

> Broc-, Brokhamtone 1166 RBE (p), 1361 Ipm
> Broc-, Brokhampton 1248 Ass, 1285 FA, 1287 Ass et freq to 1535 VE, Brokampton 1437 Pat, 1544 FF
> Brokehampton 1506 AddR, 1557 Val 42b
> Brock(e)hampton 1572, 1576 FF, 1575 TRMB, 1603 PR 15
> Brockington 1599 Comm, 1605 PR 15

This p.n. occurs elsewhere (ii, 21, 90 infra, Do, He, and as Brookhampton in Wo 33, 269, Wa 252), and denotes 'farmstead of folk dwelling by the brook', v. brōc, -hǣma-tūn, or more probably 'homestead by the brook', v. hām-tūn.

CAWCOMBE (lost), Colecumbe 1221, 1248 Ass, l. 14 ECP, Calcom(s)-felde 1532 Lanth² 130, Calcumbe 1575 TRMB 39, Calcombe 17 GR 444, Cawcomb 1772 ib. This refers to the valley in which the R. Colne rises, and the first el. is doubtless the r.n. v. Coln 5 supra, cumb. Cf. Phonol. § 26.

CLOPLEY (lost), *Cloppele* 1275 Heref, *-leye* 1280 ib, 1287 *Ass*, *Coppe-leye* (sic) 1349 Aid, *Clopley* 1575 *TRMB* 39, 1576 Pat, *Clapley* 1624 *FF*. 'Clearing on the hill', *v*. clopp(a), lēah. The first el. occurs in several Gl p.ns., cf. Clapton (198 *infra*). For the form *Clap-* cf. Phonol. § 26.

PUCKHAM FM & WOODS, (*bosco de*) *Putcumb(e)* 1274, 1276 RH, *Pulgoumbe* 1291 Tax, *Pulcomb* 14 Rudder 646, *Puckombe* 1506 *AddR*, *Puckeham* c. 1560 *Surv*, *Puckhamwood* 1575 *TRMB*, 1598 *Comm*, 1624 *FF*. Probably 'goblin valley', *v*. pūca, cumb.

ABBOTS WOOD. BESPIDGE WOOD, *Bispage hill* 1575 *TRMB* 39, *Bispedge* 17 *GR* 444, possibly a reduced form of biscop 'bishop', ME *bisp*, as in Bispham (La 136), *v*. ecg 'scarp'. BREAKNECK PLANT., *Break Neck* 1818 *EnclA*. BROCKHAMPTON PARK, *Park* 1830 M. ELSDOWN BARN, *Elsdown* 1818 *EnclA*. NASH BARN, *le Nashe*, *Nashehill* 1575 *TRMB*, *v*. atten, æsc 'ashtree'. OXLEAZE, *Oxlease* 17, 1777 *GR* 444, *v*. oxa, lǣs. SIDELANDS, *-land* 1818 *EnclA*. SOUNDBOROUGH. WHITE HALL, *Wittal* 1777 M. WHITE HILL, 1575 *TRMB*, 1723 *GR* 444, *v*. hwīt, hyll; *hwitan dic* (*infra*) is on this hill.

FIELD-NAMES

The principal forms in (*a*) are 1818 *EnclA*, and in (*b*) 1575 *TRMB* 39. Spellings dated 816[1] are (11th) BCS 356 (first set of bounds), 816[2] ib (the second set of bounds in this Hawling charter, cf. ii, 18 *infra* and Finb pp. 184–96), 1532 *Lanth*[2] 130, 17–1776 *GR* 444.

(*a*) Annis Wood (*Annyswoode* 1575, the ME fem. pers.n. *Anneis*, a variant of *Agnes*); the Barrow piece; Bentil Fields; Black acre; Blackthorn fields; the Blind Lane; Brook Furlong (*Brocke furlonge* 1532, *le Brooke forlonge* 1575, named from *Seuehampton Brok* 1532, *v*. brōc); the Burrows; Court Field (*Cort-* 1776); the Dry Leaze; Elwell; Folley; Garbidge Piece (*Gorbege Hedge* 1650); Goose Green; Granna Bottom; Harrolds Cross; Hartshill Piece; Hawthorn; Henberrow; Horsepool; Linch meadow; the Lindons (*terr' jac'* in *Lyndes* 1575, *v*. lind 'lime, linden-tree'); May Pole close; Meacham Scrubs; Millfield 1776 (ib 1575); Ninds Oxleys; Pendum piece; Perrill; Quarr Ground (*Quarrefeld(e)* 1532, 1575, 17, *v*. quarriere); Row-borough Field; Shab Hill; Sturden Hill; Stye furlong (*Stile-* 1575); Wash Brook; the Weir (*le Weareyat* 1575, *v*. wer, geat); Whitton Dean (*Wyddon Deane* 1575); Witch hasell 1751.

(*b*) *Benshill* (ib 1532); *Blacksidhill* 1532; *Bradley coppice*; *Brockforde*; *Capuls land*; *Cotehunger* 1532 (*v*. cot, hangra); *Cotomely field*; *Dongeon coppice*; *to dina more* 816¹ (*dina* is obscure, but may recur in *dinmere* 943 BCS 784 (KPN 259), *v.* mōr, located in Finb p. 190 near a marshy copse at grid 144–043206); *to þære ealdan dic* 816¹ (*v.* ald, dīc, perhaps at grid 144–054202); *to þære ealdan dune* 816² (*v.* ald, dūn, a connection with Elsdown (*supra*) (Finb p. 190) is unlikely, cf. Down's Plant 176); *ofer þa ecge* 816² (*v.* ecg); *Estfield*; *the Fordehey Closse* 1532 (*v.* ford, (ge)hæg); *Gareford* 1287 *Ass* (*v.* gāra, ford); *Gouldhey*; *to, of grimes hylle, -crimes-* 816² (from Grīm, a byname of Woden, often used in ancient earthworks, *v.* hyll, here referring to an ancient circular encampment at grid 144–047243); *Hayles Way* 1532 (the road (the Saltway) to Hailes ii, 15 *infra*); *wið þan heafdan* 816¹ (*v.* hēafod); *into hehstanes pytte* 816¹ (the OE pers.n. *Hēahstān*, *v.* pytt); *le Hitchinge close* (*v.* heccing); *Holowaye coppice* (*v.* hol², weg); *to þære hwitan dic* 816² (*v.* hwīt, dīc, at grid 144–044235 on White Hill *supra*); *Isenwell* (*v.* īsern 'iron', wella); *Kitethorne* 1532 (*v.* cȳta 'kite', þorn); *Lymepittes*; *Lymynge Hey* 1532; *Motehill*; *Northfield* (*Northefelde* 1532); *Ockeys*; *Otehill* 1532 (*v.* āte 'oats'); *Penywoode coppice* (*v.* pening); *Reves hey* (*v.* (ge)rēfa, (ge)hæg); *Roulhurst coppice*; *Shuttwode*; *the Severall pasture* 1532 (e.ModE *severell* 'private land'); *Sondayes hill* (*v.* Sundayshill iii, 108 *infra*); *Spellhonger Copice* (cf. *Swel hongre* ii, 93 *infra*, with which it may be identical, *v.* spell 'speech', hangra 'wooded slope'); *Stoneley* (*-ly* 17); *Wellhay*; *Witwellfields* (ib 17); *Woldene* 1532; *to þæs wudes efese* 816² ('edge of the wood', *v.* wudu, efes, this being Oxlease Wood at grid 144–053234).

Shipton

There were two parishes, Shipton Oliffe and Shipton Solers which were united in 1776. Shipton Oliffe was largely surrounded by Shipton Solers and the lands of the two parishes were curiously intermixed.

Shipton Oliffe (144–0318)

Scip(e)tvne 1086 DB, *Scipton(e)* 1212 RBE, 1276 RH

Stiptune (sic) 1185 Templar

Sipton' 1211–13, 1236 Fees, *Sippeton'* 1220 ib

Skipton 1216 ClR

S(c)hip-, Shypton(a) 1221 Bracton, 1236 FF, 1287 QW, 1291 Tax *et passim* to 1715 PR 4, (*-by Wydindone*) 1328 Misc, (*-Olyve*) 1371 FF, 1430 Pat, (*-Olyf(f)e*) 1439 FF, 1535 VE (*-Ollieffe*) 1621 FF

Schepton' 1221 *Ass* (p), (*-Olive*) 1349 Heref

Shupton 1354 Ipm

'Sheep farm', *v.* scēap, tūn. On the *Ship-* form (from WSax *scīep*) cf. Shipton Moyne (108 *supra*). The manor was held by the family of *Olive* (cf. Thomas *Olyve* 1347 Glouc and Rudder 656).

Shipton Solers

> *Scipetvne* 1086 DB
>
> *Sipton(a)* 1221 Eyre, *Ass* (p), 1372 Ch
>
> *S(c)hip-, S(c)hypton* 1236 *FF*, 1298 Episc, 1303 FA, 1322 WinchLB
> *et passim* to 1621 *FF*, (*-Roberd*) 1287 *Ass*, (*-Chaunflour*) 1291
> Tax, (*-Soler(e)s*) 1360 Ipm, 1481 Pat, 1540 *MinAcct*, (*-Solace*)
> 1535 VE, 1553 *FF*, (*-Solas*) 1543 LP, 1584 *Comm*, (*-Sollers*)
> 1621 *FF*, (*-Pelle*) 1374 Ipm, (*Ouer-*) 1439 *FF*
>
> *Chipton' Chamflurs* 1236 Fees
>
> *Shupton Solers* 1366 Ch

v. Shipton Oliffe (*supra*), from which it is distinguished by the
names of various holders of estates within the manor, of whom the
principal were the family of *Solers* (cf. William *Solers* 1221 Eyre 70,
Robert de *Solers* 1236 *FF* 215); *Roberd* is probably *Robert* le Archer,
also called *Robert* de Solers (1236 *FF*), who married a granddaughter
of Walter de Cormeilles, a 12th-century owner of the Shipton estate.
Chaunflour is the name of another owner John *de Chamflurs* (1236
FF) and *Pelle* doubtless refers to Robert *Pulye* who had an estate
here in 1242 (Fees).

Hampen

> *Hagepinne* 1086 DB   *Hagapennid* c. 1145 France
>
> *Hagenepene* 1086 DB, *-penne* 12 France, 1234 Cl, *Hagnepenne*
> 1194–1221, 1200, 1215 WinchLB
>
> *Haghenepenn(e)* 1221 *Ass*, 1236 *FF*
>
> *Angne-, Hangnepenn* 1221 *Ass*
>
> *Haunepenne* 1241 *FF*, 1287 *Ass*, 1327 *SR*, 1439 FF
>
> *Hennepenne* 1248 *Ass*
>
> *Haw(e)nepenne* 1274 RH (p), 1333 Ipm
>
> *Hannepenne superior'* 1285, 1303 FA, *Hanpenne* 1507 *Rent*
>
> *Havenepenn'* 1291 Tax, *Havenpen* 1527 Monast, 1535 VE, 1540
> *AOMB*, (*Over-, Nether-*) 1553 *FF*
>
> *Hampen(ne)* 1507 Rent 831, 1535 VE, 1563 *FF*, (*-inferior, -superior*)
> 1575 *FF*, (*-als. Havenpen*) 1584 *Comm*

'Hagena's pen or enclosure', *v.* penn² (found also in Pen Barn
infra). The OE pers.n. *Hagena* occurs in the poem *Waldere* ii, 15
as that of a Burgundian and as the ruler of the continental *Holm-Ryge*
in Widsith 21, as *Hagona* in Kentish charters (BCS 42, 78, etc.) and
in the p.ns. *haganan treae* (BCS 247) and Haunton (St), *Hagnatun*

942 BCS 771. It is usually regarded as an early borrowing from OG *Hagano* (Forssner 138–9) and cognate with ODan *Haghni*, ON *Hǫgni*; the ON name is considered to be the source of DB *Haganus, Hagana*, etc. (Feilitzen 282). Feilitzen thinks a native equivalent might have existed in early OE, but the sporadic occurrence of the name in much later times may be due to a memory of the legends of the heroic age, as also is the pers.n. in Withington (186 *infra*); cf. IPN 186–8, Introd. The development of *Hagene-* to *Haun-* is normal (cf. Phonol. § 35).

CLAYHILL BARN. CLEEVELY WOOD. FROG MILL, 1779 Rudder, cf. *Frogmersh* 1540 *MinAcct*, 1542 *AOMB* 447, *-mede* 1543 LP, *v.* frogga, mersc, mǣd. HILL BARN, cf. *Upthehulle* 1327 *SR* (p). PEN BARN, *Penshill Barn* 1830 M, named from *la Penne* 1285 FA, *v.* penn² 'enclosure'. SOUTHAM WOOD, 1830 M. TOTTMOOR.

FIELD-NAMES

The principal forms in (b) are 1236 FF. Spellings dated 13, 1200 are WinchLB i, 151, 156, 1507 *Rent*, 1540 *MinAcct*.

(b) *Alcotes Sich* 1200, *Holdcote(slede)* 13 (*v.* ald, cot, sīc, slæd); *Beche* 1200 (*v.* bēce² 'beech'); *Beorhforling* 1200 (*v.* beorg 'hill'); *Berleg* 1200 ('barley enclosure', *v.* bere, lēah); *Crockareshulle* (*v.* croccere 'potter', hyll); *Edricheshulle* 13 (the OE pers.n. *Ēadrīc*); *Estfeld*; *Ferncumbe, -hulle* (*v.* fearn, cumb); *le Gyres* 1507; *Hexforlong'*; *Hole(we)breche* 13, 1200 (*v.* hol², brēc); *Hordberia* 13 ('treasure barrow', *v.* hord, beorg); *Kyncotesaker*; *Longaker*; *le Mawdelyn thing* 1507 (*v.* þing 'property'); *Midlestewelle* ('middlemost well'); *Oldendun* (*v.* ald, dūn); *Pesfurlong* (*v.* pise 'pease'); *Sandputte* 13; *Sulegraue* (*v.* syle 'bog', grāf); *Suthdon'* (*v.* sūð, dūn); *Tuelueakeres*; *Westfeld'*; *Winterwelle* (*v.* winter, wella); *Wyueledenesheuede* (*v.* wifel 'beetle', denu); *Wowelande* 13 (*v.* wōh 'crooked', land).

Stowell

STOWELL (144–0913)

Stanuuelle 1086 DB, *Stanwell'* 1248 *Ass*
Stonewell' 1287 *Ass*, *Stonwell* 1327 *SR*
Stawell(e) 13 WinchLB, 1220 Fees, 1221 *Ass* (p) *et freq* to 1323 *MinAcct*
Stowell(e), -wel 1269 Episc, 1271 Ipm, 1284 Episc, 1285 FA, 1287 *Ass et passim* to 1720 PR 2, *Stowylle* 1290 Episc (p)
Stowewell 1284 Episc (p)   *Stouwell* 1303 FA

'Stone well or spring', *v.* stān, wella; there are several springs in Stowell Park. But this name, like Stowell (W 326), might denote 'a stream with a stone-built channel'. The later forms *Stawell* and *Stowell* arise from the well-evidenced loss of -*n*- before labial consonants (cf. Stafford Mills 141 *supra*, Phonol. § 37*c*).

OXPENS, 1842 *TA*, *v.* oxa, penn². STOWELL PARK, 1842 *TA*, *Deer Park* 1811 Auct 5.

FIELD-NAMES

The principal forms in (*a*) are 1842 *TA* 189. Spellings dated 1811 are Auct 5.

(*a*) Cockshoot (*v.* cocc-scīete); Cowleaze (ib 1811, *v.* lǣs 'pasture'); Cowpen bushes (ib 1811, *v.* penn²); Foss hill (on the Fosse Way); Goose grove 1811; Hangman's stone (ib 1811); Latter math meadow 1811 (*v.* mǣð 'mowing'); Lowley hill (ib 1811); Mazedown Moor 1811; Muddingham 1811; Nables coppice (ib 1811); Raybrook mead 1811; Sheep Pens 1811; Skeggs wood (ib 1811); Stowell Grove 1811.

Turkdean

TURKDEAN (144–1017)

(*on*) *Turcandene* 716–43 (11th) BCS 165, 944 ib 882, 10 KCD 1360
(*vallis qui dicitur*) *turcadenu* 779 BCS 230
ofer turcendene 816 (11th) BCS 356
Tvrchedene 1086 DB, *Turchedena* 1151–7 Oseney, 1168 P, 1199 ClR
Turkesd' Hy 1 (1267) Ch   *Turkenden'* 1191 Oseney
Turkeden(a), -*dene* 1151, 1191, c. 1220 Oseney, 1220 Cur, Fees, 1236 FF, 1248 Ass, 1273 Ipm, 1274 Cl *et passim* to 1535 VE, (-*Superiori*) 1303 FA, -*deane* 1570, 1599 FF
Thurkeden(e) 1221 Ass, 1224, 1241 FF, 1301 Ipm, (-*Sup'*, -*Inf'*) 1327 SR
Torkeden(e) 1268 Episc (p), 1287 Ass (p), 1313 WinchLB
Thorke(s)den 1284, 1295 Episc (p)
Turkden superior, -*inferior* 1587 FF, *Nether Turckden als. Turden* 1611 ib, *Turkdean* 1737 PR 13

'The valley of a river called *Turce*', *v.* denu. The r.n. *Turce* (gen. *Turcan*), which is also alluded to in *of Turcanwyllas heafde*, *on Turcanwyllas heafod* 716–43 (11th) BCS 165 'the head of the *Turce*-stream', is related by Ekwall (RN 420) to the Welsh r.n. *Twrch*; this is from Welsh *twrch* 'boar', but a figurative sense has been suggested for its use of rivers which 'form deep channels or holes into which they sink into the earth and are lost for a distance'. *v.* Addenda.

CHALKHILL BARN, *on Cealcweallas* 716–43 (11th) BCS 165, *Chalkwell spring* 1793 *EnclA*. The form suggests the meaning 'chalk or limestone walls' (*v.* cealc, wall).

BEALE'S COPPICE. BROADWATER BOTTOM, *Brod(e)-, Broadwater* 1574 *GR* 158, 1578 *BrtCt*, 1639 Inq, 'broad stream', *v.* brād, wæter, the stream which comes from Turkdean and is crossed here by Fosse Way. DOWNS COPPICE. HILL BARN, cf. *Upthehulle* 1327 *SR* (p), *v.* hyll. HOLY HILL COPPICE. LEYGORE MANOR, -*Farm* 1830, *v.* lǣge 'fallow', gāra 'gore of land'. LOWER DEAN FM, cf. *Dean Down* 1793 *EnclA*, *v.* denu 'valley'. MILKWELL COVERT. SHEW-HILL BARN, dial. *shewell* 'scarecrow'.

FIELD-NAMES

The principal forms in (*a*) are 1793 *EnclA*. Spellings dated 716–43 are (11th) BCS 165.

(*a*) Ash Furlong; Cam Mead; Cover cliff; Ditch Furlong; Gallows Furlong; the Green; Gretton, Gratton (*v.* grǣd-tūn 'stubble field'); Grindell Hill; the Hayes (*v.* (ge)hæg); Holy Bush Furlong; the Innfield; Mawbush; Nethrops Farm; Out Field; the Pen; Picked Close (dial. *picked* 'picked bare'); Seven Mens Mowth (a variant of mǣð 'mowing'); Woodend Pitt Furlong.

(*b*) *to Balesbeorge* 716–43 (*v.* beorg 'barrow', the first el. may be a pers.n. *Bælli*, cf. Wa 53); *Browninges* 1633 Inq; *Rammesdun* 1224 FF (*v.* ramm 'ram', dūn); *on seofenwyllas* 716–43 ('seven springs', *v.* seofon, wella); *þa, to þære* (*ðere*) *spelstowe* 716–43, 949 BCS 882, 10 KCD 1360 ('speech or council meeting-place', *v.* spell-stōw; Grundy unnecessarily emends to *swelstowe*; the place was on the Fosse Way near Broadwater Bottom).

Whittington

WHITTINGTON (144–0020)

Witetvne 1086 DB

Wi-, Wytinton' 1205 Cur, 1220 Fees, 1236 *FF*, 1248 *Ass et freq* to 1309 *FF*, -*ing*-, -*yng*- 1285 FA, 1287 *Ass*

Wythinton 1211–13 Fees

Whitinton, -y- 1278 Ipm, 1303, 1316 FA, 1327 *SR et freq* to 1373 *FF*, -*ing*-, -*yng*- 1303 FA, 1439 Pat, 1478 IpmR *et freq* to 1620 PR 15

Whittington, -yng- 1488 Pat, Hy 8 *Surv*

'Farmstead associated with Hwīta', from the OE pers.n. *Hwīta*, *v.* ing⁴, tūn. The spellings of this name are sometimes difficult to keep apart from those of Withington (186 *infra*). Cf. Whittington (Wo 178, where the form *Wiþindon* c. 1240 *Worc* should be deleted as it refers to Withington).

WHALLEY FM, *to weallehes weg* 800 (11th) BCS 299 (v.l. *wallehes*), *Wallaye* 1236 *FF*, *Whallay* 1236 ib (p), *Walley Fm.* 1782 Will. Probably 'clearing near the wall', *v.* wall, lēah and weg 'road'. An old embankment stands just below the farm on the opposite side of the stream.

WYCOMB, *Wickham* 1248 *Ass*, 1838 *TA*, *Wikham* 1361 Ipm. The name refers to a piece of land where Roman remains, now no longer visible, have been found (grid 144–028202, 6″ O.S. no. 27 SE); it is OE wīc-hām which usually means 'homestead with a dairy-farm' or the like. It is possible, however, that as in one or two instances of OE wīc-tūn the *wīc* denotes the Roman *vicus* (cf. EPN ii, 263–4).

ARLE GROVE, 1838 *TA*, probably named from *alre wyllan* (171 *supra*), *v.* alor, wella. SYREFORD, 1779 Rudder, *Syersford* 1777 M, *Cyford* 1792 PR 17, 45, probably the OE pers.n. *Sigehere*, *v.* ford. WOOD FM, named from *Whittington Wood* 1830 M.

FIELD-NAMES

The principal forms in (a) are 1838 *TA* 222.

(a) Burgage Hill; Conygear (*v.* coninger 'warren'); Cotton Grove; Dodwell Hill; England; Five Tree Hill; Horse Pleck (*v.* plek 'small plot'); Manlands close; Mills Hitching (*v.* heccing); Peewit Hill; Picked Hill (dial. *picked* 'picked bare'); Pitsham; Rail Piece; Sheep Cubbs (dial. *cub* 'cattle-shed, pen'); Walton (possibly 'Welshman's farm', *v.* Walh, tūn); Whatcomb.

(b) *Combe* 1361 Inq (*v.* cumb); *Ermegroue* 1236 *FF* (an OE pers.n. *Earma* or *Eorma* (cf. Armley YW iii, 210), *v.* grāf); *Tikelokeswaye* 1236 *FF* (probably a ME byname *Thikkelok* 'one with thick locks', *v.* weg).

Winson

WINSON (157–0808)

Winestvne 1086 DB, *Wi-*, *Wyneston(a)* 1224 Oseney, 1236 Fees, 1248 *Ass*, 1265 Ipm, 1276 Oseney *et freq* to 1327 *SR*
Wi-, *Wynston* 1220 Fees, 1303 FA *et passim* to 1587 *FF*
Wynneston(e) 1292 *FF*, 1312 Ipm

Wynsyngton, -i- 1552 Pat, (*-als. Winson*) 1622 *FF*
Winson 1671 PR 17

'Wine's farmstead', from the OE pers.n. *Wine* and *tūn*. The later spellings of Winson and Winstone (142 *supra*) are often difficult to separate.

CADMORE COPSE, 1830 M. DEADLANDS COPSE. EWE PEN. POOL Ho. SLON COVERT.

FIELD-NAMES (*b*) *Inthehurne* 1327 *SR* (p) (*v.* hyrne 'corner of land'); *le Merweye* 1301 AD iii ('boundary road', *v.* (ge)mǣre, weg).

Withington

WITHINGTON (144–0215)

Wudiandun 736–7 (11th) BCS 156, 774 (11th) ib 217
Uuidiandun 774 (11th) BCS 217, *Widiandune* c. 800 (11th) ib 299
Widindvne 1086 DB, *Widiendon'* 1221 Eyre, *Wi-, Wydindon(e)* 1221 *Ass*, 1275, 1287 Episc, 1327 *SR*, 1328 Misc, *Wydendonam* 1278 WinchLB, *Wydyngdon'* 1306 *Ass*
Wi-, Wythindon(a) -yn-, -d' -done 12, 1191–9, 13 WinchLB, 1209 Fees, 1221, 1248 *Ass*, 1274 RH, 1275 Episc *et passim* to 1547 Pat, (*-super le Wolde*) 1329 *FF*, *Wythingdon, -yng-* 1248, 1287 *Ass*, 1408 Pat, (*-als. Wedyngton*) 1439 ib, *Wythendon* 1291 Tax
Wi-, Wythinton, -yn- 1211–13 Fees, 1275 Episc, 1282–1314 WinchLB, *-ing-, -yng-* 1573 *FF*, 1584 *Comm et freq* to 1654 PR 8
Witindon' 1221 *Ass*
Whithindon, -y- 1255 Ch, 1287 *Ass*, *Whythyngton* 1482 Pat
Wydinton, -yn- 1274 RH, 1275 Episc, 1285, 1303 FA
Wethington 1535 VE, 1557 *FF*, *-don* 1540 *MinAcct*

'Widia's hill,' *v.* dūn. The pers.n. OE *Widia, Wudga*, which is of obscure origin, may also be found in Woodenham (213 *infra*); like *Hagena* in Hampen (181 *supra*), it is found first in OE heroic poetry as *Widia* in *Waldere* ii, 4, 9 and *Wudga* in *Widsith* 124, 130; in Germanic legend Widia was the son of Weland the Smith (cf. *Widsith*, ed. K. Malone, 198 ff). But the name appears much later as that of a moneyer in the 11th century (Redin 159), in DB, and in the 12th century (Feilitzen 417); its use for these persons as well as for the individual who gave his name to Withington would appear to perpetuate a memory of heroic story (cf. IPN 186-9, Introd.). For the affix *le Wolde*, *v.* **wald** 'high, open country' and cf. Cotswolds (2 *supra*).

LITTLE COLESBORNE, *Colesborne* 1086 DB, *Parua Coleburne* 1227 *FF*, *Parva Colesburn(e)* 1227 Pat, 1284 FA, 1291 Tax, *Little Collesbourn* 1290 Episc, *-parva* 1543 LP. *v.* Colesborne (154 *supra*) which is on the other side of the R. Churn.

CASSEY COMPTON, *Cum tún* 962 BCS 1089 (Finb 104), 982 KCD 634, 989 ib 669, *Contone* 1086 DB, *Parva Compton* 1274 Ipm, 1413 IpmR, 1610 *FF*, *Coumpton'* 1385 *Ass*, *Cassi(e)s-*, *Cassyes Compton* 1510 ECP, 1580 *Talbot*, 1608, 1623 *FF*. 'Valley farmstead', *v.* **cumb**, **tūn**. The estate belonged to the Cassey family from the time of Hy 7 (cf. Henry *Cassye* 1580 *Talbot* 72638, *v.* Rudder 839).

COTHILL, *Cotewell(e)* 1299 *RBB* (p), 1540 *MinAcct*, 1544 LP, *Cotwell* 1548 Pat. 'Well or stream near the cottage', *v.* **cot**, **wella**.

FOXCOTE, *Fuscote* 1086 DB, 1779 Rudder 839, *Foxcot(e)* 12 Glouc, 13 WinchLB, 1200 Berk, 1209 Fees, 1221 *Ass*, 1274 RH *et passim* to 1614 *Dep*, *-chotis* 1200-10 Berk, *-coate* 1586 *Comm*, *Foxecot(e)* 1214 Abbr, 1221 Eyre. 'Fox lair or den', *v.* **fox**, **cot**, and for this compound cf. EPN i, 109.

FULFORD, *Fuleford'* 1236 *FF*, *Fulford* 1274 Cl (p). 'Foul, dirty ford', *v.* **fūl**, **ford**. The ford carried a track to Andoversford over a small stream north of the farm.

HALES WOOD, 1830 M, *Hall Wood* 1544 LP, *Aleswood* 1577 M, *Alleswood* 1632 Ipm. 'Wood in the nook of land', *v.* **halh**, **wudu**. The nook is referred to in the local byname *Inthehale* 1327 *SR* (p).

HILCOT

> *Willecote* (sic) 1086 DB
> *Huldicota*, *-cote* 1209, 1220 Fees, 1327 *SR* (p), *Huldecote* 1274, 1344 *FF*, *Hudicote* (sic) 1299 *RBB*
> *Hildecote* 1221 *Ass*, 1303 FA
> *Hold(e)cote* 13 WinchLB, 1284 FA
> *Hil-*, *Hylcote* 1504 *FF*, 1535 VE, 1540 *MinAcct*, 1543 *AOMB*

This name presents phonological difficulties. If the first el. is OE **helde**, or rather late WSax *hylde* 'slope', which Ekwall suggests, the *Hulde-*, *Hilde-* spellings could be accounted for; it is doubtful whether a late WSax form would be found in regular colloquial use as far north as this, though the nearby Shiptons (180–1 *supra*) contain WSax forms. Alternatively we may have an OE *hylda* which would explain the forms; such a word, which is not otherwise known, would be a derivative of OE *hyldan* 'to flay, skin', *hold* 'carcase' and *holdian* 'cut up', and would, like another derivative *hyldere*, mean something like 'skinner' or 'butcher'; a verbal substantive *hylding* 'skinning' (which first appears in ME in Trevisa, cf. NED s.v. *hild*) would also be possible, as there is some ambiguity in the interpretation of medial -*i*- (cf. Phonol. § 49). 'Skinner's cottage' or 'shed where skinning was done', *v.* cot.

MERCOMBE WOOD, *to mærcumbe* c. 800 (11th) BCS 299, *Merescumbe* 1139–48 Glouc, *Markham grove* 1839 *TA*. 'Boundary valley', *v.* (ge)mǽre (gen.sg. (*ge*)*mǽres*), cumb, referring to a long deep valley along which the parish boundary runs, as did that of the Withington estate in BCS 299; the same boundary is named in *Meresplot* 1139–48 Glouc (but cf. *Merscplot* 190 *infra*), and in *mǽrweges* c. 800 BCS 299, which is a track going north along the boundary from the head of Mercombe.

OWDESWELL

> *Aldeswella, -welle* 1191 P, 1260 FF, 1274 Cl, 1290 Episc, 1299 RBB
>
> *Aldewell(e)* 1221 *Ass*
>
> *Oldeswell(e)* 1270 *FF*, 1287 *Ass*, 1291 Tax *et freq* to 1586 *Comm*
>
> *Oldiswell als. Odiswell* 1570 *FF*, *Owdeswell* 1779 Rudder

'Ald's spring or stream', *v.* wella. The pers.n. is an OE *Ald* found in Aldsworth (23 *supra*). The modern form has been adapted to that of the nearby Dowdeswell (167 *supra*).

UPCOTE FM, *Upcote* 1221 *Ass* (p), 1236 *FF*, 1287 *Ass*, 1327 *SR* (p), *Huppecot(e)* 1221 *Ass* (p), *Hupcote* 1299 *RBB*, *Upcottes* 1548 Pat, -*cott* 1573 *FF*. 'Upper cottage', *v.* upp, cot.

BADGERBURY PLANT., 'badger sett', *v.* burg. BARNCOMBE BOTTOM. BOGDEN BANK. BRADLEY (lost), *Bradeley* 1299 *RBB*, *v.* brād, lēah, and Bradley Hundred (163 *supra*). THE BRATCHES, *South Breach* 1811 Auct 5, *v.* brēc. BREAKNECK BANK. BROADWELL END, 1779 Rudder, *v.* brād, wella. CHATTERLEY, 1819 *EnclA*. DAY'S HILL. ELWELL, 1819 *EnclA*. FOULWELL WOOD, *Ful-*,

Fowlwell 1819 *EnclA*, 'dirty spring', *v.* fūl, wella. THE GULF SCRUBS, *Gulf Hill* 1819 *EnclA*. HILL BARN, 1830 M, cf. *Upthehulle* 1327 *SR* (p), *v.* hyll. KILKENNY, 1830 M, a transferred Irish name, cf. Kilkenny (27 *supra*). LYDE BANK, *the Lloyd* 1819 *EnclA*, the old stream-name, OE hlȳde 'the loud one', also referred to in Lyde Cottage (155 *supra*). NEEDLEHOLE, 1830 M, *Needleshole* 1814 *Rogers*, 1819 *EnclA*, the first el. is probably an adaptation to names like Needles Hole (ii, 38 *infra*) of the p.n. *Neatley* (153 *supra*), which is in the immediate vicinity, *v.* hol[1]. NORTHFIELD FM, *Northfeld* 1299 *RBB*. PINCHLEY WOOD, *-Grove* 1830 M, probably 'finch clearing', from ME *pinche*, a variant of pinca, *v.* lēah. RAVENSWELL FM, cf. *Revenesthorne* 1299 *RBB*, 'the raven's well and thorn', *v.* hræfn, wella, þorn. SHILL HILL, 1819 *EnclA*. SHORNHILL FM. SMOKE ACRE, 1819 *EnclA*, cf. Smoke Acre (70 *supra*). STAPLE FM, 1819 *EnclA*, *Staples* 1603 *FF*, cf. *atte Stable* 1327 *SR* (p), from the surname *Staple(s)*. THORNDALE, *Thornden* 1327 *SR* (p), *-dean* 1830 M, *-dale* 1819 *EnclA*, 'thorn-tree valley', *v.* þorn, denu. TURPIN'S GREEN. WALL GROVE, *Wall(ed) Grove* 1819 *EnclA*. WOODBRIDGE, 1819 *EnclA*.

FIELD-NAMES

The principal forms in (*a*) are 1819 *EnclA*, and in (*b*) c. 800 (11th) BCS 299. Spellings dated 1227, 1270 are *FF*, 1299 *RBB*, 1535 VE, 1548 Pat, 1576 *MonLand* 33, 1586 *Comm*, 1614 *Dep*, 1811 *Auct* 5.

(*a*) the Bars; Bow Wood Closes (*Bowood* 1535, *v.* boga, wudu, 'wood where bows were obtained'); Broadmead 1811; Broadnam (*v.* brād, hamm); Burnham; Butts Field (*the Butts* 1614, *v.* butt[2] 'archery butt'); the Case; Clevely (*v.* clif, lēah); Coneygree Wood 1811 (*v.* coninger 'warren'); Cow Ham (*v.* cū, hamm); Cuckoo Pen (*v.* Cuckoo Pen 43 *supra*); Dipple Bottom; the Fiddle (doubtless so called from its shape); the Folly (*v.* folie); the Forehades (*v.* fore, hēafod); the Foxalls (*v.* fox-hol); Gawlick Hill; Golden Valley; Green Stye (*v.* stīg 'path'); the Ham, Ham Hay (*v.* hamm, (ge)hæg); the Hook; Hornham Meadow; Horsham (*v.* hors, hamm); Hungerstarve Meadow, Hungry Park (names for poor land); the Inn-Field 1811; the Langate (*v.* langet); the Mill Hams 1811 (*v.* hamm); Newham (*v.* nīwe, hamm); Oil Hay; Oxleaze 1811; the Park; Prince Hay (the surname *Prince*, *v.* (ge)hæg); the Raggs (cf. the Ragg ii, 237 *infra*); Rudges; Settle ground; the Slape (*v.* slæp 'mire', cf. Löfvenberg 189); Sour Moor 1811; Stocks Hay; Stony Bridges; Walwell (FinbW 23, possibly 'Welshmen's spring', *v.* Walh, wella); White Oak Lloyd (cf. Lyde Bank *supra*); Withy Hill.

(*b*) *on beam weg* (*v.* bēam 'log', weg); *Blokoldende* 1535; *on buccan slæd* ('he-goat's valley', *v.* bucca, slæd); *to cnictes ferwege* ('the knight's cartway', *v.* cniht, fær, weg, cf. OE *fær-weg*); *innan, of denebroc(e)* c. 800, *la Dene* 1270 (*v.* denu 'valley'); *to duddan heale* (v.l. *-hale*) (the OE pers.n. *Dudda*, *v.*

halh); *on flod leah* c. 800, *Flodleye* 1270 (*v.* flōde 'gutter', lēah); *to þam fulanwege* ('the dirty road', *v.* fūl, weg); *on gatanstige* (*v.* gāt 'goat', ān-stīga 'path'); *Greendich banke* 1586; *Grenenesley* 1548; *to halgan wyllan* ('the holy well', *v.* hālig, wella); *Halyhay* 1586, *Halehaye, -hey, -lond* 1614 (*v.* halh, (ge)hæg); *on, of horsweg(e)* ('horse track', *v.* hors, weg); *in hreodcumb* ('reed valley', *v.* hrēod, cumb); *Lamphey* 1586; *innan mænanlea* ('the common clearing', *v.* (ge)mǣne, lēah); *in mærdic, andlang mærweges* (*v.* (ge)mǣre 'boundary', dīc, weg); *Merscplot* 1227 (*v.* mersc, plot); *þæs mores* (*v.* mōr); *Moreplot(t)es* 1540 *MinAcct*, 1544 LP, 1576 (*v.* mōr, plot); *the parsons peece* 1586; *Russelles* 1548; *Ruyndone* 1299 ('rye hill', *v.* rygen, dūn); *þurh þone sceagan* (*v.* sceaga 'copse'); *Southfeld* 1299; *on ealdan stanwege* ('stony road', *v.* stān, weg); *Tyckwell hedge* 1586; *Totewell* 1576; *to waclescumbe* (cf. *Waclescombe* Hundred 163 *supra*); *the bottom of Wyden* 1586; *to wohan æc* (v.l. *wogan-*) ('twisted oak', *v.* wōh, āc, dat. ǣc).

Yanworth

YANWORTH (144–0713)

Janew(o)rth(e), -wurth' 1043–66, 1216 WinchLB, 1248 *Ass*, p. 1412 GloucHist

Tenevrde (sic for *Iene-*) 1086 DB, 3*eneworþe* 1154–89 Glouc

Þ*aneword(i)am, -worthe, -worþe* (sic for 3*ane-*) 12, 1135–54, 1139–48, 1154–89 Glouc

Ianeword(am), -worþia, -orþe, -w(o)rth(e) c. 1162–1384 WinchLB (*freq*)

3*anew(o)rth(e), -wrþe* 1211–1428 WinchLB (*passim*)

Hanewurth' 1220 Cur, 1221 *Ass*

Ieanworth 1221 WinchLB

Ianesworth 1251 Ch

Yanew(o)rth(e) 1251 Ch, WinchLB, 1268 *FF*, 1282 Episc, 1287 *Ass et freq* to 1413 Pat

Yaueneworth 1287 *Ass*

Yanworth 1316 FA, 1540 *MinAcct*, 1611 *FF*

Enworth 1535 VE   *Yeaneworth* 1632 PR 7

Since OE worð 'enclosure' is often combined with pers.ns., an OE *Geana* or *Gæna* suggested by Ekwall may well be the first el.; it would be a shortened form of names like *Gænbald, Iaenbeorht* and the like; some of these pers.ns. may be merely variants of the common OE name-theme *Ēan-* as in *Ēanbald*, etc. (cf. Feilitzen 259 note). In that case we should have to assume the development of a prosthetic *y-* (ib 118). But the first el. may in fact be related to OE (*ge*)*ēan* 'in lamb' (cf. OE *ēanian* 'to bring forth (lambs, etc.)', OE **ēan,* 'lamb', and NED s.v. *yean* 'young lamb', etc.), and Yanworth would denote something like 'lamb enclosure'; such spellings as *Ʒene-, Iean-* would be normal, and those in *Jane-, Iane-, Ʒane-* represent shortened forms in the compound. For initial *Y-* cf. Phonol. § 43; *J-* is an AN variant of this (*v.* IPN 104–5).

DEAN GROVE, 1811 Auct 5, cf. *Denelane* 1457 WinchLB, *the Dean* 1839 *TA*, *v.* denu 'valley'. MILL BRAKE, *Mill piece* 1839 *TA*, cf. '*contra molendinum unam acram*' 1222 WinchLB and 'a mill called *le Gyldene Myle*' 1457 ib, 'the golden mill', *v.* gylden, myln. OAKS BOTTOM, 1811 Auct 5. STREETFOLD, 1811 Auct 5, named from the Fosse Way, *v.* strǣt. YANWORTH WOOD, 1540 *MinAcct*.

FIELD-NAMES

The principal forms in (*a*) are 1839 *TA* 232. Spellings dated c. 1190 are WinchLB ii, 334, 13 ib 318–23, 1222 ib 320, 1457 ib 550, 1811 Auct 5.

(*a*) the Bannis (ib 1811); Blackwells ground; Castle Hill (ib 1811); Church mead 1811; Clay Pitts; Culver piece 1811; Etheridge meadow; Folly Hill (ib 1811, *v.* folie); Hartley Hill (ib 1811, *v.* heorot, lēah, hyll); Great & Little Hay(e)s (*v.* (ge)hæg); Luglands (-*land* 1811); Marley pasture; Pen Piece; Radwell (ib 1811, *v.* rēad, wella); Shadwell (ib 1811, 'shady spring', *v.* sceadu, wella); Street Acre (ib 1811).

(*b*) *Bradedenverne* 1222 ('broad valley ferns', *v.* brād, denu, fearn); *le Churchehouse* 1540 *MinAcct*; *Drakenhord* 1222 ('dragon hoard', *v.* draca, hord, alluding to the folk-belief in dragons guarding treasures in barrows, of similar origin to Drake North W 400 and Dragons Ford iii, 240 *infra*); *Dudenwellerine* 1222 (the OE pers.n. *Dud(d)a* (cf. *duddan heale* in Withington 189 *supra*), *v.* wella, OE *ryne* 'stream'); *Eyleswei* 1222 (the OE pers.n. *Ægel*, *v.* weg); *domo Estrildis* c. 1190, 13 (the OE fem. pers.n. *Ēastorhild*); *Hundeshulle* 1222 (*v.* hund 'hound', hyll); *Iordanesbroke* 1457 (the ME pers.n. *Jordan* or possibly named after R. Jordan); *Maricrosse, crucem* 1457 (a cross in honour of the Virgin Mary); *le North(e)feld(e)* 13, 1457; *Scaggesforlong* 1457; *le South(e)feld(e)* 13, (-*Nevylle*) 1457; *le Valuwe* 13 (*v.* falh 'ploughed land, fallow land'); *Waitingwei* 1222; *la Welhamme* 13 (*v.* wella, hamm); *Windeberīt* 1261 ('wind-swept hill', *v.* wind, beorg).

VII. SLAUGHTER HUNDRED

LOWER DIVISION

The lower division of Slaughter Hundred is in the Windrush valley on the borders of Oxfordshire and occupies the central eastern part of the Cotswolds. At the time of the DB inquest what later constituted Slaughter Hundred was made up of the hundreds of Barrington and Salmonsbury. The former of these two included Great and Little Barrington, Widford, and Windrush and soon after was merged in Salmonsbury or, as it came to be called, Slaughter Hundred. Great Barrington was formerly partly in Berkshire and in dispute, whilst Widford has been transferred to Oxfordshire (O 384).

BARRINGTON HUNDRED (lost)

Berni(n)ton(e) hd' 1086 DB. This small DB hundred, which took its name from Great Barrington (193 *infra*), is not mentioned after 1086; *v. supra.*

SALMONSBURY HUNDRED (lost)

Sal(e)manes-, -mones-, Salesmanesberie h(vn)d' 1086 DB
Salemones hd' 1086 DB, *Salemannes hdr'* 1169 P
Salmanesburi, -bury c. 1232 AD iii, 1303 FA, (*-in libertate de Fiscampo*) 1346 FA (v.l.), *Salemanesbury* 1247 Ch, *-mans-* 1416 Pat
Salemanebur(e), -bury 1246 Cl, c. 1275 *For* 36d, 1366 Pat, *Salemannebur'* 1248 Cl, *Salemanbiry, -bury* 1290 Pat, 1364, 1379 Cl
Salomundresbur' 1247 Cl, *Salmondebir'* 1248 *Ass*, *Salmundesbur' Fiscampo* 1346 FA, *Salmondesbury* 1444, 1461 Pat
Salomonebir' 1251 Cl, *Salomonsbury* 1406 Pat
Salemonesbury, -biri Hy 3 Misc, 1274 RH, *Salmonesbury* 1316 FA, Hy 6 *AddCh*

This name, which is an alternative to Slaughter Hundred (*infra*), is taken from that of the meeting-place at Salmonsbury in Bourton on the Water (195 *infra*). Anderson 21 notes that in Hy 3 AD iii, 556 the abbots of Evesham and Fécamp agreed that the abbot of Fécamp, in whose liberty the hundred was (it had been granted to Fécamp in 1246 Cl, 1247 Ch), should hold his hundred court at Salmonsbury and in 1293 Ipm an inquisition was held there. There was, however, some flexibility in the choice of the meeting-place, for c. 1232 AD iii (D. 1054) the court was to be held at *Slohter* and in 1416 Pat 13 the coroner held an inquiry again at *Scloughter*, whilst in 1779 Rudder 303 records that a court-leet of the Liberty of Salmonsbury met twice a year at a gap in the rampart of Salmonsbury but after calling over the jury 'they adjourn to some other place to finish their business'.

SLAUGHTER HUNDRED

Sloctreshdr' 1189 P, *Hundr' de S(c)lochtres* 1221 *Ass*
Scloctrehundredo 1190 P, *hundredo de Slohtre* 13 WinchLB, *Sloghtr'*
  1221 *Ass*, *Sloctr'* 1233 Cl, *Slochtre* 1236 Theok, 1247 Ch
hundredum de Slottr' 1220 Fees
hundr' de Sloutr(e)', *Sloustr'* 1274 RH
lib' de Slouhtre 1277 Cl, *hund' de Sloughtre* 1327 *SR*, 1328 Banco
hund' de Slaughter 1535 VE, 1542 LP, 1584 *Comm*

The hundred takes its alternative name from Lower Slaughter (206 *infra*), since the latter was the chief manor, and the hundred was already annexed to it in DB (fol. 163a, Taylor 149); in 1247 the king granted the manor of Slaughter with the hundred of Salmonsbury to the abbey of Fécamp (1246 Cl, 1247 Ch).

Great Barrington

GREAT BARRINGTON (144–2113)

Berniton(e) 1086 DB, 1190–1192 P
Berninton(a), -*ton(e)*, -*tun*, -*yn*- 1086 DB, 1137 Monast, 1156,
  1196 P, 1212 Fees, 1213 Cur (p), 1254 Cl, 1287 QW *et freq* to
  1485 Pat, (*Maiore*-) 1221 *Ass*, (*Magna*-) 1290 Episc, 1291 Tax,
  1327 *SR*
Berinton 1199 Abbr, 1205 Cur, *Berington*, -*yng*- 1199 Ch, 1329
  Pat, 1354 Ipm
Bernington, -*yng*- 1221 *Ass*, 1321 Cl, (*magna*-) 1221 *Ass*
Biryton 1274 Cl
Bermithon 1292 Ch   *Berminton* 1301 Ch
Barnton Hy 6 *AddCh*
(*Great*) *Baryn(g)ton* 1461 Pat, Hy 8 *Rent*, (-*Magna*) 1535 VE
Barrington 1543 *AOMB*, (*Magna*-) c. 1560 *Surv*, 1584 *Comm*

'Farmstead associated with Beorn(a)' from the OE pers.n. *Beorn(a)*, v. ing⁴, tūn. 'Great' (Lat *magna*) to distinguish it from Little Barrington (194 *infra*). Cf. *Barrington Hundred* (192 *supra*). For the loss of -*n*- cf. Phonol. § 37(*b*).

BARRINGTON BUSHES & PARK, 1830 M. BLACKINGTON COPPICE,
1841 *TA*. BROMHAM PLANT. COOMB HILL PLANT., 1841 *TA*.
DODD'S MILL, 1830 M, *Dodde myll* Hy 8 Rent 206, cf. *Dodge
downs* 1841 *TA*, from the ME pers.n. or surname *Dodde*. DOWNS
BARN, *the Downs* 1841 *TA*, named from Barrington Downs (*infra*).
FRIEZLAND BRAKE, *Furze land* 1841 *TA*, FURZENHILL LEYS, 1841 ib,
v. fyrs(en). HILL BARN, *Hill meadow* 1841 *TA*, cf. *Upehulle* 1327 *SR*
(p), *v.* hyll. HORSECLOSE COPSE, -*coppice* 1841 *TA*. MILETREE
CLUMP, *Mile bush*, -*tree* 1841 *TA*. PARK COPSE, -*coppice* 1841 *TA*,
a litle woode called the Parke Hy 8 *Rent*. SHEEP PEN, cf. *Shepehous
close* 1543 *AOMB*.

FIELD-NAMES

The principal forms in (*a*) are 1841 *TA* 19. Spellings dated 1327 are *SR*,
1535 VE.

(*a*) Betham; Camp ground; Catsbrain hill (*v.* cattes-braʒen); Crab stock;
Ditch acre; Dropping well hill; Garsons (*v.* gærs-tūn); Hambottom (*v.*
hamm); Holly bush; Hovel downs; Lark hill; Liverage wells; the Mare;
Moonlight; Oxpen; the Sheppy (*v.* scēap, (ge)hæg); Spring hill; Wad
barrow; Washpool ground; Winterpool.

(*b*) *prat' voc' Above the bridge, beneth the Bridge* 1543 *AOMB*, *Benette-
brugge* 1535 (*v.* beneoðan 'beneath,' brycg); *atte Fortheye* 1327 (*v.* forð, ēg);
atte Hulham 1327 (*v.* hyll, hamm); *Milleham mede* 1543 *AOMB* (*v.* myln,
hamm); *Moneache Brugge* 1535; *Vicars Hamme* 1535 (*v.* hamm).

Little Barrington

LITTLE BARRINGTON (144–2012)

Berni(n)tone 1086 DB, *Parua Berni(n)ton*, -*ing*-, -*yn(g)*- 1225 Pat,
1236, 1241 FF, 1291 Tax, 1303 FA, *Parua Berneton'* 1401 Ass, *Little
Beryngton* 1446 AD iii, *Lytle Barington* Hy 8 *Rent*, *Barrington parua*
1584 *Comm*, with other spellings and meaning as for Great Barrington
(193 *supra*).

BARRINGTON DOWNS FM (*Barrington downes* 1543 *AOMB*) & GROVE
(1830 M), *v.* dūn 'hill', grāf. CAT'S ABBEY BARN, doubtless a barn
infested with cats. FOURMILE HO, 1830 M. LEYES FM, *the Leys*
1761 *EnclA*, *v.* lēah 'clearing'. SHEEP PEN.

FIELD-NAMES

The principal forms in (*a*) are 1761 *EnclA.*

(*a*) the Breach (*v.* brēc); the Byres (*v.* bȳre 'cow-shed'); Camp Wall; the Dark Lane; the Hitching (*v.* heccing); Kings Way; Lip Gate or Leap Gate (*atte Lepeʒate* 1327 *SR*, *v.* hlīep-geat); Nomans Land; the Outlands; Priors Stile; Staff Acres.

Bourton on the Water

BOURTON ON THE WATER (144–1720)

Burchtun 714 (16th) BCS 130, *-ton* 1206 Cur, 1221 *Ass*
to *Burhtune* 949 BCS 882
(*into*) *Burghtune* 949 BCS 882, *Burghton* 1221 *Ass*, 1375 Ipm, 1621 Inq, (*-juxta Sloughter*) 1496 AD ii, (*-als. Bourton super aquam*) 1601 *FF*, (*-als. Bowerton*) 1641 Inq, *Burghetone* 1428 *AddRoll*, *Burghton super Aquam als. Bowerton super Aquam*, 1610 GR 158
Bortvne 1086 DB   *Borchton(e)* 1221 *Ass*
Burton 1195 P (p), 1221 Eyre, 1235 Cl, (*-super aquam*) 1535 VE, 1557, 1592 *FF*, 1610 M, (*-upon the water*) 1690 M
Burgton 1251 Ch
Bourt(h)on 1291 Episc, Tax
Boruhton 1303 FA   *Borouton* 1327 *SR*
Bourton super aquam 1575 *FF*, *-upon the water* 1605 *FF*

'Farmstead near the fortification', *v.* burh-tūn. The 'fortification' is doubtless the encampment named in Salmonsbury (*infra*). The place is called 'on the Water' (Lat *super aquam*) from the R. Windrush which flows through the village, to distinguish it from Bourton on the Hill (236 *infra*). Cf. Bourton Way (164 *supra*).

NETHERCOTE, *Nederchote* Ric 1 (1372) Ch, *Nethercota*, *-cote* 1192 P, 1327 *SR* (p) *et freq* to 1612 *GR* 158, *Nethircote* 1496 AD ii, *Nethercott* 1617 *FF*. 'Lower cottage', *v.* neoðera, cot.

SALMONSBURY, *Sulmonnesburg* 779 (orig.) BCS 230, *Salomonesbir'* 1276 RH, *Salemanburi* 1287 QW, *Salomonesbyri* 1293 Ipm, *Salmonysbury*, *-manis-* 1435, 1465 *MinAcct.* The name refers to a large four-sided ancient encampment, of which the north-east angle is best discernible (cf. Rudder 303) and which lies north-east of Bourton village. From this Salmonsbury Hundred (192 *supra*) took its name. The OE form *Sulmonnes-* suggested to Ekwall and Anderson 20–1 that the first el. is an OE *sulh-man* 'ploughman' as the spelling is from a good original charter, and the p.n. would denote 'the encampment of a ploughman', that is, no doubt, 'one where he kept his oxen'; this interpretation would be paralleled by some examples of OE *stōd-fald* 'stud enclosure' as applied to prehistoric enclosures used by the English for their stud-horses; *v.* burh, which is also the first el. of Bourton (195 *supra*). The complete change of *Sul-* to *Sal(e)-*, *Salo-* from DB onwards is probably due to popular etymology when the rare OE *sulh-man* was obviously confused with the Hebrew pers.n. *Salomon*, which was already in use in late OE (Feilitzen 30, 351) and becomes common after DB (Reaney 281), and with its Mohammedan variant *Suliman*, which seems to be found in OG *Sul(u)man* (FörstemannPN 1368). The lost *Salmondesleg* in the nearby Upper Slaughter (209 *infra*) may have a similar origin for the first el.

BOURTON BRIDGE, formerly *on Buruhford* 716–43 (11th) BCS 165, 'ford near the fortification', *v.* burh (cf. Bourton *supra*), ford, and later *Burghtons Bridge*, *Fossebridge* c. 1603 *TRMB* 39, a bridge carrying the Fosse Way over the Windrush. BOURTON HILL FM (1830 M) & MILL (*Bourghtons mill* 1585 *BrtCt*). THE BRATCH, 1593 *BrtCt*, 1846 *TA*, *le* (*the*) *Breach* 1593 *BrtCt*, 1621 *GR* 158, *v.* brēc 'land broken up for cultivation'. BURY FIELDS, 1846 TA, *the Byrryffeld* 1581 *BrtCt*, *le Berrye feld* c. 1603 *TRMB*, *Berryfeild* 1622 *GR* 158, named from the encampment at Salmonsbury (*supra*), *v.* burh, feld. COLDPARK FM. EASTFIELD. FOXHILL FM, *Fox(h)ale* 13 WinchLB, 'fox nook', *v.* fox, halh. GILBERT'S GRAVE, a tumulus. THE GORSE, *les Gorstes* 1593 *BrtCt*, *the Gorste* c. 1603 *TRMB*, *v.* gorst 'gorse'. THE HARP, 1846 *TA*, *the Harpe peece* 1762 *GR* 892. LINCROFT HO, *le Lynckcrofte* 1593 *BrtCt*, *Lincrofte* 1621 *GR* 158, 'flax enclosure', *v.* līn, croft. MARSH FM, *the Marshe* 1581 *BrtCt*, 1621 *GR* 158, *Bourton Marsh* 1782 *EnclA*, *v.* mersc. MOOR LANE FM, named from *le* (*the*) *Moore* c. 1603 *TRMB*, 1621 *GR* 158, *the Moore hedge* 1622 ib, *v.* mōr. POCKHILL LANE, *Pock hill* 1625 *GR* 158, possibly an OE pers.n. *Poca* (cf. Pockington ii, 235 *infra*), *v.* hyll. RISSINGTON BRIDGE, *Ri-*, *Rysington bridge* 1582 *BrtCt*, c. 1603 *TRMB*, a bridge crossing the Dikler to Little Rissington (202 *infra*). SANTHILL. SWEETSLADE FM, *v.* slæd 'valley'; *slades* 949 BCS 882 is another valley to the south-east. TAGMOOR FM, *Taggmore* 1585 *BrtCt*, *v.* tægga 'teg, young sheep', mōr. WHITESHOOTS.

FIELD-NAMES

The principal forms in (*a*) are 1846 *TA* 28. Spellings dated 779 are BCS 230, 949 ib 882, 1428 *AddR* 74641, 1573–1593 *BrtCt*, c. 1603 *TRMB* 39, 1620 *GR* 665, 1621–1625 ib 158, 1762 ib 892.

(*a*) the Acre; Blindwell ('secluded well', *v.* blind, **wella**); Boswells moor; Broad Lake (*le Brodelake* 1585, *v.* brād, lacu 'stream'); Brookes marsh (cf. *betwe(e)n(e) the Brookes* 1580, 1581, *v.* brōc); Castle ground; Clarkes ground (*mess' called Clerks* 1620); Coppins lake (ib c. 1603, cf. *Coppyngeslade, -en-* 1582, 1583, the surname *Copping*, *v.* lacu 'stream', slæd 'valley'); the Crooks or Crooked ley; Deadlands; Ewe mead (*Yewe meade* c. 1603, 'ewe pasture', *v.* eowu, mǣd); the Furzen (*brueris voc' fyrsens* 1585, *v.* fyrs 'furze'); the Goss (*Gottes land* 1583, *terr' voc' Gottes* c. 1603, the surname *Gott(s)*); upper Ham (*Overhomme* 1593, *-ham* c. 1603, the Hammas, the *Vpper hamme* 1621, *v.* hamm); Kingsey meadow; Long hay (*v.* (ge)hæg); Mead close (*the Mead close* 1621); the Oxhale 1762 (*v.* oxa, halh); Rye close (cf. *Reymead* c. 1603, *v.* ryge 'rye'); Rypham (*prat' voc' Ryfame* c. 1603, *Rifham* 1762, possibly 'rough meadow', *v.* hrēof (which appears later in p.ns. as *Riv-*, etc.), hamm, cf. Riff Hills, Rifehams 209, 215 *infra*, this is preferable to a suggestion that it is from (ge)rēfa 'reeve' in O 463); Slaughter house ground (*terr' voc' Slaughters* c. 1603, a surname derived from Slaughter 206 *infra*); Smiths mill (*mess', terr' voc' Smythes* 1577, c. 1603, *Smith Hill* 1625, the surname *Smith*); Southlake (ib 1625, *v.* sūð, lacu 'stream'); the Swilly (*v.* swelg 'pit, whirlpool'); Town ground (*le Towne feld* c. 1603, 1621); Weir ground; Wick Moor (named from Wyck 203 *infra*).

(*b*) *Alsettes hous(s)e* 1573, c. 1603; *Asshfeld* 1583; the *Axehale* 1622; *le Bottome* 1583; *le Bridge meade* c. 1603; the *Brod Fyrses* 1581, the broad *Ferzes* (*v.* brād, fyrs); *Burghton Downe* 1582 (*v.* dūn); *Butt(e) fyrsens* 1585, *-furze* 1621; *Choriham* 1217 Oseney; *Churchberrye* 1621 (*v.* beorg 'hill, barrow'); *le Cote acre* c. 1603, *Cotemulles* 1428 (*v.* cot 'cottage'); *Curputt* 1583, *-pit* c. 1603, *-pittes* 1621 ('pit haunted by curs', from ME *curre*); *Frogholdes* 1575; *le Grene ditch* 1593 (cf. *grenan dic* 223 *infra*); *le Hadde* 1577 (*v.* hēafod 'headland'); *Hobbeschotes* 1428, *Hobbyes meadow* 1622 (the ME pers.n. or surname *Hobbe*); *Honycak furlonge* 1625; the *lordes moore* 1622; *Lote Meade* c. 1603, the *lott meadowe* 1621 (*v.* hlot 'allotment'); *Ludwelle* 1428 ('loud stream', *v.* hlūd, **wella**); *Micklehill* 1590; *Morter pitt ley* 1585; *Mounclane* 1584; *le Neite* c. 1603 (*v.* atten, ēgeð 'island'); (the spring called) *Nicolles barrell, Nicholls-* 1593, 1621, *Nicholls well* 1622 (ME *barel* 'tub, barrel', obviously here used of a well); *the olde forge* c. 1603; the *Parsons Fyrses* 1581 (*v.* fyrs); *le Pigge down* 1593 (*v.* pigga 'pig', dūn); *to pippenespenne* 949 (probably the OG pers.n. *Pip(p)en* or an OE equivalent (Forssner 204), *v.* penn² 'enclosure'); *Reddewell Lacke* 1577 (*v.* hrēod, **wella**, lacu); the *South field* 1621; *le Staple stone* 1590 ('pillar stone', *v.* stapol, stān); *Temple ham(me)* c. 1603, 1621 (cf. Temple ham 202 *infra*); *Warlock Stone* 1585 (*v.* wērloga 'traitor, reprobate', stān); *le Wellheade* 1584; *in winesburg* 779 (the OE pers.n. *Wine* and burh); *uuithigford* 779, *on, of wiðigford(a)* 949 ('willow ford', *v.* wīðig, ford); *le Wythis* c. 1603 (*v.* wīðig 'willow').

Clapton on the Hill

CLAPTON, formerly CLAPTON ON THE HILL (144–1617)

Clopton 1171–83 AC, 1221 Eyre (p), 1234, 1251 Ch, 1327 *SR et freq* to 1611 *Rec*, (*-super montem*) 1590 *FF*, (*-super le Hill*) 1611 ib, *Clapton* 1577 M, 1679 PR 17, (*-on the Hill*) 1641 Inq, (*-on Hill*) 1678 Will. The el. OE *clopp(a), which seems to denote 'a lump, a hill', has been fully discussed by Ekwall, *Studies*[2] 136 ff (cf. EPN i, 99–100 s.v.); it appears to have a WSax provenance and is found several times in Gl, *Clopley* (179 *supra*), Clopton (241), Clapley (258), and Clapton (ii, 224 *infra*). On the later forms in *Clap-* which are dialectal cf. Phonol. § 26.

GOMM'S HOLE, *Combs-*, *Gomb's Hole* 1774 *EnclA*, *Gounes Hole* 1777 M, from the surname *Gomme*. HILL BARN, *the Hill* 1774 *EnclA*, *Clapton Hill* 1830 M. NEW BRIDGE, 1777 M, *Newebrigge* 1481 *MinAcct*, *v.* nīwe, brycg.

FIELD-NAMES

The principal forms in (*a*) are 1774 *EnclA*, and in (*b*) 1621 Inq.

(*a*) Quickham Lane; The Swilley (cf. the Swilly 197 *supra*).

(*b*) *Churchhayes*; *Hallen, mess'* 1662 GR 892 (*v.* hall, ende); *Hillinge*; *Lott medowe* (*v.* hlot).

Eyford

EYFORD (144–1425) ['eifəd]

Aiforde 1086 DB
Hey-, *Heiford* 1220, 1236 Fees, 1327 *SR*, *Hayford(e)* 1316 FA, 1551 Pat
Eyford(e) 1272 Episc, 1303 FA, 1327 *SR*, 1360 Ipm *et passim* to 1752 PR 14, *-vorde* 1318 WinchLB (p)
Exford als. Eysford 1618 *FF*

'Ford by an island or water-meadow', *v.* ēg, ford, cf. Ayford (iii, 60 *infra*). The ford carried the Stow–Andoversford road across the Slaughter stream which has been dammed to form a lake.

BROCKHILL BARN. MILTON'S WELL. SALTER'S POOL. SKINNERS HILL.

FIELD-NAME. (a) *Seven Springs* 1777 M.

Naunton

NAUNTON (144–1123) ['nɑ:ntən]

> *Niwetone, -tune* 1086 DB, 1185 Templar
> *Newynton, -in-* J Monast, 13 Misc, 1287, 1375 Ipm, 1480 Pat, (*-super Codeswold*) J Monast, (*-on le Wolde*) 1378 AD iii, (*-de la Wolde*) 1379 FF, 1380 Ipm
> *Newenton(e)* 1235 Fees, 1248 *Ass*, 1284 Episc (p), 1287 QW *et freq* to 1501 Ipm, (*-in Cotswold*) 1289 Episc, (*-super Coddeswolde*) 1303 Pat, (*-als. Nawnton super Cottesold*) 1570 FF
> *Neweton* 1303 FA, *Neuton on Coteswolde* 1304 Pat, *Newton als. Naunton* 1591 FF
> *Niwenton super Coteswalde* 1307 Pat, *Niwenton* 1328 Misc
> *Newnton* Hy 6 AddCh
> *Nawinton, -en-* 1484 Rogers, 1545 LP, (*-upon Cottesold*) 1544 ib, (*-upon Cottiswolde*) 1597 FF, (*-als. Nawneton on Cotteswoulde*) 1625 Inq
> *Naun-, Nawnton* 1476 IpmR, 1535 VE *et freq* to 1683 PR 4, (*-super Cott(e)swo(u)lde*) 1566 FF, 1642 Inq

'(At) the new farmstead', v. nīwe (wk.dat. *nīwan*), tūn. On the dialectal change of ME *-ewen-* to *-aun-*, which occurs in other Nauntons (ii, 34, 105 *infra*, Wo 158, etc.), Frampton (ii, 32), Brawne (ii, 153 *infra*), etc., cf. Phonol. § 22. For the affixes v. wald and Cotswold (2 *supra*).

AYLWORTH

> *Ailwrde* 1086 DB, *Ailewurda* 1182 P, *Eile-, Eylewurth, -w(o)rth(e)* 1220 Fees, 1230 Cl, 1248 *Ass*, 1279 FF *et freq* to 1535 VE, *Ayl(e)worth* 1476 IpmR, 1497 AOMB *et freq* to 1587 FF
> *Elewrde* 1086 DB, *-w(o)rth* 1262 Ipm, 1291 Tax
> *Ailes-, Ayles-, Eylesw(o)rth(e), -wurth* 12 Tewk 80b, 1241 FF, 1248 *Ass* (p), 1327 SR, 1557 *Val* 140b, *Eyllisworth* 1306 *Ass*
> *Elleswrth* 1291 Tax

'Ægel's enclosure', v. worð. The first el. is an OE pers.n. *Ægel*, which is not on record, but is assumed from p.ns. like Aylesbury

(Bk 145), Aylesbeare (D 580), Aylesford (K 145), Ailsworth (Nth 228), etc. Some of the spellings of Aylworth suggest a weak form *Ægla*, but they can be accounted for as an uninflected genitive of *Ægel*. Most examples of *Ægel-* as a pers.n. theme occur in late OE and are in fact developments of names which contain OE *Æþel-* (cf. Feilitzen 103–6, E. Ekwall, *Early London Personal Names* 197); others like *Egelmund* (LVD) can be explained as OG names (Forssner 12 ff). But the theme occurs in OG *Agil-* and in the monothematic names OG *Aigil, Egil*, ODan *Eghil*, ON *Egill*; in view of p.ns. like Aylesbury and Aylesford which are evidenced as *Ægelesburh* and *Ægelesford* at an earlier date than the change of *Æþel-* to *Ægel-* it must also be presumed to have existed in OE; it would appear to have been a theme that fell into disuse at a very early stage in OE since it finds no place in the records.

HARFORD, HARFORD BRIDGE

> *on Heortford* 716–43 (11th) BCS 165, *æt Heortford, to heort forda* 963 (11th) ib 1105
> *Hvrford* 1086 DB
> *Hertford* 1220 Fees, 1285 *FF*, 1287 QW, 1327 *MinAcct et passim* to 1435 *GR* 444, *Herteford* 1253 Ch, 1400 Ipm
> *Hartefford in Nawenton* 1545 LP, *Hartforde als. Harford* 1588 *FF*, *Harforde* 1610 ib, (*-Bridge*) 1830 M

'Stag ford', *v.* heorot, ford; cf. Hartford (Ch), -forth (YN 289).

THE BRAKE. CHURCH FM, cf. *Abouechirche* 1327 *SR* (p). CLOUD HILL. DOWNS BRAKE, 1830 M, *v.* dūn 'hill'. THE FOLLY, 1830 M. GRANGE HILL, -*Barn* 1830 M. HILL BARN, 1830 M. NAUNTON DOWNS, 1779 Rudder. PARKER'S BARN & COPPICE, named from the family of William, Samuel or Richard *Parker* (1679, 1695, 1737 PR 15, pp. 94, 96). ROUNDHILL FM, 1779 Rudder 560. SUMMERHILL, 1830 M.

FIELD-NAMES

The principal forms in (*a*) are 1841 *TA* 137, and in (*b*) 1540 *Rogers*. Spellings dated 716–43 are (11th) BCS 165, 963 ib 1105, 1640 Inq; cf. also Eales 94 ff.

(*a*) Barrow ground (possibly identical with *Bearuwe* 716–43 (11th) BCS 165, *v.* bearu 'grove', at grid 144–117224); Cow Bank; Cuckoo pen (*v.* Cuckoo Pen 43 *supra*); Holt (*v.* holt); Lady Picked Hill (dial. *picked* 'pointed'); Scot ground; Seven Wells; Sideland.

(b) on *ælfrices gemæro* 963 (the OE pers.n. *Ælfrīc, v.* (ge)mǣre); *Ayleworth Downe & feild* 1640; *Clyntons hey* (*v.* (ge)hæg); *the Conigree* 1640 (*v.* coninger 'warren'); *Culvyr hey* (*v.* culfre 'dove'); *andlang furu* 963 (*v.* furh); *on þa healdan stige* 963 (*v.* hald² 'sloping', stīg 'path'); *Hide meadow* 1640; (*andlang*) *hrycges* 716–43, *hricweges* 963 ('ridgeway', *v.* hrycg, weg); *Lady Hayes* 1640; *Magottys heys* (*Magotte*, a pet form of *Margaret*); *Mallbarnys hey*; *on mylen weg* 716–43 (named from *æt þære ealdan mylne* 963, *v.* myln); *Rose Courte* c. 1525 ECP (the surname *Rose, v.* court); *Schypphey* (*v.* scēap, (ge)hæg); *Shittengitten* 1620 FF; *on stanford* 963 (*v.* stān, ford); *Water hey*; *the West feild* 1640.

Great Rissington

GREAT RISSINGTON (144–1917)

> *Risendune, -duna, -don*(*e*) c. 1075 Monast, 1086 DB, c. 1115 (1333) Ch, Hy 1 (1267) Ch, 1200 Cur, 1211–13 Fees, 1221 *Ass et freq* to 1333 Ch, (*Brade-*) 1220 Fees, (*Brode-*) 1488 Pat
>
> *Ri-, Rysindon*(*e*), *-yn-, -dun* 12 Glouc, 13 WinchLB, 1200 Cur (p), 1221 *Ass*, 1252 Ch, (*Magna*) 1291 Tax, 1298 Episc, 1327 *SR et freq* to 1435 *MinAcct*, (*Brod*(*e*)-) 1346, 1395 *FF*
>
> *Rysyngdon, -i-* 1328 Banco, (*Magna-*) 1303 FA, 1381 FA, (*Brode-*) 1392 Ipm, 1482, 1571 *FF*, (*Greate-*) 1584 *Comm*
>
> *Magna Risinton* 1218 FF, *Brode-* 1577 M, *Risington magna* 1584 *Comm, Rissington Magna* 1705 PR 13
>
> *Rissenden* 1221 *Ass, Ryssingdon* 1279 Abbr
>
> *Rusyn*(*g*)*don*(*e*) 1332, 1345 Ipm, (*Brode-*) 1349, 1385 ib
>
> *Magna Resyngdon* 1444 Pat, 1465 *MinAcct*, (*-als. Broderysyndon*) 1499 *FF*

'Hill overgrown with brushwood', *v.* hrīsen, dūn. It is described as *Brode-* (*v.* brād 'broad'), *Magna* or *Great* to distinguish it from Little and Wyck Rissington (202, 203 *infra*).

BURFORDHILL, 1815 *EnclA*, near a track leading to Burford (O 31). DICK BRIDGE. THE FOLLY. HORSEHILL COPSE, *Horsehill* 1815 *EnclA*. NEW BRIDGE, *v.* 198 *supra*.

FIELD-NAMES

The principal forms in (*a*) are 1815 *EnclA*, and in (*b*) 1623 Inq.

(*a*) Bambury Hay (*v.* (ge)hæg); Barhill (*v.* bere 'barley'); Bellhay; Chestle (*v.* ceastel 'heap of stones'); Chitton; the Green; Greenway; Hadborough Furlong; the Hardis meadow (cf. *Hardesmull* 1375 GR 1375, the

surname *Hardy*); the Heath; Heaven; Hillinge Cross; Infield; Langett
(*v.* langet); Laynes (*v.* leyne 'arable strip'); Oatlands; Oldacre; the Pikes
(dial. *pike* 'a pointed land in a ploughed field', *v.* NED s.v. *pike* 10); Pry;
Tythingmead; Woad ground.

(*b*) *the Chaunterye lande* 1584 *Comm*; *Cookeseyes*; *Niles* (*Nyles or Neld*
c. 1565 ECP).

Little Rissington

LITTLE RISSINGTON (144–1919)

Risedvne 1086 DB, *Ri-*, *Rysindon*(*a*), *-yn-* 1151, 1151–7, 1167–98
Oseney, c. 1180, c. 1220 Godstow *et passim* to 1320 Ch, (*-Basset*(*h*),
-ett) c. 1200 Godstow, 1236 Cl, 1269 Ch, 1275 Ipm *et freq* to 1330
FF, (*Litell-*) c. 1230 Godstow, (*Parua-*) 1271 Oseney, 1278 Episc
et freq to 1571 FF, *Parva Resindon* 1284 Episc, *Ris*(*s*)*ington Parva*
1683 PR 4, 1705 ib 13, with other forms and meaning as for Great
Rissington (201 *supra*); *v.* lȳtel, parva. The manor was acquired by
Ralph *Basset* t. Hy 1.

BOBBLE SPRING.　　CATE BRITAIN, *Kates Britton* 1830 M.　　COLLIER'S
HILL BARN, probably named from the family of John *Collier* 1803
PR 17, p. 133.　　FORTY COPSE, named from a local family of *Forty*
(cf. William *Forty* of Slaughter 1806 PR 17, 121).　　FOULWELL
COPSE.　　FURZECOMB COPSE.　　HANK'S COPPICE, named from the
family of Alice or John *Hank*(*e*)*s* 1568, 1779 PR 17, pp. 126, 132.
RISSINGTON MILL, 1830 M.

FIELD-NAMES

The principal forms in (*b*) are Godstow.

(*a*) Temple ham 1843 *TA* (ib 1328 Ipm, possibly the same place as
Templehamme 197 *supra*, *v.* tempel, hamm).

(*b*) *the Ashen causey* c. 1180 (*fraxinum cawlsi* ib, *v.* æscen, caucie 'path');
Exeshale 1217 (*v.* halh); *Gorst* 1217 (*v.* gorst 'gorse'); *Henoure* 1327 SR
(*v.* hēah, ofer[2] 'slope'); *Holdeya, aqua* 1217 ('old water-course', *v.* ald, ēa);
Pilehulle c. 1180 (*v.* pīl, hyll); *Ten-*, *Threeacre* c. 1180; *Walterislake* c. 1230
(the ME pers.n. *Walter*, lacu 'stream'); *Wytheryndeham* c. 1180 (*v.* rind(e)
'ridge', hamm, the first el. is possibly wið 'near, beside').

Wyck Rissington

WYCK RISSINGTON (144–1921)

Risendvne 1086 DB, *Ri-*, *Rysindon*, *-yn-*, *-en-*, *-dun* 1281 Ch, (*Wyk(e)-*, *Wik(e)-*) c. 1170 Monast, 1227 *FF*, 1236 Fees, 1291 Tax *et passim* to 1492 Ipm, *Wikeresindon* 1236 Fees, *Wik' Risinton* 1290 Episc, *Wyke Rusyndon* 1294 Ipm, *Wyke Risington*, *-y-* 1558 *Surv*, 1575 *FF* with other forms and meanings as for Great Rissington (201 *supra*). For the affix *v*. Wyck (*infra*).

WYCK BEACON & MILL, WYCKHILL HO, *Wik(e)*, *Wyk(e)* 1220 Fees, 1269 Ch, 1275 Ipm, 1327 *SR et freq* to 1575 *FF*, (*-juxta Stowe*) 1286 Episc, 1302 Ipm, 1424 IpmR, *Wikstowe* 1287 QW, *le Wike Milne* c. 1603 *TRMB*, *Wick Hill House* 1784 PR 13, *Wick Beacon & Mill* 1830 M. From OE wīc 'dairy-farm, outlying farm'. From its location in the north of the district Wyck was probably a secondary settlement from Great Rissington; it may indeed be the original name of Wyck Rissington (*supra*).

FOX HOLE COPPICE, 1830 M. THE GROVE. HEATH HILL, *Heath Hill Gate* 1826 GR 368, *Ethel* 1830 M, *v*. hǣð. STOW BRIDGE, 1750 GR 1375, a bridge leading to Stow (225 *infra*).

FIELD-NAMES

Spellings dated 1575 are *TRMB* 39, 1763 *GR* (D. 45).

(*a*) the Double Dole 1763 (*v*. dāl 'share'); Millars 1763; Vitock's-Ham 1779 Rudder 627 (*Vytcockysham* 1510 GR 1365, *v*. hamm); Wick Crook 1763.

(*b*) *Campiunmedwe* 1227 FF (the ME surname *Campion*, *v*. mǣd); *pastur' le Markes* 1575; *Saltforde* 1327 *SR* (p) (possibly a surname from Salford (O 373), 'ford on a salt-way', *v*. salt, ford); *le Townesend* 1575.

Sherborne

SHERBORNE (144–1714)

Scirebvrne 1086 DB, *Scyreburn(a)* c. 1245, 1257, 1278 WinchLB *Si-*, *Syreburn(e)*, *-burna* 1166 RBE (p), 1175–1286 WinchLB (*freq*), 1201 Cur, 1221 *Ass*, 1269 Episc, 1279 Heref (p) *Sirburne* 1221 WinchLB, *Syrbourn* 1291 Tax

S(c)hire-, Shyreburn, -bo(u)rn(e) 1193 P, 1221 *Ass*, 1251 Ch, 1251
WinchLB, 1289 Episc *et passim* to 1729 PR 17
Schiresborn 1249 BM *Chyreburn* 1288 Episc
S(c)hir-, Shyrburn(e), -bo(u)rne 1300, 1384, 1404 WinchLB, 1406
Pat *et freq* to 1535 VE
Shurbourne 1552 *FF* *Sherborne* 1601 *FF*, 1659 PR 14

'The bright clear stream', *v.* scīr[1], burna, a common stream-name.
The stream is Sherborne Brook, an affluent of the R. Windrush.

BROADMOOR FM, *Broadmore, -moores* 1622, 1652 Sherb, *v.* brād, mōr.
BUDGEHILL WOOD. CROOKMOOR ASH, *Crookes* 1652 Sherb, probably
the surname *Crook*. DUCKLESTONE MILL. FOLLY COPSE. THE
FORK. GROVE BARN, cf. *Grovestanidelve* 13 WinchLB, *v.* grāf,
stān, (ge)delf 'quarry'. HAYCROFT FM, *Heycroft* 1248 *Ass* (p),
v. hēg 'hay', croft. HILL BARN, cf. *la Hulmede* 13 WinchLB,
Upehulle 1327 *SR* (p), *Vndehill, Hill howse* 1540 *MinAcct*. HUNGRY-
HILL. LANGOTT HILL, *v.* langet 'long strip'. LAUGHCROFT, *Leure-
croft* 1186 WinchLB, *Leverecrofth* 13 ib, *Leverescroft* 1319 ib, *Leycrofte*
1540 *MinAcct*, from lǣfer 'rush-bed' or possibly the OE pers.n.
Lēofhere, v. croft. LEASOW FURLONG. MARESLAID COPSE. NORTH-
FIELD BARN, *Campo Aquilonari, -Boreali, -Septentrionali* 13 WinchLB.
OUTLANDS PLANT., *Utlong(e)* 12, 1184–94 WinchLB, *v.* ūt, lang[2]
'long strip'. PICARDY COPSE, *Picard(i)es* 1622, 1652 Sherb, the
surname *Picard(y)*. QUARRY WOOD, *Quarreriam* 13 WinchLB,
Quar piece 1622 Sherb 6, *v.* quarriere. SANDY HILL BOWSEN, Gl
dial. *bowsen* 'cow-shed'. SHERBORNE BROOK (*Shireborne Brook* 1777
EnclA), COMMON (1830 M) & PARK (*the Park* 1622 Sherb, *the New-,
the Old Park* 1652 ib). SNOWBOTTOM. TRUL'S PIECE, *terr' voc'
Trylles* 1540 *MinAcct, Tull Elms piece* 1622 Sherb, *Turl's Lane &
Piece* 1777 *EnclA, Trull Fm.* 1790 Will, probably a surname *Trill*,
cf. Trillis (123 *supra*). VICAR'S BRAKE, cf. *the Vicars or Clarks Close*
1777 *EnclA*. WOEFUL LAKE FM, 1830 M, *the Woodpoles* 1652
Sherb 15, 'pools in the wood', *v.* wudu, pōl, lacu 'stream', cf.
Woefuldane Bottom (99 *supra*) for a similar adaptation.

FIELD-NAMES

The principal forms in (*a*) are 1777 *EnclA*, and in (*b*) 12–1319 WinchLB.
Spellings dated 1182, 1484 are Sherb, 1540 *MinAcct*, 1622, 1651, 1652 Sherb.

(*a*) Ashcroft (*Essecroft* 13, *v.* æsc, croft); Cowham (*Cuham* 1221–32,
Couhomme 1282–1314, *Cowham* 1484, 1652, *v.* cū, hamm 'meadow'); Downs

Piece; Middleham Meadow (*Medelham* 1484, *Middleham mead* 1622, *v.* middel, hamm, mǣd); the Mill ground; Onewell; Smiths; South Field (*campo Australi* 12, 13); Tight Lane; Wadlings Hill (*Overe-, Neþer Wadelinghull* 12, 13, *-welle* 12, the OE pers.n. *Wædel, v.* -ing⁴, hyll).

(*b*) *Ailburuhomme, Heilbureham, Helburghom* (the OE fem. pers.n. *Æþelburg,* hamm); *Aldeswrþeweie* ('the road to Aldsworth (23 *supra*)', *v.* weg); *Andrewesmede* (named from its owner, William *Andrew* of Windrush 1282–1314 WinchLB ii, 249, *v.* mǣd).

Berentenhulle; Bikewrð (the OE pers.n. *Bica,* worð); *Blakemulde(ne)londe* ('black-earth land', *v.* blæc, molde, land); *Bowling Alley piece* 1622; *Brenhulle* (doubtless 'burnt hill'); *Brondrid* (possibly OE *brand-rēod* 'burnt clearing', cf. *wowe brondred* ii, 7 *infra*); *Burymille* 1540 ('the town mill').

Caldewelle lake, fons de Kaldewelle ('cold spring', *v.* cald, wella, lacu 'stream'); *Chapellacre* 13, *Chapel close* 1622; *la Chivesee; Clopbemesti* (probably an error for *Clophemesti* 'path of the dwellers at Clapton (198 *supra*)', *v.* hǣme, stīg, cf. Weston Subedge 261 *infra* for the name-type); *Conygree* 1651 (*v.* coninger 'warren'); *the Copes* 1622 (*v.* copeiz 'copse'); *Cote* (*v.* cot); *Cowruge* 1540 (*v.* hrycg); *Cur(i)elond(e).*

(*la*) *Dedemore* (*v.* dēad 'dead', probably in the sense 'disused', mōr); *Dene* (*v.* denu); *Dichacre; Drakewell* ('dragon well', *v.* draca, wella).

Egemundesgastone (the OE pers.n. *Ecgmund, v.* gærs-tūn 'pasture'); *le Eyt* (*v.* ēgeð 'island'); *terra Elfrunne* (the OE fem. pers.n. *Ælfrūn*); *Erleslond* (*v.* eorl, land); *Evedefurlonge, Evedelonde, Yvedeford* (possibly OE *ēowd, ēfod,* 'sheep-fold'); *Eurelonde* (probably an error for *Oure-* 'upper').

Ferancumbe (*v.* fearn 'fern', cumb); *Forth-, Vortheye* (ib 1327 *SR*) (*v.* forð, ēg).

Galonge (*v.* lang²); *Gertona* (probably an error for gærs-tūn); *la Gitford; Goose Acre* 1540; *Gore* (*v.* gāra).

Hasilles 1540 (*v.* hæsel 'hazel'); *Herewinewell* (the OE pers.n. *Herewine*); *Hickcombehey* 1484 (probably a surname from Icomb 220 *infra, v.* (ge)hæg); *Holecumb(e)* 13, *Howcoms* 1622, *the Holcombs* 1652 ('hollow valley', *v.* hol², cumb); *Hommuk* 1286 (an early example of e.ModE *homoke, hummock* 'hillock' first recorded c. 1556 NED s.v.); *Horestone* ('boundary stone', *v.* hār, stān); *Hundestoft* (the OE pers.n. *Hund, v.* topt, a rare instance of the ON word in Gl); *Huscombe* 12, 13, *Hiscombes* 1652 (*v.* hys(s)e 'scion, shoot, tendril', cumb).

Kenesberwe (the OE pers.n. *Cēn,* bearu 'grove'); *Krauling, Graweling.*

Leonardes medowe 1540; *Lidersedegore* (*v.* gāra); *Liyacra; Luckewelle* (the OE pers.n. *Luca*); *Lut(t)lecumbe* (*v.* lȳtel, cumb).

Maggedeslone; Mang-, Nangwell 1622, 1651; *Medweye* (*v.* mǣd, weg); (*la*) *Meracre; Mokles-, Mukelslad* (*v.* micel, slæd).

le Nerecroft ('the near croft'); *Neþerhomme, Netherhamme* (*v.* hamm); (*le*) *Newemede.*

Oldenhulle, þoldenhulnaker (*v.* ald, hyll); *Otenefurlong* (*v.* āte 'oats' or an adj. *āten*); *Overhomme* (*v.* hamm).

Penedich (*v.* penn² 'pen', dīc); *Petelonde; the Picked close* 1622 (cf. Picked Lease 40 *supra*); *Pigstye piece* 1622; *Pipeleswel* 1182 (possibly ME *pipel,* a variant of ME *popel* 'bubbling spring' as in Popplewell YW iii, 17, e.ModE *pipple* 'to ripple' or OE *Pyppel* as in Peopleton Wo 216).

la Rug(g)eweie, -weye ('ridge-way'); *Rustusfe.*

Segina Lug, a messuage (probably ME *lugge* 'a pole, branch', used later in the sense of 'a square pole or perch', first el. uncertain); *Syrdeshulle* (probably an error for foll.); *Syriecheshulle* (the OE pers.n. *Sigerīc*); *Smalelonde, -mede, -weye* (*v.* smæl 'narrow'); *Som-, Samehavedlond* (the ME pers.n. *Samme, v.* hēafod-land); *Spelecrondele* (*v.* crundel 'quarry', first el. uncertain); *Suannewell* ('swan stream', *v.* swan[1], wella).

Thornhills 1652; *Trayfurlonge* 1540; *Twenewawe, betwene Wawes* ('between the walls', *v.* betwēonan, wāg); *Twiseledeweie* ('forked road', from OE *twislian* 'to fork').

(*les*) *Vactes*; *Varnslad* ('fern valley', *v.* fearn, slæd).

Wei-, Weydene (*v.* weg, denu); *Welfende* (doubtless an error for *Westende infra*); *Werkeshulle* (the OE pers.n. *Weorc*); *Westcroft*(*e*); *le Westende Capell* 1550 Pat (*v.* capel 'chapel'); *Wille(l)mes-, Williamesdene* (*v.* denu 'valley'); *la Wite Dicg*; *Wythyham mead* 1622 (*v.* wiðig 'willow', hamm).

Lower Slaughter

LOWER SLAUGHTER (144–1622) [ˈslɔːtə, ˈslɑːtə]

The forms for LOWER & UPPER SLAUGHTER include:

Sclostre 1086 DB   *Sloustr(e)'* 1252 Ch, 1274 RH

Sclotris 1159 P   *Slouctres* 1174 P

Slochtre(s) 1168, 1190 P, *Slochtr'* 1221 Eyre, *Slouchtre* 1286 FF

Scloctre(s) 1195 P, *Sloctres* 1204 P, 1211–13 Fees, 1219 ClR, 1220 Fees

Scloutres 1195 P, *Sloutre* 1274 RH, (*-superiori*) 1290 Episc, (*Over-*) 14 AD ii, *Sloutr' Inferiori* 1286 Episc

Slohtre(s), *-ter* 13 WinchLB, 1221 *Ass*, c. 1232 AD iii, c. 1275 *For*

Slokhter, Slogtre, Schlochtres 1221 *Ass*   *Slouthtre* 1275 Ipm

Sloghters, -tre, -tir' 1229 Pat, 1276 Cl, 1459 *MinAcct*, (*Ouer-*) 1398 *MinAcct*

Slouhtre, -ter 1266 FF, 1277 Cl, *Slouȝter superiori* Hy 6 *AddCh*

Slougehtre superior' 1291 Tax

Sloughtre, -ter 1328 Misc, 1355 Ipm, 1391 *FF et passim* to 1496 Pat, (*-sup^r, -superior(i)'*) 1291 Tax, 1327 SR (*-Inf^r, -inferior'*) 1327 SR, 1535 VE, (*Over-, Ouer-*) 1328 Banco, 1411 *Ass et freq* to 1504 FF, (*Nether-*) 1328 Banco, 1435 *MinAcct et freq* to 1504 FF

Slaughter c. 1560 *Surv*, 1584 *Comm*, (*Ouer-, Over-*) 1572, 1627 FF, (*Nether-*) c. 1560 *Surv*, 1572, 1627 FF

Uper-, Lower Slater 1698, 1699 PR 3, 13

The spellings for Upper and Lower Slaughter are included here, as in earlier documents the two parts of the manor cannot easily be differentiated; indeed the grouping of the two parts accounts for the early plur. forms like *Slotris, Slochtres*, etc., as well as the present-day usage, The Slaughters. The spellings clearly point to an OE *slōhtre* and this is confirmed by the OE spelling of the lost *Slaughterford* (*infra*). OE *slōhtre* is known only from these p.ns. and possibly Slaughterford (Sx 177–8), though spellings of the latter (*Sloghtreford* 1276, etc.) are not early enough to rule out OE slāh-trēow 'sloe-tree' for the Sx name. The word has been connected with a MHG **sluohter*, which is the source of several German p.ns. like *Schlochtern*, etc. (FörstemannON ii, 810), and with the Du p.n. *Slochteren*; the German *sluohter* is stated to mean 'uneven ground with pools, holes and ditches' (cf. Bach ii, § 290) and LG *slochter* is equivalent to Lat *fossa* 'ditch' (Middendorff 118). It appears to be connected with OE slōh 'slough, mire' (esp. 'a miry place in a road'), which occurs in one or two Gl p.ns. The name Slaughter may be the old name of the stream which runs through both villages to join the R. Dikler, and have denoted some patch of muddy ground in its lower reaches, or, if the meaning of *slōhtre* was more that of LG *slochter*, a ditch, possibly one which carried the water of the stream across the Fosse Way in the neighbourhood of *Slaughterford*. The local topography is no longer decisive.

SLAUGHTERFORD (lost), replaced by SLAUGHTER BRIDGE, *slohtran ford* 779 (orig) BCS 230, *wið slohterword* 949 ib 882, *Slahteruesford* 1320 *Ass. v.* Slaughter (*supra*), ford.

CHESSELS, *the Chestles* 1732 *Encl, Davis's-, Lawrence's Chestles* 1750 *GR* 1375, *v.* ceastel 'heap of stones'; it is an ancient site where Roman coins have been found (BG vii, 71–2). PENNSHILL, cf. *Penn close* 1648 *GR* (D. 45), the surname *Penn*.

FIELD-NAMES

The principal forms in (*a*) are 1732 *Encl* (*GR* 45). Spellings dated 1436 are *MinAcct*, c. 1603 *TRMB* 39, and others *GR* (D. 45). Some earlier field-names cannot be separated as being in Lower Slaughter or Upper Slaughter (*infra*).

(*a*) Angerman (*Angermansham* c. 1603, a surname *Angerman* from the ME pers.n. *Anger, v.* hamm); the Bayliffes Crookes; Bicks Well; Bigway hill; Calves Ditch; Culverham Brook (*v.* culfre 'dove', hamm); Dodmore; Frogwell greens; Fulwell ('dirty stream', *v.* fūl, wella); the Furzes (*le Firsen*

c. 1603, *v*. fyrs); Gallowes piece (*le Gallowes* c. 1603, *v*. galga); the Harbour (*le Harbour* c. 1603, *v*. here-beorg 'shelter'); Hay Meade (*v*. hēg 'hay'); Hem Leasowe; Househam; Kingsham, -hay, -well (*Kingesey meadowe* c. 1603, the surname *King*, (ge)hæg); Knave Castle (*Cnauecastell* 1392 *MinAcct, le Knaves Castle* c. 1603, a name doubtless parallel to the common *Maydes Castle* (233 *infra*) or Maiden Castle (cf. YW iv, 70), 'earthwork frequented by youths', *v*. cnafa, castel); Kytes Lane (*Kytes close* c. 1603, from the surname *Kyte* ib); the Mill Lays (*Mylne furlonge* c. 1603); the Mortar pitt Hitching (*v*. heccing); the Parke; Red Herring; the Severall Lot meades (*v*. Severals 28 *supra*, hlot); Sturt (*v*. steort 'tail of land'); Tomlins (*mess' voc' Tomlyns* 1481 *MinAcct, le Tomlyns well* c. 1603, the surname *Tomlin*); the Varundels (the common f.n. *Farendel, v*. fēorða, dǣl); Williamslads Way.

(*b*) *Benehull* 1436 (*v*. bēan 'bean'); *to þan ealdan sice* 949 BCS 882 (*v*. sīc, here the Slaughter brook); *Fosse peace* c. 1603 (near the Fosse Way); (*le*) *Hall(e) place* 1548 Pat, 1567; *Hawe* 1436 (*v*. haga 'enclosure'); *Hollow Hitches* 1649 (probably the same as Hollow-sack 209 *infra*).

Upper Slaughter

UPPER SLAUGHTER (144–1523)

The spellings and interpretation are given with those of Lower Slaughter (206 *supra*).

BECKS HILL. COPSE HILL, *Coppice* (*Lays*) 1755 *EnclA*, 1847 *GR* 297. THE DINGLE, 1847 *GR* 297, *v*. dingle 'dell'. JOINER'S DOWNS, 1847 *GR* 297. KIRKHAM, -*Farm* 1830 M, *Kercomb close* 1755 *EnclA*, *Kerkam-* 1847 *GR* 297. REDDITCH BOWSING, *Redditch* 1847 *GR* 297, *v*. hrēod, dīc, dial. bowsen 'cow-shed'. THE RIDGE. SLAUGHTER WOODS, 1830 M. WAGBOROUGH BUSH, 1732 *EnclA*, -*barrow-* 1824 M, a tumulus, *v*. beorg 'barrow'. WALES BARN, *Wales* 1755 *EnclA*.

FIELD-NAMES

The principal forms in (*a*) are 1755 *EnclA*, and in (*b*) c. 1603 TRMB 39. Spellings dated 1392–1425 are *MinAcct*, 1435–76 *GR* (D. 444), 1481 *MinAcct*, 1547 Sherb 171, 1649 *GR* (D. 45), 1779 Rudder, 1847 GR (D. 297).

(*a*) Anthill; Arkills ground 1847 (the local surname *Arkell*); Aston close (cf. *Astonesmull* 1395, *Astons Myll* 1481, a corn-mill on the Aston Blank boundary); Barn Lotts 1847 (*v*. hlot); Bell Acre 1847; Black bush; Blacknell 1847; Broad Quarrs; the Brook Furlong (*le Broke* c. 1603, *Brookway Hill* 1847); Buslet; Bustill 1847; Church pitts; Combhill (*Nether-, Overcombe leys* c. 1603, *v*. cumb); the Crooks; Crowbush; the Downs; Ewe Hill 1847; Foxdenhill (*Foxdene* 1435, *Foxstones Hill* 1847, *v*. fox, denu); Furze Bank 1847; Gomes Hole (cf. Gomm's Hole 198 *supra*); the Gores, Goors 1847 (*v*. gāra); Gooseham (*v*. gōs, hamm); the Hallow; Hear Stone 1847; Hewhill; Hollow-sack 1847 (*Holwaysiche* c. 1603, *Hollows Hitches* 1649, *Hallows hitch* 1755, 'stream in the hollow way', *v.* hol², weg, sīc); Langet 1847 (*v.* langet); the Lime Kiln Plot; Long Fryday (doubtless used of unproductive land, associated with the day of fasting, esp. Good Friday, cf. Sr 279); Millway; No Man's Lands 1779 (ib Hy 8 *Rent*); Pease hill (*v.* pise 'pease'); Pitty Holt 1847; Portway; Riff Hills 1847 (cf. Rypham 197 *supra*); Ryelands 1847 (cf. *le Rye Peece* c. 1603); Seven Wells ground 1847; Sidland 1847; Stony Nap 1847 (-*Knapp* 1755, *v.* cnæpp 'hillock'); Stow Stones, Stoway (*Stowe waye Peace* c. 1603, named from Stow (225 *infra*), the adjoining parish); Thiesden 1847 (*Theeve denn* 1755, 'thief's valley', *v.* þēof, denu); Tylands; Vardnil-bank; Vineyard hill, the Winyard; Woodin Pitts (*Woddene* 1435, 'wood valley', *v.* wudu, denu); Woodway.

(*b*) *Burywey* 1392; *Casteleslond* 1392 (*v.* castel, referring to a mound in the village); *Chirche-*, *le Churchewey* 1392, c. 1560 *Surv*; *Dernewell(e)* 1392, 1435 ('hidden well', *v.* derne, wella); *Etilbarowe pece* (*v.* beorg 'barrow'); *Eveshams Wayes* (the road to Evesham Wo, probably the same as Buckle Street 15 *supra*); *Feir-*, *Fayrewellhull*, -*hill* 1412, 1547 (*v.* fæger, wella); *Gosewell* 1392 (*v.* gōs, wella); *le Grene Meeres*; *Ickombeshey* 1440 (a surname from Icomb 220 *infra*, *v.* (ge)hæg); *Joumpes thorne*; *Langford* (possibly identical with *Langan ford* 224 *infra*); *Lowsebarowe* ('little barrow', *v.* lūs 'louse, something small', beorg); *the Marylondes* 1440; *Mounesleyse* 1481 (the ME byname *Moun*, *Mun* 'monk', *v.* lǣs); *Mullelond* 1392 (*v.* myln); *Northfeld*; *Pyrrymanslond* 1481 (the ME surname *Piriman*); *Pope hill* (the local surname *Pope*); *Renhulles* 1425; *Salmondesleg'* 1425 (cf. Salmonsbury 195 *supra*, with which it is no doubt connected); *Seuenacre* 1392; *Syndulbergh* 1392, *Syndurbury* 1392, *Simblebarowe* c. 1603 (*v.* beorg 'barrow, hill'); *le Southfelde*; *Stirke leys* (*v.* stirc, lēah); *Venhey* 1440 (*v.* fenn, (ge)hæg); *Wicke broke* (named from Wyck Rissington 203 *supra*); *Wollehous* 1457 ('a wool house', *v.* wull, hūs).

Windrush

WINDRUSH (144–1913)

> *Wenric(a)* 1086 DB, 1175 WinchLB, 1201–3 Cur
> *Wenrich(e)* 12 WinchLB, 1166 RBE (p), 1199 *FF*, 13 WinchLB, 1216 ClR, 1271 *FF et freq* to 1398 Ipm, -*ruch* 1346 FA
> *Wenriz* 1186, 13 WinchLB, 1207 Abbr, 1220 Fees
> *Wenrige* 1216 ClR, *Wenerigge* 1250 Fees, *Wenrugg* 1291 Tax
> *Wenerishe* 1280 Cl   *Wehenriz* 1287 QW
> *Wynrych(e)*, -*riche* 1295 Episc, 1303 FA *et freq* to 1557 *FF*
> *Wynrys(s)he*, -*risshe* 1409 Ass, 1465 *MinAcct*, 1501 Ipm
> *Wyndriche* 1562 FF, (-*als. Wyndrishe*) 1599 ib, *Windrishe* 1604 FF
> *Wyndridge* 1590 FF, *Wynrige als. Wynrushe* 1593 FF
> *Windrush* 1657 PR 17, 1765 ib 13

Named from the R. Windrush (14 *supra*).

CAMP BARN, *Camps-* 1830 M. OLDPOOL BARN, possibly identical with *Mere de Wenriz, Wenrichesmere* 13 WinchLB, *v.* mere 'pool'. PINCHPOOL FM, *Pynchepole* 1547 Sherb 171, 1597 *FF*, the manor was held by William *Pinchpool* 1316 FA and by John *Pinchpool* in 1501 Ipm; the surname means 'finch pool', from ME *pinche, v.* pōl. QUARRY PLANT., *the Stone Quarrs* 1777 *EnclA, Quarry* 1830 M. SALTWAY PLANT. WINDRUSH CAMP, 1830 M.

FIELD-NAMES

The principal forms in (*a*) are 1777 *EnclA*.

(*a*) Broadmead; Budge hill; Cockbury; the East Field; Elberham; the Gospel Ground (doubtless where the gospel was read on beating the bounds); Kings Park; Nosebury Camp; Racknap; Whithole End; Windrush Downs.

(*b*) *le Court Place* 1501 Ipm; *Cowham* 1535 VE (*v.* cū, hamm).

VIII. SLAUGHTER HUNDRED

UPPER DIVISION

The upper division of Slaughter Hundred lies north of the lower division and occupies the hilly country between the Evenlode (which here forms the eastern boundary of the county abutting on Oxfordshire) and the Dikler. It is centred on Stow on the Wold. Upper Swell parish was in Lower Kiftsgate Hundred (in DB in *Witelai* Hundred) but is included here in the topographical arrangement. Daylesford, Evenlode and Church Icomb were formerly in Worcestershire but were transferred to Gloucestershire in 1931 (Wo 120, 123, 143) and Church Icomb in 1844; Church Icomb and Icomb now form one civil parish. The detached Little Compton (a detached parish of Deerhurst Hundred) was transferred to Warwickshire in 1844 (Wa 299). For the hundred-name *v.* 192 *supra*.

Adlestrop

ADLESTROP (144–2427) ['ædlstrəp]

>   *Titlestrop* 714 (16th) BCS 130   *Tedestrop* 1086 DB
>   *Tatlestrop(e)* 11 (c. 1200) KCD 1367, 1251 Ch, 1276 RH, 1374
>   Rent 248, *-throp(e)* 1315 HMC v, 327, 1338 Ipm, 1376 *FF*, 1392
>   Ipm, *-thorp* 1327 *SR*, 1337 BM, *Tattlest(h)rop* 1291 Tax, Episc,
>   *Tattelestrop* 1292 ib, *Tatelesthorp(e)* 1338 Orig, 1590 FF, *Tatils-
>   trope* c. 1603 *TRMB*
>   *Tetlestropt* 1221 Eyre (p), *-trope* e. 13 ChronEv
>   *Thatlestrope, Thetillestroppe* 13 ChronEv
>   *Tadelecthorpe* (sic) 1287 QW, *Tadelest(h)rop* 1298 Episc, 1328
>   Banco, 1413 AD iii, *Tadlestrop* 1334 Heref, *Tadilthorp* 1577,
>   1610 M
>   *Attlesthorpe* 1330 Heref
>   *Athilthorp(e), -yl-* 1535 VE, 1545 LP, 1552 *FF*, (*-als. Addelstroppe*)
>   1627 FF, *Athilthroppe* 1597 *Talbot*
>   *Edelstrop* 1599 PR 14
>   *Adlesthrope als. Adelsthorpe als. Tatelsthrope* 1626 FF, *Ad(d)lestrop*
>   1684 PR 14, 1685 ib 5

In view of the early spellings with initial *T*- there can be little doubt that the original form of the name was *Tat(e)les-throp*; the later form *Attle-, Adle-*, etc. arises from a wrong analysis of phrases like 'at Tatlesthrop' (cf. æt, atten in EPN i, 6, 13 and Phonol. § 45). 'Tǣtel's dependent farmstead', *v.* þrop (cf. Hatherop 36 *supra*).

The OE pers.n. *Tǣtel* is not on record, unless the name of a Mercian moneyer *Tatel* (Searle) is a variant of it, but it occurs in p.ns. like *Tetilles wode* (iii, 172 *infra*), Talton (Wo 173), which is 9 miles north of Adlestrop, and Tatsfield (Sr 337), and is a derivative in -*el* of the recorded OE *Tāta* (Redin 54).

BAYWELL WOOD, *on bæganwellan* 718 (11th) BCS 139, *to, of Bægen-welle* 979 (11th) KCD 623, *on beagan wylle* c. 1050 (c. 1200) ib 963, (*riuulum de*) *Beiwelle* 11 (c. 1200) ib 1367, *Baywell* 1712 GR 892. '*Bæga*'s spring or stream', *v.* wella. Baywell was on the bounds of the land granted at Daylesford by Æthelbald king of the Mercians to *Bægia* 'servo Dei' for a monastery (BCS 139). This is, of course, not to be confused with the origin of Bibury and *Bywell* (26, 28 *supra*).

HARCOMB WOOD, *Hertescumbes welle* 11 (c. 1200) KCD 1367. 'The stag's valley', *v.* heorot, cumb. Harcomb Wood is on the north boundary of the parish (grid 144–241289) and the coomb runs down west towards Evenlode. The *welle* (called *to heort wellan* 969 (11th) BCS 1238) is without doubt the spring just below the wood near Horn Fm. The stream, a nearby hill and a spring are called *on heort broc'*, *Heortdune*, and *heortuuelle* (213, 220 *infra*), and there was a bridge called *Hertesbrugge* (*infra*).

CONYGRE LANE, *Coney Gree lane* 1775 *EnclA*, *v.* coninger 'warren'; it was called *on þa stige* in 949 BCS 882, c. 1050 KCD 963, *v.* stīg 'path'. COOMB WOOD. FERN FM, formerly *New Farm* 1777 M, cf. *Fern Old Inclosures* 1775 *EnclA*. THE NAITE, *le Neyte* c. 1603 *TRMB* 39, *v.* atten, ēgeð 'island'; this place is high on the hillside, and the name must therefore have had the sense of dial. *ait, nait* 'osier bed', rather than the usual 'island'. NORTON GAP, 1775 *Encl*, on the road to Chipping Norton (O). PEASEWELL WOOD.

FIELD-NAMES

The principal forms in (*a*) are 1775 *EnclA*, and in (*b*) c. 1603 *TRMB* 39. Spellings dated 949 are BCS 882, 979 (11th) KCD 623, c. 1050 (1200) KCD 963, 11 (1200) ib 1367, 1712 GR 892.

(*a*) Banbury Lane (formerly *to þære oðere stræt* 949, *to cynges ferdstrete* 979 and *regiam stratam de Norhamtun* 11, the Cotswold Ridgeway from Stow to Northampton, *v.* stræt); Blundalls (*terr' voc' Blundells* c. 1603, the surname *Blundel*); Bridge Lot (*v.* hlot); Church furlong 1712 (ib 1633 Inq);

Cross Green; Green Hill; the Upper, Lower Hide (v. hīd 'hide of land'); Kites Green; Langett 1712 (v. langet); Newball's (*terr' voc' Neweboldes* c. 1603, the surname *Newbold*); Parish Brook furlong; Pool Meadow (*le Poole meade* c. 1603); Spartswells (*Sparteswelle more* 11, *Spartwell close* 1712); the Town Street.

(b) *Asterne hole* 11; *riuulum de Beiwelle* 11 (also called *broces* 949, *sices* 979, the stream running from Baywell to the R. Evenlode); *Cheyle*; *le Cottes* (*the Coatland* 1633 Inq, v. cot); *Goodgrumsthornes* ('good groom's thorns', from ME grome, v. þorn); *on heort broc* 949, c. 1050 (the stream from Harcombe *supra* to the R. Evenlode); *Hertesbrugge* 11 (possibly a bridge over *Heortbroc* prec.); *le Horse crofte*; *Lodreswei* 11 ('robber's road', v. loddere, weg, also called *on þa str(æ)t* 949); *Monneswalle* 11 (the OE pers.n. *Mann*, v. wall); *le Northfelde*; *Rahulfes furlung* 11; *Rede mede*; *Soperholdes*; *le Southfelde*; *le Towne mershe*; *le Webwell*.

Bledington

BLEDINGTON (144–2422) [ˈblediŋtən]

Bladintvn, -yn-, -ton(a) 1086 DB, 1169 P, 1175–1404 WinchLB (*freq*), 1221 *Ass*, 1251 Ch, 1275 Episc *et passim* to 1428 *AddRoll*, -ing-, -yng- 1251 WinchLB, 1303 FA, 1405 Pat *et freq* to 1771 PR 13

Bladitona 1175 WinchLB

Bledington, -yng- 1424 Pat, 1535 VE *et freq* to 1728 PR 14

Bleddington, -yng- 1577, 1690 M, 1586 FF

'Farmstead on the R. *Bladon*', v. tūn. The river is now called the Evenlode (v. *Bladon* 3 *supra*). For the modern form, cf. Phonol. § 3.

WOODENHAM, *Wodenham* 1287 *Ass*, 1327 *SR*, 1540 *MinAcct*, *Withenham* 1540 ib. Probably 'Wōda's water-meadow', v. hamm; the farm is on the low-lying ground near the junction of the R. Evenlode and Westcote Brook. The pers.n., an OE *Wōda*, is not recorded but is a weak form of *Wode*, the name of a moneyer, which Redin 80 associates with OE wōd 'mad' and the pers.n. *Wod* in *Widsith* 30. But OE *Wudia*, a variant of *Widia*, is also possible, as in Withington (186 *supra*).

THE BANKS, *ripis voc' the Free bankes* 1540 *MinAcct*. BLEDINGTON HEATH, *le Hethe* 1575 TRMB, *le Comon Heath* 1626 Inq, v. hǣð 'heathland'. BLEDINGTON MILL, cf. *the lordes mille*, *Mille close*, -parke 1540 *MinAcct*. MICKLANDS HILL. PEBBLY HILL, *Pibley Hill* 1770 EnclA.

FIELD-NAMES

The principal forms in (a) are 1770 *EnclA*, and in (b) 1575 *TRMB*. Spellings dated 1540 are *MinAcct*, 1626 Inq.

(a) Bettertons; Bondlands furlong (*Banne Landes furlonge* 1575, probably from (ge)bann 'summons' or bēan 'bean'); Broadenham (*Brodnam* 1575, v. brād, hamm); the Bull Plott; Claydon (*Cley-* 1540, v. clæg, dūn); Cowham (v. cū, hamm); Coxmore; Dunstall (v. tūn-stall 'farmstead'); Foscott Inclosure (*Foxcote hayes* 1540, near Foscot (O 357), v. (ge)hæg); Fromdon (*Framedeane* 1575, the OE pers.n. *Frama*, v. denu); Grayhursts; Hammer Lands (*-longe* 1575, probably the ME byname *Hammere*, v. lang²); Hangerson (*Handgaston* 1575, v. gærs-tūn 'pasture'); the Home Stall; Horseham (1540, v. hors, hamm); Lanes furlong (*le Laynes* 1575, v. leyne 'arable strip'); Lord's Land Meadow (*le Lordes medowes* 1540); the Oar; Quickham (*Quickham* (*-broke, -waye*) 1575, v. cwic 'quickset hedge', hamm); Roughborough (ib 1540); Sandway; Shetnam Bridge; Smeenham; Spark Field; Spursborough Leys (*Sputtesborough* 1540, perhaps the OE pers.n. *Sprot*, with metathesis).

(b) *le Beastes pastur*; Blakemore (ib 1540, v. blæc, mōr); *le Buryland* 1540; *Chitenshall*; *Courte Close* 1540; *Coweford* (v. cū, ford); *Disbarowe filde* 1575, *Discombe Yates* 1626 (possibly an AN form of dīc 'ditch', v. beorg, cumb, geat); *le Drovewaye* (dial. drove 'unenclosed road'); *le Heardes house* 1626 (v. hirde 'herd'); *Hennebreche* (v. henn, brēc); *Kench Leyes* 1626; *Landwaye*; *le Leis* 1540 (v. lēah); *le Lottemeade* (v. hlot 'allotment'); *Mirtlandes* 1626; *le Parke* 1540; *Portwaye*; *Rostheye*; *Stutham*; *Teithing waye*; *Thornes* 1626; *Threeman meade*; *Twoe Thornedells* 1626 (doubtless 'two quarters', from the ME *farendel*, v. fēorða, dæl, cf. Phonol. § 41 b); *Whetehill filde*; *Whetney filde*; *Whight Landes*; *Woldlande* (v. wald 'wold').

Broadwell

BROADWELL (144–2027) ['bradəl]

> Bradewell(e) 11 (c. 1200) KCD 1367, 1086 DB, 1221 FF, *Ass*, 1251 Ch, 1276 RH *et passim* to 1428 *AddRoll*
> Bradwell 1433 Pat, 1535 VE *et passim* to 1675 Og
> Brodwell 1605 Comm, 1611 Rec
> Broadwell 1684 PR 14, 1715 ib 4

'Broad spring', v. brād, wella, referring to 'the large spring which rises near the manor-house' (Rudder 311). It is a common p.n. (cf. 188 *supra*, ii, 109, iii, 214 *infra*, O 308, Wa 139, etc.).

CAUDWELL BROOK, *on cealdwillan lace*, *on ða*, *of ðære cealdan wyllan* 11 (c. 1200) KCD 1365, *Cawelle broke* 1559 *AddR*. 'Cold spring', *v.* cald (ceald), wella, lacu 'stream'. The OE reference is from the Maugersbury charter; the spring is near the north-east corner of that parish (grid 144–210260) and the stream runs east on the Broadwell–Oddington boundary to the R. Evenlode.

COWNHAM, 1793 *EnclA*, *v.* cū 'cow' (gen.pl. *cūna*), hamm. CRAB ORCHARD, 1830 M. FIELD BARN, 1830 M, named from *Bradwellfeld* 1552 *AddR* 74142, *v.* feld 'common field'. MILL BROOK, 1830 M, cf. *atte Mulne* 1327 *SR* (p), *Mill place* 1552 *AddR*, *Mill Plot* 1793 *EnclA*, *v.* myln. PLUM'S BARN, 1830 M, *Plumb's Farm* 1793 *EnclA*, from the surname *Plum(b)*. RED HILL FM, *Redhill* 1793 *EnclA*. STOW WELL, 1793 *EnclA*, a well on the outskirts of Stow (225 *infra*). SYDENHAM, (*pratum*) *Sidenham* 11 (c. 1200) KCD 1367, 1770 *EnclA*, 'the extensive water-meadow', *v.* sīd, hamm.

FIELD-NAMES

The principal forms in (*a*) are 1793 *EnclA*, and in (*b*) 1552, 1556, 1559 *AddR* 74142. Spellings dated 779 are BCS 229, 949 BCS 882, 11 (12th) KCD 1359, c. 1050 (12th) ib 1365, and 1596, 1597, 1602 *Talbot*, 1639 Inq.

(*a*) Ally's Brook furlong; Bitham Corner (*v.* bytme 'bottom'); Black bush furlong; Bradman Lays (*Bradlame* 1596, *Burybradnam* 1779 Rudder, *v.* brād, hamm); Canscombe piece; the Combs (*Combe furlonge* 1639, *v.* cumb); Ditchland; Droveway; Fitmoor meadow (*on fittig mor* 11, *Fytmore* 1559, *Fittmore* 1597, the first el. might be associated with OE *fitt*, 'contest, fight', 'moorland subject to dispute', *v.* mōr); Flaxhill Butts; Galley Knap (*Gal(l)owefurlong* 1552, 1639, 'gallows hill', *v.* galga, cnæpp 'hill'); Garston furlong (*v.* gærs-tūn 'pasture'); the Heath (*on ðene hæðhyll* 11, *le Heth edyshe* 1556, *v.* hǣð, edisc, the same heathland being referred to in the adjacent Heath Barn 218 *infra*); Hides lake (*v.* lacu 'stream'); Holwell furlong; Humble Bee Well; the Lot meadow (*v.* hlot 'allotment'); Matchcroft furlong; Mawlays; Millham (ib 1797 *GR* 334, *v.* myln, hamm); Morden Quarter (*into mórdene* 779, *on mordene* 11, 'moorland valley', *v.* mōr, denu, cf. Mordens 227 *infra*); Oathill; the Parsonage ground (cf. *Parsonage Lane* 1556); the Picks (dial. *pick* 'a corner of a field'); Quinmoor Lane (the first el. probably identical with that in *on cwenena broce* 949, *on cwenna broc* 11, *innan cwenan bróc* c. 1050, 'the women's brook and moor', *v.* cwene, bróc, mōr); the Rifehams (*Rifeham plot* 1632, cf. Rypham (197 *supra*), *v.* hrēof, hamm); Slade Acres (*Slade* 1552, *v.* slæd 'valley'); Smoke Furlong (cf. Smoke Acre 70 *supra*); Stains Bridge; Stoney Knap (*v.* cnæpp 'hillock'); Turnham; Varendels (*v.* fēorða, dǣl).

(*b*) *Mess' called Beene*; *on deopan cumbe* 949, 11 (*v.* dēop, cumb); *mess' called Ferthyng*; *on ðene greate þorn* 11 (at grid point 144–214267, cf. *greatan þorne* 223 *infra*); *Hales* (*v.* halh); *Hamfurlong* (*v.* hamm); *Hariettes hey* (*v.* (ge)hæg); *on ðæt heafodland* 11 (*v.* hēafod-land); *Hobbesselle heornes*; *on*

ðon horpytt 11 (v. horu, pytt, at grid point 144–221266, Black Pit 224 infra
is 300 yards south-west, cf. horpyt 223 infra); Quermelhey; anlong ðere
sæltstræte 11 (v. salt, stræt, cf. Saltway 19 supra, part of the Stow–Evesham
road); Sandeshill plot 1632 (v. plot 'plot of land').

Condicote

CONDICOTE (144–1428) ['kundikət]

Cundicotan c. 1052 KCD 807.

Connicote 1086 DB   Cunnecote 1154–89 Glouc

Condicote 1086 DB, 1185 Templar (p), 1287 Ass, 1403 Pat et freq
    to 1760 M, Condycote 1407 Pat, Hy 6 AddCh, 1535 VE

Cundikote 1128 Glouc, Cundicot(e), -y- 1154–89 ib, 1166 RBE (p),
    1195 P, 1201 Cur (p), c. 1218 AD iii, 1220 Fees et passim to 1675
    Og, -cott 1291 Tax, 1327 SR, -coat 1751 PR 14

Gundicote 1242 Theok (p)

Cundecote 1303 FA, 1315 Ch, 1577, 1646 M

Condecote p. 1412 GloucHist

'Cunda's cottage', v. -ing⁴, cot. The pers.n. is OE Cunda (Redin 62);
it occurs also in Cundall YN 181. The medial -i- may be a reduced
form of OE -an- (v. Phonol. § 48).

HINCHWICK

Hunchewic, -wyk Ric 1 (1372) Ch, c. 1218 AD iii, 1366 Ch
Hinkewyke 1205 ClR, -wik 1205 Ch
Hi-, Hynchewike, -wyke 1258 Madox, 1571 FF, Hynchwicke 1584
    Comm
Henchewike, -wyke 1495, 1524 Rent, -weke 1585 FF

'Probably 'Hȳnci's dairy-farm', v. wīc. The spellings with Hinke-
point to the recorded OE Hȳnca, but the weight of evidence is against
a non-palatalised form. If this is a related Hȳnci we have to assume
assimilation of the gen.sg. -es (which occurs once) by the preceding
palatal.

EUBERRY CAMP, Camp ground 1856 TA, an ancient encampment.

FIELD-NAMES

The principal forms in (a) are 1856 TA 57.

(a) Debden meadow; the Hangings; North Furze; Nun-heys 1779
Rudder (named from the nuns of Coleshill (Wa), v. (ge)hæg); Picked ground
(cf. Picked Lease 40 supra); Scarlet hill; South Furze; Wash pool meadow.

(b) *Cumbwellslade* 1258 Madox (v. **cumb, wella, slæd**); *Fildeneway* 1258 ib ('road of the open-country dwellers', v. **filde²**, **weg**, cf. EPN i, 172–3; this section of the road forms the west boundary of Condicote and continues south on the Upper Swell–Temple Guiting boundary as *fildene wege* 228 *infra*, cf. *Fielden Way* 16 *supra*).

Daylesford

DAYLESFORD (144–2425)

Dæglesford (*vadum*) 718 (11th) BCS 139, 841 (11th) ib 436, 875 (11th) ib 540, 979 (11th) KCD 623, *Deilesford* 777 (14th) BCS 222, c. 1050 (c. 1200) KCD 963, *Dæiglæsford* 914 (12th) BCS 1135, *Degilesford* 979 (11th) KCD 623, *Dagelesford* c. 1050 (c. 1200) KCD 963, *Eilesford* 1086 DB, with other forms as cited in Wo 121. 'Dægel's ford', v. **ford**. OE *Dægel* is not recorded but it would be an -*el* derivative of a hypocoristic *Dæga* (from OE *Dægbeorht*, *Dægfrið*, etc.), corresponding to OG *Dagalo*; it occurs also in Dallington (Nth 81).

FIELD-NAMES

This parish was formerly in Wo. Spellings in (b) are 718 (11th) BCS 139, 979 (11th) KCD 623, c. 1050 (12th) ib 963.

(b) *to Babban beorge* 979 (the OE pers.n. *Babba*, v. **beorg** 'hill, barrow'); *to dunemannes treowe* 979 (an OE pers.n. *Dūnemann*, v. **trēow**); *on fearhom* 718 ('fern meadow', v. **fearn** (with a not uncommon loss of -*n*- cf. Phonol. § 37 b), **hamm**); *on nunnena beorgas* 718, *to Nunnena beorge* (v. **nunne** 'nun', doubtless in allusion to the monastery here for which land was granted, v. BCS 139 and Baywell 212 *supra*, **beorg**).

Donnington

DONNINGTON (144–1928)

Doninton, -*yn*- c. 1195 Godstow (p), 1284 Episc (p), 1359 AD ii, -*ing*-, -*yng*- 1262, 1296 Ipm, 1327 *SR*, 1418 Pat *et freq* to 1590 *FF*
Dunninton(e), -*yn*- e.13 ChronEv, 1234, 1251 Ch, -*yng*-, -*ing*- 1585 *FF*, 1761 PR 4
Donnington 1597 *Talbot*

'Farmstead associated with Dunna', v. **ing⁴**, **tūn**. The well-evidenced OE pers.n. *Dunn(a)* occurs in other local names, Duncombe, the f.ns. *Dunne(n) dic* and *Dunnes sleade* (*infra*) and *Dunnestreatun*, *into Dunnestreattúnne* 779 (c. 1200) BCS 229, that is 'farm on the Roman road belonging to *Dunna*', v. **stræt**, **tūn**, the road being the Fosse Way, near which remains of a Roman villa have been found; *Dunnestreatun* may in fact be the older name of Donnington, as the bounds in BCS 229 are those of Donnington.

DUNCOMBE HO (144–177279), *innon* (*of*) *dunnen cumbe* 779 (c. 1200) BCS 229. 'Dunna's valley', *v.* Donnington (*supra*), cumb.

HEATH BARN, 1830 M, preserves the name of *to ðam hǽðe, on, ofer ðene hǽð* 779 (c. 1200) BCS 229, *le heath* 1559 *AddR. v.* hǽð 'heathland'; it was the land (part of which is still heathy) at 144–205291. Cf. the Heath (215 *supra*).

CRAWTHORN WOOD, 1830 M, *v.* crāwe, þorn, cf. Crowthorne 47 *supra*. DONNINGTON MILL, 1765 *EnclA, atte Mulne* 1327 *SR* (p), *v.* myln. LAMING HOOKS BARN, 1830 M, *Lemming Hooks* 1765 *EnclA*. LITTLE BARROW, *Lutliburia* 1258 Madox, *Littleborough* 1830 M, *v.* lӯtel, beorg 'barrow'; this is probably *grenebeorhas sice* 779 BCS 229, 'green barrow' (*v.* grēne[1], beorg). MIRE SPRING, 1830 M. THE OAKS, 1830 M. STONEHILL QUARRY, *Stone Hill* 1765 *EnclA*. WATERHEAD BARN, *to ðam héafde* 779 BCS 229, *the Water Head* 1765 *EnclA*. WEASEL BARN.

FIELD-NAMES

The principal forms in (*a*) are 1765 *EnclA*, and in (*b*) 779 (c. 1200) BCS 229. Spellings dated 1597 are *Talbot* 72648, 1639 InqM.

(*a*) Bampit Way; Bitten Wall (possibly identical with *into ðére bytine* (sic for *bytme*) 779, *v.* bytme 'bottom'); Breech Leys (*Bratchelles Hamme* 1597, *v.* brēc, lēah, hamm); Castle furlong; Cownam (*v.* cū, hamm); the Drift Way; Fosse Leys (named from Fosse Way); Ganborough (cf. Ganborough 247 *infra* and Little Barrow *supra*); Hoar Stone ('boundary stone', *v.* hār, stān); Imple furlong; Madcombe Gate; the Neight furlong; Tackleys.

(*b*) Adkins Loume 1639; *on áthylle* ('oat hill', *v.* āte, hyll, possibly to be identified with Oathill Slad 220 *infra*); *to ðére blinde wylle* ('the secluded well', *v.* blind, wella); *in cærswylle* ('cress well', *v.* cærse, wella); *in ðæt óðer clif*; *Crakettes peece* 1597; *Donnington Church Waye & Fittmore* 1597 (*v.* Fitmoor 215 *supra* which is adjacent); *Donnington Towne feilds* 1652 *ParlSurv*); *in(non) dunne(n) dic, of dunne dic, innon dunnes sleade* (*v.* Donnington *supra*, dīc, slæd); *Farr Hill* 1597; *into ðam fox hole* (*v.* fox-hol); *to ðére fureh* (*v.* furh); *to gices díc* (possibly an OE pers.n. *Gic*, related to *gicce* 'itch'); *innon hæssucmór* (*v.* hassuc 'clump of coarse grass'); *to ðám heafodlonde* (*v.* hēafodland); *to ðám héafodstocce* (*v.* stocc); *innon, of headeboldes þorn(e)* (the OE pers.n. *Heaðubald, v.* þorn); *the Home* 1597; *in hrisc pyt* (probably the same quarry as *Hrisc pytte* 228 *infra, v.* risc 'rush', pytt); *innon meoson móre* (*v.* mēos 'moss, bog', mōr); *Loue topps* 1639; *Norehill peece* 1597; *innon ðére saltstret* (*v.* salt, strǣt, the Stow–Evesham road, cf. Saltway 19 and *sæltstræte*

216 *supra*); *innon ðám sandséaðe* ('sand pit', *v.* sand, sēað); *innon ðone stane* (*v.* stān); *to ðam twám stáne* ('the double stone', *v.* twā, stān); *in twise beorg* ('the twin barrow', *v.* (ge)twis, beorg); *Whytinges peece* 1597; *innon wudeweig* (*v.* wudu, weg, possibly the same road as *Wodeweye* 227 *infra*).

Evenlode

EVENLODE (144–2229) ['emloud, 'iːvənloud]

> *æt Eu(u)langelade* 772 (16th, 11th) BCS 209, 210, *Eowengelad* 784 (11th) ib 244, (*æt, to*) *Eowlangelade* 969 (11th) ib 1238
>
> *Eunelade* 777 (14th) BCS 222, c. 1050 (c. 1200) KCD 912, 1221 *Ass*, -*lode* c. 1050 (c. 1200) KCD 1367
>
> *Eownilade* 779 (c. 1200) BCS 229, *Eowniglade* c. 957 (12th) ib 1317
>
> *Eowenland* (sic) 964 (12th) BCS 1135
>
> *Eunilade* 1086 DB, c. 1086 *EveB*, 1221 Eyre
>
> *Evenlade* 1185 P, 1275 Episc, *Evinlade* 1209 Fees
>
> *Ewenelod(e)* 1284 Episc (p), 1291 Tax, 1331 *Ass*
>
> *Emlade* 1378 *Hailes*[1] (p), -*lod(e)* 1428 *AddRoll*, 1549 Pat, 1611 *Rec*, 1723 PR 3
>
> *Evenelod* 1369 Episc, 1712 PR 16

Other spellings are given in Wo 123 (from which county the parish was transferred in 1931). Evenlode is also the name of the river near which the village stands, but that is a back-formation; the old name of the river was *Bladen* (3 *supra*). 'Eowla's water-course or river-crossing', from an OE pers.n. formed from *Eowa* and equivalent, as Ekwall notes, to a ContGerm *Avila* (cf. Schönfeld 40), and OE gelād, on the interpretation of which *v.* EPN ii, 8–9; the *lode* is doubtless the second eastern channel or cut of the river here. The later *Even-* is an inversion which could arise when OE *efen* 'even' had been assimilated to *em-* (cf. Phonol. § 34*b*).

FOUR SHIRE STONE, 1690 M, *The Shire Stones* 1607 M, so called because it marks the point at which the counties of Gloucester, Oxford, Warwick, and Worcester once met. In 969 (12th) BCS 1238 the bounds of Evenlode include four stones at this point (*to þane stane*, *to þan operan stane*, *to þan þriddan stane*, *to þan feorðan stane*); cf. Wo 124.

ILDEBERG (lost), *Gildbeorh* 969 (12th) BCS 1238, *Ildeberga* 1086 DB, *Gildeneberga* 13 ChronEv. 'Hill of the guild or guildsmen', *v.* gild, gilda, beorg, and for a discussion of names of this type, cf. Wo 124.

BROOKEND WOOD, *Brookend Slad* 1766 *EnclA.* COLDICOTE HO, *Coldecote* 1270 Ipm, 'cold cottage', *v.* cald, cot, cf. Calcot (122 *supra*). EVENLODE GROUNDS & MANE, 1830 M, *v.* main 'demesne lands'. HEATH END BRIDGE, -*Brook* 1766 *EnclA*, *la Hethe* 1275 *Ass*, *Heathen Farm* 1830 M, *v.* hǣð, ende. HORN FM, *Horn Brook* 1766 *EnclA*, -*House* 1830 M, *v.* horn 'corner of land'; it is in an angle of the parish boundary. NORTHFIELD FM, *Northfield* 1699 *GR* 687. STOCK BRIDGE, 1766 *EnclA*, 'bridge made of logs', *v.* stocc, brycg. STUMPER FURZE, 1830 M.

FIELD-NAMES

The principal forms in (*a*) are 1766 *EnclA*, and in (*b*) 969 (11th) BCS 1238. Spellings dated 772 are BCS 210, 949 ib 882, c. 1050 (12th) KCD 963.

(*a*) Broad Mear & Pleck (*v.* mere 'pool', plek 'small plot'); Butterwell Hill; Cats brain furlong (*v.* cattes-braʒen); Green Gap, Lane & Lays; Haines's Ford; the Hale gate; the Lays; the Lots (*v.* hlot 'allotment'); Muncer Slad; Oathill Slad (cf. *áthylle* 218 *supra*); the Peer; Pesshill; Picked Lotts; the Picks (cf. the Picks 215 *supra*); the Poors Knap; Ray Meadow; Red Ford; Ridgway; Sedgey Butts; Sidelong; Stratford (cf. Saltway (1) 19 *supra*); Stuphill Gate; Surr Slad; Thatcham (*v.* þæc, hamm); Yarnsboroughs.

(*b*) *Ælfera mere* 772 (probably the OE pers.n. *Ælfhere*, if not an error for *ælfitu* 'swan', *v.* mere 'pool'); *ofer þone broc*; *to þan brocenan beorge* ('the broken hill', *v.* brocen, beorg); *Cenepes mor* 772 (cf. Kempley iii, 172 *infra*); *æt cettantreo* 772 (an OE pers.n. *Cetta* (cf. Cheddington Bk 90), *v.* trēow); *onlang dune* (*v.* dūn); *to þan ealdan slo* (*v.* slōh 'slough, bog'); *bi þan earðlande* (*v.* erð 'ploughing', land); *Fowerley Acres* 1699 *GR* 687 (*v.* fēower 'four', lēah); *on fugel mere* (*v.* fugol 'bird', mere 'pool'); *to þære grenan stige* ('green path', *v.* stīg); *bi heafdon* (*v.* hēafod); *to Heortdune* 949, *to heordune* c. 1050, *heortuuelle* 772, *to heort wellan* 969 (cf. Harcombe 212 *supra*, which is nearby, *v.* heorot, dūn, wella); *to hwettan stanes wylle* 949, *to hwete wellan* 969, *to wettan stanes wylle* c. 1050 (the OE pers.n. *Hwetta*, *v.* stān, wella); *to lafercan beorh* ('lark hill', *v.* lāwerce, beorg); *to þan lytlan beorhe* ('little barrow', *v.* lȳtel, beorg); *æt, on mules hlæw(e)* 772, 949, *to mules hlawe* 969, *on mules hlaw* c. 1050 (the OE pers.n. *Mūl*, hlāw 'mound'); *andlang riþiges* (*v.* rīðig 'small stream'); *andlang sealt stræte* ('salt-way', *v.* salt, stræt, cf. Saltway (1) 19 *supra*).

Icomb

ICOMB, CHURCH ICOMB (144–2122) [ˈikəm]

> *Ican-, Iccacumb* 781 (11th) BCS 240, *Iccacumb* 964 (12th) ib 1135
> *Iccecumb* 11 Heming   *Icecumb'* 1221 Eyre
> *Iacumbe* 1086 DB, *Iecumbe* 1221 *Ass*, *Jacomb* 1291 Tax

Iccvmbe, -cumb(e), -comb(e) 1086 DB, 1181–91 WinchLB, 1221 *Ass*,
1261 *FF*, 1282 Episc *et passim* to 1675 Og, *Ickumb'*, *-kombe* 1221
Ass, 1353 Ipm *et freq* to Hy 6 *AddCh, Iccoumbe* 1348 Misc (p)
Icvmbe, -combe 1086 DB, 1220 Fees, 1611 *Rec, Ycomb* 1303 FA
Hichecumb, Hichumb 1221 *Ass*
Hiccumbe, -comb 1269 Ch, 1287 QW, *Hickumbe* 1327 *SR* (p)
'Ic(c)a's valley', *v.* cumb. An OE pers.n., which occurs also in
Icangæt (infra), is discussed s.n. Ickford (Bk 124). The church is
mentioned in 1271, 1289 Episc, 1291 Tax, etc. The spellings *Ia-,
Iecumbe* may be misreadings of *Ia, le Cumbe* and refer to foll.

Combe Baskerville (lost), *la Cumbe* c. 1086 *EveB, Cumba* 1144,
c. 1180 Glouc, *Cumb(e)* 1216 ClR, 1261 *FF*, 1265 Misc, *Comb(e)* 1287
QW, (*-Baskirvile*) 1499 Ipm, 1830 M, (*-Baskerville*) 1515–29 ECP,
Combaskervyle 1568 *FF, cum Basket Feild* 1774 PR 13. *v.* cumb
'valley'. It was held by Bernard *de Baskerville* in the 12th century
(Glouc) and Walter *de Baskerville* in the 13th (1216 ClR); Sir John
Baskerville was seised of the manor in 1499 Ipm 123. Mr C. R.
Elrington points out that this lost place was without doubt in the
parish of Westcote (228 *infra*).

Camp, *Icomb Camp* 1830. Guy's Fm, *Guys Tower* 1830 M, named
from the family of Thomas *Guy* 1619 PR 13, 148. Icomb Place,
1731 PR 14. The Park. Weasel Coppice, *uuilesuuelle* 781 (11th)
BCS 240, *on Wulfilde wyllan* c. 1050 (12th) KCD 1365, *Wylles Welle*
14 WoHS (1911), *Wheeslye Hill* 1649 ParlSurv; the oldest form
suggests an OE pers.n. *Wil*, which has been proposed for Wilsham-
stead (Bd 85) and Wilson's (Sx 479); the second OE spelling *Wulfilde
wyllan* is from the fem. OE *Wulfhild, v.* wella.

FIELD-NAMES

The principal forms in (*a*) are 1810 *EnclA*, and in (*b*) 14 WoHS (1911).
Spellings dated 781 are (11th) BCS 240, 949 BCS 882, c. 1050 (12th) KCD
1365, 1598 *Comm*, 1649 ParlSurv, 1842 *TA*.

(*a*) Abbington Pool; Ash Farm; Berry Hill; Burnt bush furlong; the Cow
Pen; Dingle (*v.* dingle 'dell'); Dustlett Wood (*Durslade* 14, 'deer valley',
v. dēor, slæd); the Green hill; the Headland; the Hill; the Meer Ditch Wood
(*Merediches Ynde* 14, 'boundary ditch' *v.* (ge)mǣre, dīc, ende); Oxney Gate
(*v.* oxa, (ge)hæg); Plumb bush furlong; Ridge mead; Staple Road.

(b) *land called Browne* 1649; *Callow Knappe* 1649 ('bare hill-top', v. calu, cnæpp); *Cokkescombe* (v. cocc², or an OE pers.n. *Cocc* derived from it, cumb); *land called Deykes, -Dyes* 1649; *Godewelle* ('the good spring', v. gōd, wella, identical with *saltuuelle infra*); *Gouldes house* 1598; *the Grewey* (probably for 'green way', v. grēne¹, weg); *Haythornes Horne* (OE hæg-þorn 'hawthorn', v. horn 'bend, nook'); *Icangæt* 781 (v. Icomb *supra*, geat 'gate'); *Leches house* 1598; *the Mere* (v. mere 'pool'); *Merestones* ('boundary stones', v. (ge)mǣre, stān); *Saltuuelle* 781, *on sealter wille* 949, *innan sealtera wyllan, of sealtera wyllan lace* c. 1050 ('the salters' well', v. saltere, wella, the well is on the bank just above the Stow–Burford road, which was doubtless an old salt-way, cf. Saltway (1) 19 *supra*); *Smale Thornes* (v. smæl 'small, narrow', þorn); *land called Tibbetts* 1649; *Wyndeȝate* (v. wind-geat 'a wind-swept gap' or 'a swing-gate'); *Uuynheres stig* 781 (the OE pers.n. *Wynhere*, v. stig 'path').

Maugersbury

MAUGERSBURY (144–2025) ['mɔːgəzberi]

Meilgaresbyri' 714 (16th) BCS 130

æt Mæþelgares byrig 949 (orig.) BCS 882, *into Mædelgares byrig* 11 (c. 1200) KCD 1365

Maðelgæresbyri 1016 (14th) KCD 723

Malgeresberie 1086 DB

Malgaresbur(i), -biria, -byr', -bury(e) e.13 ChronEv, 1234, 1251 Ch, 1291 Tax, 1327 SR *et freq* to 1590 FF, *Malgarsbury* 1374 Rent 248, 1548 FF, 1575 TRMB, *Malgarysburye* 1543 AOMB

Melgeresbiria, -biry 1230 Bracton, 1260 FF

Malgerbury(e) 1544 LP, 1584 *Comm*

Maw-, Maugersbury(e) 1557, 1572 FF, 1682 PR 4

Malgersbury 1635 Inq

'Mæthelgar's fortified place', v. burh. There might have been an OE pers.n. *Mæþelgār*, but, though *mæþel* 'speech, council' is a common noun, it is not found as an OE name-theme as the cognate word is in OG pers.ns. like *Madalger*; *Mæþelgār* might well be an OE adaptation of the OG name (cf. Mangotsfield iii, 98 *infra*, which presents similar difficulties); the OG name was certainly common in England from the time of DB (Forssner 184). The site of the *burh* is still visible; cf. *Northbury* (224 *infra*).

DINGLE WOOD. DOWER FARM BARN. FISHPOND COPPICE, 1750 GR 1375. FOSS LANE, *the Foss Lane* 1766 EnclA, a lane leading

to the Fosse Way, formerly called *holan weg* (*infra*). HIDE FM &
MILL, THE HYDE, *Hydemylle* 1543 *AOMB*, *the Hide* (*Mill*) 1766
EnclA, *v.* hīd 'a hide of land'; this hide of land, which is that part
of the parish west of the Fosse Way, is doubtless the hide restored in
1016 by King Æthelred to Evesham (KCD 723). LARKHILL BARN.
MANTLET. MARGERY COPPICE, -*Quar* 1766 *EnclA*, *v.* quarriere
'quarry'. MAUGERSBURY GROVE, 1830 M, *Malkersbury Grove* 14
WoHS (1911), *Malgarysburye groue* 1543 *AOMB*, *v.* grāf 'copse'.
MEADOW HO, cf. *Maugersbury Meadow* 1766 *EnclA*, *v.* mǣd. MILL
POND, *the Mill Pond* 1766 *EnclA*. THE OLD COPPICE, 1830 M.
OXLEAZE. THE RETREAT, 1830 M. ROCK HO. SADDLE BOW.
ST EDWARD'S WELL, 1766 *EnclA*, for St Edward cf. Stow (225 *infra*).
STOW BRIDGE, 1766 *EnclA*, the bridge carrying the Fosse Way
towards Stow (225 *infra*) across the Dikler.

FIELD-NAMES

The principal forms in (*a*) are 1766 *EnclA*, and in (*b*) 1374 *Rent* 248. Spellings
dated 949 are BCS 882, 1016 (12th) KCD 723 (cf. Finb 150), c. 1050 (12th)
ib 1365, 1543 *AOMB*, 1575 *TRMB*, 1634 Inq.

(*a*) Angerman; Black pit furlong (*on ðone blacan pytt* c. 1050, *v.* blæc,
pytt, cf. *horpyt infra*); Blind Lane; the Camp; Cadnill Close (*Cadnell close*
1634); Egdon Hill; Fulbrook Ground ('dirty stream', *v.* fūl, brōc, cf. *on ðene
fulan ford* 1016, *v.* ford); the Green (*Malkersbury Grene* 14 WoHS, -*gars*-,
le Grene 1575, *v.* grēne²); the Ham (*v.* hamm); Haremore grounds; Heathill
Field; Hill Mead (*Hylmeade* 1543); Holy Well Head (*v.* hālig, wella);
Lammas Meads (cf. Lamas mead 77 *supra*); the Long Hedge; the Marsh;
the Oxneys (*Oxney* 1634, *v.* oxa, (ge)hæg); Sandle Piece; Small Wells; Stow
Hill; Well Lane (Well Lane 225 *infra*).

(*b*) *Benhull* ('bean hill', *v.* bēan, hyll); *to þam beorgan* 949 (*v.* beorg 'hill');
on Bicanford c. 1050 (the OE pers.n. *Bica*, ford); *Bleyneslond* (probably a
byname from OE *blegen*, ME *bleyne* 'blain, sore'); *on ðone bradan þorn* 1016
(*v.* brād, þorn); *on ða braðan strette* 1016 (*v.* brād, strǣt); *Colyneslond* (the
ME pers.n. or surname *Colin*); *Dedefordesse* ('disused ford', *v.* dēad, ford,
æsc 'ash-tree'); *Delelond* (*v.* dǣl 'share of land'); *Doune iuxta Foss*' (*v.* dūn
'hill, down' and Fosse Way 17 *supra*); *oð ðone garan* 949 (*v.* gāra 'gore of
land'); *of ðes grafan heafdon, to ðere grefes heauedon* c. 1050 (*v.* grafa, grǣf
'trench, ditch', hēafod); *to þam greatan þorne* 949 (at grid point 144–192229,
v. grēat, þorn, cf. *greate þorn* 215 *supra*, Great Thorns 225 *infra*); *on ða
grenan dic* 1016 (*v.* grēne¹, dīc, cf. Greneditch 197 *supra*), Grenhull; *Harries-
lond* (the ME pers.n. *Harrie*); *onlong hecge* c. 1050 (*v.* hecg 'hedge-row');
on ða hócihtan dic 1016 ('the hooked ditch', from an OE *hōciht* formed from
hōc 'hook, bend' with the adj. suffix -*iht*, *v.* dīc); *innan ðone lytlan holanweg,
onlong ðere holan weges* c. 1050 (*v.* hol², weg, cf. Foss Lane *supra*); *on horpyt*

949 (*v.* horu 'filth', pytt, probably at grid-point 144–183245, and the same pit as Black pit f.n. *supra*, but not identical with *Horpytt* 216 *supra*); *in hriswyllan lace* c. 1050 (identical with *on siscwille* 949, 'spring near the brushwood', *v.* hrīs, wella, lacu 'stream'); *on langan ford* 1016 (*v.* lang, ford, cf. *Langford* 209 *supra*); *on ða litlan dic* c. 1050 (*v.* lȳtel, dīc); *to mærðorne* c. 1050 ('boundary thorn', *v.* (ge)mǣre, þorn); *on mæswille* 949 (possibly an error for *mærwille* 'boundary stream', *v.* prec., wella); *Malgarsbury feild* 1575 (*v.* feld); *Maremede* 1543; *Northbury* (*v.* norð, burh); *Remede* 1543; *on þorn beorh, of þorm beorge* (sic) 949 ('thorn hill', *v.* þorn, beorg); *on ðone ðyrlan stan* c. 1050 ('stone with a hole in it', *v.* þyrel (adj.) 'pierced', stān); *innan ða wæter-furh* c. 1050 (*v.* wæter, furh 'furrow').

Oddington

ODDINGTON (144–2225)

Otintone, -ton(a), -tune, -yn- 862 (l. 13) BCS 535, 1066–87 Glouc, 1086 DB, 1139–1189 Glouc (*freq*), 1221 *Ass*, 1268 Pat *et passim* to 1340 Misc, *-ing-* 1138 Glouc

Otindon(a), -yn- 1086 Glouc, 1254 Cl, 1283 Ch, 1291 Tax, *Otendon* 1306 Pat

Othinton 1205 ClR   *Ottinton* 1233, 1242 Cl, 1267 Pat

Odynton p. 1412 GloucHist, *Odyngton, -ing-* 1535 VE, 1545 LP, 1553 *AOMB*, *Oddenton* 1609 PR 4

'Farmstead associated with Ot(t)a', *v.* ing⁴, tūn. OE *Ot(t)a* is not recorded but is known from such p.ns. as *Otanhyrst* 811 BCS 339 or *Ottanford* 909 ib 627 (cf. Totford Sr 211). Ekwall suggests that *Otta* is a hypocoristic form of dithematic names in *Ōht-* (*Ōhthere*, etc.), as is the recorded *Ōhta* (Redin 77). The spellings in *-don* may be due to some confusion with Oddington (O 233), which contains the same pers.n. with dūn 'hill'. On the later form in *Od-* cf. Phonol. § 40(*a*).

ASH FM, 1766 *EnclA*.   BANKS FM, 1787 *TA*.   BLACK PIT, 1787 *TA*, *v.* blæc, pytt, possibly identical with *horpytt* 216 *supra*, cf. Black pit 223 *supra*).   FERN BANK, 1787 *TA*.   MARTIN'S HILL.   OAKLANDS.   ODDINGTON ASHES, *-Lower, -Upper Ashes* 1830 M, *v.* æsc. SMENHAM.

FIELD-NAMES

The principal forms in (*a*) are 1787 *TA* 146.

(*a*) Bull Acre; Compt hill field; Corsham field; Cow leasow (*v.* cū, lǣs 'meadow'); Ditch field; Embrook Ford 1777 M (*Hembrook* 1693 GR 334, *v.* hemm 'edge, border', brōc, on the Maugersbury boundary); Fowl-moor 1779 Rudder; Great Thorns (cf. *greatan þorne* 223 *supra*, the location is at 144–224239, but the places are not the same); Haremoors; Horse fair; Horsebridge meadow; Jail close; Longton hill field; Maw leasow; Oven Pitts (*v.* ofen 'oven, furnace', pytt); Quinmoor field (near Quinmoor Lane 215 *supra*); Sise ground; the Spotted Pig; Sweetmoor; Townshends.

(b) *Curnock* 1693 *GR* 334; *Mon-, Mundaylandes* 1543 *MinAcct*, 1553 *AOMB* (cf. Sundayshill iii, 108 *infra*).

Stow on the Wold

STOW ON THE WOLD (144–1925)

> *Eduuardesstou* 1086 DB, *Ead-, Edwardestowe* Hy 1 (1241) Ch, c. 1107 BM, *Stowe S(ci') Edwardi* 1260 *FF*, 1316 FA, 1330 Ch, 1395 *FF et freq* to 1585 *FF*
>
> *Stoua* 1213 WinchLB (p), *Stouwa, -e* 1258 Madox, 1284 Episc, 1327 *SR*
>
> *Le Stauwe* 1221 *Ass*   *Estow* 1221 *Ass*
>
> *Stow(e)* 1221 Eyre, 1236 *FF*, 1276 RH *et passim* to 1733 PR 4, (*-super le Olde*) 1557, 1571 *FF*, (*-on the Olde*) 1574 *FF*, (*-on the Wowld*) 1577 M, (*-the Olde*) 1585 *FF*, 1597 Will, (*-le Old*) 1611 *Rec*, (*-in ye Would*) 1701 PR 3

v. stōw 'place', here in the sense 'place where people gathered for the practice of religion' and later 'a church dedicated to the service of a particular saint' (cf. EPN ii, 159). Stow was probably originally part of the Maugersbury estate which was given to the monastery at Evesham (Wo) before 714 (cf. BCS 130); it is named from the church which was dedicated to St Edward, king and martyr (975–8) and which is called 'the church of St Edward' in DB (cf. Finberg 64); the name *Edward* in the oldest forms of the p.n. appears also in St Edward's Well (223 *supra*). Stow stands on the high exposed hill-top above Maugersbury and the affix 'on the Wold' refers to this (*v.* **wald**, Cotswolds 2 *supra*).

STOW ON THE WOLD STREET-NAMES

CHURCH ST., 1729 *GR* 1375, *Church-streate* 1575 *TRMB*, *v.* cirice, strǣt. HIGH ST., 1662 *GR* 1375, *Alto Vico de Stowe* 1575 *TRMB*, *v.* hēah 'chief'. MARKET PLACE. NEW ST., *Newstrete* 1575 *TRMB*, *v.* nīwe. SHEEP ST., 1684 *GR* 334, *v.* scēap 'sheep'. WELL LANE, 1575 *TRMB*, 1696 *GR* 334, *v.* wella 'well'. Lost streets include *Burford streate* 1575 *TRMB*, 'the street leading to Burford (O 310)', probably the street now called Foss Rd. (part of the Fosse Way), *Duck Bath Street* 1714 *GR* 334, 'duck pond', *v.* dūce, bæð, *Noon Lane* 1723 *GR* 334, *Raggs Row* 1684 *GR* 892, 1766 *EnclA* (cf. also *Ragges place* 1575 *TRMB*), from the surname *Ragg* and rāw 'row of houses'. Old tenements include *Beesones Barne* 1575 *TRMB*, *le Corner House* 1575 ib, *the Courthouse* 1634 Inq, *the Crosse house* 1634 ib, *Inn called the Quart Pot* 1707 *GR*, 334, *ten' voc' Ringaldes* 1575 *TRMB*, *Ringed Hall* 1634 Inq, *Ring Hawle* 1636 *GR* 1375, *le Swan* 1446 AD, *the Swan Inn* 1705 ib 334.

FIELD-NAMES

The principal forms in (*a*) are 1750 *GR* 1375, and in (*b*) 1575 *TRMB* 39.

(*a*) Bayliffs Plat (*v.* baillie, plat² 'small plot'); Dodmore; Edmund's little hill; Granhams-Bank; the Gores (*v.* gāra); the Hangings; the Harbour; King's-well; the Mores; the Rays; Red lands; Sladway (*v.* slæd, weg); Small-way (*v.* smæl 'narrow'); Stow Pits 1819 *GR* 334.

(*b*) *Burnameʒ Mile*; *la Dele in Stowe* 1374 *Rent* 248 (*v.* dæl 'share of land'); *Gill Stephens hay* (*v.* (ge)hæg 'enclosure'); *le Horspoole* (*v.* hors, pōl).

Lower Swell

Lower Swell (144–1725)

The forms for Lower & Upper Swell include:

Swelle 706 (16th) BCS 118, *æt Suella major* 714 (16th) ib 130, *æt Suuelle* 1055 KCD 801

Sv(v)elle 1086 DB, *Su(u)ella* 12 *Tewk* 75a, *Suelle* 1221 *Ass*
Suwell' 1221 *Ass*, *Sowell'* 1291 Tax, *Sewell* 1584 *Comm*
Swell(e) 1221 *Ass*, 1248 *FF*, 1251 Ch, 1255 *FF*, 1261 Ipm *et passim* to 1597 *Talbot*, (*Over(e)-*) 1274 RH, 1325 *FF*, 1336 BM, 1536 *Rent*, (*-Abbatis*) 1221 *Ass*, (*Nether(e)-*) 1274 RH, 1287 *Ass*, QW, 1301 Ipm *et freq* to 1575 *FF*, (*Magna-, Parua-*) 1287 *Ass*, (*-Superior, -Inferior*) 1291 Tax, 1327 *SR*, 1535 VE, (*Upper-*) 1611 *FF*, 1692 PR 4, (*Lower-*) 1699 ib 3

From OE (*ge)swell* or **swelle* 'swelling', which Ekwall discusses in Studies² 151. The word *swell* is not independently recorded in the sense 'rising ground' until the 18th century (NED s.v.), but p.ns. like this Swell and Swell (So) demand such a topographical extension of meaning. The latter place is at a point where the land begins to rise rapidly to a long ridge; Lower Swell and Upper Swell are similarly situated where the ground begins to rise steeply to Swell Hill. Lower Swell is a little way from the R. Dikler and Upper Swell is on the river but further up its course. Upper Swell is also distinguished as Lat *magna*, *major*, and Lower Swell as Lat *parva* and *Abbat* (the latter from the Abbot of Hailes).

BOWL FM, (le) Bowlde 1535 VE, 1540 MinAcct, 1542 LP, Bould (Mill) 1628 Inq, 1669 GR 444, Swell Bowl 1830 M. From OE bold, a Merc variant of bōðl 'mansion, dwelling'. Cf. Bould (O 357).

ABBOTSWOOD, Abbotts wood 1628 Inq, v. abbat, wudu; the manor was held by Hailes Abbey from the late 13th century. CAMP COVERT. CONDICOTE LANE, cf. Condicote Lane (16 supra), Stret beorge (228 infra). DITWELL, -Lays 1790 EnclA. FROG WELL. HORESTONE, 'boundary stone', v. hār, stān. HUNTSHILL. OLD-FURZE COVERT, cf. Swell Furze Hill 1790 EnclA, v. fyrs. QUARWOOD. SEARCHAM COPPICE. STAYT'S SPINNEY. SWELL HILL FM, 1830 M. SWELL WOLD, 1790 EnclA, v. wald. WHITTLESTONE or WHISTLESTONE.

FIELD-NAMES

The principal forms in (a) are 1790 EnclA. Spellings dated 1255 are FF, 1540 MinAcct, 1545 LP, 1628 Inq.

(a) Brunts Hill; Crabtree Leys; Gallows piece; half penny meadow (one paying ½d. rent); Hell-Fire Gate & Lotts; Mill lays; the Mordens (Morden 1535 VE, Murden 1545, -lessue 1540, -leasowes 1628, 'marsh valley', v. mōr, denu, læs 'meadow', cf. Morden 215 supra); the Sheep Hill; Stand Hill; the Town Green.

(b) Gannow(e) 1540, 1545, the sheepcote of Gannow 1628 (probably ME gannowe, a secondary form of gannok in some such sense as 'shelter', in this case a sheep-cote); le Park 1321 Misc, Swell park 1628; Wildmore Medowe 1540 (v. wilde, mōr); le Wodeweye 1255 (v. wudu, weg, cf. wudeweig 219 supra).

Upper Swell

UPPER SWELL (144–1726)

For spellings and meaning v. Lower Swell (226 supra).

CONDICOTE LANE, a Roman road (16 supra). FOX FM, 1830 M. PITMAN'S BARN. POLE'S PLANT.

FIELD-NAMES

The principal forms in (b) are c. 1055 Finb 171. Spellings dated 1374 are Rent 248.

(b) in þa bradan furh (v. brād, furh 'trench'); le Clump 1575 TRMB (e.ModE clump 'a clump of trees'); on norþ halde codes byrig (v. hald 'shelter', burh, Cōd is an OE pers.n., possibly that of the man who gave his name to

Cutsdean (ii, 7 *infra*); Dr Finberg identifies the site with Fox Fm in Upper Swell); *innon þam ealdan dic* (*v.* ald, dīc 'ditch'); *into fildene wege* ('road of the dwellers in the open country', *v.* filde², weg, here the lane from Hinchwick over Kineton Hill, on the Temple Guiting boundary, the same lane as *Fildeneway* 217 *supra*); *Fraunkeleyneslond* 1374 (ME *frankelein* 'a freeholder, a freeman'); *in þ' fule ric* ('dirty ditch', *v.* fūl, ric); *into þam grenan wege* (*v.* grēne¹, weg); *be suðan hættes lawe* (an OE pers.n. *Hætt* is not known, though a ME byname *Hatte* occurs as a later metonymic form for 'hatter' (Reaney 156); possibly in this name it is hætt 'hat-shaped hill', *v.* hlāw 'mound'); *æfter ðam heafde* (*v.* hēafod 'headland'); *into hrisc pytte, of hris pytte* ('rushy pit', *v.* risc, pytt, identified by Finberg with a f.n. Rush-pit field at grid 144–160276, cf. *hrisc pyt* 218 *supra*); *into huntes hylle* (possibly an OE pers.n. *Hunt* a strong form of *Hunta*); *Hurne* 1374 (*v.* hyrne 'nook, corner'); *innon ðene litle beorh* (*v.* lȳtel, beorg 'barrow'); *be suðan þam longam beorge* ('the long barrow', identified by Finberg with the one at grid 144–167263); *into mær wylle* ('the boundary spring', *v.* (ge)mære, wella); *ofer þeos hylle* ('pease hill', *v.* pise (*peosu*), hyll); *into þam slæde* (*v.* slæd 'valley', the same valley as Mordens 227 *supra*); *be ðere stige* (*v.* stīg 'steep path'); *to stret beorge* (*Stratburgdich' 1255 FF*, 'barrow near the Roman road', *v.* strǣt, beorg, near Condicote Lane on the Lower Swell boundary at grid 144–155267, cf. Finb p. 236); *innon þa ðreo beorgas, of þam ðreom beorgum* (*v.* þrēo 'three', beorg 'barrow', probably the traces of three barrows at grid 144–190270, cf. Finb p. 236); *into twam beorgum* (*v.* twēgen (*twā*) 'two', beorg); *in ðone twislede beorh* ('the forked or divided barrow', from OE *twisled* (cf. twisla), beorg); *be wulfweardinge lea* ('the clearing of Wulfweard's folk', from OE *Wulfweard, -ingas*, lēah).

Westcote

WESTCOTE (144–2220)

Westcote 1315, 1382 *MinAcct*, 1499 Ipm *et freq* to 1726 PR 13, (*Over-, Nether-*) 1515–29 ECP, *Wescote* 1457 AD ii, (*Nether-, Ouer-*) 1547 *FF*; the identification of *Westcot(e)* c. 1220 Berk, 1232 Ch is doubtful. 'West cottage', *v.* west, cot.

COMBE BASKERVILLE (lost), *v.* 221 *supra*.   GAWCOMBE, 1830 M, *Gocombe* 1779 Rudder.   HAWKWELL.   WELL HO.

FIELD-NAMES

The principal forms in (*a*) are 1840 *TA* 215. Spellings dated 1701 are *GR* 334.

(*a*) Berton (*v.* bere-tūn); Bushy Ham (*v.* hamm); Corn Dingle (*v.* dingle); Duckpits 1701; Homestall (*v.* stall 'site'); Lanket (*v.* langet); March; Oakham; Picket Mead 1701 (dial. *picked* 'cleared, pointed'); Reed Hill; Rivacre; Tabury Field; Totwell ground; Unkham.

(*b*) *Fynditch* 1633 *GR* 892 (*v.* fin 'heap (of wood, etc.)', dīc).

IX. KIFTSGATE HUNDRED

UPPER DIVISION

(With detached parts of WESTMINSTER, DEERHURST and TEWKESBURY HUNDREDS)

The Upper Division of Kiftsgate Hundred occupies the north-east of the county and includes the northern Cotswolds and part of the low-lying lands in the Avon valley, the Avon forming the northern boundary almost to Stratford on Avon (Wa 236). It lies between Warwickshire on the east and Worcestershire on the west and at one time it was almost detached from the county by the Worcestershire parishes of Broadway and Blockley; the latter parish was transferred to Gloucestershire in 1931. The parishes of Sutton under Brailes (an isolated parish transferred to Warwickshire in 1844, *v.* Wa 301), Moreton in Marsh, and Todenham were detached parts of Westminster Hundred (iii, 146 *infra*); Clifford Chambers, Shenington (an isolated parish transferred to Oxfordshire in 1844, *v.* O 402), Bourton on the Hill, and Lemington were detached parts of Tewkesbury Hundred (ii, 48 *infra*); and Little Compton (transferred to Warwickshire in 1844, *v.* Wa 299), Preston on Stour and Welford were detached parishes of Deerhurst Hundred (ii, 75 *infra*). The parishes of Admington, Clifford Chambers, Clopton, Dorsington, Long Marston, Milcote, Preston on Stour, Quinton, Welford on Avon, and Weston on Avon were in 1934 and 1935 transferred to Warwickshire, and Cow Honeybourne and Pebworth in 1931 to Worcestershire. At the time of the DB inquest, there were (apart from detached parts of other hundreds and counties already mentioned) three hundreds, *Celfledetorn* (which comprised Admington, Aston Subedge, Clopton, Dorsington, Hidcote Bartrim, Cow Honeybourne, Long Marston, Mickleton, Pebworth, Quinton, Weston on Avon, and Weston Subedge), Kiftsgate (which included the manor of *Langeberge* and Meon (251, 254), cf. Finberg 49 and Addenda), and *Witley* (which included Batsford, Chipping Campden, Ebrington, Lark Stoke in Admington, part of Longborough, Saintbury, Sezincote, and Willersey). Before 1220 these three hundreds had been united to form Kiftsgate Hundred. On these hundreds *v.* esp. Anderson 15–19 and Lower Kiftsgate Hundred (ii, 1 *infra*).

CELFLEDETORN HUNDRED (lost)

Celfledetorn(e), *Celfle(o)de*, *Ceolflede hd'* 1086 DB. 'Cēolflǣd's thorn-tree', *v.* þorn. The pers.n. is the OE fem. *Cēolflǣd*. The loss of the final el. or its ellipsis in *Ceolflede* occurs also in the DB spellings of Brightwell's Barrow and Salmonsbury (22, 192 *supra*). The site of this place has not been discovered.

KIFTSGATE HUNDRED

Cheftesihat 1086 DB

Keftesgate (*hundredum*) 1183, 1187 P, 1274 RH, 1284, 1484 Pat,
Keftegate 1303 FA, 1485 Pat

Ki-, Kyftesgate (*hundredum*), *-gat'* 1193 P, 1220 Fees, 1233 Pat,
1248 *Ass*, 1255 Cl, 1259 WinchLB, 1274 RH, 1279 Ipm, 1285
FA *et passim* to 1568 *Comm, Kiftesygate* 1221 *Ass, -gwat* 1221
Eyre, *-iate* 1221 *Ass, -y(h)ate* 1248 ib

Kuftesgat(e) 1227–1230 Pat, *Kufteseyte* 1236 Theok, *Skuftesgat(e)*
1223, 1228 Pat

Khyftesyate 1248 *Ass*

Ki-, Kyftegate 1251 Pat, 1287 *Ass*, 1316 FA, *et freq* to 1395 Pat

Kyfhyate 1495 *Rent, Kyfgate* 1536 ib

Kippisgate 1518 Glouc   *Kuesgate* c. 1560 *Surv*

The hundred is named from Kifts Gate (250, 261 *infra*). Cf. also
Spelsbury (250 *infra*).

WITLEY HUNDRED (lost)

Witelai hundredum (*hd', hvnd'*) 11 Heming, 1086 DB, *Widelei, -les
h(vn)d'* 1086 DB, *Wichtele hdr'* 1169 P. This may have a similar origin
to Witley (Wo 183), and be a compound 'forest-glade or clearing in a
bend', *v.* wiht (which denoted a river-bend or a hollow in a hillside),
lēah (cf. Anderson 17). The site of the place has not been discovered.

HENMARSH (lost)

Hennemerse 1235 Ipm, 'marsh haunted by wild hen-birds (moor-
hens or the like)', *v.* henn, mersc. From its use as an affix, this was
the name of a district characterised by much marshland centred on
Moreton in Marsh (251 *infra*) and extending from Bourton on the
Hill and Chipping Campden (236, 237 *infra*) on the west to Lemington
(246 *infra*) as well as Barton on the Heath, Little and Long Compton,
and Sutton under Brailes in Warwickshire (Wa 298, 299, 301) on
the east.

Admington

ADMINGTON (144–1945)

Edelmintone, -tona 1086 DB, 12 WinchLB, 1221 Plea

Ethelmintona 1175 Monast (WinchLB)

Adel-, Adilminton(a), -yn- 1184–94, 1251, 1257 WinchLB, 1271
Pat *et freq* to 1440 WinchLB, *-ing-* 1251 Ch, 1251 WinchLB,
(*-als. Admyngton*) 1587 *FF*

Edelinton 1221 *Ass*
Edelmeton 1221, 1287 *Ass, Adelmeton'* 1287 ib
Athelminton 1221 WinchLB, *-yng-* 1287 *Ass*
Adelyngton 1287 *Ass, -in-* 1291 Tax
Admington 1704 PR 4

'Farmstead associated with Athelhelm', *v.* -ing[4], tūn. The pers.n.
is OE *Æþelhelm*.

LARK STOKE, *Stok(e)* 716 BCS 134, 1220 Fees, 1248 *Ass, Stoch* 1086
DB, with the prefix *Lauerke-* 1227 *FF,* 1287 *Ass,* 1409 *MinAcct,*
Lauirke- 1236 Fees, *Lark(e)-* 1287 *Ass,* 1319 Ch, 1345 *FF et freq* to
1540 *FF, Laverstokes* 1274 RH, *Lark(e)stocke* 1350 Ipm, 1587 *FF,*
-stowe 1374 AD, *-stowke* 1563 *FF. v.* stoc 'place', often in the sense
'dependent outlying farmstead'; the occasional use of the ME plur.
stokes might suggest 'the farm buildings'. Occasionally *stoc* seems to
have had a religious connotation and that may be the case with Lark
Stoke (cf. EPN ii, 153 ff). It may be noted that Lark Stoke was in the
DB hundred of *Witley* but the main part of Admington was in *Cel-*
fledetorn hundred; Lark Stoke may therefore have been an outlier of
some other neighbouring village. The affix is from OE lāwerce (lāferce)
'lark', and the compound 'farmstead frequented by larks' is repeated
in *Laverkestoke,* the old name for Langley (Bk 241 n), and Laverstock
(W 381, Ha); in some of these there is a similar variation between
stoke and an occasional *stow* (*v.* stōw 'place').

BOG MILL STALLS. BRUTON. HARBOUR HILL, *Harberyll',* *-hill*
1575 *TRMB* 39, *v.* here-beorg 'shelter, lodging', hyll. OXHOUSE
STALLS. SMALL BROOK.

FIELD-NAMES

The principal forms in (*b*) are 1575 *TRMB* 39. Spellings dated 1409, 1540
are *MinAcct*, 1642 Inq.

(*b*) *Adylmington heye, le Heye* 1540 (*v.* (ge)hæg); *Eleaven Lands* 1642;
Fordefeld 1409 (*v.* ford, feld); *Frissen lesowe* 1540 (probably a metathesised
form of fyrsen 'growing with furze', *v.* lǣs); *Kyngesfeld* 1409 (a local surname *King*, found later in *terr' voc' Kynges* 1540); *the Leys* (*v.* lēah ' clearing');
Mo(o)re le(a)sowe 1540, 1575; *le Neght feld, -Nete-* (perhaps nēat 'cattle');
Neowenham 1184–94 WinchLB (*v.* nīwe, hamm); *the Overground* 1642;
Perins Yard, mess' voc' Perins (from a local surname *Perrin* found also in
terr' voc' Peryns 1540); *Pollis yarde* (a local surname *Pooley* found also in
mess' voc' Poolley 1540, *v.* pōl, lēah); *Sharpegore* 1409 ('sharply pointed
triangle of land', *v.* scearp, gāra); *Smythes yarde, cotag' Smythes; Soundwell*

Leyes (possibly OE (*ge*)*sund* 'sound, healthy' used of a spring of health-giving properties); *Swaynesfeld* 1409 (the ME pers.n. *Swain*); *Uptonesfeld* 1409 (named from Will' *Upton*); *Windfore lesowe* 1540; *Wynson field* 1642; *Wynterbournefeld* 1409 ('spring flowing chiefly in winter', *v.* winter, burna).

Aston Subedge

ASTON SUBEDGE (144–1341) [ˈastən ˈsubidʒ]

in easthammore 709 (c. 1200) BCS 125, *Estvne* 1086 DB, *Eston'* 1221 Eyre, 1248 *Ass* (p), 1274 RH, (*-Johannis*) 1221, 1236 Fees, *Aston* 1273 Ipm, (*-sub Egg(e)*) 1284 Episc, 1287 *Ass*, 1327 *SR et freq* to 1535 VE, (*-subtus Egge*) 1297, 1309 *FF et freq* to 1506 *FF*, (*-under Egge*) 1362 *FF*, 1378 AD iii, 1438 Pat, (*-Underedge*) 1563 *FF*, (*-Subedge*) 1608 *Harrowby*, 1682 PR 4. 'East farmstead', *v.* ēast, tūn; it is east in relation to Weston Subedge (261 *infra*). The OE form is clearly an error for *ēasthǣma-*(*ge*)*mǣre* 'boundary of the men of Aston', as Aston Subedge parish lies against the southern boundary of Church Honeybourne (Wo), which the charter is dealing with; on the elliptical form cf. Chipping Campden and Weston Subedge (237, 261 *infra*), *v.* hǣme, (ge)mǣre. The affix in Aston, Weston and Norton (262 *infra*) refers to their location below the steep escarpment at the northern extremity of the Cotswolds (*v.* ecg, 'edge, scarp'). The place was called *Johannis* because it was held at the time by *Johannes* le Brun of the Bishop of Rochester.

ASTON HILL, 1830 M. LITTLE LONDON. MANOR HO. POORS PIECE.

FIELD-NAMES

The principal forms in (*a*) are 1772 *EnclA*. Spellings dated 1607–1668 are *Harrowby*.

(*a*) Ashbrook furlong (*Ashbrooke* 1647, *v.* æsc, brōc); the Boll Gap; Brack furlong (*Bratch-*, *the Brechfurlong* 1647, 1667, *v.* brēc 'land broken up for cultivation'); Butt meadow (ib 1647, *v.* butte); Chilwell furlong (*Chillwell* 1668, 'cold spring', from e.ModE *chill* 'cold'); Cold Ash ('exposed ash-tree', *v.* cald, æsc); Dowry meadow; Easter meadow (doubtless one brought into use at Easter or otherwise associated with Easter, cf. Sundayshill iii, 108 *infra*); Ham Green (named from *the Homm* 1667, *the ham* 1668, *v.* hamm 'water-meadow'); Henhouse furlong; Huntsgrave (*-graue* 1647, the surname *Hunt*, *v.* grafa 'trench, ditch'); the Linches (*v.* hlinc 'ridge'); Marbrook furlong (*Marebrooke-* 1668, probably 'boundary brook', *v.* (ge)mǣre, brōc); Parsonage Lane (*the Parsons Lane* 1647); Pool furlong; Powder Corner; Thoroughts; Weaver furlong (*Weavers more* 1667); Withyrow furlong (*v.* wiðig 'willow').

(b) *the Beegarden* 1607 (v. bēo, gardin); *Brech Layes* 1667, *Breach Meadow* 1647 (v. Brack furlong *supra*); *Corcombe* 1647, 1668; *Elme leyes* 1668; *Flaxehades* 1647 (v. fleax, hēafod); *the Halefurlong* 1647 (v. halh); *le Hoder close* 1608; *Lott grounde* 1668 (v. hlot 'allotment'); *Maydes Castle* 1667 (a late name usually applied to an ancient encampment, 'one frequented by maidens', v. mægden 'maiden', castel, cf. Maiden Castle (YW iv, 70), Maidenhill (247 *infra*), and Knave Castle 208 *supra*); *Pery way* 1668 (v. pirige 'peartree', weg); *le Shephouse Close* 1608.

Batsford

BATSFORD (144–1833)

(æt) *Bæccesore* 716–43 (11th) BCS 163 (v.l. *Bæcces(h)oran* 11th Heming), *Bæceoran* 961–72 Finb 112

Beceshore 1086 DB, *Bechesore* 1196, 1199 FF, *-hor'* 1249 FF, *-oure* 1220 Fees, 1273 FF, *-ofere* 1236 Fees, *-ouere* 1248 *Ass*

Begesoure 1235 Ipm   *Bagessoure* 1291 Episc

Bagesovere 1236 Fees, *Baggeshor(e)* 1274, 1276 RH, 1287 *Ass*

Bac(c)hesor(e) 1235, 1268 Ipm, 1269 Episc, 1284 *Ass*, 1287 FF *et passim* to 1535 VE, *(-als. Battesforde)* 1610 FF, *Bachesour* 1277 Episc, *-hore* 1285 FA, 1309 FF, *Bacheser* 1303 FA

Batysore 1541 FF, *Battisore* 1547 Pat, *Batsore als. Batshore als. Bachesore* 1577 FF, *-als. Battesford* 1630 Inq

Bat(t)esford(e) 1577 M, 1587 FF, 1610, 1695 M, *Batsford* 1685 PR 4

Batchford als. Battisford 1646 FF

'Bæcci's slope', v. ōra[1]; the ME spellings in *-ofere*, *-ou(e)re* represent a substitution of OE ofer[2] 'slope, ridge' (cf. EPN ii, 54, 55). It refers to the steep hillside rising to the north-west of the flat terrain of Moreton in Marsh. The pers.n. is an OE *Bæcci* (a derivative of the recorded *Bacca*), evidenced only in p.ns. like Batchmere's Fm (Sx 80) and Batchworth (Hrt 81). The modern form Batsford is an inverted one, which arose when ME *-ts-* was assimilated to *-ch-* (cf. Phonol. § 44a); *-ford* is due to popular etymology, but there is no ford here.

BATSFORD HEATH FM, *the Heath* 1630 Inq, *Bat(t)esford Heath* 1630 ib, 1682 PR 5, 143, v. hǣð 'heathland'. BATSFORD PARK, 1830 M. BLENHEIM, *Blenham* 1830 M. BORAM FM, *Boreham Meadow* 1630 Inq, 'boar meadow', v. bār, hamm. CADLEY HILL, 1830 M, *Cadlow Hill* 1630 Inq, probably 'Cada's mound', from the OE pers.n. *Cada*, v. hlāw. COLD WELL LAKE, *Cawdle* 1838 *TA*, 'cold spring', *v.* **cald, wella, lacu** 'stream'. Furze Heath, 1830 M. Parson's Heath, 1838 *TA.* Sisters Pool. Townsend Hovel, *-ground* 1838 *TA.*

FIELD-NAMES

The principal forms in (*a*) are 1838 *TA* 20, and in (*b*) 1630 Inq. Spellings dated 1642 are InqM.

(*a*) Blackall meadow (*Blackham-* 1630, *v.* blæc, hamm); Bradley piece; Catley arbour 1777 M (*the Arbor close* 1642, *v.* Cadley *supra,* erber 'garden, orchard'); Church hill (*Churchyard hill* 1630); Draw rails; Knotts heath; big & little Knowl (*v.* cnoll 'hillock'); Lady holm (*Lady Hame* 1630, *v.* hamm); Langate (*v.* langet); Monka meadow (*Monke meadow* 1630, named from the monks of Tewkesbury Abbey, cf. Rudder 266); Red gate ground; Sally meadow; Slang (dial. *slang* 'a narrow strip of land separating two larger divisions); Stud field (*Stutford Meadowes* 1630); Wharf.

(*b*) *Broad meade; broad Meare; Hemp grounde* 1642; *Hurtes Leyes* 1642; *Lampe lande* 1550 Chant (cf. *Lampehousse* 67 *supra); Sheep howse close.*

Blockley

This large parish was formerly in Worcestershire and its names are dealt with in Wo 98 ff. They are summarised here.

Blockley (144–1534)

> *Bloccanleeh* 855 (11th) BCS 488, *-lea,* n.d. (11th) ib 1320, 978 (11th) KCD 620   *Bleccelea* (sic) 964 (12th) BCS 1135
> *Blochelei* 1086 DB
> *Blokele(ia), -lege* 1195 Abbr, 1221 Eyre, 1255 Ch
> *Blockele(ia), -ley(e)* 12 WinchLB, 1206 Abbr, 1209 Fees *et passim*
>   to 1348 WinchLB, *Blokkele(y)* 1242 Theok, 1291 Tax, 1306 *Ass*
> *Blocleg* 1270 Ch, *Bloklei* 1404 WinchLB

'Blocca's forest-glade or clearing', *v.* lēah; the pers.n. is an otherwise unknown OE *Blocca,* a weak form of the *Blocc* found in Bloxham (O 394).

Aston Magna, *Easttune* 904 ASChart xviii, *Eastune* 977 (11th) KCD 615, *Estona* 1208 Fees, 1327 *SR, Hangynde Aston* 1282 *FF, Hanging(e) Aston* 1549 Pat, 1626 InqM, *Aston Magna* 1626 ib, 1830 M. 'East farm', *v.* ēast, tūn, so called from its situation in the east of the parish; it was called 'hanging' (*v.* hangende 'steep') because it is on a steep hillside; *Magna* 'great' probably to distinguish it from Aston Subedge (232 *supra*). The OE form from KCD 615 was identified in Wo 88 with White Ladies Aston, but Finb 90, 123 shows that the OE forms refer rather to Aston Magna.

DITCHFORD ON FOSSE, *Dicford* c. 1052 ASChart cxi, 1086 DB, *Dicheford*' 1221 Eyre, *Dicheforde* 1661 GR 368. 'Dike ford', *v.* dīc, ford. Here the Fosse Way crosses Paddle Brook or Knee Brook; OE *dīc* may here be used as a translation of the Lat *fossa* 'ditch' of the road-name.

DORN

> *Dorene* 964 (12th) BCS 1135, 1346 FA, *Doron* 1482 IpmR
> *Dorne* 11 Heming, 1190 *EveB*, 1208 Fees, *Dorn* 1356 Pat

This is probably a British name, a derivative of the el. duro- 'gate, fort'; Ekwall (Wo 99) notes a Gaulish *Duronum* in France. Roman foundations have been found here; the hamlet lies just west of the Fosse Way.

DRAYCOTT, *Draicota* 1208 Fees, *Draycote* 1275 Wo. This common p.n. (which occurs also ii, 216 *infra*) probably means 'shed where a dray was kept', *v.* dræg, cot (cf. EPN i, 134–6).

NORTHWICK PARK, *Norðwica* 964 (12th) BCS 1135, *Northwike* 1221 Eyre (p), *-wyke* 15 Rent, *Norwyk juxta Blockele* 1254 FF. 'North dairy-farm', *v.* norð, wīc; it lies north of Blockley and was doubtless a secondary settlement from that place; cf. *The Wick* (51 *supra*) and Finberg 8–11.

PAXFORD, *Paxford* 1208 Fees, 1248 *Ass*, 1274 RH, 1287 *Ass et passim* to 1759 PR 4. 'Pæcc's ford', from an OE pers.n. *Pæcc* (cf. ME *Pake* in the surname *Paxman*, Reaney 245). *v.* ford. The ford was across Knee Brook.

UPTON WOLD FM, 1830 M, *Uptune* 897 BCS 575 (cf. Finb 63), *Huppeton* 1182 Wo, *Upton* 1208 Fees, *Upton Old(e)* 1549 Pat, 1628 Inq. 'Upper farmstead', *v.* upp, tūn, and wald 'wold, hill'; cf. Phonol. § 42(*b*).

ASTON HALE, 1830 M, *v.* halh 'nook of land'. BANK FM. BLAKE-MORE COVERT, *Blackmore Coppice* 1830 M, *v.* blæc, mōr. BLOCKLEY DOWNS & PARK FM, 1830 M. BOGS BARN. BRAN MILL, *Braundes Mill* 16 VCH (Wo) iii, 271, the ME pers.n. or surname *Brand*. THE CAM. THE DINGLE. DITCHFORD MILL, 1830 M. DOVEDALE, 1830 M, *-Cottage* 1826 *EnclA*. FURZE BANK. HAILSTONE FM.

HANGMAN'S HALL FM. HIDE BARN. HILL BARN, *Hill Meadow-*
1830 M. THE HOLT, 1830 M. KETTLE'S BARN. KNEE BRIDGE,
1830 M, *v.* Knee Brook (9 *supra*). MARBROOK. MILL ROW,
cf. *yᵉ Mille ground* 1661 *GR* 368. NORCOMBE WOOD, 1830 M,
Northcumbe 1299 *RBB, -comb dean* 1746 *GR* (P. 52), *v.* cumb, denu.
OLDBOROUGH. SANDPIT BRIDGE. SHALES COPPICE, *Shells-* 1840
TA. SNUGBOROUGH MILL. STAPENHILL FM, *Stapenhull* c. 1300
Wo 100, *Stapenell Farm* 1830 M, 'steep hill', *v.* stēap, hyll. WAL-
LAND BARN. WARREN FM, 1830 M. WELLACRE FM, 1830 M.

FIELD-NAMES

The principal forms in (*a*) are 1840 *TA* 39, 21. Spellings dated 1661 are
GR 368, 1745 ib (P. 52).

(*a*) Bonds Hill; Cowlease; Dogtails als. Bogtails 1746; Gratton (probably
from grǣd-tūn 'stubble field'); Hurdlers 1746; the Lots (*v.* hlot 'allotment'); Old Oven; Picked ground (dial. *picked* 'cleared, pointed'); Pool
Ground; the Several (cf. Severals 28 *supra*).

(*b*) *yᵉ Bridge ground* 1661; *yᵉBroode ground* 1661; *la Le* 1221 Eyre (p)
(*v.* lēah).

Bourton on the Hill

BOURTON ON THE HILL (144–1732)

Bortvne 1086 DB

Burton' 1173 P, 1206 Abbr, 1221 Eyre, 1231 Cl, 1287 *Ass et freq*
to 1536 *Rent,* (*-in Hennemeyrs'*) 1274 *FF,* (*-in Henmarsh*) 1500–15
ECP, (*-iuxta Campedene*) 1291 *FF,* (*-super montem*) 1535 VE,
1541 *FF,* 1577 M, (*-upon the Hill*) 1552 Pat

Bourton c. 1195 Godstow, 1287 *Ass,* 1291 Tax *et freq* to 1495 *Rent,*
(*-in Hen*(*n*)*emersh*) 1415 IpmR, AD iii, (*-in Hemmarsh*) 1421
Pat, (*-on the Hill*) 1741 PR 4

Borghtone 1331 Ipm   *Boorton* 1434 *MinAcct,* (*-in Hennemershe*)
1393 Cl

Borton super Montem als. Borton in Henmarshe 1590 *FF, -on the
Hill* 1714 PR 4

'Fortified farmstead', *v.* burh-tūn. It is distinguished from Bourton
on the Water (195 *supra*) by the affixes *Henmarsh* (230 *supra*) and 'on
the Hill' (*v.* hyll, Lat *mons*).

BOURTON CLUMP (1830 M), DOWNS (*Burton Downe* 1557 *FF*), FIELD
(1777 M) & WOODS (*-Wood* 1830 M). PEBBLE GROVE, *Pebblestone*

Grove 1826 *EnclA*. RECTORY FM, 1830 M. SLATE BARN, cf. *the Lower, Farther Slaits* 1826 *EnclA*, *v*. slæget 'sheep-pasture'. THE SNUBBS. TUCKWELL LODGE.

FIELD-NAMES

The principal forms in (*a*) are 1826 *EnclA*. Spellings dated 1435–1479 are *GR* 1099.

(*a*) Arm Scot; Blindwell furlong (*v*. blind 'hidden', wella); Bouton Hill (if not an error for *Bourton*, this is *terr' voc' Boueton'* 1435 'land above the town', *v*. būfan, tūn); the Bratch furlong (*v*. brēc); Caldicote (*v*. cald, cot); Cony ground (*le Conyng'* 1474, *v*. coninger 'warren'); Fenhill close; the Great Gorstall; Hallow Street furlong; Middle & Upper Holm; Kilsdown Bottom (*Kyllesdown* 1472, an OE pers.n. *Cylle*, *v*. dūn); Kinsonwell Leys; Lady Ham (*v*. hamm); the Langate (*v*. langet); the Mortar Pits; Small Thorns; Stockwell (*v*. stocc, wella); Thorn'd Leasow Gate; Water Gap Way; Wood Slaite (*v*. slæget 'sheep-pasture').

(*b*) *Bernerdesplace* 1435; *Burton Mershe* 1557 *FF*; *Mykkelbarowe* 1474 (*v*. micel, beorg 'barrow'); *le Milweyfurlong* 1435; *Morton' Berowe* 1472 (named from Moreton in Marsh 251 *infra*, *v*. beorg); *Oxlesowe* 1479 (*v*. oxa, læs); *Sharpemersh* 1472; *Shepehous* 1472; *foss' voc' Townedych* 1469; *Walshehey* 1470 (the surname *Walsh*, *v*. (ge)hæg).

Chipping Campden

CHIPPING CAMPDEN (144–1538)

> *on Campsætena gemære* 1005 (12th) KCD 714
> *Campedene, -dena* 1086 DB, 1190 P, 1211–13, 1220 Fees, 1221 Eyre (p), *Ass*, 1232 Cl, 1233 Berk, 1236 Fees, 1247 Ch *et passim* to 1492 Pat, (*Chepyng-*) 1287 *Ass*, 1403 *FF et freq* to 1446 Pat, *Kampedene* 1233 Cl, 1236 Fees
> *Compeden'* 1221 *Ass*, 1234 Cl
> *Caumpeden(e)* 1225 *FF*, 1274 Cl, RH, 1275 Episc, 1284 *FF*, 1285 FA *et freq* to 1442 Pat, (*Cheping-, -yng-*) 1287 *Ass*, 1315 BM, 1323 Misc, 1324 *FF*, *Kaumpeden'* 1248 *Ass*
> *Campden* 1517 InqEncl, 1535 VE, 1586 *Comm*, (*Chepyng-, -ing-*) 1451 Pat, 1461 *MinAcct et freq* to 1608 *Harrowby*, (*-mercatus*) 1590 Camd, (*Chipping-*) 1689 PR 4

'Valley with enclosures', *v*. camp (gen.pl. *campa*), denu. The town lies at the head of a valley formed between The Hoo and Westington Hill; the stream is called The Cam, but this appears to be a back-formation from Campden. The early forms with medial -*e*- in *Campe*- (*Caumpe*- is an AN variant) do not favour a derivation from OE *camp* 'fight, battle', and Rudder's report of a tradition of a great battle between West Saxons and Mercians is not relevant to the history of the name (Rudder 319, BG ix, 354). The OE form *Campsætena gemære* is elliptical, 'the boundary of the inhabitants of Campden' (with loss of the second el. of the p.n. which is frequent in folk-names in sǣte). In 1287 *Ass* 275, m. 9, Osbert de Staneby stated: 'there is no place in the county called *Caumpedene* by itself, only *Cheping Caumpedene* and *Brode Caumpedene*'. To distinguish it from Broad Campden (*infra*), it is called 'Chipping' from OE cēping 'market, market-place' (cf. the 1590 Lat equivalent *mercatus*), as in Chipping Sodbury (iii, 51 *infra*) or Chipping Norton (O 368); market rights were granted to Hugh de Gondeville c. 1180 and confirmed in 1247; the market is referred to in *foro de Campedene* 1248 *Ass* 4d. The alternative affix 'Henmarsh' is from the district-name (230 *supra*).

BERRINGTON MILL
> *Berinton* 1205 OblR
> *Byri-, Biryton* 1273 Ipm, 1274 Cl
> *Buri-, Buryton* 1287 *Ass*, 1350 AD, 1506 *FF*
> *Buryngton* 1546, 1574, 1600 *FF*, *Byrryngton* 1549 Pat
> *Berington als. Burington* 1616 *FF*

'Borough farmstead', from OE *byr(i)g, byrh*, gen.sg. of burh, and tūn; medial -*ing*- is a later substitution for -*i*- (cf. Phonol. § 49).

BROAD CAMPDEN
> *Parva Campedene* 1216 ClR
> *Bradecampeden(e)* 1224 *FF*, 1248 *Ass*, 1273 Ipm, *Bradecompeden* 1225 *FF*, *Brode Caump(e)dene* 1313 AD ii, 1327 *SR*, -*campedene* 1378 *Ass*, 1391 *FF*, *Brodcampden* 1460 *MinAcct*, 1494 Ipm
> *Large Campeden* 1291 Episc

v. Chipping Campden (*supra*); 'Broad' (*v.* brād, OFr *large*) because it is spread out in comparison with Chipping Campden, which is a long narrow village built along the main street.

COMB BUILDINGS, OLD COMB BARN, *Cumba* c. 1145 BM, 1156 (1266) Ch, *Cumbe* 1221 *Ass*, 1274 RH, (-*juxta Campdene*) 1342 Ipm, *Combe* 1454, 1553 Pat, (-*Campden*) 1620 *Rec. v.* cumb 'a valley'; it was the old name of the head of the Campden valley, now called Tilbury Hollow.

WESTINGTON, *Westington, -yng-* 1225 *FF*, 1267 Misc, 1272 Ipm *et freq* to 1686 PR 4, (-*super Waldas*) 1273 Ipm, *Westinton, -yn-* 1267 Pat, 1295 *FF*, 1327 *SR*, -*done* 1274 RH, *Westondon* 1484 ECP, 1493 FF. '(Land) west in the village', *v.* west or westan, in, tūn, and cf. Eastington (54 *supra*); for the affix *v.* wald.

CAMPDEN ASHES & HILL FM, 1830 M.   COMPTON WOOD, 1830 M. CONDUIT HO, named from *Westington Conduit* 1830 M, *v.* conduit. COURT PIECE, 1830 M, -*piece*, -*Paces* 1824 M.   FURZE HEATH, 1830 M.   GREYSTONES FM.   THE HOO, *Ho* 1220 *FF*, *the Hooe* 1830 M, *v.* hōh 'spur of land, ridge-end'.   HULLAND HO.   KINGCOMBE LANE.   THE LEASOW, *v.* lǣs.   LEYSBOURNE.   LITTLEWORTH. PYE MILL, *Peomull* 1383 VCH (Wo) iii, 271, *Pie Mill* 1830 M, from pēo 'insect' or the ME byname *Pie* (cf. Reaney 251), *v.* myln. SEDGECOMBE FM, -*Wood* 1830 M, *v.* secg 'sedge', cumb.   SHERNAL PLANT.   SNAKE BANK.   SPRINGHILL LODGE, 1830 M.   TILBURY HOLLOW, 1830 M.   WESTINGTON MILL, *le Ouer mille in Westyngton* 1546 *FF*, a water-mill.   WOLD'S END, *Worlds-end* 1824 M.

FIELD-NAMES

The principal forms in (*a*) are 1845 *TA* 38. Spellings dated 1225 are *FF*, 1777 M.

(*a*) Box hedge close; Campden Down & Field 1777; Cherry orchard; Marsh 1777; Mill orchard; Sheepy (*v.* scēap, (ge)hæg).

(*b*) *East Hitchins* 1660 *GR* 76 (*v.* heccing); *Godeswand* 1225; *Hall close* 1626 InqM; *Meredich* 1225 ('boundary ditch', *v.* (ge)mǣre, dīc); *Pynckeheyes* 1608 Harrowby (the surname *Pink, v.* (ge)hæg); *Senewell'* 1225 (possibly a shortened form of *Seven-wells*); *Shexestrete* 1553 Pat (probably for the modern Sheep Street).

Clifford Chambers

CLIFFORD CHAMBERS (144–1952)

> *æt Clif(f)orda* 922 (17th) BCS 636, 966 (11th) ib 1181
> *Clifort* 1086 DB
> *Clifford(e), -ia(m), Clyfford(e)* 1086 Glouc, c. 1127 AC, 1138–1267 Glouc (*freq*), 1163 P (p), 1220 Fees, 1221 *Ass et freq* to 1625 *FF*, (-*on Stoure*) 1328 Banco, (*Chaumberes-*) 1388 Cl, (-*Chamberer*) 1526 Glouc, (-*Chamberleyne als. Chamberer*) 1580 *FF*, (-*Chambers*) 1723 PR 4

'Ford near the cliff or steep bank', *v.* clif, ford; the ford was no doubt one which carried the road to Stratford on Avon across the R. Stour. The manor was given in 1099 to St Peter's Gloucester for the use of the *camerarius* or chamberlain (ME *chamberere*, OFr *chamberier*); Francis *Chamberlayne* was party to a fine in 1625 *FF*

WILLICOTE HO

Wilcot(e) 1086 DB, 1212 Abbr, 1325 *MinAcct*
Wile-, Wylecot(e) 1176 France, 1284 Episc, *et freq* to 1363 *Ass*
Willecota, -cote c. 1200 France, Hy 3 BM, 1401 Ch
Wili-, Wylycote 1267 Glouc (p), 1287 *Ass*, 1295 Episc, *Wi-,*
  Wyllicote(s), -cott 1411 Ipm, 1416 AD iv *et freq* to 1615 *FF*

'Cottage by the willow', *v.* wilig, cot. Little Willicote is just over the parish boundary in Quinton.

WINCOT

Wenecote 1086 DB   *Woncote* 1416 AD iv
Wi-, Wynecot(e) 1221 *Ass* (p), 1260 *FF* (p), 1362 AD iv
Wi-, Wynnecote 1267 Glouc (p), 1319 *FF* (p)
Wyncote, -cott 1362 AD iv, 1494, 1541, 1620 *FF*

'Wina's cottage', *v.* cot. The pers.n. is OE *Wina* or *Wynna* (Redin 58). Probably Shakespeare's *Wincot* (*Taming of the Shrew* Ind. ii, 22).

CLIFFORD HILL (*the Hill* 1777 M) & MILL.   COLD COMFORT.
SHEEPLEYS FM, *Shiplease* 1777 M, *Sheep Lays* 1824 M, *v.* sceap, læs.
STARVEALL.

FIELD-NAMES

The principal forms in (*a*) are 1842 *TA* 49. Spellings dated 922 are (1643) ASChart xxi (BCS 636), 1525 *Surv* 11, 254, 1641 Inq.

(*a*) Aarons leys; Clifford Bushes 1777 M; Long & Short Lengths; Morris ground; Stand hill; Sunday meadow (cf. Sundayshill iii, 108 *infra*).

(*b*) *in ða dic* 922 (*v.* dīc); *Fyldeslond* 1525; *Firzen heath* 1641 (*v.* fyrsen, hǣð); *on ðone herepað* 922 (*v.* here-pæð 'highway'); *Muncke close* 1641 (named from the monks of St Peter's, Gloucester, cf. Clifford Chambers *supra*); *Rye peeces* 1641; *Stonbridg* 1525 (*v.* stān, brycg).

Clopton

CLOPTON (144–1744)

Cloptvne 1086 DB, -*ton* 12 WinchLB, 1201 P (p), 1220 Fees, 1248 *Ass* 4 *et passim* to 1686 PR 4, (-*subtus Mune*) 1401 *FF*, (-*on the Hill*) 1590 *FF*. 'Farmstead on the hill' (here Meon Hill 254 *infra*), *v.* clopp, tūn, cf. Clapton (198 *supra*). It may be noted that *Will' Sakespere* is mentioned as living here in 1248 *Ass*, a very early reference to the local family of Shakespeare.

BEECH'S NUT.   JARRETT'S BROW, cf. *Jarrets Leys* 1756 *GR* 892, from the surname *Jarrett*.   WHITE HOUSE BARN.

FIELD-NAMES

The principal forms in (*a*) are 1756 *GR* (892, T. 52), and in (*b*) 1621 Inq. Spellings dated 1577–84 are *BrtCt*, 1698 *M*.

(*a*) Ashetts (*v.* æscett 'clump of ash-trees'); Ashill Meadowes (*v.* æsc, hyll); Gibbs Leasow (*v.* læs 'meadow'); Smellesdell als. Smallysdell (the surname *Small*, *v.* dell); Stratford Leasow ('meadow on the road to Stratford on Avon' (Wa 236), *v.* læs).

(*b*) *Churchayes* (*v.* (ge)hæg 'enclosure'); *Clapton fieldes* 1577; *Heardmans house*; *Hillinge* (*v.* hyll, hlinc 'ridge'); *Hurdley peice* 1698 (*v.* hirde 'herd', lēah); *Kaymedowe* 1521 *FF* (the surname *Kay*); (*le*) *Lew(e)land(es)* 1577, 1584 ('sunny lands', *v.* hlēow, land); *the Lott meadow* (*v.* hlot 'share of land granted by lot'); *Smithes Mill*; *the Walk* 1698; *Whites Close* 1698.

Dorsington

DORSINGTON (144–1349)

Dorsitune c. 1060 KCD 964

Dorsinton(e), -*tvne* 710 (16th) BCS 127, 1086 DB, 1203 Abbr, 1220 Cur, Fees, 1221 *Ass*, c. 1230 *DJ* 4, 1236 Fees *et freq* to 1535 VE, -*ing*-, -*yng*- 1234 Bracton, 1311 Fine, 1315 Ipm *et passim* to 1753 PR 4

Dersinton' 1203 Cur, 1221 *Ass*, 1245 Ch *et freq* to 1336 Ipm, (*Parua-*) 1330 FF, -*ing*-, -*yng*- 1236 Fees, 1248 *Ass et freq* to 1359 Berk, (*Magna-*) 1381 *FF*

Dorston 1525 *Surv*

'Farmstead associated with Dēorsige', *v.* ing⁴, tūn. The pers.n. is OE *Dēorsige*. On the *Dor*- form cf. Phonol. § 21.

BRAGGINGTON, 1779 Rudder, *Braginton* 1618 *FF*, the first el. is possibly an OE pers.n. *Brac(c)a* suggested for Bragenham (Bk 83) which has a similar voicing of *-k-* to *-g-*, *v.* -ing⁴, tūn.   UDDE WELL.

FIELD-NAMES

Spellings dated c. 1230 are *DЈ* 4.

(*a*) Dorsington Fields 1777 M.

(*b*) *Bevekesforlong* c. 1230; *Boundmedow* 1525 *Surv*; *Middelforlung* c. 1230 (for the *-lung* forms cf. Phonol. § 6).

Ebrington

EBRINGTON (144–1940) [ˈjæbətən]

> *Bristentvne* 1086 DB   *Edbrihttona* 1155 (1340) Ch
> *Edbricton'* 1200 Cur, 1248 *Ass*, -*brich*-1211–13 Fees, -*brigh*- 1248, 1320 *Ass*, -*britton* 1282 Episc, -*brethon* 1332 Ch
> *Eadbrithona* 1220 Fees, -*brithton* 1274 Episc
> *Ebrihton*, -*yh*- 1274 RH, 1327 *SR*, *Ebrighton*, -*ygh*- 1301 *FF*, 1314 Ipm, 1328 Banco *et freq* to 1692 PR 4, (-*als. Eburton*) 1503 Ipm, (-*vulg. Ebberton*) 1675 Og
> *Ebriton*, -*y*- 1270 Ipm, 1274 RH, 1287 QW, 1301 FA
> *Ebriston*, -*ys*- 1276 Ipm, 1350 BM, *Ebrizton* 1316 FA
> *Eberton* 1371 BM, -*bre*- 1380 ib, -*bur*- 1404 Ipm, -*bar*- 1542 LP
> *Ebrington* 1383 BM, c. 1560 *Surv*, (-*als. Ebrighton*) 1581 FF

'Ēadbeorht's farmstead', from the OE pers.n. *Ēadbeorht* and tūn. The DB form is erratic, but the medial *-en-* might suggest that originally the name had the medial connective -ing⁴, which is, however, mostly lost.

BATTLE BRIDGE (1779 Rudder), BATTLEDENE FM, *on badelan broc* 1005 (12th) KCD 714, *Badles* 1815 *M*. 'Bædela's brook', *v.* brōc, and a wk. form of the pers.n. in Battlescombe (118 *supra*), Battledown (ii, 97 *infra*); as in the latter the modern form is due to the influence of the word *battle*.

CHARINGWORTH

> *Chevringavrde* 1086 DB
> *Chedringewurda* 1160, 1163 P (p), -*wurða* 1166 P (p), *Chadelinge-worth* 1200 Cur (p)

Chaveringewurd, -wrth' 1190 AD iv, 1201 Cur (p)
Chev(e)ringew(o)rth' 1196 Finberg 114, 1201 Cur (p), 1220 Fees
Cauelewrd', Cauelengwrd', Cheuelingwrd' 1221 *Ass*
Chauelingewurth', Chauelligwrth' 1221 *Ass* (p)
Chaveringworth(e), -yng- 1277 Episc (p), 1287 *Ass*, 1316 Ipm, 1328
   Banco, *Cheveringworth, -yng-* 1285 FA, 1287 *Ass*
Charyngworth(e), -ing- 1353 *FF*, 1355 Ch *et freq* to 1677 PR 3
Chalingworth, -yng- 1397 *Ass*, 1535 VE

'Enclosure of Ceafor's folk', *v.* **ingas, worð**. The first el. is an OE
pers.n. *Ceafor*, which is not recorded, but it would be originally a
nickname from OE **ceafor** 'beetle'. The older forms in *Ched-* (if correct) probably arise as AN spellings from the confusion of *-v-* and *-ð-*
in pronunciation; spellings with medial *-el-* for *-er-* are AN (cf. IPN
107), and persisted for a time in the contracted form *Chalingworth*.

HIDCOTE BOYCE

Hudicota 716 (14th) BCS 134, *-cot(e)* 1196 Finberg 114, 1221, 1248
   Ass, (-Boys) 1327 *SR, Hudecote* 1314 Ipm
Hedecote 1086 DB, 1404 Ipm
Hidecot(e) 1200 Cur, *Hydecote Boys* 1556 *FF*
Hodykote 1287 *Ass*   *Hydycote Boys* Hy 6 *AddCh*
Hidcott Boys 1601 *FF, Great Hidcote* 1683 PR 4
Hittcott Boys 1620 *FF, Hitcote Boyce* 1688 PR 4

The first el. of this name and Hidcote Bartrim (244 *infra*) is probably an OE pers.n. *Hydeca*, a derivative of *Huda* (as suggested by
Ekwall), but there is some evidence for medial *-i-* being a reduced
form of OE *-an* (cf. Phonol. § 48), so that the first el. could be the
OE pers.n. *Huda* itself, with fronting of *-u-* to *-i-* before the dental
(cf. Phonol. § 29). 'Hydeca's or possibly Huda's cottage', *v.* **-ing**[4],
cot 'cottage'. The affix *Boyce* is from the surname of the feudal
tenant *Ernolf de Bosco* (1200 Cur) or *Ernald de Bosco* (1212 Fees),
from Lat *boscus*, OFr *bois* 'wood'.

BLACK DOWNS, 1830 M, *v.* **blæc, dūn** 'hill'.   EBRINGTON FORD,
1830 M, *v.* **ford**.   FURZE LANE, cf. *Furze ground* 1844 *TA, v.* **fyrs**.
GOOSE HILL, 1830 M.   THE GROVE.   HOARSTON, *Hoarstenbanke*
1631 Inq, 'boundary stone', *v.* **hār, stān**; it is on the county boundary.
LITTLEWORTH BARN.   LONGMORE, *Longmoor* 1815 *M, v.* **lang, mōr**.
MANOR HO, 1830 M.   MAREFURLONG, *-furland* 1830 M, *Moor-*

furlong 1824 M.   MILL POND, named from *Ebrington Mill* 1830 M.
OAKHAM FM, *-field* 1815 M.   THE ORCHARDS, 1844 *TA*.   PUDLICOTT
MILL, 1830 M, *Pudlicot(e)* 13 WinchLB (p), 1777 M, probably a
derivative of puddel (ME *podel*) 'a dirty pool, a puddle', as in Puddle-
worth (ii, 195 *infra*), but in view of the medial -*i*- which may represent
an earlier -*an*- (Phonol. § 49) we may here have an OE pers.n.
Pud(d)el(a) (formed from OE *Puda*), *v.* cot.   RYEPIECE BARN, *-furlong*
1815 *M*.   STARVEALL, 1830 M.   STOWHILL BARN, *Stow(e) hill* 1754
Will, 1844 *TA*, *v.* stōw (perhaps as a surname), hyll.   TYSLIDE
BARN, *Tyslade* 1844 *TA*.

FIELD-NAMES

The principal forms in (*a*) are 1844 *TA* 43. Spellings dated 1631 are Inq,
1815 *M*.

(*a*) Beanhill Hays 1815, Benfurlong 1815 (*v.* bēan 'bean', (ge)hæg);
Black hill, -moor; Black Pits 1815; Broad Moors 1815; Cloud Field 1815,
Upper Cloud 1815 (*v.* clūd 'rock'); the Clump; Long Coleston 1815;
Connigre 1815 (*v.* coninger 'warren'); Duck's Nest 1815; Ebrington Bratch
1815 (*v.* brēc); Elkham 1815; Elm Hole 1815; Ferney Butts 1815; Fernhill
Leys; the Ferriss; Gravelly hill; the Green 1815; Ham (*v.* hamm); Hays
Ends 1815; great & little Heath; Homestall; Millers Ham 1815; the Moors
1815; New Diging 1815; Oakleys close; Old Maids 1815; Oxway; the Pingle
(*v.* pingel 'small enclosure'); Portway furlong 1815; Redlands (ib 1815);
Red Pool 1815; Sallowtree furlong 1815 (*v.* salh 'willow'); Slade Furs 1815
(*v.* slæd, fyrs); the Sling (dial. *sling* 'a narrow strip, a narrow road'); Smith's
Ham & Leys 1815; Stratford way furlong 1815 (near the road to Stratford
on Avon Wa); Tadpole furlong 1815; Water Grip Furs 1815 (*v.* grype
'ditch', furh); Wattle Moor Lays 1815; Windmill hill (*Windemill ground*
1631).

(*b*) *Hauekescumbe* 1301 *FF* ('hawk's valley', *v.* hafoc, cumb); *the horse
closes* 1631.

Hidcote Bartrim

HIDCOTE BARTRIM (144–1742)

> *Hidicote* 1086 DB, *-cot'* 1248 *Ass*
> *Hudicot(a)*, *-cote*, *-y-* 1175 WinchLB, 1190, 1195 P (p), 1221 *FF*,
>   1248 *Ass et freq* to 1305 WinchLB, (*-Bertram*) 1274 RH, 1287
>   *Ass*, 1302 *FF*, (*-Bartram*) 1327 *SR*, 1385 *Ass*
> *Hodicote* 1236 Theok   *Hedycote* 1449 *Rent*
> *Hydcwte Bertram* 1517 InqEncl, *Hydecote Barthram* 1564 *FF*,
>   *Hitcote Bartram* 1688 PR 4

v. Hidcote Boyce (243 *supra*). 'Bartrim' from the feudal tenant *Bertrannus* de Hudicota (1190 P) or, more probably, Philip *Bertram* (1221 Eyre 91).

HIDCOTE COMBE & HO, *Hitcote-* 1830 M, *v.* cumb. WEST HEYS, cf. *Uuerheia* 1221 *FF, v.* uferra, (ge)hæg.

Cow Honeybourne

COW HONEYBOURNE (144–1043)

> *Heniberge* 1086 DB
> *Huniburn(a), -y-* 12, 1221 WinchLB, 1221 *Ass,* 1251 Ch *et freq* to 1292 WinchLB, (*-Abbatis*) 1221 *Ass*
> *Honiburn(e), -y-* 1274 *FF,* 1275 WinchLB, 1285 *FA et freq* to 1305 WinchLB, (*Calewe-*) 1374 Episc, (*Cal-*) 1529 WorcWills, *-born(e)* 1316 FA, 1375 WinchLB, 1540 *MinAcct,* (*Caw(e)-*) 1577, 1646 M, 1610 *FF,* (*Cow-*) 1596 *FF,* 1687 PR 4

'Honey stream' or 'stream by which honey was found', *v.* hunig, burna. The stream is called *Hunigburna* in KCD 1368 (Wo) and from it is also named Church Honeybourne (Wo 264). There are also other examples of the compound in *Huniburnan* in Dowdeswell, Honeyband, *Honniburne* (171 *supra,* ii, 23, iii, 248 *infra*). The spellings *Cal(ewe)-, Caw-* suggest that the affix is OE calu 'bare, lacking vegetation', for which *Cow-* is a later popular substitution in the p.n.

COOMBE FM, *le Combe lees* 1575 *TRMB, v.* cumb 'valley'. HONEYBOURNE LEASOWS, 1830 M, *Honyborne-, Honiburne le(a)sowe* 1540 *MinAcct,* 1575 *TRMB, v.* læs 'meadow'.

FIELD-NAMES

Spellings dated 1540 are *MinAcct,* 1575 *TRMB* 39, 1637, 1641 Inq.

(b) *Barns* 1540; *Browns acre* 1637 (*terr' voc' Brownes* 1540); *Cotmandcroft* 1540, *Cotemanscroft* 1575 (the surname *Cotman* 'cottager', *v.* croft); *terr' voc' Cropthorns* 1540 (a surname from Cropthorne Wo 119); *Dinge furlong* 1641 (*v.* dyncge 'manured land'); *Fordehouse* 1575 (*v.* ford); *Forgehouse* 1540 ('smithy'); *the Ham* 1575, *Ham acre* 1637 (*v.* hamm); *Hogyerde* 1540 (*v.* hogg, geard); *Honiborne Grove als. the Grove* 1641; *le litle leasowe* 1575 (*v.* læs); *the Milham lees* 1575 (*v.* myln, hamm); *the More* 1641; *le Parke* 1575; *Ram close* 1641; *Rigge Waye filde* 1575 ('ridge-way field'); *Sheppards house* 1641; *Wateringe Place* 1641.

Lower Lemington

Lower & Upper Lemington (144–2234)

> *Leminingtvne* 1086 DB, *Lemelinton'* 1220 Fees, *Lemeninton'* 1221 Eyre
> *Limentone* 1086 DB, *Lyminton* 1303 FA, (*Nether*) *Lymyngton*
> c. 1560 *Surv*
> *Lemeinton* 12 (1496) Pat   *Leomintona* 1105 *Tewk* 94d
> *Lemmintone* 1236 Theok, *Lemmyngton'* 1287 *Ass* (p)
> *Lemiton'* 1248 *Ass*
> *Lemynton(e)* 1287 QW, 1291 Tax, 1327 *SR*, 1481 *FF*, (*North-*)
> 1287 *Ass*, (*-iuxta Todenham*) 1307 *FF*, (*-Power*) 1328 Banco,
> (*-Hennemersh*) 1373 *FF*, (*Ouer-*) 1493 *FF*
> *Lemyngton, -ing-* 1426 Pat, 1540 *AOMB*, (*Nether-, Over-*) 1587,
> 1627 *FF*

The first el. of this obscure name is probably, as Ekwall proposed, an old stream-name; this might be *Limen*, from Brit *lemo- 'elm' such as we have in Lympne (K) or R. Leam (Wa 4), from which Leamington (Wa 138) is named. The OE forms of those names have *Lim-, Leom-*, and in Leamington (as in Lemington) the ME spellings in *Lem-* predominate. 'Farmstead near the stream called *Limen'*, v. ing⁴ (usually lost partly through dissimilation), tūn. The stream is that which runs by Lemington to Knee Brook; it can hardly be Knee Brook itself as that stream was called *Doferburna* in 977 KCD 614. The place was called 'Power' from Ralph *de Power* (1328 Banco). Over or Upper Lemington survives as Lemington Manor.

Black Heath, 1830 M.   Oldbrough Fm, 1797 PR 4, 45, *-bury* 1777 M, v. ald, burh, cf. *Oldbury* (ii, 66 *infra*).

Longborough

Longborough (144–1829)

> *Langeberg* 1086 DB, 1193, 1195 P, 1195 Abbr, 1199 *FF*, 1205
> ClR, 1220 Cur *et passim* to 1296 WinchLB, *-bir'* 1204 P, *-burgum*
> 1217 Bracton, *-birge* 1221 *Ass*, *-berth* 1287 QW, *-bergh* 1287 *Ass*,
> 1289 AD ii, 1303 FA
> *Lang(e)ber(u)we, -berwe* Hy 3 AD ii, 1236 Fees, 1241 *FF et freq*
> to 1392 Ipm, *Langberew, -borow(e)* 15 Rent, 1584 *Comm*, *-barowgh*
> Hy 6 *AddCh*, *-barowe* 1535 VE

Long(e)berg(h) 1301, 1304 Ipm *et freq* to 1361 *Ass, -ber(o)we* 1316
FA, -barow(e) 16 WinchLB, 1585 *Talbot, -borowe* 1571, 1592 *FF,*
-bury 1700 PR 4, *-borough* 1731 ib

'The long hill or barrow', *v.* lang, beorg. But it may refer more
precisely to a long barrow; one stands ½ mile above the village
(144-174290). Another DB *Langeberge* denotes the Cotswold scarp
(251 *infra*).

BANKS FEE, *Banckesfee* 1585 *Talbot,* 1599 FF (*-als. Fee Bancke*) 1598
Talbot, (*-als. Free Banckes*) 1601 FF. According to Rudder 532, this
is named from Richard *le Blanck* who held land here in 1287; the
second el. is ME *fe,* OFr *fé,* 'a landed estate'.

FROGMORE FM, *Frogghemor* 1275 Ipm, *Froggemor* 1287 *Ass, Frogmore*
1302 Inq aqd. 'Frog-infested marsh', *v.* frogga, mōr.

HORSINGTON COVERT, *of Horsendunes slead* 779 (c. 1200) BCS 229,
Horsynden 1495 *Rent, Horsenden* 1524 ib, 1525 *MinAcct, Horssinton,*
Horsing- 1597, 1598 *Talbot.* 'Horsa's hill', *v.* dūn. On the OE pers.n.
Horsa cf. Horsenden, -don (Bk 169, Mx 34). But the repetition of
so rare a pers.n. in p.ns. of this type may point to OE hors 'horse',
with OE gen.pl. *horsa* developing an inorganic *-n* (cf. Tengstrand 177).

MAIDENHILL FM, *Medenhulle* 1275 Ipm, *Maiden hill* 1692 *GR* 536.
'Maidens' hill', *v.* mægden, hyll. The significance of p.ns. con-
taining 'maiden' is uncertain; occasionally they denote 'land owned
by maidens', but other possibilities include 'places where maidens
gathered', or 'easy obstacles (such as maidens could overcome)',
cf. Medbury (Bd 71), Maidenford (D 26), *Maiden Castle* (YW iv, 70).
Maiden Hill (ii, 190 *infra*) is the name of a hill with an ancient
encampment. Cf. also Maiden Hill, *Maydes Castle* (94, 233 *supra*).

STRATFORD BRIDGE, *Stratford* 1540 *MinAcct,* (*-Ford*) 1830 M. This
old ford carries a small field-track across the R. Evenlode to the
Fosse Way, which is a mile distant. It probably therefore means
'ford leading to the Roman road', *v.* strǣt, ford.

THE CROOK. DEBDENE. GANBOROUGH, 1777 M, *-boro* 1830 M,
cf. also *Grandborough* 1842 *TA.* LONGBOROUGH HEATH, 1766
EnclA, Hethende 1540 *MinAcct, v.* hǣð. LUCKLEY FM, 1830 M
possibly an OE pers.n. *Luca* as in *Lugdown* (ii, 230 *infra*), *v.* lēah.

NEW PARK, 1842 *TA*. SALTMORE COPPICE, *Saltemor* 1277 Inq,
v. salt 'salt', mōr, cf. Saltway (2) 19 *supra*. SOUTHFIELD BARN,
1830 M, (*le*) *Southfeld* 1547 Pat, *-field* 1598 *Talbot*. STOW BRIDGE,
1830 M, named from Stow (225 *supra*).

FIELD-NAMES

The principal forms in (*a*) are 1842 *TA* 16. Spellings dated 1277 Inq, 1535
VE, 1540 *MinAcct*, 1589–1601, 1615 *Talbot*, 1633 Inq.

(*a*) Banstead piece; Chapel close (*Chappell-* 1633); Clump hill (e.ModE
clump 'cluster of trees'); Freeboard; Grange hays (*v.* (ge)hæg); Landgate
(*v.* langet); Lay hill; Madcomb (*-combe* 1601, *v.* cumb, the first el. may be
an OE pers.n. *Māda*); Millway hill (ib 1615); Northead pool; the Shaves;
Stall ground; West brake (*v.* bræc[1] 'thicket').

(*b*) *Aswelle* 1277 (*v.* æsc, wella); *Baggemor* 1287 *Ass* (the OE pers.n. *Bacga*
or bagga, some kind of animal, *v.* mōr); *Bolnam* 1535, *Bolnaham* 1540 (the
first el. possibly a byname from ME *bollen* 'swollen (with wind)', *v.* hamm);
Buribrugge 1277 (*v.* burh, brycg); *Colemede* 1277; *Horstoune peece* 1597
(probably 'boundary stone', *v.* hār, stān); *Lampelande* 1589 (a field of which
the rent maintained a lamp in church); *Merwelle* 1277; *Sappewelle* 1277 (the
first el. is possibly OE sæppe 'fir-tree' (cf. Sapley Hu 208) but in this compound it may well be OE *sæp* 'sap', used in a stream- or spring-name like
the adj. sæpig in Sapey Brook Wo 75); *Smythmore* 1535, 1540; *Watergall*
1277 (a name repeated elsewhere (EPN i, 192), *v.* wæter, galla 'wet spot in
a field'); *Westcombe* 1601; *Whatewell* 1277; *Wylmore* 1535.

Long Marston

LONG MARSTON, formerly DRY MARSTON or MARSTON SICCA (144–
1548)

 Merstuna 1043 KCD 916, *Merston(e)* c. 1043 KCD 939, 1198 *Cur*,
  1221 *Ass*, 1233 Berk *et passim* to 1340 Ch, (*Drey(e)-*) 1248 *Ass*,
  1255 *FF*, (*Dri(e)-*, *Dry(e)-*) 1250 WinchLB, 1267 Ch, 1282 Episc
  et freq to 1540 *MinAcct*, (*Dru(e)-*) 1255 *FF*, 1282 Episc, 1291
  Fine, (*Druy(e)-*) 1315, 1317 Ipm, (*Longa-*) 1285 FA, (*Lunge-*)
  1287 *Ass*, (*-Sicca*) 1291 Tax, 1384 WinchLB *et freq* to 1535 VE
 Merestone 1086 DB *Meyrston* 1287 QW
 Dr(e)yemershton 1318 Orig, 1319 WinchLB, 1362 AD iv, *Drey-*
  merschetone 1365 WinchLB
 Marston Sicca 1535 VE, 1540 *MinAcct et freq* to 1822 M, *Drye*
  Marston als. Longe Marston 1583 *Talbot*, *Longe Marston als.*
  Marston Sicca als. Dry Marston 1610 FF

'Farmstead near the marsh', *v.* mersc, tūn. To distinguish it from Broad Marston (253 *infra*), it is described as 'long' from the length of the village (*v.* lang), and as 'dry' (*v.* drȳge, Lat *sicca*), because it stands above the level of the marshy ground of Noleham Brook; on the use of this contrasting term Rudder 540 remarks that it 'is not unaptly applied to this place, for notwithstanding its superabundance of water in the winter, it is frequently very much distressed for want of it in dry seasons'. On the forms *Lunge-* and *Dreye-* cf. Phonol. §§ 6, 30.

COURT FM, cf. *the Court mead(ow)e* 1577 TRMB, 1633 Inq, *v.* court 'manor house'. THE GRANGE. MERE'S BARN.

FIELD-NAMES

The principal forms in (*b*) are 1575 *TRMB* 39. Spellings dated 1255 are *FF*, 1540 *MinAcct*, 1632–9 Inq, 1725 *GR* 76.

(*a*) Ox close 1725; Shepherd's close 1725.

(*b*) *Attebenelandeshendes, Estbaneland* 1255 (*v.* atte, bēan, land); *New Bechefurlong* 1255; *Chep aker* 1286 WinchLB, *-acr'* 1540, *-acres, -meadowe* 1575, *the Cheepe acres* 1632 (probably 'acres of low rental', *v.* cēap, æcer; there were 33 *chepacres* in Long Marston Ed 3 WinchLB i, 251 note); *Cley-furlung* 1255; *la Gore* 1255 (*v.* gāra); *Hardinges lane*; *la Hole* 1255; *Innesmore* (probably the OE pers.n. *Ine* as in Innsworth ii, 159 *infra*, *v.* mōr); *Linfurlong* 1255 (*v.* līn 'flax'); *Logmeade*; *Longe leyse* 1540, *the Long leasowe* 1575 (*v.* lǽs); *la Mose* 1255 (*v.* mos 'bog'); *Mulneputtis* 1255 (*v.* myln, pytt); *Parsons leasowe*; *Sydeshale* 1255 (*v.* halh); *la Slade* 1255 (*v.* slæd); *the Slatted pigscote* 1633; *Smithes croftes*; *the Stocke* (*v.* stocc 'stump'); *le Talehouse* (probably 'a counting-house'); *le Westfilde.*

Mickleton

MICKLETON (144–1643)

Micclantun, to Mycclantune 1005 (12th) KCD 714

Muceltv[n]e 1086 DB, *Mucleton(a)* 1109 Monast, 1183 AC, 1221 Ass, *Mukelton(e)* 1274 RH, 1291 Tax, 1313 FF *et freq* to 1428 WinchLB

Mic-, Mik(e)letun(a), -ton 1091 Monast, 1221 Ass, c. 1560 Surv, 1584 Comm, *Mi-, Mykelton(e), -ul-, -yl-* 1248, 1287 Ass, 1402 Ipm *et freq* to 1540 FF, *Mickleton* 1587 FF

Muclinton' 1195 P, *Mukelinton(a)* 1220 Bracton, Cur, 1221 Ass

Mikelinton' 1221 Ass   *Mokelton* 1287 Ass

Mekelton(a) 1278 WinchLB, *-ul-* 1475 Pat, *-il-* 1535 VE

'The great farmstead', *v.* micel (with the wk.obl. *miclan* giving the ME -*in*- forms, cf. Phonol. § 49), tūn. In DB Mickleton had a hidage of 24 against Aston Subedge 4, Dorsington 2¼, Pebworth 12 and Quinton 14, and it was by far the largest manor in this area.

ATTLEPIN, -*Lane* 1772 *EnclA.* BAKER'S HILL, 1679 *Harrowby*, 1698 *M*, named from the family of Anthony *Baker* (1619 PR 3, 43) or William *Baker* (1670 ib 45). BATH COPPICE, 1841 *TA.* CARTER'S LEYS, 1841 *TA.* FURZE LANE, cf. *Furze hill* 1841 *TA.* KIFTSGATE COURT, *v.* Kifts Gate (261 *infra*). LONG HILLS FM, *Longhills* 1679 *Harrowby*, 1698 *M*, *v.* lang, hyll. LONGLANDS FM, *Longlands* 1698 *M*, *v.* lang, land 'a land in the common field'. MICKLETON HILLS FM (-*Hills* 1830 M) & WOOD (1698 *M*). NINEVEH, 1777 M, a common transferred biblical name. THE PARK, *the Parks* 1698 *M*, *v.* park. PAUL'S PIKE, cf. *Pauls House* 1830 M. SPELSBURY BARN, 1841 *TA*, *Spellborough* 1698 *M*, probably 'speech hill', *v.* spell, beorg; the latter is more likely than burh 'fort', as it refers to the highest local point of the Cotswold scarp where no evidence of old fortifications occurs; the place is adjacent to Kiftsgate Court and the name therefore clearly refers to the meeting-place of Kiftsgate hundred. STARVEALL, 1841 *TA.* TADPOLE.

FIELD-NAMES

The principal forms in (*a*) are 1841 *TA* 130, and in (*b*) 1698 *M*. Spellings dated 1005 are (12th) KCD 714, 1574 *TRMB*, 1666 *GR* 892, 1673 ib 76, 1679 *Harrowby*, 1683, 1742, 1756 *GR* 892.

(*a*) Ash hill; Ashbrook; Barley orchard (*Barly*- 1698); Bearcroft (*v.* bere 'barley', croft); Berry meadow; Bushy meadow (cf. *Bushie Leasow* 1698); Butter hill (ib 1679, 1698, 'hill with rich pasture', *v.* butere, hyll); Church Meer (-*meres* 1698); Combs bank; Coppice (*the Coppice* 1698, *v.* copeiz); Cowpen; Cutthroat lane; Fishpool meadow; Foul Quabb (*foulquab* 1698, 'dirty bog', *v.* fūl, cwabba); Getleys; Glide hill; the Hangings; Harbors (*the Arbour ground* 1683, *v.* erber 'garden'); Horstone 1779 Rudder ('boundary stone', *v.* hār, stān); the Horne 1742 (*v.* horn 'nook, bend'); Horse croft (ib 1698); Langate (*the Langett* 1673, *v.* langet); Lilleys; Malaga Slade; Four-, Five Days Math (*v.* mǣð 'mowing'); Midnell hill; Milsington; the Oven; Overton close (*Vuer-*, *Overtone* 1221 *Ass*, *Overton closes* 1679, 'upper village', *v.* uferra, tūn); Ox close (*Oxe*- 1698); Pitchill meadow; Plat pool (*v.* plat[2] 'small plot'); the Pool ground 1742; Rye furlong; Sally grove (*v.* salh 'willow'); Smennell; Stone hill; Stratford Leys (ib 1756, -*lane* 1666 'the lane to Stratford on Avon (Wa)', *v.* also lēah); Summers hill; Washpool Leys (-*leyes* 1698); Windmill leasow (ib 1698).

(b) *on Aðulfes treow* 1005 (the [OE pers.n. *Æþelwulf*, v. trēow); *Bonners Leassowe* 1679; *Cowlane-meadows*; *on ða dic* 1005; *le Halle medowe* 1574; *Hemmers Gate or Norton Gate* 1679; *on Hengesðes cumb* 1005 ('the stallion's valley', v. hengest, cumb); *on Hysemannes þorn* 1005 (the OE pers.n. *Hyse-mann*, v. þorn); *Langeberge* 1086 DB ('the long scarp', v. lang, beorg, cf. Finberg 49, different from Longborough 246 *supra*); *on mærcumbes wylle* 1005 ('boundary valley', v. (ge)mǣre, cumb, wella); *Mott meade* 1679, *Moat-meadow* 1698 (v. mote 'moat'); *on oppan broc* 1005 (an OE pers.n. *Oppa* corresponding to OHG *Oppo*); *the Oxe-eye* (v. oxa, ēg 'island, water-meadow'); *atte Pleystude* 1327 SR (p) ('the sport place', v. pleg-stede, -styde); *Ratton Plot* 1683 ('rat-infested plot', v. ratoun, plot); *on ðæt slæd* 1005 (v. slæd); *on ðone stan* 1005; *on ða stræt* 1005; *oð ða twicelan, andlang broces* 1005 (an old stream-name from an OE *twicele 'the forked one, the twin-stream', cf. twicene 'road-fork'); *on Wulfgyðe bricge* 1005 (the OE fem. pers.n. *Wulfgȳð*, v. brycg); *Wulstone* 1558 BM.

Milcote

Milcote (144–1852)

Mulecote 710 (14th) BCS 127 *et freq* to 1325 *FF*, (*-upon Avene, -upon Esture*) 1245, 1246 Ch, *Mel(e)cote* 1086 DB, 1167 P, 1287 Cl, *Mulcote* 1330 *FF* with other spellings as given in Wa 236. 'Mill cottage', v. myln, cot; it is near the confluence of the Avon and the Stour.

Moreton in Marsh

Moreton in Marsh (144–2032)

Mortun 714 (16th) BCS 130, *Mortvne* 1086 DB, *-ton(e)* 1226 ClR, 1280 Ch, 1287 *Ass et passim* to 1327 SR (*-& Henemers'*) 1248 *Ass*, (*-in Hennemersh*) 1253 Ch, (*-in Hennmerss*) 1287 *Ass*, (*-Hennemersh*) 1407 ib, (*-Henmershe*) 1494 *FF*, 1500–15 ECP, 1524 *Rent*, (*-Henmarshe*) 1577 M, 1587 *FF et freq* to 1779 Rudder, (*-Inmarsh*) 1648 *FF*, (*Noua-*, *Veteri-*) 1287 *Ass*, Old-, *Newemorton in Henmerssh* 1484 Rogers, *Murton Henmarsshe* 1541 *FF*, *Mourton en le Marshe* 1570 *FF*, *-Hinmarsh* 1681 PR 4, *Murton in Mershe* 1572 *FF*, *Moreton in Marsh* 1711 PR 4, *Moreton in (the) Marsh* 1732 PR 4. 'Farmstead in the marshland or moor', v. mōr, tūn. The affix 'in Marsh' is an adaptation of the affix *Henmarsh* (230 *supra*) in *Morton Hennemarsh*, *-Inmarsh*, etc., whilst 'in the Marsh' which is sometimes found in more recent times is an erratic substitution. *Old Morton* survives only in the street-name Old Town (*infra*).

Coldicote Fm, *Caldecot(e)* 1248, 1287 *Ass*, *Caldicote* 1310 *FF*,

Cauldicott 1587 *FF*. 'Cold, exposed cottage', *v.* **cald, cot**, and cf. Calcot (166 *supra*).

OLD TOWN (1821 *EnclA*, 1830 M), the older part of Moreton which was formerly called *Veteri-* or *Oldmorton* 1287 *Ass*, 1484 *Rogers*. *v.* Moreton (*supra*), **ald** (Lat *vetus*) 'old'.

DUNSTALL, *the Dunstall farm* 1821 *EnclA*, a not uncommon form of tūn-stall 'farmstead'. LANGATE LODGE, *the Langate* 1821 *EnclA*, *v.* **langet** 'long strip'. MORETON COMMON, 1830 M. OSIER SPINNY, -*Spiny* 1830 M. UPPER FIELDS, 1830 M.

FIELD-NAMES

The principal forms in (*a*) are 1821 *EnclA*.

(*a*) Berry gore; Broad Lent; Cockpit meadow; Croft Holm; Davids well; Fossway ground; Gostalls; Greenhill 1779 Rudder; Hunts Moor; Long Sitch (*v.* **sīc** 'stream'); Moreton Heath 1746 *GR* 892 (*Murton hethe* 1540 *MinAcct*, *v.* **hǣð**); Stockwell (*v.* **stocc, wella**); the Swan Hill.

Pebworth

PEBWORTH (144-1346)

> *Pebewrthe* 848 (14th) BCS 453
> *æt Pebbewurðy* 1012-23 (orig.) KCD 898
> *Pebeworde* 1086 DB, -*wrda* 1140 BM, -*w(o)rth(a)* 1154-8 (1340) Ch, 1287 *Ass*, c. 1560 *Surv*
> *Pebbew(u)rda* 1140 Monast, 1154-8 (1340) Ch, -*w(o)rth(e)*, -*wurth* 1211-13 Fees, 1248 *Ass*, 1269 Pat, 1270 Ipm, 1291 Tax *et passim* to 1533 *FF*
> *Pebworte* 1176 France, -*worthine* 1278 Cl, -*worth(e)* 1286 WinchLB, 1535 VE *et freq* to 1743 PR 4, (-*als. Pedworthe*) 1583 *Talbot*
> *Pubbeworth* 1285 FA   *Pobbeworth* 1303 FA

Pedmore (Wo 305) is parallel to Pebworth and has a similar change of *Peb-* to *Ped-* as that in the form *Pedworthe*. It has been derived from the OE pers.n. *Pybba* which is that of a Mercian king, the father of Penda (cf. Redin 108). But the very regular spellings for the two p.ns. cannot be directly from this; there may have been, however, a form *Peobba* from a different grade (PrGerm **peuƀ-*) as in OE *Peuf(a)*. 'Peobba's enclosure', *v.* **worð**; the OE spelling -*wurðy* is WSax (*v.* **worðig**) and is due to the dialect of the document, and the ME -*worthine* is from Merc **worðign**.

BROAD MARSTON

> *Merestvne* 1086 DB
> *Brademerston'* 1224, 1241 FF, *Brod(e)merston* 1306 *Ass*, 1396
>   WinchLB *et freq* to 1504 AD iii, *-mershton(e)* 1362 AD iv, 1392
>   Ipm, 1401 WinchLB, *-Marston* 1571 *FF, Bradmaston* 1517
>   InqEncl, *Broade Marston* 1583 *Talbot*
> *Mersshton Boys* 1327 *SR, Marston Boyes als. Brodemeston* 1533 *FF*

v. Long Marston (248 *supra*). As in Broad Campden, 'Broad'
(*v.* brād) refers to the shape of the village site. The affix *Boys* refers
to a 13th-century tenant Ernald *de Bosco*, as in Hidcote Boyce
(243 *supra*).

ULLINGTON

> *Wenitone* 1086 DB
> *Olinton(e), -yn-* 1212 RBE, 1286 Ipm, 1402 Pat, 1403 *FF*
> *Ullin(g)ton', -yn-, Vll-* 1220, 1236 Fees, 1327 *SR et freq* to 1607 *FF*
> *Wulinton'* 1236 Fees
> *Ollin(g)ton, -yn(g)-* 1285 FA, 1287 *Ass*, 1307, 1375 Ipm

On the evidence of the *Weni-* and *Wulin-* spellings, this would
seem to be 'farmstead associated with Willa', *v.* -ing[4], tūn. The OE
pers.n. *Willa* is recorded and this could become *Wylla* through the
influence of *w-* (cf. Bülbring § 283), ME *Wull-, Ull-* (cf. Phonol.
§ 42*b*). Ullingswick (He) is similarly from *Willa* (cf. DEPN s.n.).

THE LEASOW, *v.* lǣs 'meadow'.   PEBWORTH DOWNS & FIELDS.

FIELD-NAMES

The forms in (*b*) are c. 1603 *TRMB* 39. Spellings dated 1543 are *AOMB*.

(*b*) *le Gardener; Grenehill; Hobbyns hold* 1552 *FF* (ME *hold* 'tenure');
le Mere 1543 (*v.* mere 'pool'); *le More; Senslande; le Sheaphouse; le Syche*
(*v.* sīc 'stream'); *the greate Yellowes* 1629 Inq.

Preston on Stour

PRESTON ON STOUR (144–2049)

> *Preston* 1086 DB, 13 Misc, 1221, 1248 *Ass et passim* to 1467 Pat,
> (*-super Steuram*) 1291 Episc, (*-super Sturham*) 1291 Tax, (*-super
> Stauram*) 1292 Episc, (*-super Storam*) 1320 *Ass*, (*-super Stoure*) 1379,
> 1496 *FF*, (*-upon Sture*) 1504 Pat, (*-super, -on Stower*) 1535 VE, 1587

FF *et freq* to 1775 PR 3. 'The priests' farmstead', *v.* prēost, tūn, and R. Stour (11 *supra*). The reference may be to the monks of Deerhurst, for in 804 lands *æt Sture* 'at the Stour' and Todenham (258 *infra*) were to be given to Deerhurst (BCS 313).

ALSCOT PARK

> *Ælf-, Alf-, Elfsiescota* 1186, 1190 P (p)
> *Alscot(e), -kote* 1221 *Ass*, 1255 *FF*, 1327 *SR*, 1495 Ipm
> *Alsiscote* 1248 *Ass*
> *Ales-, Asselecote* 1287 *Ass*
> *Alu-, Alvescote* 1308 AD iv, 1360 Ipm, 1401 Ch, 1411 Ipm
> *Alvescott als. Allyscott als. Alscott* 1591 *FF*

'Ælfsige's cottage', from the OE pers.n. *Ælfsige* and cot; cf. Alstone (ii, 41 *infra*).

CHURCH FM, *the Churche house* 1569–83 *AddR*.

FIELD-NAMES

(b) *le commen Backhouse* 1569–83 *AddR* (*v.* bæc-hūs 'bake-house'); *le Cribberd* 1477–1557 ib; *Dunstall* 1569–83 ib (*v.* tūn-stall 'farmstead').

Quinton

QUINTON (144–1846)

> *Quentone, -ton(a), -thon* 840 (14th) BCS 453, 1168 P, 1183 AC,
>   1195 P (p), 1200 FF, 1215 ClR, 1220 Fees *et passim* to Hy 6
>   *AddCh*, (*Nether-*) 1292 Ch, 1325 *FF*, (*Uuer-*) 1248 *Ass*, (*Over(e)-*)
>   1274 RH, 1292 Ch, (*Lan-*) 1303 FA, (*-Marmion*) 1327 *SR*
> *Qvenintvne* 1086 DB, *Queninton* 1221 *Ass*
> *Quyn-, Quinton* 1416 Pat, 1440 WinchLB *et passim* to 1751 PR 4
> *Queynton(a)* 1428 WinchLB, 1587 *FF*, (*Quer-*) 1471 Cl (for *Ouer-*)

'The queen's farmstead', *v.* cwēn, tūn. The *Quenin-* forms arise from confusion with Quenington (45 *supra*). *Nether-* and *Over-* refer to the two villages of Lower and Upper Quinton, and *Marmion* to the family of *Marmion* (cf. Robert *Marmion* 1236 Fees, *v.* also 1327 *SR*).

MEON HILL

> *Mene, Mena* 1086 DB, 1157 P, 1158 RBE, 1221 Plea, 1236 Fees,
>   1287 QW, 1335 Orig, 1405 *Ass*

Mona 1160 RBE, *Mones* 1220 Fees
Muna 1158–9 *et freq* P, *Mune* 1211–13 Fees, 1221 *Ass* (p), 1252
Ipm, 1274 RH *et freq* to Hy 6 *AddCh*
Mina 1190 P   *Miene* 1195 P
Muena 1191, 1192, 1195, 1201, 1204 P
Meone 1221 *Ass*, 1306 Ipm *et freq* to 1594 *FF*, (-*als. Mune*) 1253
Ipm, *Meones* 1221 Eyre (p), *Meeon*(*e*) 1600, 1631 *FF*
Moene 1361 *Ass*, 1443 *FF*   *Morne* (sic) 1406 Pat
Meene 1517 *InqEncl*, 1581, 1634 *FF*, *Meen-hill* 1779 Rudder
Myone 1537 *FF*   *Mean*(*e*) 1631 Inq, 1692 *M*

The various spellings are best explained by an OE *Mēon-*, of which the ME developments would in this area be [mø:n], represented by *Mona, Muna, Moene, Meone*, and [me:n], represented by *Mene, Miene* and (with raising of the close *ē* to *ī*) by *Mina* (cf. Phonol. §§ 16, 21). The name has therefore an original form similar to that of the R. Meon (Ha), *Meonea* a. 790 BCS 258, *Meóne* 824 ib 377, *Méone* 932 ib 689, etc., and East and West Meon (Ha), *Meanuarorum provincia* c. 730 Bede, *æt Meone* c. 880 BCS 553. Ekwall (RN 288) explains the Hampshire names as from a Brit r.n., possibly related to the Gaulish r.n. *Moenus* (R. Main); its origin is doubtful, but it might be connected with the root of OIr *moin* 'treasure'. Meon Hill is, however, the name of a very prominent hill at the northern end of the Cotswold escarpment and on its summit are the remains of an extensive ancient encampment; it is to this hill we should expect the name to refer rather than to a river, for only a couple of insignificant streams rise on the lower slopes. But this does not rule out an etymological connexion with the Hampshire r.n. The manor was held in 1201 by William de Gamages, who also held a manor of Dymock (cf. Gamage Hall iii, 168 *infra*), and so Meon is sometimes associated with Dymock in the records.

RADBROOK, *Rodbroc, -brok*(*e*) 1260 *FF*, 1292 Ipm *et freq* to 1419 IpmR, *Radbrocke* 1574 AD v, *Meene Radbrooke* 1649 ParlSurv. 'Stream where reeds grew', *v.* hrēod, brōc. On the forms cf. Phonol. §§ 21, 26. *Meene* is from (ge)mǣne 'common' or Meon Hill (prec.).

BOOKER'S BARN, cf. *the Brookers Meadow* 1698 *M*.   COLEMAN'S HILL, 1698 *M*.   GREEN, *la Grene de Quenton* 1320 *Ass*, *atte Grene* 1327 *SR* (p), *v.* grēne². HILL BARN, cf. *atte Hulle* 1327 *SR* (p), *the Hill ground* 1698 *M*. REEVE'S FM. SNOW'S HO. WINDMILL HO.

FIELD-NAMES

The principal forms in (*a*) are 1839 *TA* 162, and in (*b*) 1698 *M*. Spellings dated 1631 are Inq.

(*a*) Austins Leasow; the Coombs (*the Combes* 1698, *v.* cumb); Cow Pen; the Hangings; Loose Hill; Rushy Leasow; Sling (dial. *sling* 'narrow strip'); Sungate; White Hill.

(*b*) *Cowes leasowe* 1631 (*v.* læs); *the Green Leasesow*; *Lodbrookes piece* 1631; *Lowes hill*; *the Slingett* (dial. *slinget* 'a long narrow strip', its use being carried back nearly 100 years by this f.n.); *Wyllaleynslond* 1449 *Rent* ('Will Aleyn's land').

Saintbury

SAINTBURY (144–1139)

Svineberie (sic) 1086 DB
Sei-, Seynesberia, -bir', -bur(ia), -bury 1186, 1190 P (p), 1199 *FF*, 1203 Cur, 1276 RH, 1287 *Ass et freq* to 1501 Ipm
Sei-, Seynebur(ia), -bir', -bury 1220 Fees, 1248 *Ass*, 1269 *FF*, 1272 Ipm, 1274 RH, 1284 Episc *et freq* to 1303 FA
Senesbir', -byre 1233 Cl, 1264 Ipm
Saynebire 1274 Cl (p)
Sevenesbyry 1279 Fine
Seneburi 1285 FA, *Senbury(e)* 1496, 1547 Pat, 1622 *FF*
Seynbury Hy 6 *AddCh*, 1484 AD iv, 1535 VE, (-*als. Seyntbury*) 1570 *FF*, *Saynbury als. Sayntbury* 1621 *FF*
St. Berry 1675 Og, *Saintbury* 1707 PR 4

'Sǣwine's fortified place', from the OE pers.n. *Sǣwine* and burh; beside the DB *Svine-* and the 1279 *Sevenes-*, this is regularly contracted here to *Seine-*. The *burh* may refer to the remains of ancient entrenchments on the higher ground just south of the village near the church and Buckle Street, cf. Wall Fm and *Oldeburidich'* (*infra*).

GUN'S COTTAGES, *Guns cottage, hill & meadow* 1841 *TA*, named from the family of Jeffery *Gun* 1675 PR 4, 65. MIDDLE HILL FM, *Middle hill* 1841 *TA*. NEWCOMBE, 1760 BM, 1776 Will, *v.* nīwe, cumb. SAINTBURY GROUNDS (1830 M) & HILL (*Seynesbury Hill* 1529–32 ECP). WALL FM, near ancient intrenchments (cf. Saintbury *supra*), *v.* wall.

FIELD-NAMES

The principal forms in (*a*) are 1841 *TA* 170. Spellings dated 1269 are *FF*, 1543 LP, 1638 Inq.

(*a*) Amblers lays; Barn hill; Blake moor; Calves pen; Castle bank (ib 1779 Rudder 635, an intrenchment, *v.* castel); Claywell; Comb house; Coney green (*le Connyger* 1539 BM, *v.* coninger 'warren'); Coney holt ('rabbit wood', *v.* coni, holt); Dry lays; Godwells; the Hales (*v.* halh); Larkborough; the Leys; the Moors; the Nap (*v.* cnæpp 'hill'); Sandfords meadow; Spring hill; Tundish (so called from its shape).

(*b*) *Courteland* 1543; *Dewes close* 1638; *Gygollesmedenetherende* 1269 (the ME pers.n. *Gigelle* (cf. Reaney 181 s.n. *Jekyll*), *v.* mǣd, neoðera, ende); *Greene close* 1638; *the Lynches* 1484 AD iii (*v.* hlinc 'ridge'); *leʒ Lottes* 1543 (*v.* hlot); *Nonemonneslond* 1269 (probably the same area as *Nan(n)esmonnes land* 709 (c. 1200) BCS 125, 972 (10th) ib 1282, *nones-monnes-lond* n.d. KCD 1368, which is in Broadway (Wo 191) near the Saintbury boundary at Fish Inn, such names usually referring to lands on ill-defined boundaries); *Oldburidich'* 1269 (*v.* ald, burh, dīc, cf. Saintbury *supra*); *la Oldewelde* 1269 (*v.* ald, **wald** (WSax *weald*) 'wold'); *Shepe close* 1638.

Sezincote

SEZINCOTE (144–1731) [ˈsiːziŋkout]

Ch(i)esne-, Cheisnecot(e) 1086 DB, *Chesnecothe* 1236 Theok
Cinctecote 1166 RBE (p)
Sesnecot(e), -choth 1185 Madox, e.13 BM
Senescot(e) 1195 P, 1204 Cur, 1291 Tax, *Senecote* 1221 Plea
Suinescote 1201 P, *Swenecota* 1220 Fees
Snesnechoth e.13 BM, *Snescota* 1220 Fees
Scenescot Hy 3 AD ii, *Shenescote* 1401 Ipm, *Schenecote* 1374 Ipm
Sessecot' 1221 *Ass*
Shesnecote 1236 Fees, *Scesne-, S(c)hesnecot(e)* 1196 Finberg 114, 1236 Fees, 1248 *Ass*, 1268 Ipm *et passim* to 1380 *FF*, *Schesen(e)-cot(e)* 1248 *Ass*, 1291 Tax, 1297 Episc
Sesencote 14 AD ii, *-yn-* Hy 6 AddCh, 1535 VE, *-on-* 1498 AD i, *Seasencott* 1597 *FF*, *Sezingcott als. Seseencott als. Sesencott* 1610 *FF*

A good many of the spellings are erratic, but there can be no doubt of Ekwall's derivation from OE cisen 'gravelly' and cot 'cottage'. The variation in the initial consonant is due to the AN substitution of *s-* for OE *c-*, ME *ch-*, a change similar to that in Cirencester (60 *supra*), cf. IPN 100–3, Phonol. § 32.

CLAPLEY, 1830 M, *Cloppeleye* 1269 Pat, 1347 *FF*, *Clopley* 1576 *FF*.
'Hill clearing', *v.* clopp(a), lēah, and cf. Clapton (198 *supra*).
THE BLACKTHORNS. CAMP, *Camp ground* 1830 M, an ancient
encampment. GOLD BARROWS. HANS BRAKE, 1830 M. HOME
FM, cf. *Home close* 1692 *GR* 536. RODMORE COPPICE, *Rudmore* 1241
FF, *Radmore* 1692 *GR* 536, 'reed marsh', *v.* hrēod, mōr. RYE FM,
1830 M, *Greate Rye*, *Rye meadow* 1692 *GR* 536, probably ME *atter
eye* 'at the water-meadow (*v.* ēg); it lies on land in the angle formed
by the confluence of two streams. SEZINCOTE HILL (cf. *Hill meadow*
1692 *GR* 536) & PARK (*Lowe-*, *Vpper Parke* 1692 ib). THICK-
LEATHER COPPICE, *Thicke Leather* 1692 *GR* 536, possibly of the same
origin as Dikler (6 *supra*), 'dense reed-bed', *v.* þicce², lǣfer; the
copse is not near the Dikler and cannot be named from it. THE
WARREN, 1692 *GR* 536, *Chapmans Warren* 1777 M.

FIELD-NAMES

The principal forms in (*b*) are 1692 *GR* 536 (T. 29). Spellings dated 1241
are *FF*.

(*a*) Sezincot lane 1842 *TA*.

(*b*) *Calves close*; *Cranmore* ('crane marsh', *v.* cran, mōr); *Cumbeshull'* 1241
(*v.* cumb, hyll); *Green hills Rye* (cf. Rye Fm *supra*); *Hetine hill* 14 AD ii;
Hobbes meadow; *Lylyes ground*; *Longeforlong'* 1241; *Mutmers close*; *Nodwell
close*; *the Padock*; *Poole Rye* (cf. Rye Fm *supra*); *Scoweweye* 1241 (probably
for *Stoweweye* 'the road to Stow'); *Syrlonecroft* 1241; *Smithmore* 1692; *the
two Langetts* (*v.* langet).

Todenham

TODENHAM (144–2363)

Todanhom 804 (11th) BCS 313
Teode-, *Toteham* 1086 DB, *Teudenham* 1221 Eyre (p)
Thudenham 1221 *Ass*   *Thodeam* 1241 Theok
Todeham 1231 Theok, 1248 *Ass*, 1263 Episc, 1275 Heref, 1300
    Abbr, -*hamme* 1327 *SR*
Todynham 1287 *Ass*, 1298 Episc, *Todenham* 1291 Tax, 1294 Episc,
    1307 FF *et freq* to 1707 PR 4
Tuddenham c. 1560 *Surv*   *Toddenham* 1566 FF

The occasional *Teod-*, *Teud-*, *Thud-* spellings suggest that the first
el. is the OE pers.n. *Tēoda*. 'Teoda's water-meadow', *v.* hamm
(indicated by the spellings -*hom*, -*hamme*), which is appropriate for
the large low-lying tract between Knee Brook and Nethercote Brook.

From CAMBRIDGE UNIVERSITY PRESS

We have pleasure in enclosing

1 E.P.N.S. Vols. XXXVIII-XLI (Glos. 1-4)

BIRCH HEATH. COOPER'S COPPICE, named from the family of George *Cooper* 1787 PR 4, 151. CRAB ORCHARD, 1830 M. DUNSDEN FM, -*Barn* 1830 M, *Todenham Dunson* 1777 M. MANOR FM, 1784 *CirenP.* MOUNT SORRELL, 1830 M. PALLINGS COPPICE, 1830 M. PHILLIP'S FM, named from the family of Henry or Grace *Phil(l)ips* 1741, 1784 PR 4, 148, 151. TIMM'S COPPICE, named from the family of Richard or Francis *Tims* 1728, 1729 PR 4, 147. TODENHAM MILL, -*Mills* 1638 GR 1099. TUNBRIDGE HO, -*paddock* 1840 *TA*. WATER SLADE COPPICE, 1830 M, *v.* wæter, slæd 'valley'. WOODHILLS, 1830 M.

FIELD-NAMES

The principal forms in (*a*) are 1840 *TA* 200. Spellings dated 1610–1779 are GR 1099.

(*a*) Black Pit close; Bratch (*v.* brēc); Catbrain ground (*v.* cattes-braȝen); Chinslade grounds 1779; Copped hill (*v.* copped 'peaked'); Dadnam meadows; Dean; Dean's Slade; the Digings; Football Butts (ib 1715); North & South Gotion; Gigbridge meadow; Goss hill (*v.* gorst, hyll); Gratton (Butts) (*v.* grǣd-tūn 'stubble-field'); Green Sands; Han Acre; Hand hill; Heel Lands; Heep Barrow; Hemstall End 1767; Hen Lands; Hillborough; Horne ground; Lanes 1748 (*v.* leyne 'arable strip'); Langate (*v.* langet); Long Ham (*v.* hamm); Mill Ham; the Myfield; Nibden; Nollands; Notchill; Nothams Slade; Oxney (ib 1616, *v.* oxa, (ge)hæg); Sallow Bed (*v.* salh 'willow'); Slingate (dial. *slinget* 'narrow strip'); Steep Barrow; Stockinghole; Summers hill; Wells close (*Welles* 1610); Whorestone ('boundary stone', *v.* hār, stān, cf. Phonol. § 42*a*); Wormbridge; Wormshill.

(*b*) Beale Yate 1624 (*v.* geat 'gate'); *the Church house* 1693; *the Pinfold* 1682 (*v.* pynd-fald); *Welley* 1649 (*v.* wella, ēg).

Welford on Avon

WELFORD ON AVON (144–1451)

> *Welleford* 1086 DB, 1187, 1190 P, 1203 Cur, 1221 Eyre, 1227 *FF*, 1233 Berk (p), 1248 *Ass et freq* to 1325 *MinAcct*
> *Welneford* 1177 P, 13 Misc, Hy 3 Monast, 1221 *Ass*, *FF* 1291 Tax, 1316 FA *et passim* to c. 1560 *Surv*, (-*als. Welford*) 1575, 1603 *FF*
> *Wylneford* 1248 *Ass*   *Welleneford* 1287 *Ass*
> *Weleford* 1261 Ipm   *Whelforde* 1309 Abbr
> *Welford* 1314 Ipm *et freq* to 1691 PR 4, (-*super Auene*) 1433 *FF*

'Ford near the spring or springs', v. wella (gen.sg. wellan, gen.pl. wellena), ford; it has a meaning similar to Wansford (Nth 245) from welm 'spring'. The ford may have been across the Avon.

RUMER HILL, Ruwemere 1255 FF, Rumour (Hill) 1777 M, 1840 TA, probably 'pool in rough ground', v. rūh, mere. WESTON HILL.

FIELD-NAMES

The principal forms in (a) are 1840 TA 153, and in (b) 1575 TRMB 39. Spellings dated 1227 are FF, 1624, 1634 Inq, 1779 Rudder.

(a) Aggets gate; Ayte (Neytes 1634, v. ēgeð 'island'); Bedlam pasture (Bedlam 1779, a transferred name from the Bedlam or Bethlehem Hospital in London); Blacklands; Dove house close; Homeage; Milham Mead (v. myln, hamm, mǣd); the Nook; Quar Gate Hill; Ram Hill; Slingate (dial. slinget 'narrow strip'); Stople hill; Synderham 1779; Weedlet ('weedy conduit'; v. wēod, (ge)lǣt); Wessons close (Weston close 1624).

(b) Blakelete 1227 ('black conduit', v. blæc, (ge)lǣt); Blackemans house; Bromlyes close 1624; terr' voc' Cockes, -Cookes; Cornefilde; Downe meadowe; Fursinhill (v. fyrsen 'furzy'); Hades 1634 (v. hēafod); Leyes 1634; Myddlebarowe fild (v. beorg 'barrow'); Ordrichesorchard 1227 (the OE pers.n. Ordrīc, v. orceard); Pooledole, -meade (v. pōl, dāl, mǣd); Sholebreade filde (the common f.n. Shoolbread, v. scofl, brǣdu); Sta(w)broke fild(e) (possibly 'stone brook', v. stān, brōc, with loss of -n- before the labial, cf. Phonol. § 37 c); le Westfild.

Weston on Avon

WESTON ON AVON (144–1651)

Westona juxta Avenam 716 (14th) BCS 134
to *Westuninga gemǣre* 922 (17th) ASChart xxi
Weston(e), -tvne 1086 DB, 1176 France, 1220 Fees et passim,
(i) (-(Roberti) Mauduit, -duyt) 1221 Plea, 1236 Fees, 1274 Ipm et freq to 1327 SR, (-Mauduth) 1242 Ipm, (-Maudit) 1396 ib, (-Mawdytt) 1517 InqEncl, (ii) (-Cantelov, -loo, -lou) 1274, 1276 RH, 1287 Ass, (-Cantelupi) 1316 FA, (-Cauntelo) 1324 FF, (iii) (-super Auene) 1287 Ass, (-super Abonam) 1291 Tax, 1363 Ass, (-on Avene) 1406 Pat, (-super, -on Avon) 1535 VE, 1596 FF, (-super aquam) c. 1603 TRMB

'West farmstead', v. west, tūn; the OE form means 'boundary of the men of Weston' (v. -ingas, (ge)mǣre). There were two manors in Weston, one Weston on Avon itself which was held by Evesham

Abbey and then later held of them by John *de Cantilupe* (cf. 1285 *FF*, 1316 FA ii, 267, also Walter de *Cantilupo* 1324 *FF*), and the second called Weston Maudit from the feudal tenants Robert *Maudit* (1221 Plea), William *Maudit* (1284 FA), etc. The two manors were separate in DB, Weston on Avon being in *Witley* and Weston Maudit in *Celflede* hundred.

KNOBS FM, *Hobs Fm.* (sic) 1777 M.　WESTON SANDS.

Weston Subedge

WESTON SUBEDGE (144–1240)

Wæsðæma [gemære] 1005 (l. 12th) KCD 714
Weston(e) 1086 DB, 1220 Fees, 1221 Eyre (p), 1236 Fees, 1248 *Ass et passim*, (*-Marmiun*) 1235 Fees, (*-Pen(e)bregg'*) 1248 *Ass*, (*-sub Egge*) 1255 *FF*, 1274 RH, 1278 Ipm *et freq* to 1535 VE, (*-under Egge*) 1303 FA, 1312 Ipm, 1314 Pat, 1319 Ipm *et passim* to 1478 Pat

'West farmstead', *v.* west, tūn, so called from its location in relation to Aston Subedge (232 *supra*), which has the same affix. On the elliptical OE form *wæsðæma* 'dwellers at Weston', *v.* hǣme and cf. similar OE forms for Campden (237 *supra*), Aston (ii, 3), Ashton (ii, 42), Hinton on the Green (ii, 45), Elberton (iii, 113), cf. Durdham Down (iii, 142 *infra*). The manor was held by Henry de *Penbrugge* in 1235 Fees; Robert *Marmiun* had half a carucate in Quinton which is hard by. It lies under the Cotswold scarp (*v.* ecg).

DOVER'S HILL, 1830 M, named from Robert *Dover*, who (according to Rudder 24) lived in the time of James 1 and 'instituted certain diversions on the Coteswold, called after his name, which were annually exhibited about Willersey and Campden...every Thursday in Whitsun-week at a place called Dover's Hill'; an account of the games (which ceased in 1852) is given in *Annalia Dubrensia* (1638), cf. also BG xiii, 103 ff and *The Times* 25 May 1961.

KIFTS GATE, *Kyftesgate* 1354 Ipm, *Kyftesgate* 16 WinchLB ii, 441; the first reference is to the taking of an inquisition here and the second to 'þe Kynges court' held here. Many other spellings are given for the names of the hundred of Kiftsgate (230 *supra*) which presumably met here or at Kiftsgate Court or Spelsbury (250 *supra*). This site is 1″ O.S. 144–135390 on the ridgeway on the top of the Cotswold escarpment a mile west of Chipping Campden. The second el. is OE **geat** 'gate, gap'; the topography suggests the meaning 'gate' (across a road), as in Rapsgate (155 *supra*) rather than 'gap in the hills', though this would suit Kiftsgate Court. The first el. has been explained by Ekwall in RES (NS) viii, 408. In this interesting note he takes the first el. to be an OE *cȳft which would have a meaning similar to that of the related Goth *gaqumþs* 'meeting, conference' and ON *samkund* 'meeting'. It is cognate with OHG *cumft* 'coming', which, like the related words, is from the verbal root *kum-with an original -*ti* suffix. Kiftsgate would thence mean 'gate or gap where meetings (presumably of the hundred) were held', a close parallel to Rapsgate. *v.* Addenda.

BURNT & MIDDLE NORTON, NORTON HALL

per norðamere 709 (c. 1200) BCS 125, *Nortvne* 1086 DB, *Norton(a)* 1220, 1236 Fees, 1248 Ch, 1287 *Ass et passim*, (*-Gyffard*) 1276 RH, 1285 FA, 1287 *Ass*, (*-sub Egg(e)*) 1278, 1302 Ipm, 1326 *MinAcct et freq* to Hy 6 *AddCh*, (*-under Egge*) 1303 FA, 1320 *Ass et freq* to 1478 Pat, (*Over-, Nether-*) 1582 FF, *manerium sub Egge de Nortune* 1274 RH, *Northton' sub Egge* 1294 Episc. 'North farmstead', *v.* norð, tūn, so called from its location in relation to Aston Subedge (232 *supra*) with the same affix. On the OE spelling cf. Aston Subedge (232 *supra*); it is not to be confused with *norðhomme* (265 *infra*) later in the same charter. It was called *Gyffard* from the feudal tenant (cf. John *Gyffard* 1303 FA), and 'Burnt' from the burning down of the hall in 1741 when Sir John Keyt, the owner, lost his life in the fire.

BOLD GAP.   THE DINGLE.   EDEN'S FOLLY, *-ground* 1839 *TA*, named from the family of John *Eden* 1747 PR 4, 119.   GREEN HILL. KINGCOMB, 1830 M.   KNAPP COTTAGES, *the Knap* 1839 *TA*, *v.* cnæpp 'hill'.   LONG HILL.   LONG STRETCH FM, *Longstretche* 1689 *Harrowby*, *v.* lang, strecca 'stretch of land'.   THE LYNCHES, 1830 M, *the Linchfield* 1689 *Harrowby*, *v.* hlinc 'ridge'.   PODEN COTTAGES, *Podoun* 1687 PR 4, *Poden Hedgefield* 1689 *Harrowby*, 'toad valley' (from ME *pode*) or 'Pod(d)a's valley', *v.* denu or dūn 'hill' and cf. Podsmead (ii, 166 *infra*); Poden (Wo 264) is nearby, but it is not to be confused with Puddenham (264 *infra*).   THISTLEY HILL, *Thysteleye* 1287 *Ass* (p), 'thistle clearing', *v.* þistel, lēah.   WESTON

PARK, 1830 M, *parc' episcopi Wygorn' in villa Weston sub Egge* 1287
Ass 42, a park of the Bishop of Worcester, *v.* park.   WHITE'S FM,
named from the family of Richard *White* 1685 PR 4, 116.

FIELD-NAMES

The principal forms in (*a*) are 1839 *TA* 218, and in (*b*) 1689 *Harrowby*.

(*a*) Applebers Orchard; Beckford; Brook Furlong (cf. *the Brookefield*
1689); Coney Gree (*v.* coninger 'warren'); Cotty Croft; Curst land; Fox-
borough ('fox-earth', *v.* fox, burg); Hind Field; Homeage; Inn Field; Lambs
Heads (*le lower Lamsett* 1625 Inq); the Lawn (*v.* launde); Lench Field
(*v.* hlenc 'hill-side'); Leys Field (*Lower Leyes* 1689, *v.* lēah); Mill Butts;
the Oven; Pill Bottom; Pitchill Meadow; Rumbles; the Sling (dial. *sling*
'narrow strip'); Wheatleys Meadow (*Wetleys* 1689, *v.* hwǣte 'wheat', lēah).

(*b*) *Aishbrooke* (the same stream as Ashbrook 232 *supra*); *the Elbow-land*;
the fetche ground (ME *fecche* 'vetch'); *Gasons hedge*; *Rowbottom* (*v.* rūh,
botm).

Willersey

WILLERSEY (144–0939)

Willersey(e), *-ei*(*a*) 709, 714 BCS 125, 130, *-ei* 1086 DB, 1386 Ipm,
    Wyll- 1445 Pat, *Long Willersey* 1662 *Harrowby*
æt Willereseie, into, on Wyllerese(i)ge, of þere ege 840–52 (c. 1200)
    BCS 482, *Willerese* 1195 P, *-heye* c. 1220 GlR (p)
on Wyllersege, of Wylleresegge n.d. KCD 1368
Wylardeseye c. 1220 GlR (p), 1286 Episc, 1287 *Ass*, *-heye* 1248
    Ass, *Wi-*, *Wyllardeseye* 1274 RH, 1291 Tax, 1303 FA
Wi-, *Wyllarsey(e)* 1269 FF, 1274 RH, 1291 Tax *et passim* to 1577
    FF, *Wi-*, *Wylarsey(e)* 1327 SR, 1342 Heref

The first el. is probably a reduced form of the OE pers.n. *Wilheard*;
the OE forms are from documents of too late a time to carry much
weight against the many *Wyl(l)ard-* spellings; it is hardly likely to
be from OE *wi-*, *wyllere* 'salt-boiler' as that is a WSax form (corresponding to Angl *wellere*). 'Wilheard's water-meadow or island',
v. ēg, probably a piece of higher and drier ground above marshland.

CAMP, *the Camp* 1767 *EnclA*, an ancient encampment on Willersey
Hill, referred to in *burhwal* (*infra*).   CONDICUP FM, *Contercope
Corner* 1662 *Harrowby*, *Condercup* 1767 *EnclA*, *Condicop Barns* 1830
M; this farm is on the parish boundary where it makes a sharp bend
towards Badsey and it is therefore possible that the name is a late

adaptation of Fr *contre-coup* 'cut back'. THE FIELD. FURZE HILL, 1767 *EnclA*, *Fursy hill* 1637 Inq, *Furzen hill* 1662 Harrowby, *v.* fyrs(en), hyll. POOL FM.

FIELD-NAMES

The principal forms in (*a*) are 1767 *EnclA* (PRO). Spellings dated 709 are (13th) BCS 125, c. 850 (c. 1200) ib 482, 972 (10th) ib 1282, 11 KCD 1368 (bounds to 709 ib 61), c. 1603 *TRMB*, 1626, 1637 Inq, 1662, 1667 *Harrowby*, 1779 Rudder. KCD 1368 is undated but indicated as 11.

(*a*) Beward (ib 1662, *-furlong* 1637); Blind Lane; Bretforton Field (ib 1662, named from Bretforton Wo); Broad Brook; Carbage Hill (*Carbeseech* 1637, *Cerby Sich* 1667, *v.* sīc 'stream'); Chamber de Key; Chipping Furlong; Colley (*Colehillfield* 1637, *v.* col¹ 'charcoal', hyll); the Court Close; Goody Gore (*Goody Gore furlong* 1637, *Goods Gore-* 1667, *v.* gāra); the Ham (*le Home* c. 1603, *v.* hamm); Hawksmore; Horseham (*Horsham* 1637, 1667, *Horsome* 1662, *v.* hors, hamm); Hurst Furlong (ib 1637, *the Hurst* 1662, *v.* hyrst 'wood'); Lowherd (*Loward* 1637, 1667); Meadow Ditch Hades (*v.* hēafod); Midsummer Leys; Moss Furlong (*Mossefurlong* 1662, *v.* mos 'marsh'); Park Furlong (*le Parke* c. 1603); Parsons 1779 (ib c. 1603, 1626); Pillcroft; Puddenham (*Poddenhomme* 709, *on Pudanhammesbroc* 850 (Birch wrongly reads *Wudan-*), *on Wudanhomme* (sic) 11, *Pudnam field* 1637, the OE pers.n. *Puda*, *v.* hamm, at grid point 144–102413); Sandbrook (*in, on sondbroc* 709, 850, *on sandbroc* 972, 11, *Sambrook* 1637, *Sandbrooke* 1662, *v.* sand, brōc); Shewill; the Sidelongs; Spragges's (*Spragges* c. 1603, 1626, from the surname *Spragg*); Stanchhill; Stewards Mear; Swire Hedge (*le Swere* c. 1603, *v.* swēora 'neck of land, col'); the Town Ham (*v.* hamm); Windmill Leys; Wool Furlong (ib 1662).

(*b*) *in boerges* 709, *to ðe beorges* 11 (*v.* beorg 'barrow'); *on blacanpytt* 11 (*v.* blæc, pytt); *on ða blacan þyrne* 11 ('the black thorn', *v.* blæc, þyrne); *in blechemere* 709, *on bleccan mære* 850, *Blackmeare* 1637, 1667 (the first el. may be the OE pers.n. *Blæcca*, *Blecca*, *v.* mere 'pool'); *onlong broces* 11; *Brodemore* 1637; *in buregwalles* 709, *þone burhwal, on ða burhwalles* 850, *on burwalles* 11 ('the wall of the fort', *v.* burh, wall, the name of the long upper bank of an old encampment); *in buregwelle* 709, *on burhwellan* 850, *on burhwyllen* 11 ('spring below the fort', *v.* burh, wella, cf. prec.); *in Cademunstre* 709, *on Cadanmynster* 972, 11 (the OE pers.n. *Cada*, *v.* mynster 'church'); *in ealdegare* 709, *ombutan eadulfing garan* 850, *on Eadelming garan* 11 (from the OE pers.n. *Ēadwulf* or *Ēadhelm*, *v.* -ing⁴, gāra, which here denotes a projecting piece of land on the parish boundary ½ mile south-east of Fish Inn); *on þa ealdan dīc* 850, 972 (*v.* ald, dīc); *oð ða egge* 850, *on þa ecge* 972 (*v.* ecg, here the Cotswold escarpment); *Evisham Way* 1662 (the road to Evesham Wo); *the Fallowfield* 1662; *the Ferm' medowe* c. 1603; *Fordehey* 1637 (*v.* ford, (ge)hæg); *on Fugelmære* 11 ('wild-fowl pool', *v.* fugol, mere); *on furena* 11 (*v.* furh); *Haylond* c. 1603 (*v.* hēg, land); *be ðan heafdon* 854 (*v.* hēafod); *in hegeweie* 709, *on heig weig* 850, *on hegweige* 11, *Higheway furlong* 1637, *hayway-* 1667 ('the road for carrying hay', *v.* hēg, **weg**, the name survives as Hayway Fm (Wo 191) nearby); *Keys house* c. 1603; *the Lott* c. 1603 (*v.* hlot); *in merebroc* 709, *on mærebroc* 11 ('boundary stream', *v.* (ge)mǣre, brōc); *Myll knapp* c. 1603 (*v.* myln, cnæpp 'hill-top'); *in norð-homme* 709, *on norðhommes broc* 850, *on north ham* 972, *on, of norðom(me)* 11 (*v.* norð, hamm); *on polðorne* 709, 11 (*v.* pōl 'pool', þorn); *the pulse field* 1662 (ME *puls* 'pulse, peas, beans'); *on pycrestan* 11 (an OE pers.n. *Pīchere* or *Pīcer* as in Pixham (Wo 225) or Pickersom (ib 266), *v.* stān); *onlong riðies* 850, 11 (*v.* rīðig 'stream'); (*Sally*) *Sandfurlong* 1637, 1662 (*v.* salh 'willow'); *Shepcrofte* c. 1603; *Shirefilde* c. 1603; *stanitun hullessyce* 709 (perhaps identical with Stanchhill *supra, v.* stāniht 'stony', hyll, sīc); *Stertfurlong* 1667 (*v.* steort 'tail of land'); *the Stiringfield* 1662; *le Towne Medow* c. 1603; *on tun(e)wealdes stan* 850 (the OE pers.n. *Tūnwald, v.* stān); *on þeoua dene* 11 ('thieves' valley', *v.* þēof, denu); *onlong walles* 11 (the rampart of the *burhwal supra*); *Wheatefield* 1662.

INDEX OF PARISHES IN PART I